MW01627289

CONTEMPORARY
Sailors' Valentines
Romance Revisited

CONTEMPORARY

Sailors' Valentines

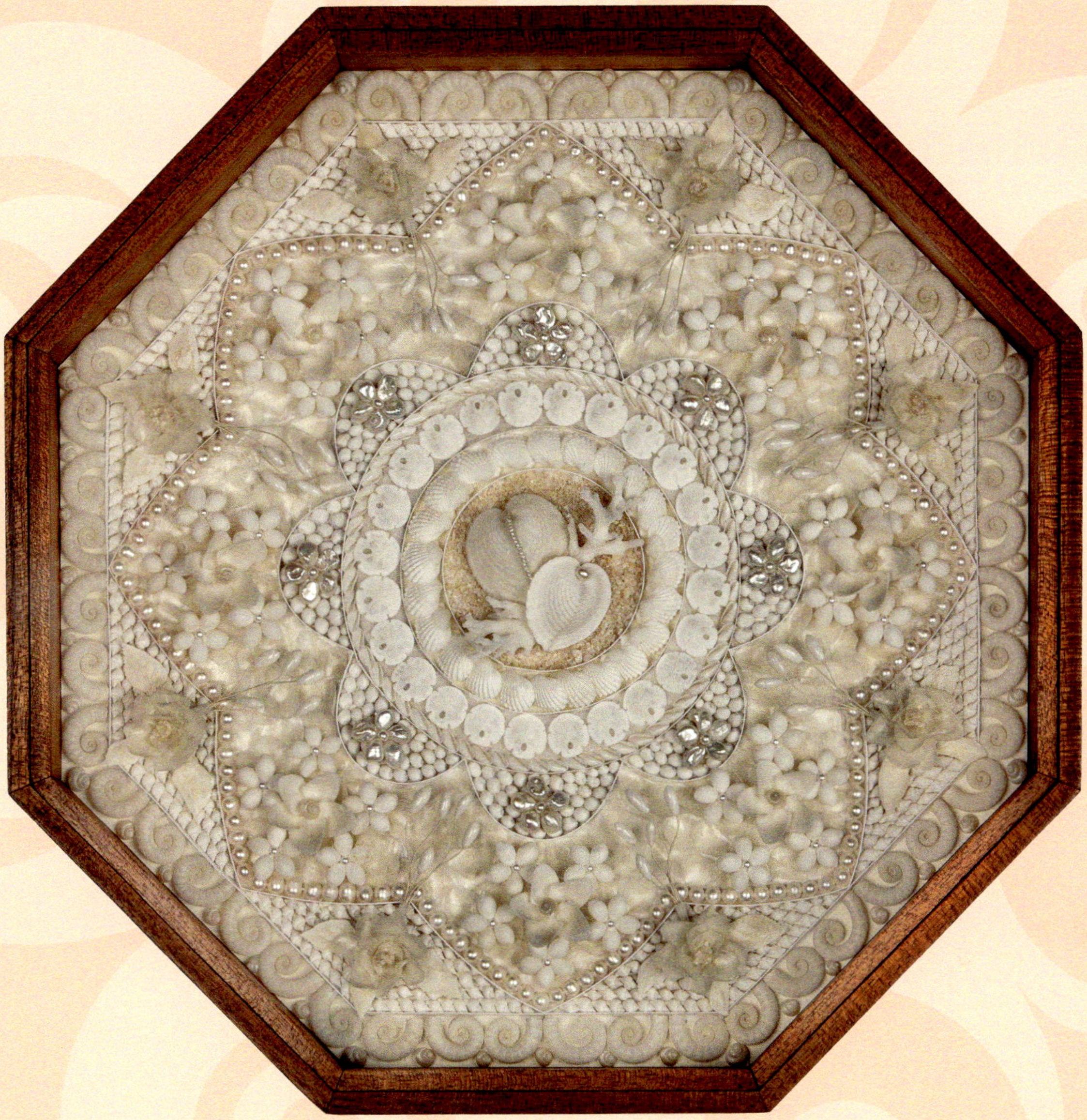

Romance Revisited

PAMELA BOYNTON

To my dear old friend BEV! XOXO

Pamela Boynton
July 2016

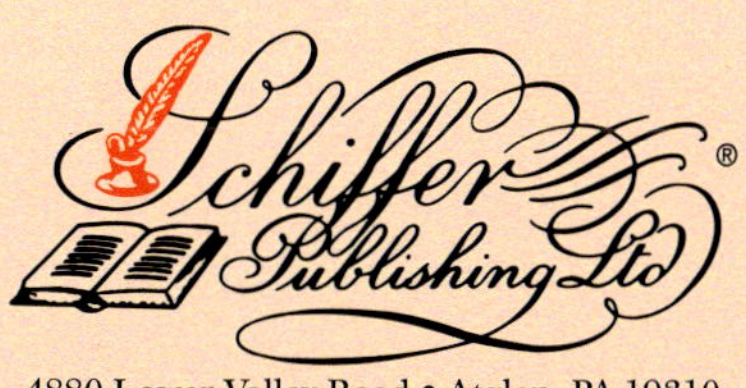

4880 Lower Valley Road • Atglen, PA 19310

Other Schiffer books on related subjects:

Sailors' Valentines: Their Journey Through Time, Grace L. Madeira, Constance Marshall Miller, Mary S. Page, & Ann T. Schutt, 978-0-7643-2378-2

Folk Art of Cape Cod and the Islands, Jeanne Marie Carley, 978-0-7643-4526-5

Contemporary Scrimshaw, Eva Halat, 978-0-7643-3049-0

Library of Congress Control Number: 2015956765

Published by Schiffer Publishing, Ltd.
1880 Lower Valley Road
Atglen, PA 19310
Phone: (610) 593-1777; Fax: (610) 593-2002
E-mail: Info@schifferbooks.com

Designed by Justin Watkinson
Cover design by Brenda McCallum

Type set in Great Vibes/Agenda-Light/GoudyOlSt BT
ISBN: 978-0-7643-5102-0
Printed in China

Front cover: *With My Love* by Daphne Hunte. Photo by Andre Williams
Back cover: *Up, Up and Away* by Judy Dinnick. Photo by Lasting Impressions, Ft. Myers
Spine: Mermaid painting by Carolyn Hunte, from *A Mermaid's Garden* by Daphne Hunte
Title page: *Entwined Hearts* by Pamela Boynton. Photo by Lasting Impressions, Ft. Myers
Angel wing and heart cockle images adapted from drawings in *Index Testarum Conchyliorium* by Nicolaus Gaulterius, published in 1742 (used on dedication and introduction pages).

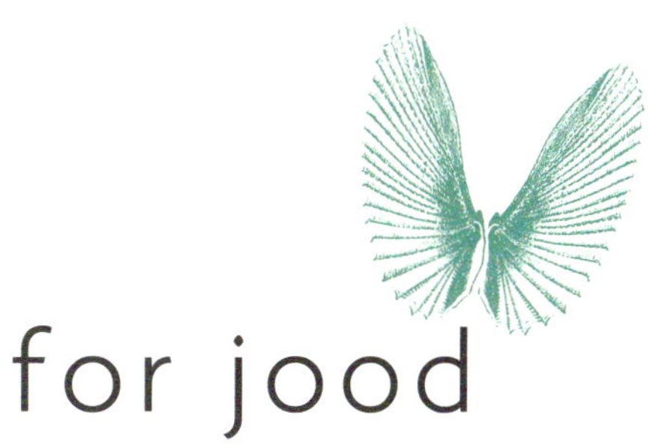

for jood

"it's always ourselves we find in the sea"

e. e. cummings

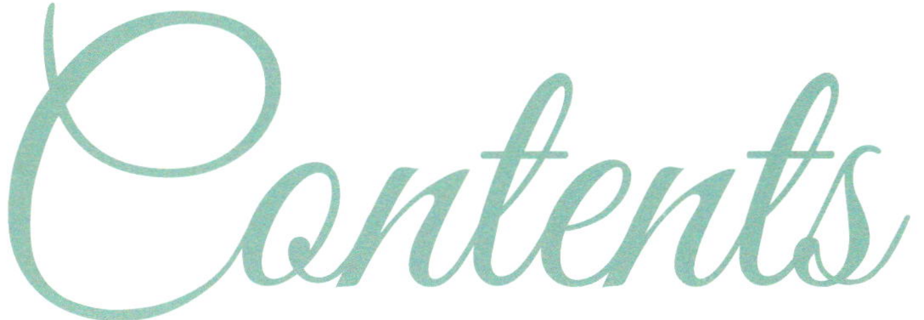

Foreword

Little did the Englishman Mr. B. H. Belgrave ever dream when he brought the concept of Sailors' Valentines to Barbados and taught the local ladies to create them with local shells that they would be so sought after by collectors from all over the world a century later.

Seeing my first Valentine in 1981 at the Sanibel Shell Show, and learning that they were an integral part of Barbadian history, sparked my interest as a lifelong Barbadian in studying and creating them. Until then I had been making three-dimensional floral arrangements with shells, but when I returned from the show that year I decided to try my hand at a traditional-style Valentine. I entered it in the Sanibel show the following year and also entered one or two more shows in the early 1980s.

In the late 1980s, I opened a small business called Daphne's Sea Shell Studio on our historic plantation on Barbados. It grew in size over the years and proved to be a successful venture and therefore a very busy time in my life. In the midst of all of this activity, I was not able to take the time to travel to Sanibel for the show.

After seeing an article about Sailors' Valentines in the February 2003 issue of *Martha Stewart Living*, I decided to return to Sanibel in March of that year. Witnessing the change in the Valentines from traditional to contemporary, and seeing the work of many new artists, I was inspired to join them in creating more three-dimensional pieces and also inspired to begin a collection of the remarkable work being done. I was elated to purchase at that show the piece done by Sandy Moran that I had seen in the *Martha Stewart Living* magazine. In 2005, tired of the demanding life of an entrepreneur, I closed my business and built a personal studio where I could focus solely on my own Valentines and take life at a slower pace.

As wonderful as the thought of relaxing was, I had had a vision for years that began to occupy my thoughts more frequently. I was passionate about teaching Barbadians and visitors to our island the relevance of the history of Sailors' Valentines to our culture. In order for that to happen, I wanted to bring some of the most talented artists to the island with their work. The planning took almost a year, but in February of 2011, six of the finest Sailors' Valentine artists traveled to Barbados to showcase their Valentines along with my own. They are all featured in this book: Pam Boynton, Judy Dinnick, Connie Miller, Gerda Reid, David Rhyne, and Jane Santini.

The two-day event began with an exhibition at Gallery NuEdge in the brand-new, upscale Limegrove Lifestyle Centre. Each artist's work was displayed on individual tables, and more than 200 guests attended the event. For the second day of the event, my husband and I had given permission to the Barbados National Trust to open our 300-year-old plantation to the public for viewing; it was Valentine's Day, which seemed most appropriate. Several large tents were erected on our property where the artists displayed their work. More than 700 people attended and had a chance to see and learn about Sailors' Valentines from the artists themselves. At the conclusion of the two days, the historical and contemporary forms of this unique art form had gained well-deserved exposure with Barbadian locals and visitors alike.

During the planning of this exhibition, the Philatelic Society of Barbados asked if I would allow them to create four stamps with my Valentines on them. Instead, I suggested that the stamps should include two of my pieces, an antique Valentine from a local collection, and a piece from my collection done by Pamela Boynton (this book's author), as I thought her Valentine *Evermore* was the best reproduction of an antique piece. Thus, on February 14, 2011, the day our plantation home was open to the public, the Philatelic Society was there selling the commemorative issue of four stamps featuring Sailors' Valentines. The stamps are still being sold today.

In 2014, I had the pleasure of taking Sailors' Valentines one step further. The Barbados Horticultural Society was taking a team of florists and Barbadian flowers to the Chelsea Flower Show in England. I had a vision that Sailors' Valentines could be done using our exotic and colorful local flowers to create the society's entry for that year. We had several meetings and decided we needed to create four 6-foot-wide

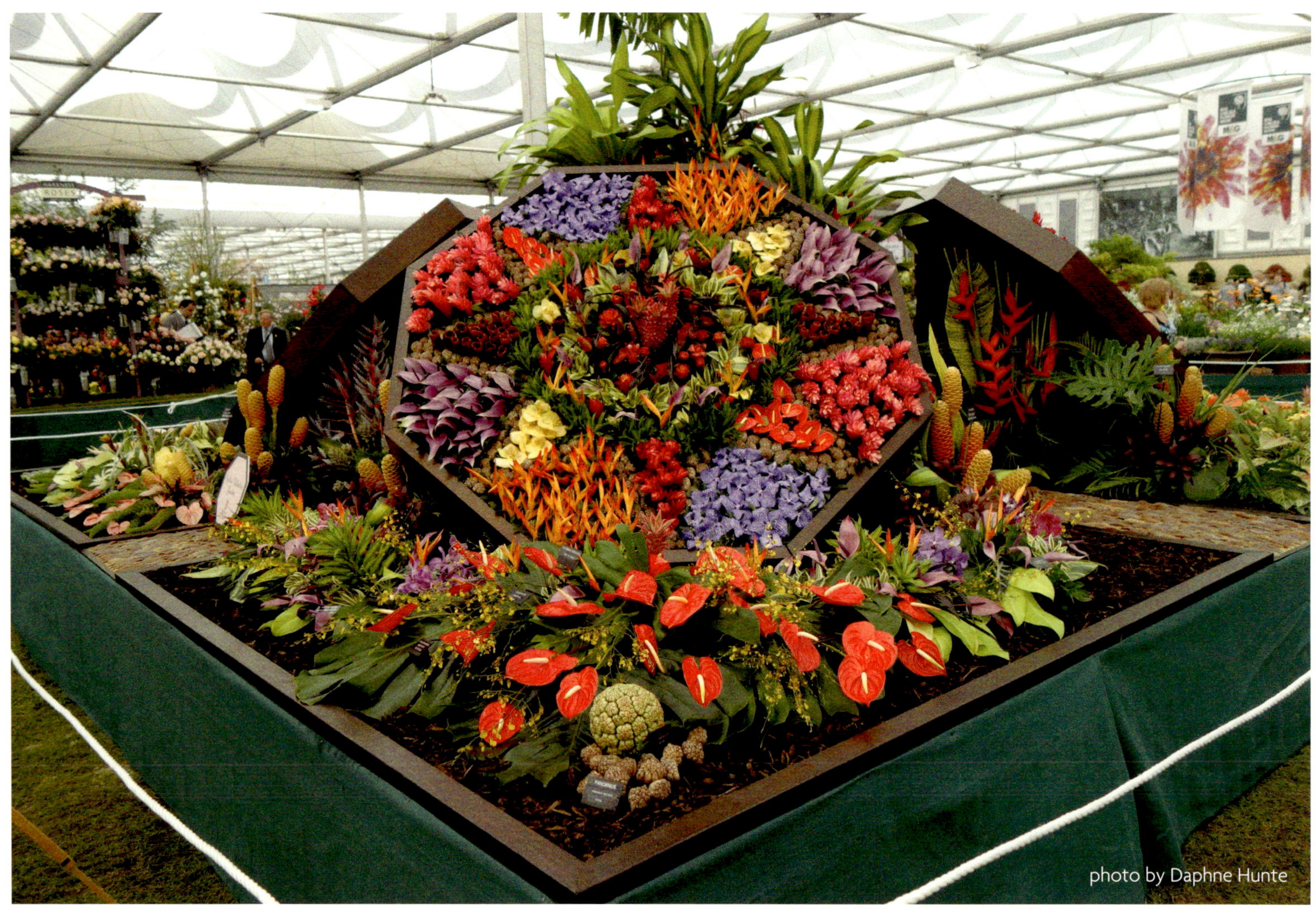

photo by Daphne Hunte

Valentine boxes and design geometrical patterns inside them within which the flowers would be arranged. After months of planning, in May 2014 the team flew to England to set up for the show; my husband and I joined them. The florists did a magnificent job of bringing to life the designs I had conceptualized, for which they were awarded a coveted gold medal. The display was funded in part by Sir Martyn and Lady Arbib (see her work on pages 12–21). Sailors' Valentines had been exposed to their largest audience ever, with remarkable success.

Many of the shell floral arrangements I have done over the years I may never see again. Pieces I created for President and Mrs. Ronald Reagan and a piece done for Betty Ford are among these treasures. Other work, however, still decorates the hallways and rooms of my home. Included in these are the bridal bouquets created for my daughters and granddaughters. They are part of a larger collection: my cherished collection of shell art, and Sailors' Valentines in particular, made by artists from all over the world.

Today's artists, whose exceptional pieces you will have the pleasure of seeing in this book, are a talented and diverse lot. Each person has a unique vision and feeling, and each demonstrates a need to move away from the structured traditional style and bring a new perspective to this old craft. The movement, dimension, and colors of today's work are staggering. When we all get together at shell shows or gatherings, discussions are lively and impassioned, and the sharing of new ideas and shell discoveries is plentiful. For me, the time I spend with these artists is as precious a way as time can be spent.

—Daphne Hunte
Barbados, 2016

Acknowledgments

A book does not come about without many people providing support and encouragement, some of them unknowingly.

With gratitude to:

Daphne Hunte, without whom this book would not have happened. She has taught me so much about the art of working with shells, and she has been a steadfast advocate for promoting awareness of Sailors' Valentines and those who make them. I never hesitated to lean on her during this project, and she never failed to be there for me. What would I do without you?

All the artists in this book who worked so diligently to get me what was needed. I am most appreciative.

John, my patient and agreeable husband, for his constant willingness to serve as my courier and sounding board for this book, and for his tenacious efforts to get my computer to behave more agreeably as well.

Emily, Robb, and Ash, just for being practically perfect in every way.

Lisa Story, copy editor extraordinaire, but so very much more than that to me.

Sir Martyn and Lady Arbib, Larry and Carolyn Alexander, Daphne Hunte, and Natalie Manning, for graciously allowing the Sailors' Valentines in their collections to be photographed for this book.

Larry Strange and his family (seashells.com), Sue Hobbs and Phil Dietz (suehobbs@verizon.net), Jim and Rose Prestigiacomo (seashellsandwood.com), and Ken Wye (eatonsseashells.co.uk), a few of our shell suppliers, for successfully satisfying our insatiable need for seashells.

Those who make our magnificent wooden cases; their names appear beneath their work on the pages that follow.

. . . and to Bella, for creature comforts.

A Tribute to Artists Who Paved the Way

Many thanks to the following Sailors' Valentine artists who paved the way for those of us in this book and beyond. Some of these people are gone; some are no longer creating Sailors' Valentines. They are all an integral part of the history of this art form.

The Barbadian Cottage Industry

Helen Nemirow Beck

Ralph Cahoon

Shirley Farley

Paula Fisher

Priscilla Huston

Jean Karabin

Mary S. Page

L. Rodman Page

Humbert (Bert) Porecca

Ann T. Schutt

Bernard Woodman

Judith Coolidge Hughes and her family:

- Helen Coolidge Woodring (sister)
- Louise Coolidge Carpenter (sister)
- Judith Coolidge Carpenter Herdeg (niece)
- Cooper Coolidge Woodring (nephew)

Preface

History

The definitive history of Sailors' Valentines has been somewhat of a mystery. That mystery began to unravel when an article appeared in the February 1961 issue of *The Magazine Antiques*. Written by Judith Coolidge Hughes (who came from a family of shell collectors, shell art collectors, and shell artists*), this article remains the seminal piece on the origin of Sailors' Valentines. It led people to the conclusion that they were not made by sailors, as folklore had told, but rather were made by Barbadian women and purchased by sailors as gifts for their loved ones—wives, sweethearts, mothers—before returning home after years at sea.

Prior to her article being published, collectors and scholars alike thought that sailors made these octagonal shell works to while away the hours during their long voyages at sea, much as they did scrimshaw. Judith Hughes gave several indisputable reasons why this could not have been the case.

First, while scrimshaw required only whalebone and a few tools, shell mosaics required far too many materials—shells, wood, glue, cardboard, paper, cotton, nails, screws, hinges, glass, and small tools—to make it feasible for them to have been done aboard a ship while at sea.

Second, unlike scrimshaw, examples of which show widely varying and unique styles, the early Sailors' Valentines showed a lack of individuality; similar patterns and techniques were common among almost all pieces. How could sailors aboard different ships have created such similar work?

Third, 35 types of shells have been identified in all known antique Sailors' Valentines, and all of those shells are native to the West Indies and particularly to its easternmost island, Barbados.

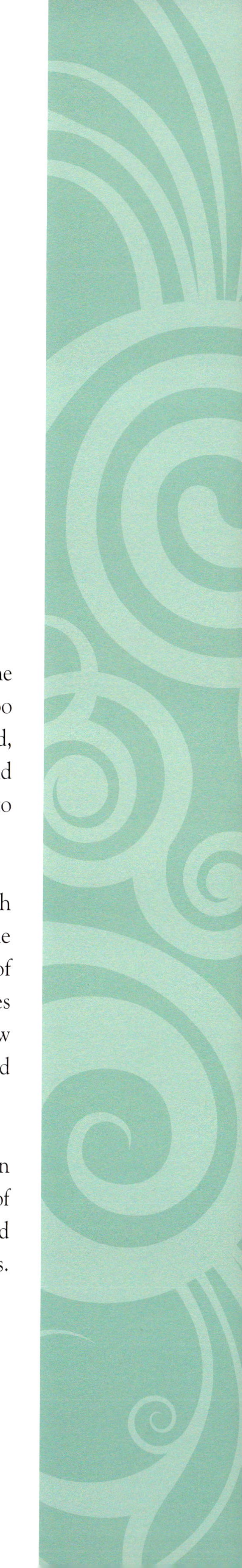

* Much of the work owned by this family can be viewed in the book *Sailors' Valentines: Their Journey Through Time.*

Fourth, while restoring a damaged Sailors' Valentine, a woman from Massachusetts found a Barbadian newspaper dated 1833 used as backing in the box.

Following the publication of the Hughes article, people began to accept that the making of Sailors' Valentines had been a cottage industry on Barbados. It was thought that Mr. B. H. Belgrave, an Englishman, had migrated to Barbados with his brother George and opened The New Curiosity Shop in Bridgetown. Coming from England in an era when shells and other exotica were extremely popular and abundantly displayed, Mr. Belgrave had been exposed to the shell work being done by women there, including what were called shell mosaic plaques, undoubtedly the precursor to Sailors' Valentines.

It was further presumed that once on Barbados, Mr. Belgrave proceeded to have octagonal wooden cases made and then distributed them, along with templates of various geometric patterns and local shells, to the women of Barbados, hoping to engage them in shell work. Evidently his plan proved successful. Once in his shop, these pieces were purchased as souvenirs by sailors for whom the island was a final port of call before returning to their homelands of America, England, and Holland, the places where most of these works were later discovered.**

There is, however, no evidence to support that what we now call Sailors' Valentines were called that during the 1800s in either England or Barbados, the two places they are known to have been made. Mr. Belgrave's New Curiosity Shop used only the words "shell mosaics" and "fancy work" to advertise these shell-related objects. It does not seem too great a stretch to imagine that at some point along the way, someone referred to them as Sailors' (i.e., the purchasers and gift givers) Valentines (they were romantic tokens of love) . . . and the name stuck.

More details about the history of Sailors' Valentines can be found in:

John Fondas, *Sailors' Valentines*, Rizzoli International Publications, 2002.

Grace L. Madeira, Constance Marshall Miller, Mary S. Page, and Ann T. Schutt, *Sailors' Valentines: Their Journey Through Time*, Schiffer Publishing, 2006.

** Shell artist Bill Jordan hired researchers to further investigate the history of Sailors' Valentines. They found evidence that the Belgrave family dates back to the 1700s on Barbados, and that Caribbean natives were creating mosaic forms of art as early as the 1750s. To follow the still unfolding history, visit Bill's blog at www.sailors-valentine.com/blog.

Author's Notes

Shell names

We all use the same shells, and as artists most of us are not inclined to call a wentletrap an epitonium, as a more scholarly person would. But as far as common names of shells go, we often refer to them by different names. I have done my best to keep the common names of shells we use consistent for this book.

Where *does* that apostrophe go?!

As I reviewed my folders of material and articles about Sailors' Valentines before beginning this book, I noticed a lot of inconsistency as to where the apostrophe was placed. I know that some use the word "Sailor" in this situation as a possessive:

one piece by one sailor = Sailor's Valentine
multiple pieces by one sailor = Sailor's Valentines
multiple pieces by multiple sailors = Sailors' Valentines

Since sailors didn't actually make these works, the use of an apostrophe as a possessive seems unwarranted to me, and since the artists are not sailors, the possessive seems unnecessary in that case as well.

Because the term "Sailors' Valentine" came about decades after this artwork was first created (they were previously referred to as shell mosaics or fancy work), I regard the term as defining a particular style of artwork, and as such the apostrophe remains static. So after careful consideration and several somewhat mundane conversations with editors about language usage, for the purposes of this book, the work will be referred to in all instances as Sailors' Valentines.

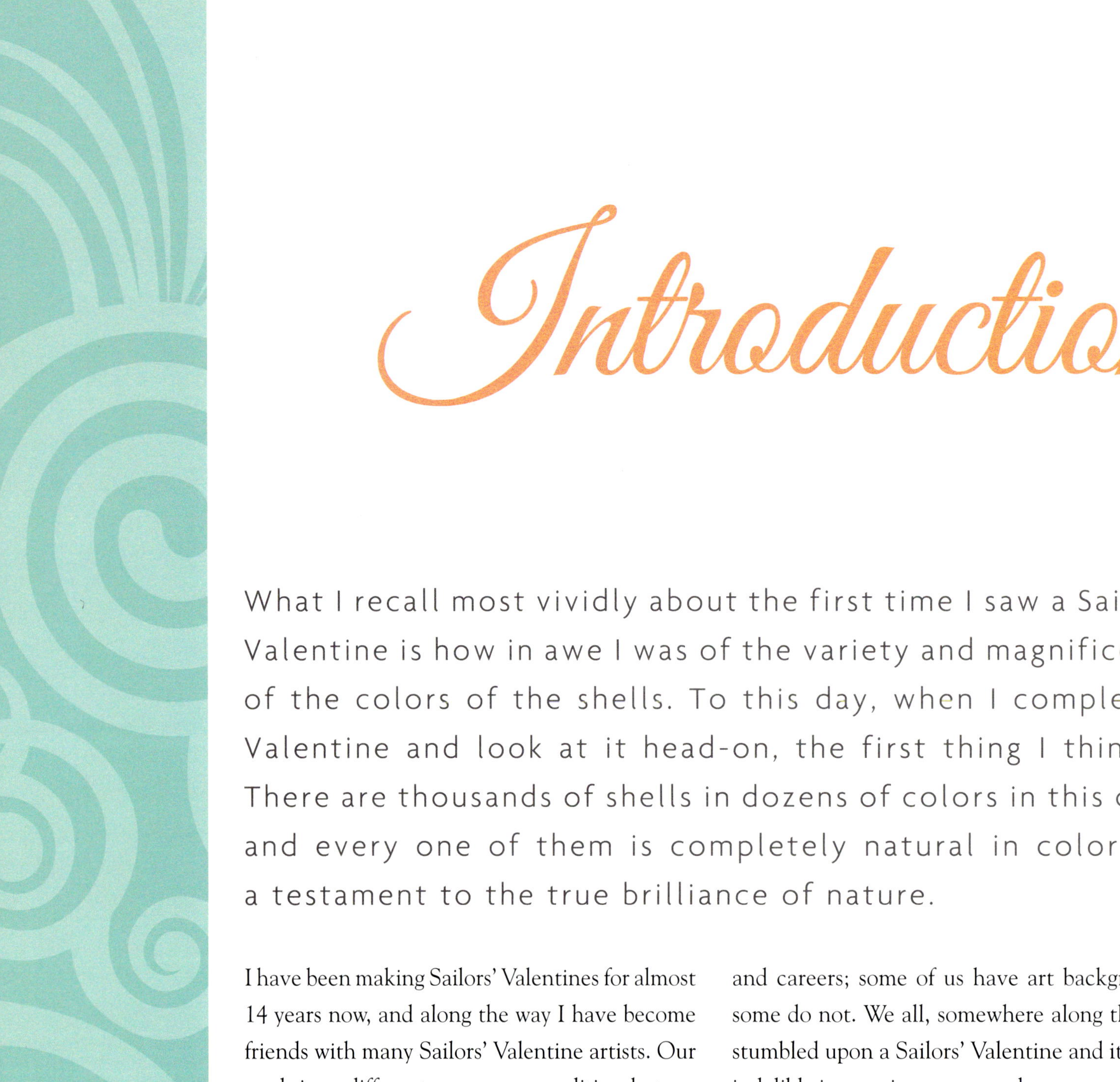

Introduction

What I recall most vividly about the first time I saw a Sailors' Valentine is how in awe I was of the variety and magnificence of the colors of the shells. To this day, when I complete a Valentine and look at it head-on, the first thing I think is: There are thousands of shells in dozens of colors in this case, and every one of them is completely natural in color . . . a testament to the true brilliance of nature.

I have been making Sailors' Valentines for almost 14 years now, and along the way I have become friends with many Sailors' Valentine artists. Our work is as different as our personalities, but we share one thing in common: a passion for shells and sea life and a love of arranging them in an octagonal shadowbox. When I first began to think about authoring this book, I wanted to offer readers a place where they could not only study new visions of an old craft, but also get to know the artists as people. We come from varying backgrounds and careers; some of us have art backgrounds, some do not. We all, somewhere along the line, stumbled upon a Sailors' Valentine and it left an indelible impression on us; we knew we would be creating one someday.

Every time I begin the process of creating a Valentine, I lay out an endless array of shells on my work space. Though I have done so many times before, I am always struck by how ingenious their many characteristics are:

the whorls of a whelk
the curl of a spirula
the "tendrils" of a yoka star turban
the apex of an olive shell
the spines of an urchin
the color of a strawberry top
the iridescence of an abalone
the chambers of a nautilus
the spires of a latiaxis
the stripes of a zebra nerite
the fragility of a janthina
the perfect heart shape of a heart cockle
the pearl of an oyster
the sheer magnificence of a sunburst star turban

That a mollusk could create such marvels astounds me. I am reminded first and foremost that the beauty of the materials we use for our art is inherent. We, therefore, as artists, can only take partial responsibility for any beauty observed in our work—a humbling truth.

I hope you do find beauty in the pages ahead, and I hope that beauty reminds you, too, that in the midst of all that unsettles us in life, something as simple as a seashell can be a reminder that there is much in the natural world to delight us and bring us a little joy.

I invite you to enter our world.

Artists
AND THEIR WORK

photo by Tatevik Mirzakhanyan

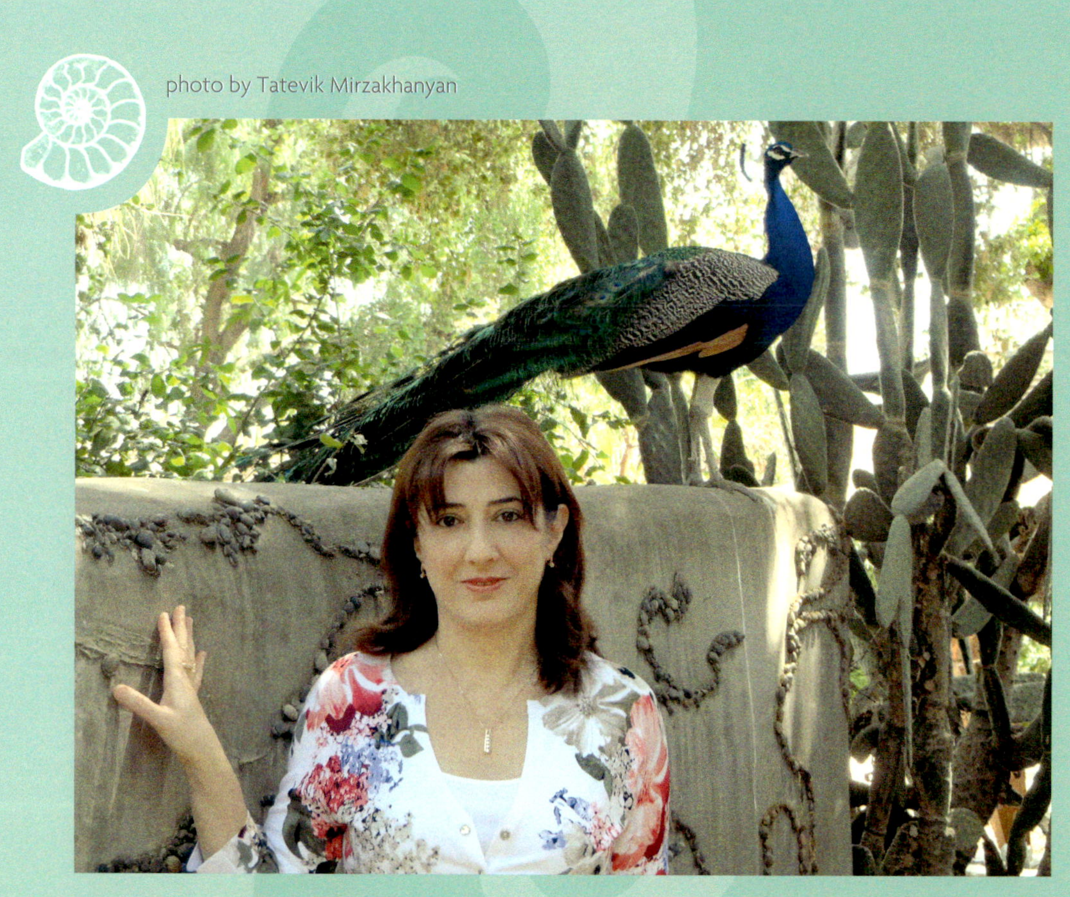

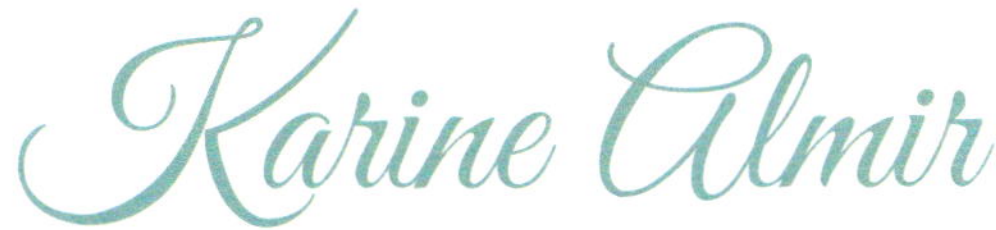

Glendale, California

I was born and raised in Armenia and spent my summer vacations at the seaside of Sochi. It never occurred to me then that seashells could be used to create wonderful works of art, or that my childhood pastime of shell collecting would evolve into an art form and passion years later.

In 1996 I moved to Southern California with my husband and two daughters. Though educated as an engineer, I started working as a sugar artist making gum-paste flowers and bouquets for wedding cakes.

After watching an episode of the *Martha Stewart Show* about the Sanibel Shell Show, I was inspired to create shell art. A few years later, I happened across another *Martha Stewart* episode that featured several Sailors' Valentine artists who had won awards at the Sanibel Shell Show, and I was blown away. I felt as if all my life I had been waiting for that one moment, and that I had discovered my true calling . . . being a shell artist.

In March 2009, I participated in the Sanibel Shell Show for the first time with mosaic-style shell art. While I was at the show, one of the artists encouraged me to try my hand at making a Sailors' Valentine. It seemed like a daunting process. I began with a simple sketch for my first piece, but I had so many ideas running through my head that I had no idea what the final piece would look like.

Once I started making Sailors' Valentines, I couldn't stop. I invest hundreds of hours in each piece, and by the time I have finished I feel as though my creation is like my own child. I adore working with tiny shells, though it can be very challenging at times. The most enjoyable piece I have made was a micro-mosaic Sailors' Valentine done with tiny pieces of sea urchin spines. While working on one piece my head is always filled with ideas for future pieces, just as it was the time I made my first Valentine. I feel so fortunate to have found my true calling.

www.shellartbykarine.com

The flowers, plants, and peacock capture the spirit of the Los Angeles County Arboretum: flowering trees, perennials, shrubs, and a peacock roosting in a tree. The tiny flowers are made of apple blossom shells, lilac shells, and baby whelks. The peacock is crafted from operculums, gooseneck barnacles, and rice shells. Crushed painted shells are used for the background.

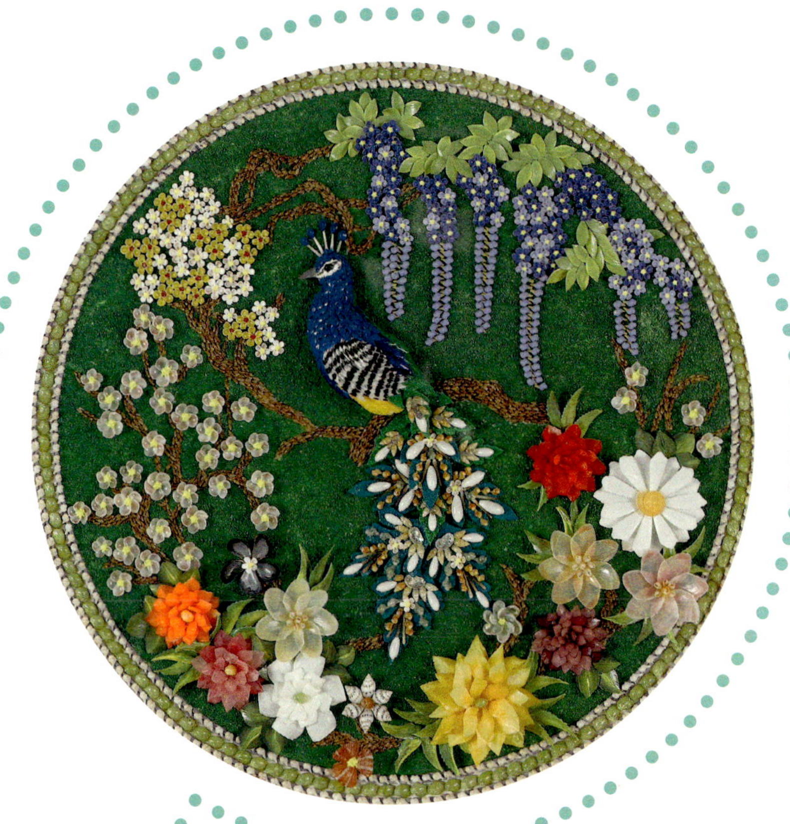

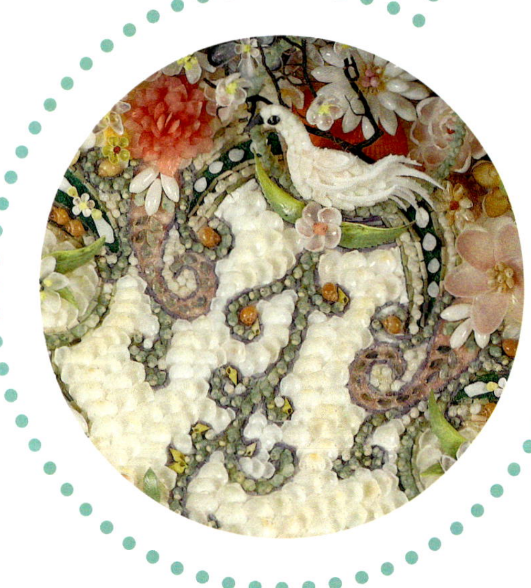

Eight small swans sit in the eight corners of the Sailors' Valentine. Each dainty swan is made of tiny operculums and coquina shells.

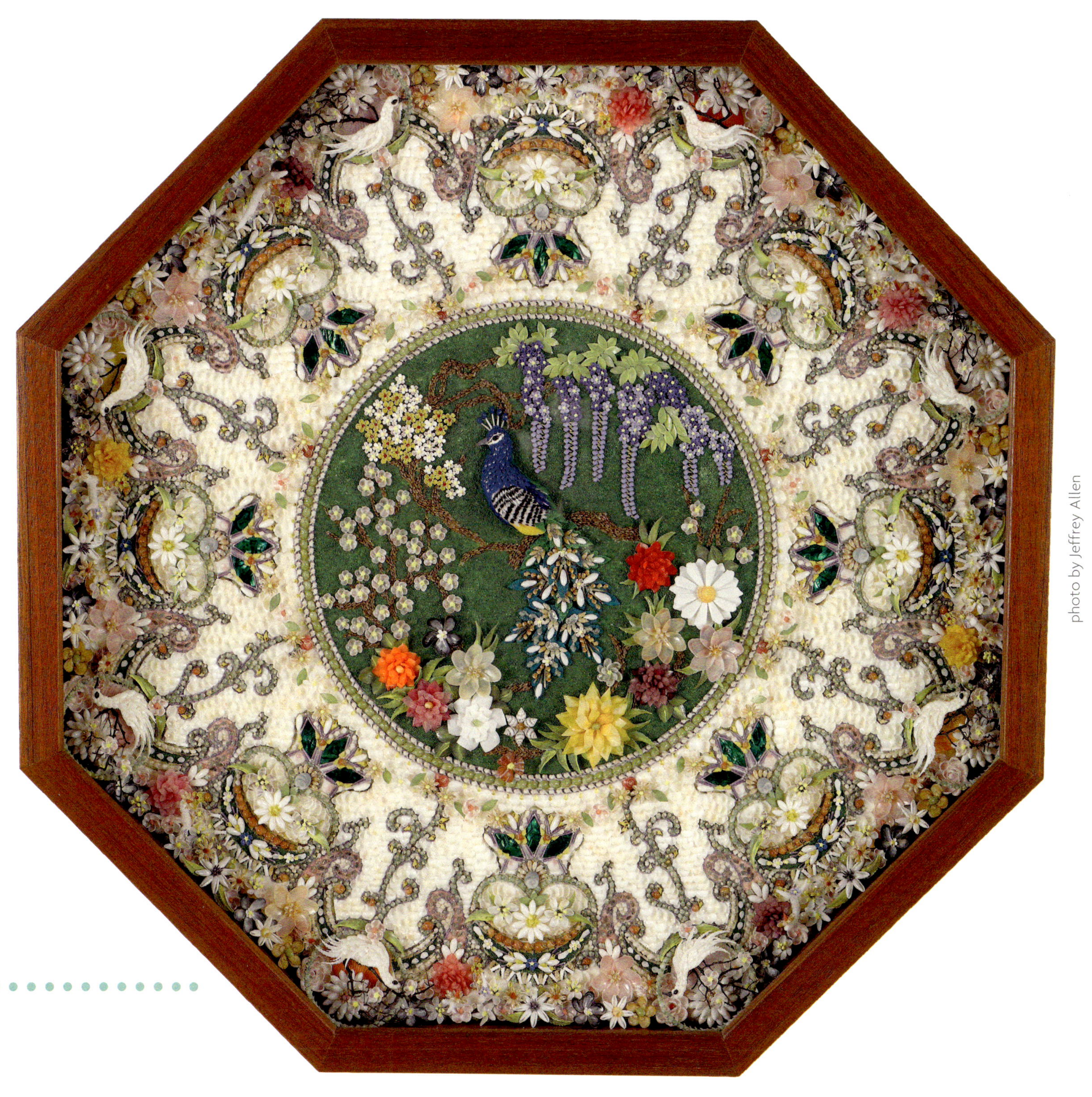

photo by Jeffrey Allen

Peacock

Inspired by the peacocks at the Los Angeles County Arboretum.

20-inch mahogany case made by Jim Prestigiacomo

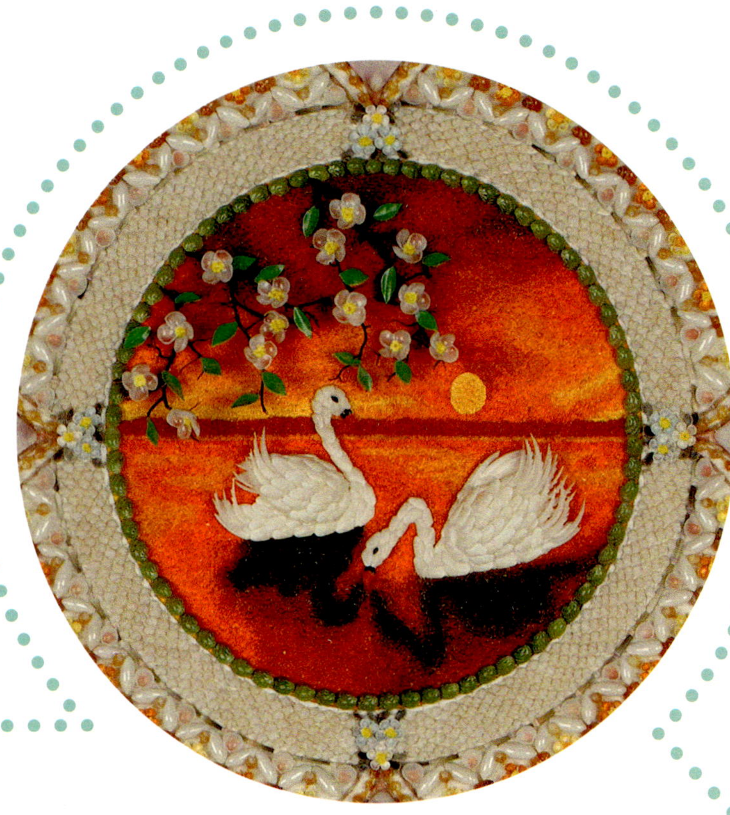

As the sun sets upon the lake, painting everything with a red-orange hue, two swans, made of tiny coquinas and gooseneck barnacles, rest under the hanging branches of a flowering tree. The tree is made of sea fans with apple blossom shell flowers and leaves of painted garfish scales placed on top of them.

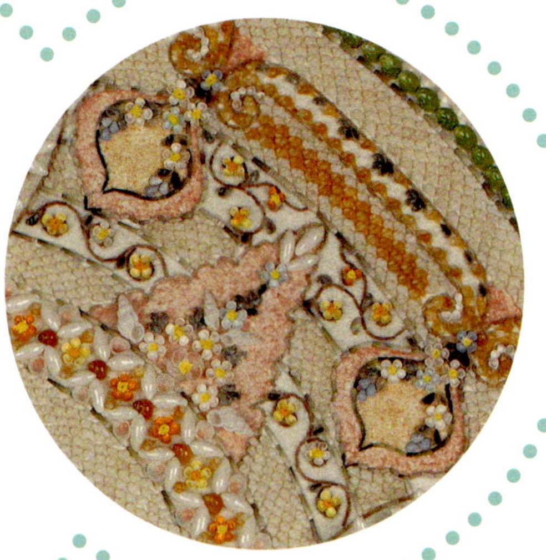

A scrolling ornamental pattern is made of cut sea urchin spines. Tiny lilac shell flowers accentuate the delicate design.

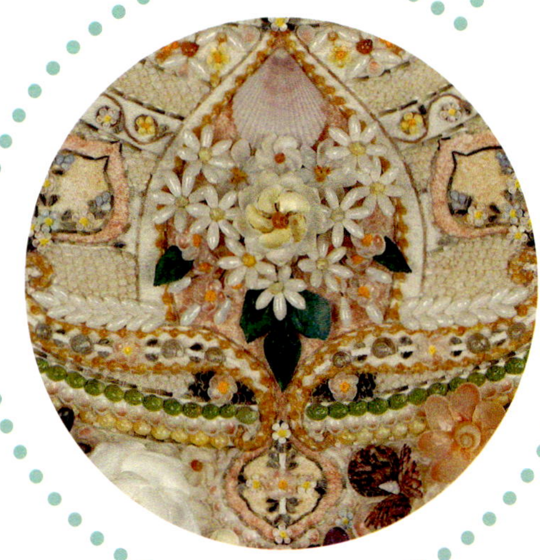

A pecten vase holds a bunch of flowers made of rice shells, apple blossom shells, cup shells, and cockles. Crushed pink tellins are used for the background.

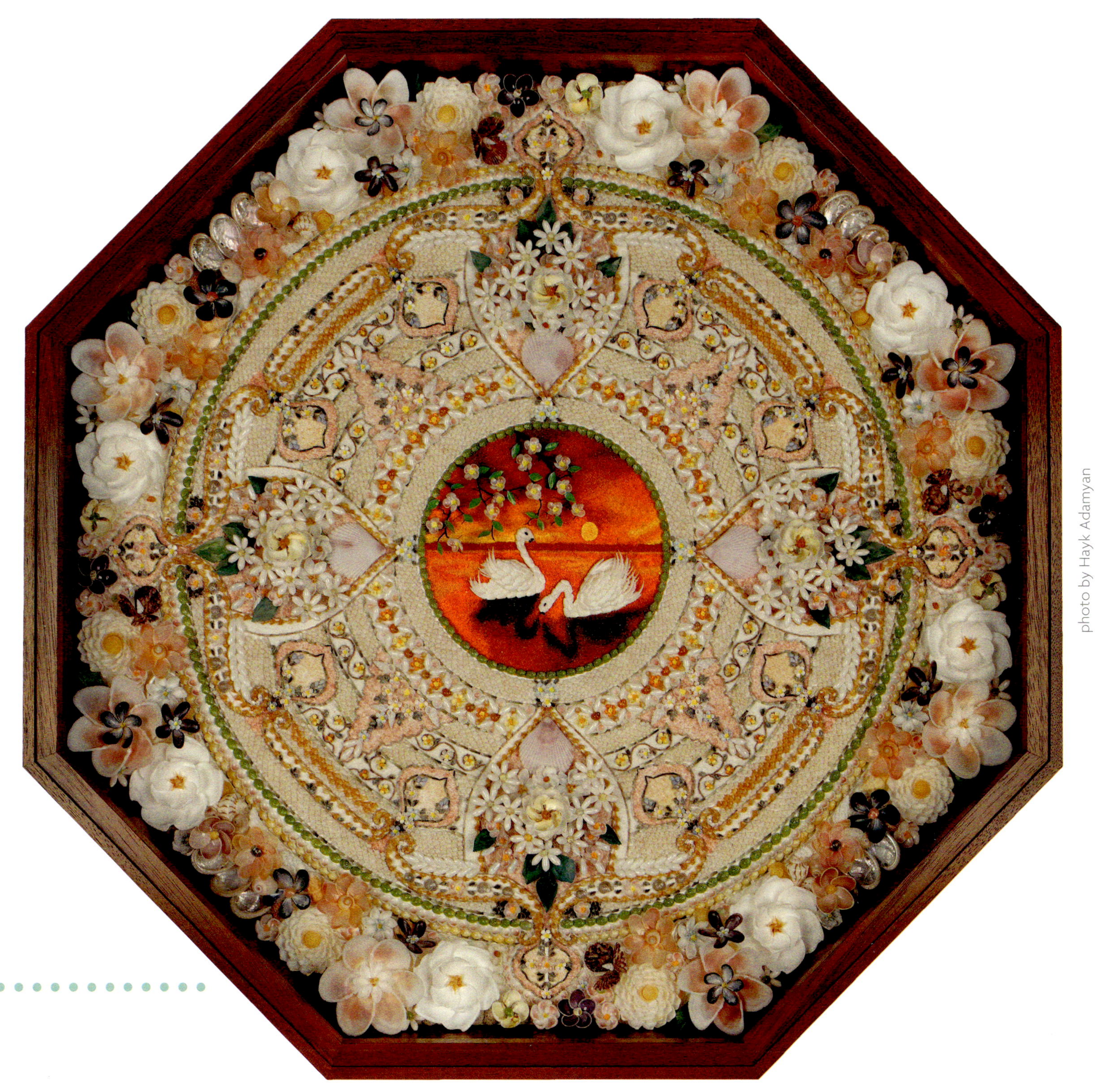

photo by Hayk Adamyan

Swans

Inspired by a small lake in Yerevan, Armenia, that is frequently visited by swans.

21-inch mahogany case made by Jim Prestigiacomo

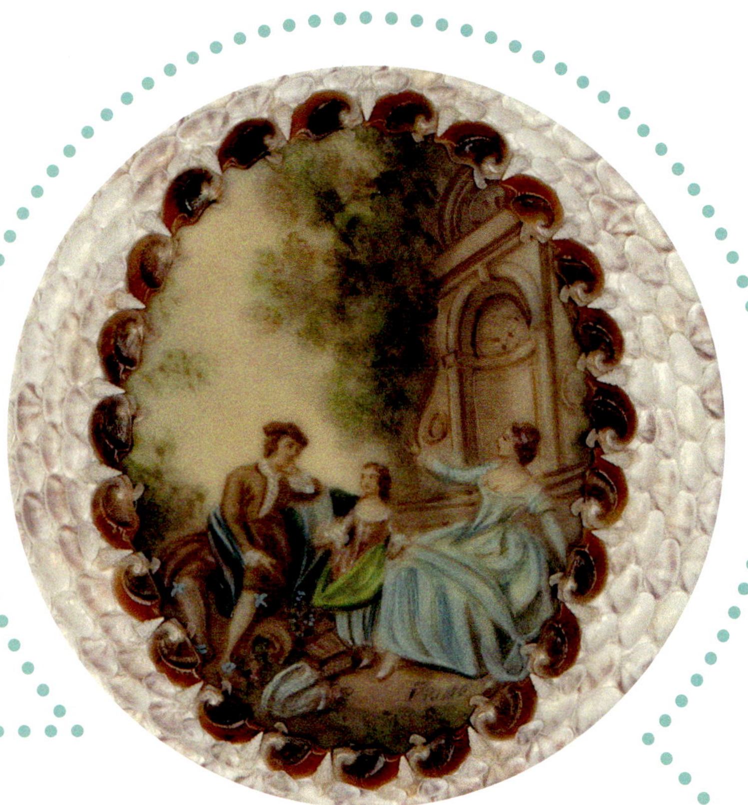

The image in the center is a vintage Italian original miniature painting, framed with operculums.

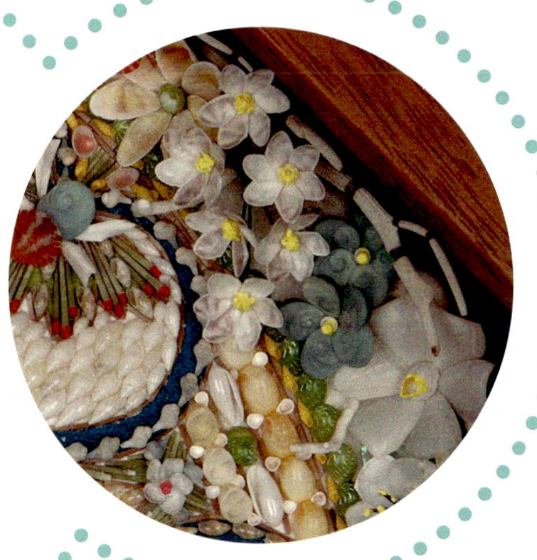

The borders are decorated with tiny flower arrangements. Delicate baby coquina shells are used to make six-petal flowers, which are bordered by other flowers made from red brachiopods and blue operculums. Rare banana coral from Hawaii is placed between the flowers.

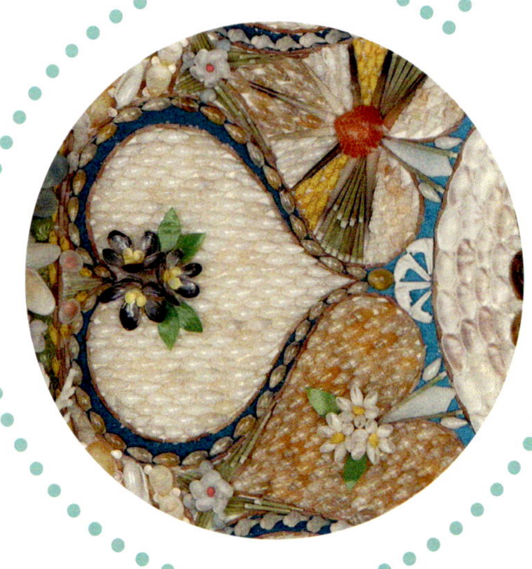

The center of the piece is surrounded by hearts done with white rice shells. Tiny blue mussel shells (collected from California beaches) form flowers that decorate the interior of the hearts. Painted fish scales are used for leaves.

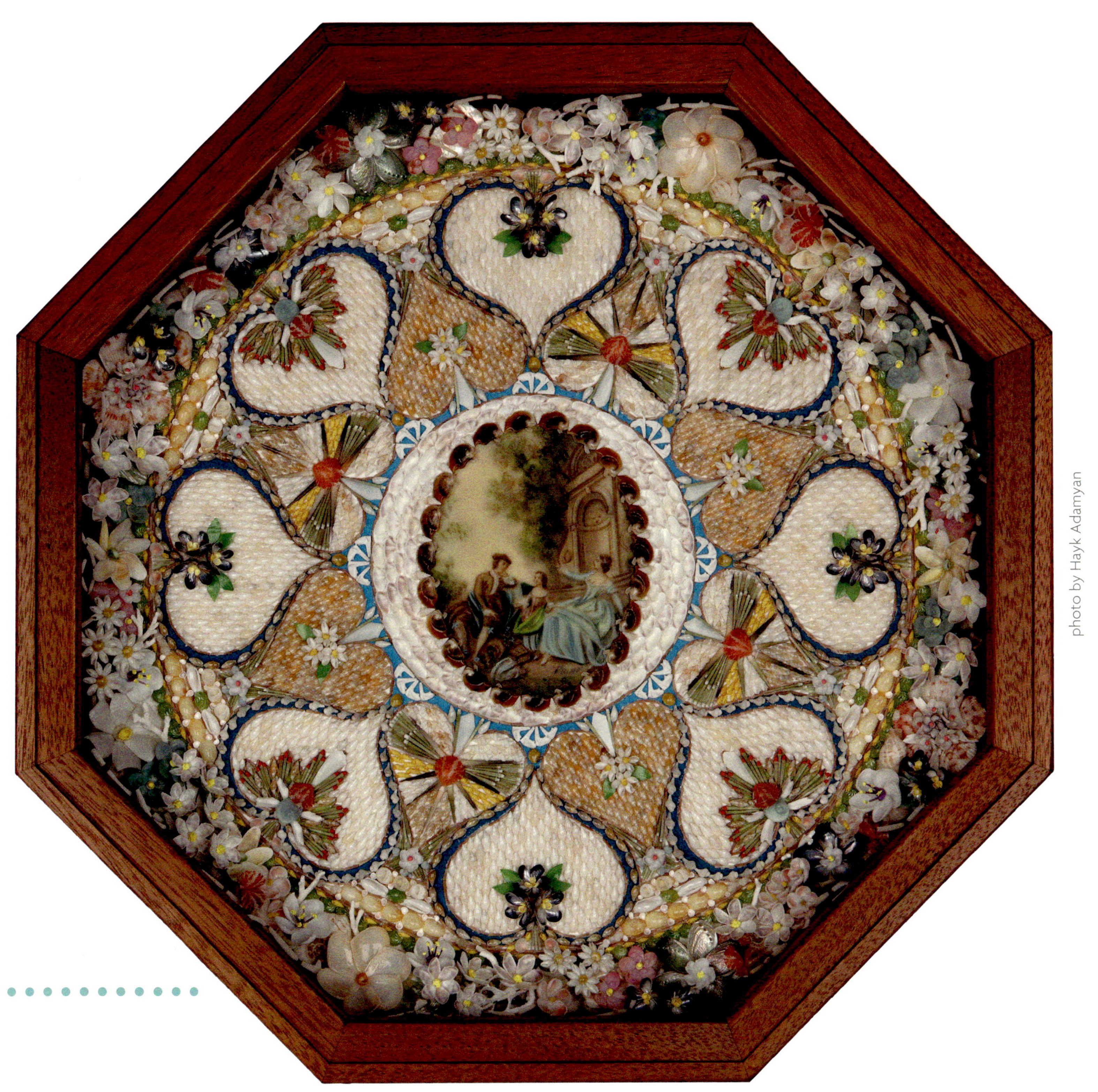

photo by Hayk Adamyan

Conversation in a Park

Inspired by the art of Romanticism.

12-inch mahogany case made by Jim Prestigiacomo

After shell artist Bill Jordan taught the artist how to make sea urchin letters, she wrote a romantic message using sea urchin spines on a disk of real ivory.

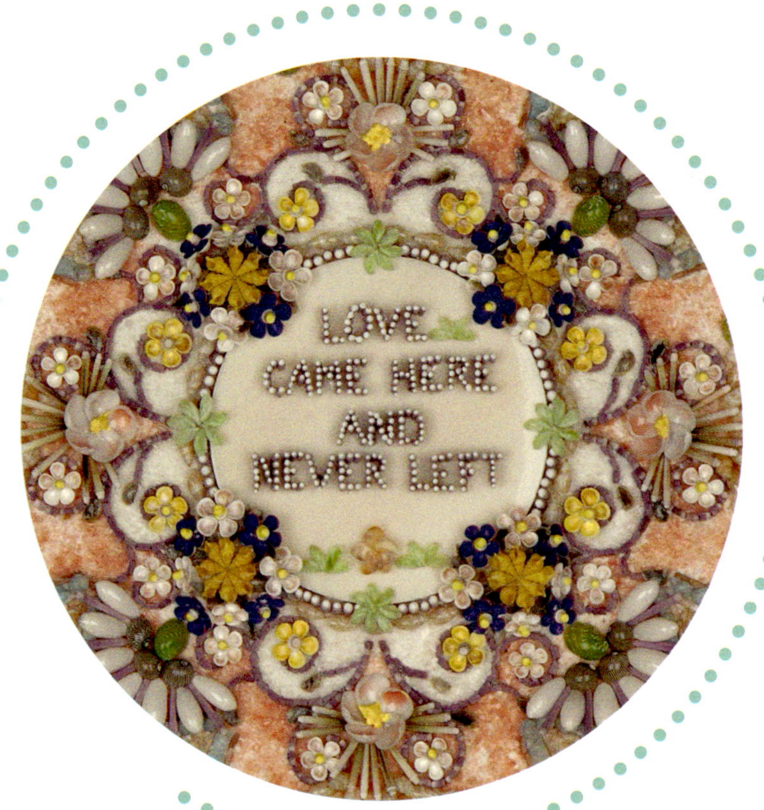

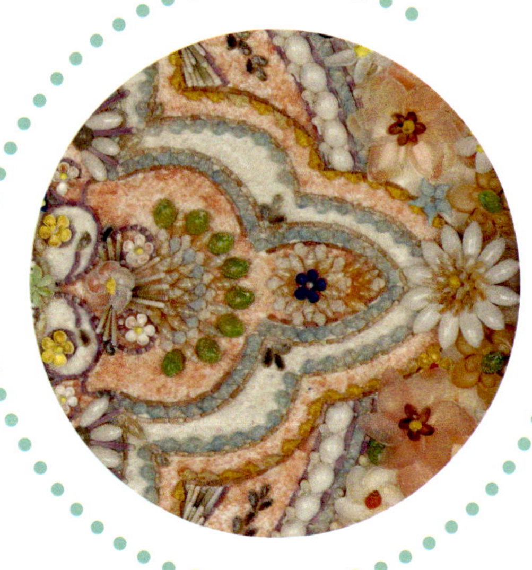

The four corners of the diamond are filled with emerald nerites, rice shells, and flowers made from lilac shells that have been dyed yellow and purple. They lie on a background of crushed pink tellins.

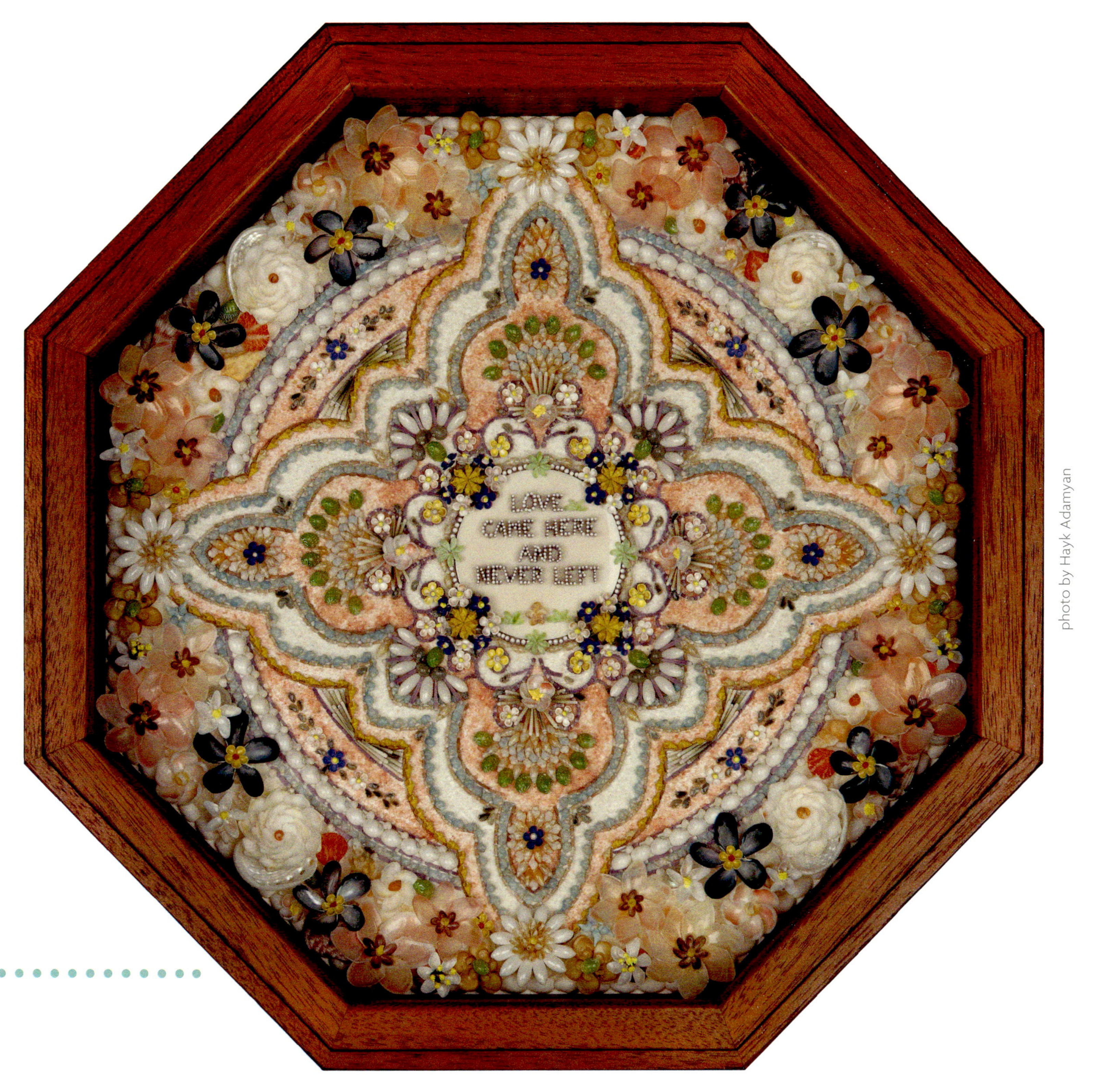

photo by Hayk Adamyan

Love Came Here ...

Inspired by the detailed work of shell artist Bill Jordan.

10-inch mahogany case made by Jim Prestigiacomo

photo by Andre Williams

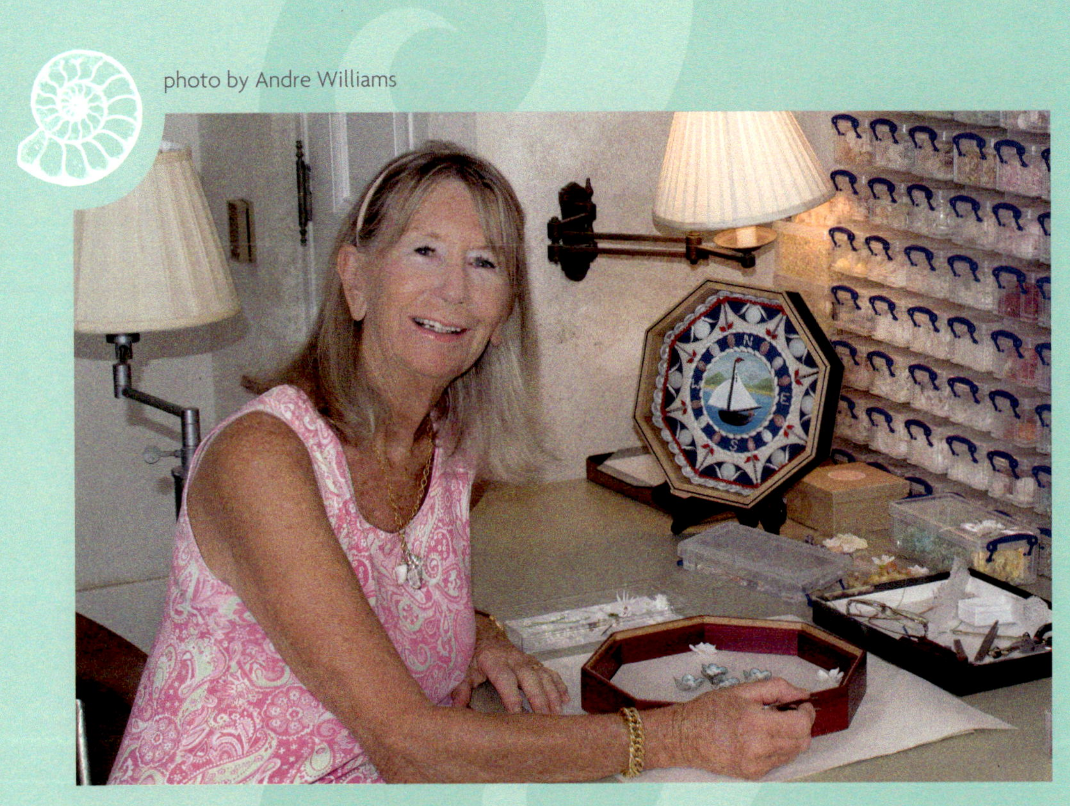

Sally Arbib

Wiltshire, England

I was born and raised in the South of England and currently spend my summer months in Wiltshire and the winter on Barbados. When my husband and I were building our house on Barbados, I discovered Sailors' Valentines in an auction catalogue while looking for antique furniture with a seaside feel. I started buying old Valentines whenever I saw them and now have a significant collection.

I always enjoyed shelling on the beach, and having found a good variety of shells on the beaches of Barbados, I began to think about having a go at a Sailors' Valentine. I found someone to make me a box, bought a few more shells from The Shell Gallery, and made my first Valentine for the millennium with the date as the centerpiece.

When I met Daphne Hunte* in 2012, I discovered the magnificent modern world of Sailors' Valentines and was immediately enthralled. I added several new pieces to my collection and then visited Daphne in her studio. She is such an enthusiast, and she gave me lessons on the various techniques of making shell flowers. I was hooked.

I proceeded to make Valentines for each of my 15 grandchildren. Those for the girls were the more typical flowery ones, but then, inspired by Connie Miller,** I began to design animals and boats for the boys.

In England I work in a bright conservatory overlooking the River Kennet, but on Barbados I have to share an office with my husband Martyn—not ideal! Martyn met my box maker, Paul Swan, on the golf course. Paul had never heard of Sailors' Valentines, but was a skilled carpenter who had made boxes of various shapes and sizes. He has become a great enthusiast and finds unusual woods and veneers for my boxes.

I am delighted to have discovered this compelling art form that occupies so much of my time and thoughts and that has led me to new friends from across the world who share a common passion.

* Daphne Hunte's work can be seen on pages 90–101.
** Connie Miller's work can be seen on pages 134–145.

The artist painted the face of a lion and sprinkled it with sand, then added pieces from gooseneck barnacles that were dyed in tea. Surrounding Leo is a row of sea urchin pieces and oat grain margin shells.

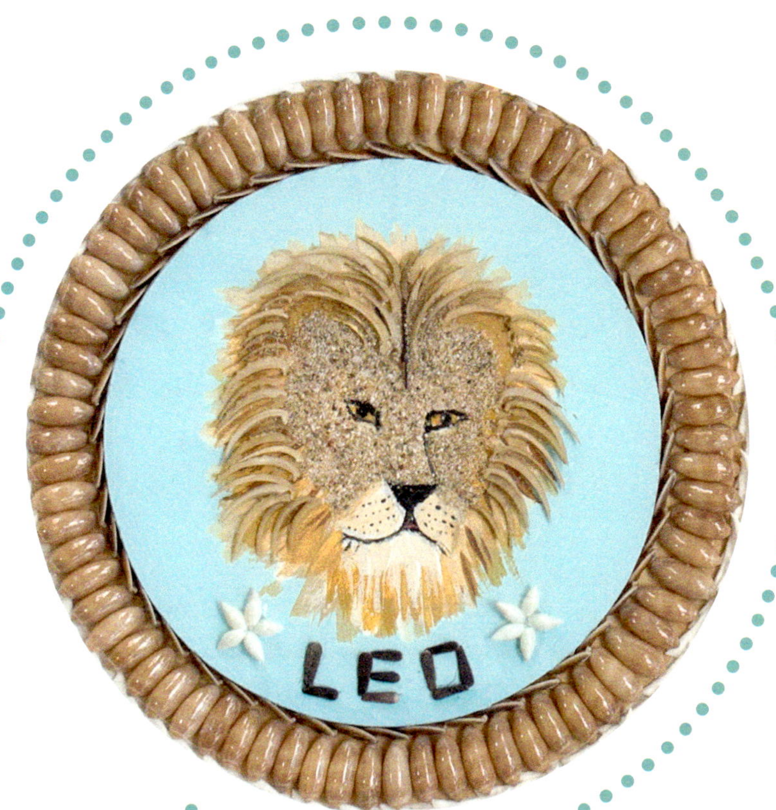

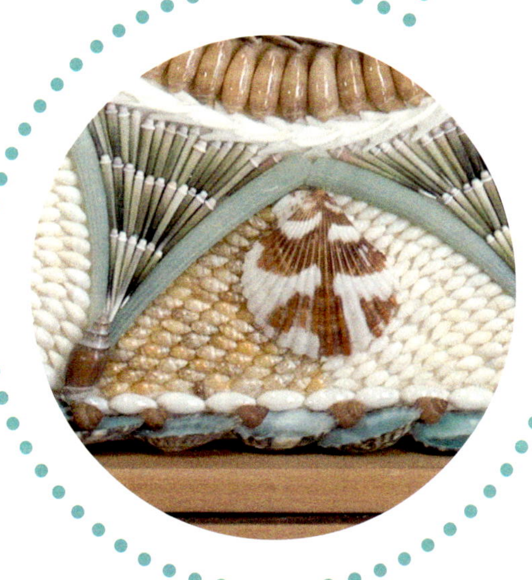

The outer sections have two colors of rice shells and a line of blue-green limpets and tiny Philippine melissas. Alternating in the eight sections are striped cerith shells and calico scallops.

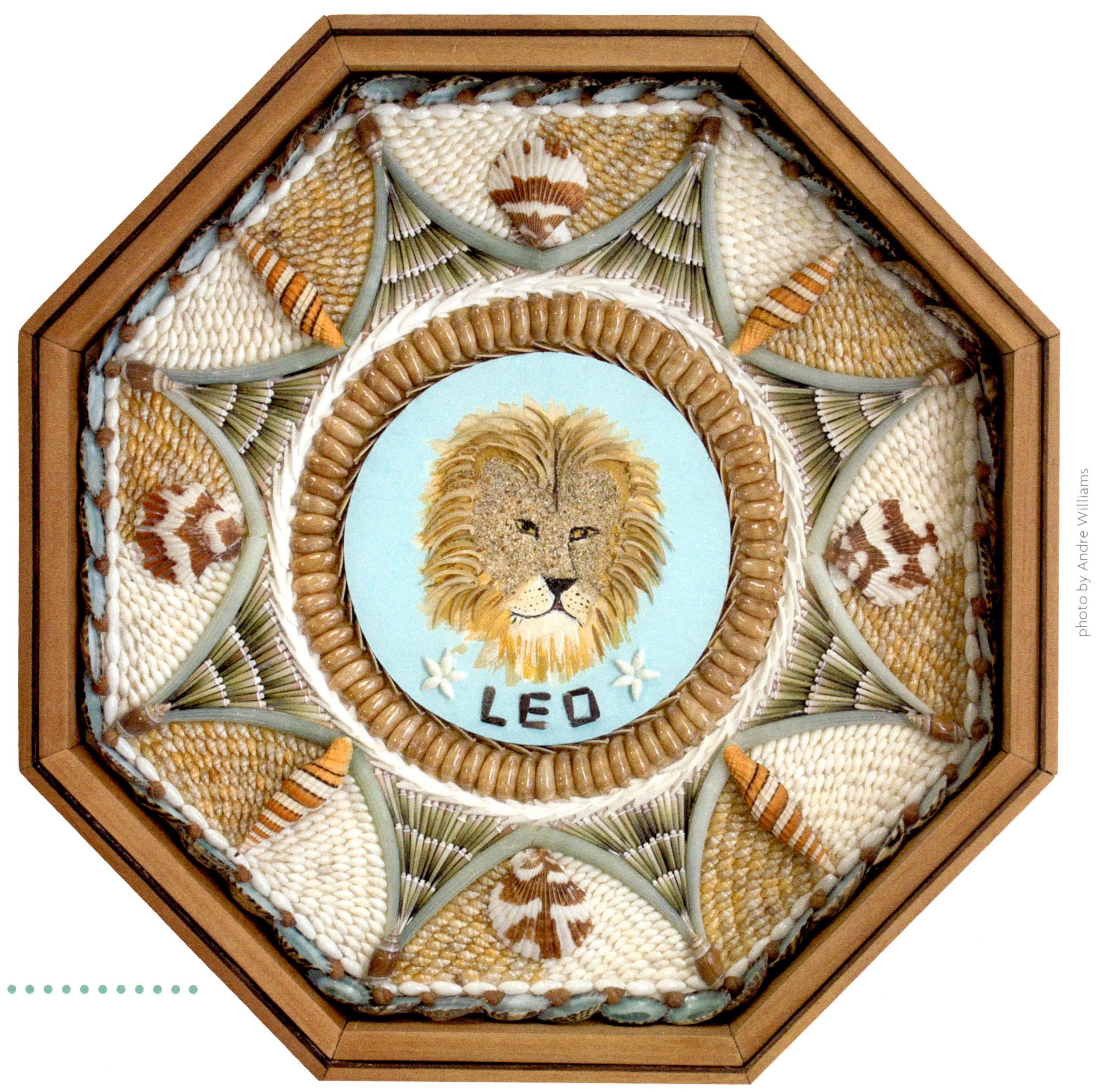

photo by Andre Williams

Leo

It had to be a lion for the artist's grandson Leo
—a simple design like a circus poster.

10-inch steamed pearwood case made by Paul Swan

Small pieces of abalone shell are used to create the background water effect. The swan's neck is made from tiny rice shells, with lima shells as the next layer, and then the bones of the sea urchin for the wing and tail feathers. The beak is a little piece cut from a smooth dove shell.

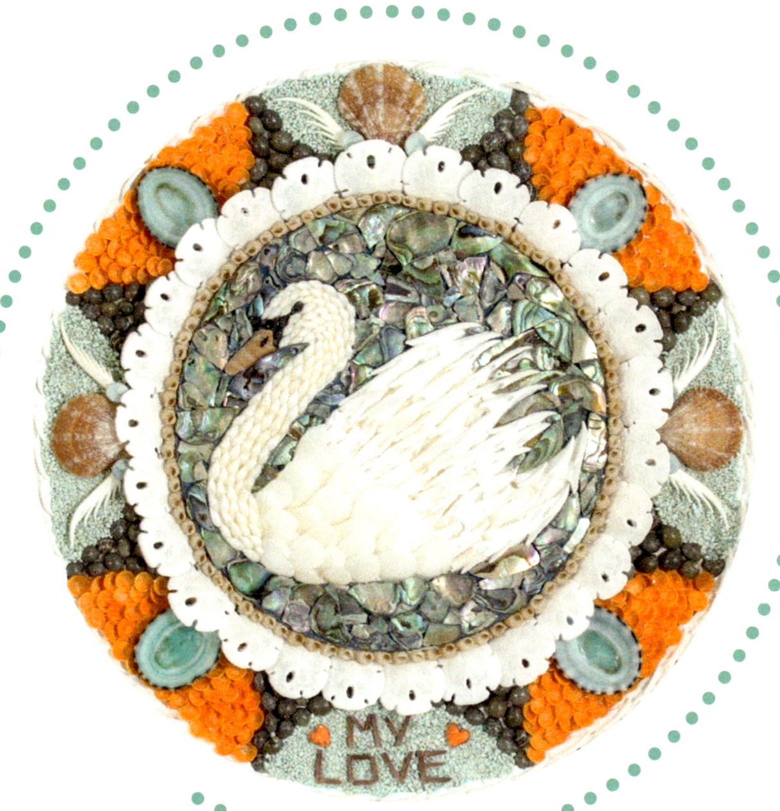

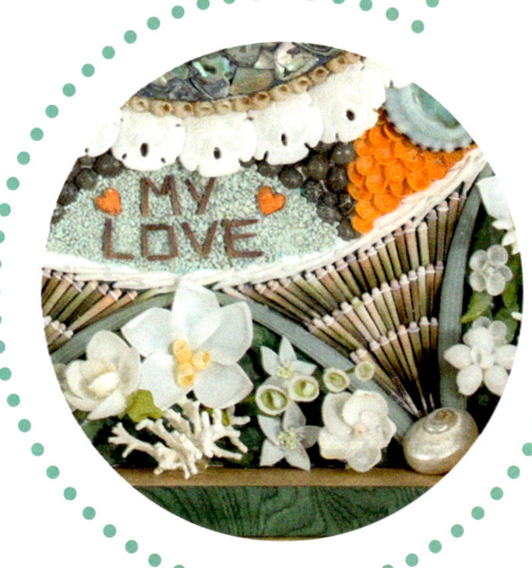

To complement the beautiful green of the case, the artist used coordinating shells: dyed green garfish scales, green tusk shells, green sea urchin spines, green limpets, and dyed green sand.

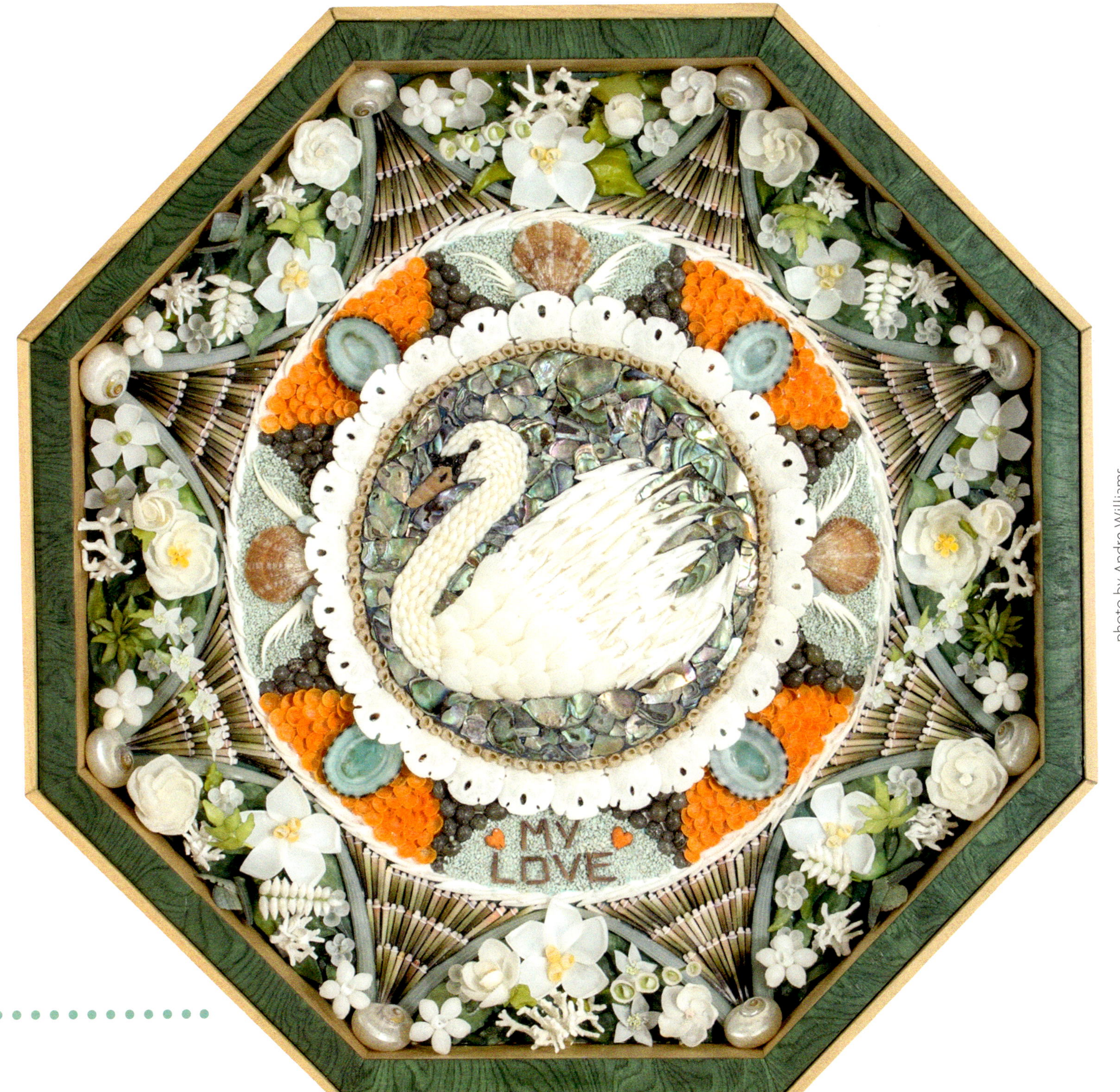

photo by Andre Williams

My Love

Inspired by a pair of swans gracefully swimming on the Kennet River in the view from a window of the artist's studio in Wiltshire, England.

10-inch lemonwood case with green veneer from Italy made by Paul Swan

This rather unusual fish has fins and lips of blue mussel shells. The body is created with three colors and sizes of cup shells and a band of white tusk shells; the eye is a keyhole limpet. Sand, sea fans, and small pieces of coral were used to create the sea floor.

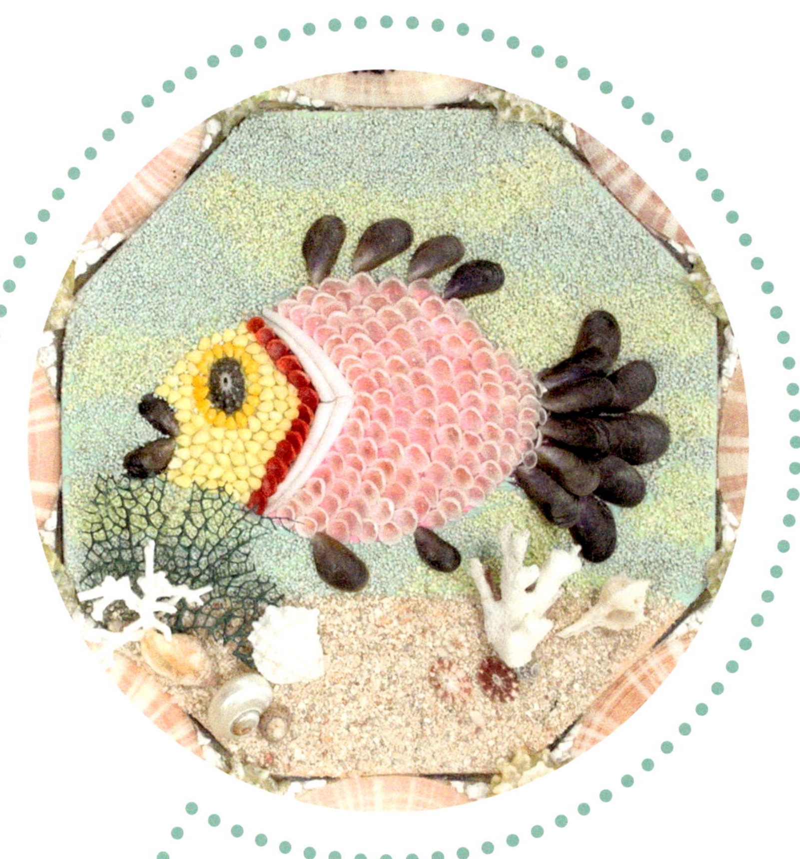

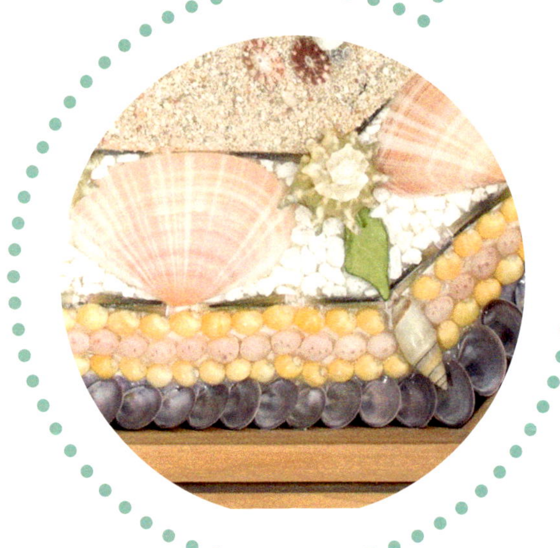

The color theme continues in the outer rim using yellow nerites, pink trivia shells, and a row of purple venus clams.

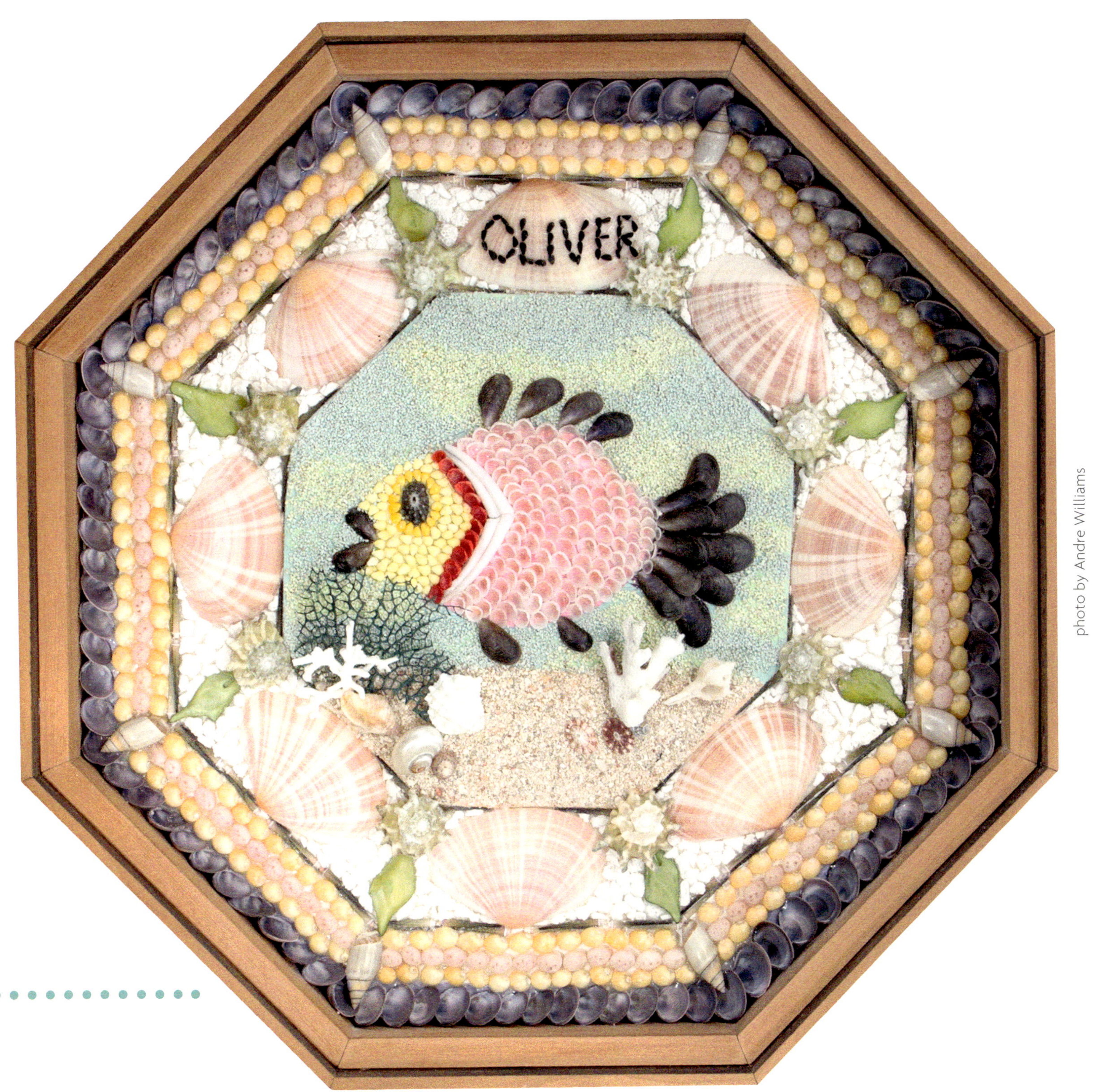

photo by Andre Williams

Oliver's Fish

The artist's grandson chose the colors for the fish in this Valentine made as a gift for him.

10-inch steamed pearwood case made by Paul Swan

The sea urchin vase is filled with tiny flowers made from natural and dyed cup shells. The green leaf is made from dyed garfish scales. Surrounding the vase are slices of ringtop cowries showing their purple insides, emphasized with apple blossom shells.

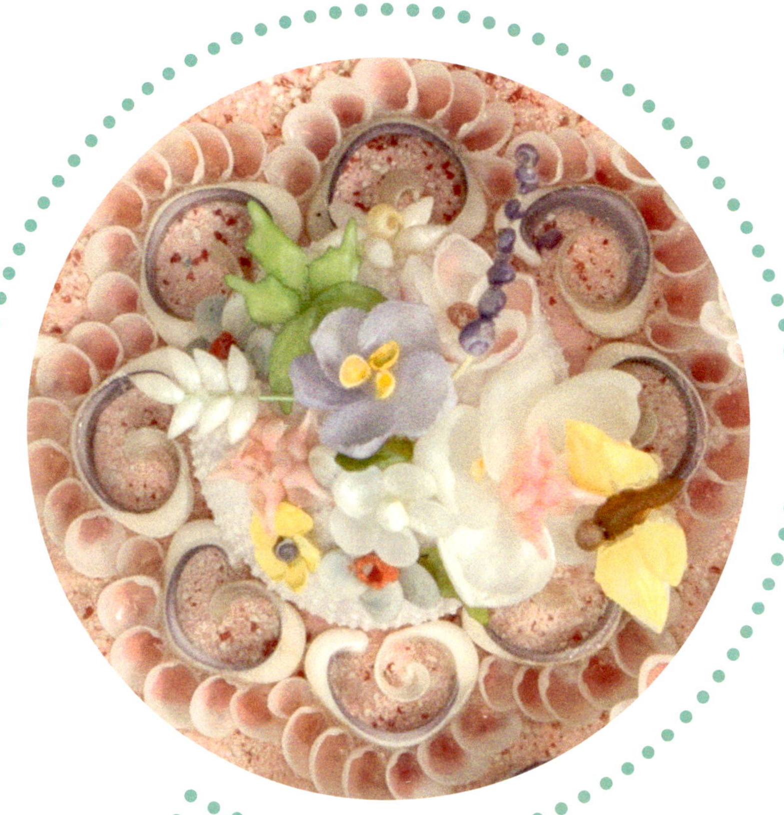

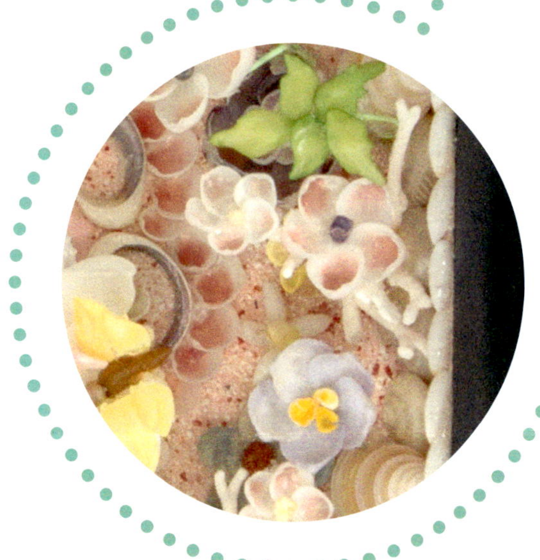

These same flowers are repeated at the edges with the addition of some white coral and a row of pearl umboniums.

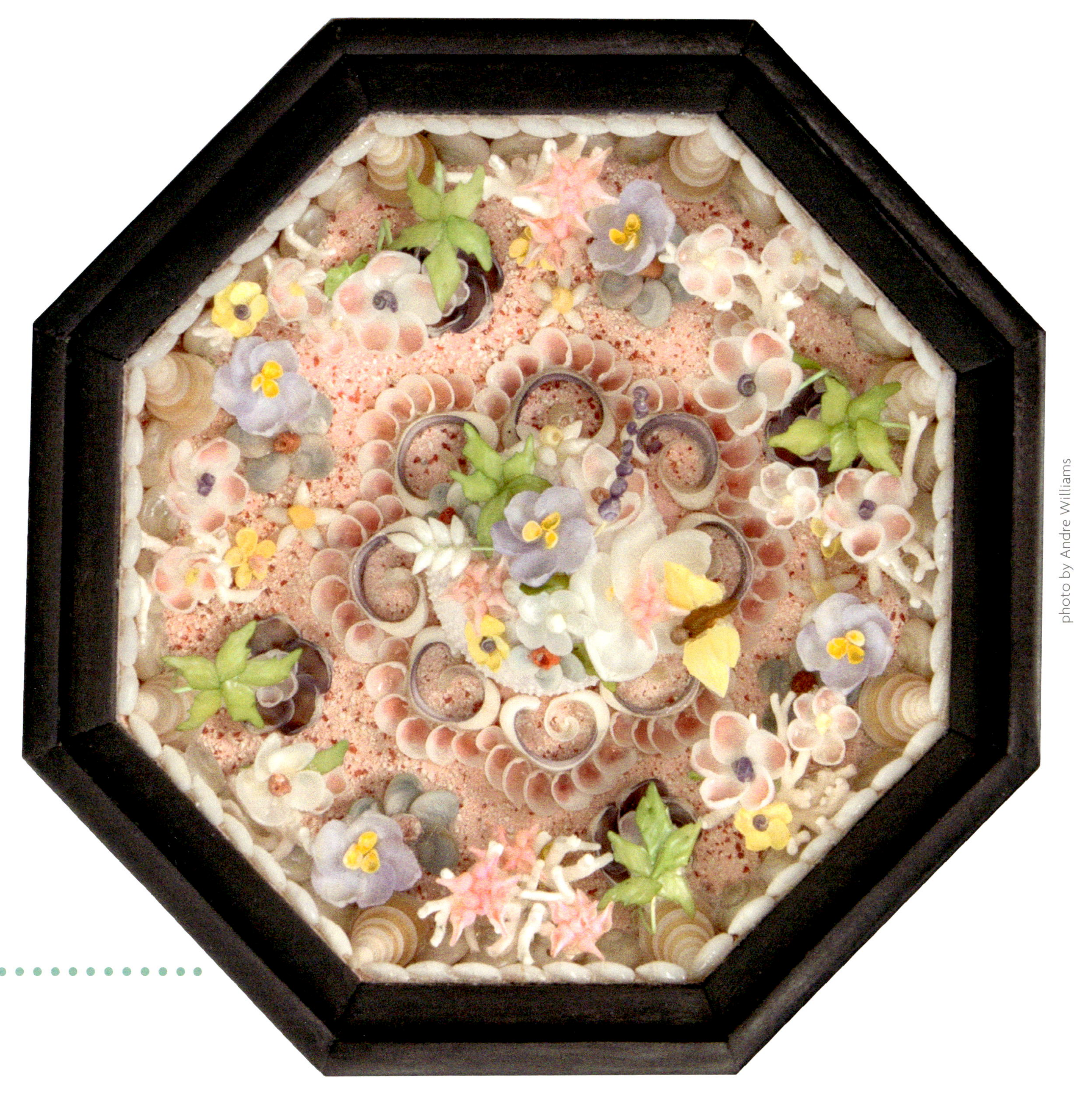

photo by Andre Williams

In the Pink

Created as a gift for a good friend with colors the artist imagined she would love.

5-inch case, wood and maker unknown

photo by Glenn Bassett

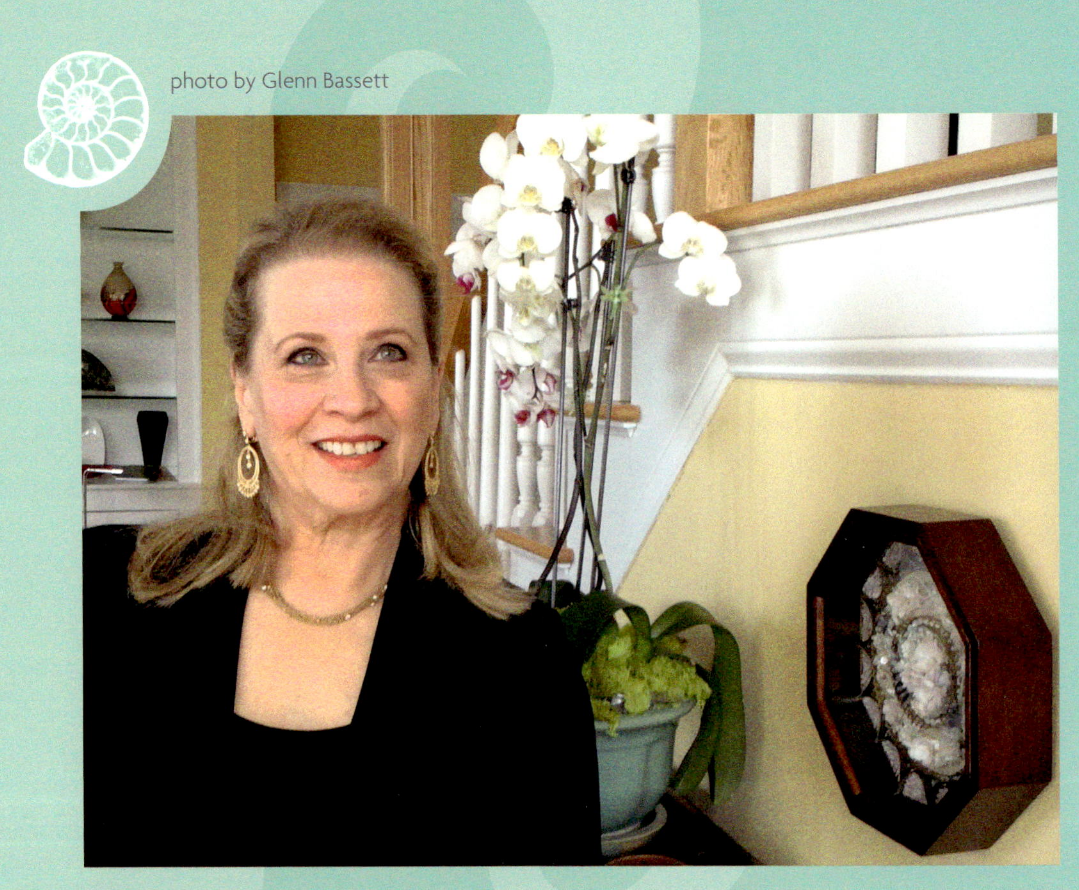

Sandi Blanda

Plymouth, Massachusetts

I saw my first Sailors' Valentine in 1983 when a friend purchased one at a gallery on Nantucket. I fell in love with it and did some research, finding photographs of the original primitive designs. I knew then that I wanted to take the art form to a different level, in particular by incorporating a multitude of shell flowers of varying colors surrounding the center. Because I had been misinformed that sailors made them at sea, I expected the process to be quite simple. That was not the case, and I struggled to create my first pieces. But the Aaron Faber Gallery, prominent in New York City to this day, encouraged me to produce a dozen pieces in six months and offered to sponsor a show of my work if I achieved that goal . . . and so I did.

For more than 20 years I worked in the basement of my Long Island home, covering every horizontal space with shells. Sea urchins and their many pieces are, to me, the most interesting to work with. Not only can beautiful flowers be made from their parts, but I also use them to create the lacy fill that is a key component of my work.

The first Sailors' Valentine I made remains my favorite. Though it was done in a poorly constructed 17-inch pine box, my personal style was evident from the beginning. I decided early on that I would use only shells that were completely natural, not wanting to lacquer and oil them to enhance their colors as some had recommended. I love bold colors, but when I need to cleanse my palette, I design an all-white Valentine. I have created more than 80 all-white Valentines in my career and have never duplicated one.

In addition to making Sailors' Valentines, I have done considerable research on their history, and I am proud to have consulted with John Fondas, who wrote the first book on them in 2002. I have also restored antique pieces from both museum and personal collections, which always yields insightful information.

If my work enriches the lives of others, I am flattered. If my work transports people to our country's rich maritime past, that's even better. But sharing my passion by teaching others is by far the greatest joy my work provides.

www.christina.com/artist/sandi-blanda

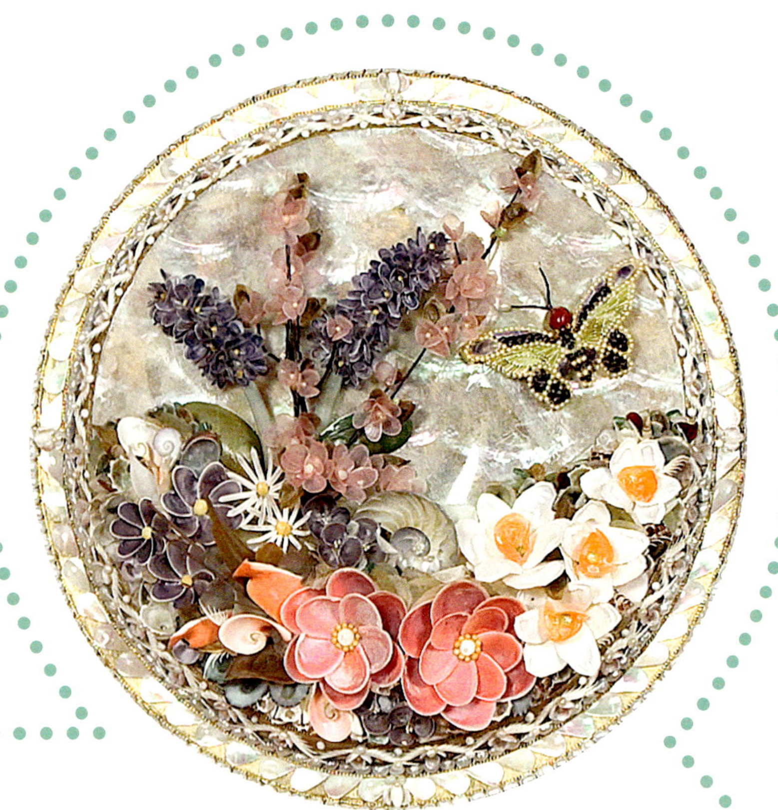

Deep pink rosecup shell flowers add a resplendent burst of color at the bottom of the centerpiece.

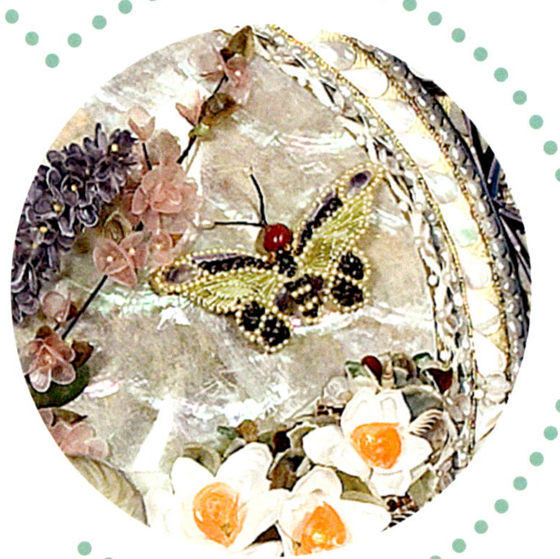

The butterfly is made from green sea urchin spines, seed pearls, tiny blue mussel shells, black snails, and black coral dotted with pearls for the antennae. The head is a rare burgundy snail.

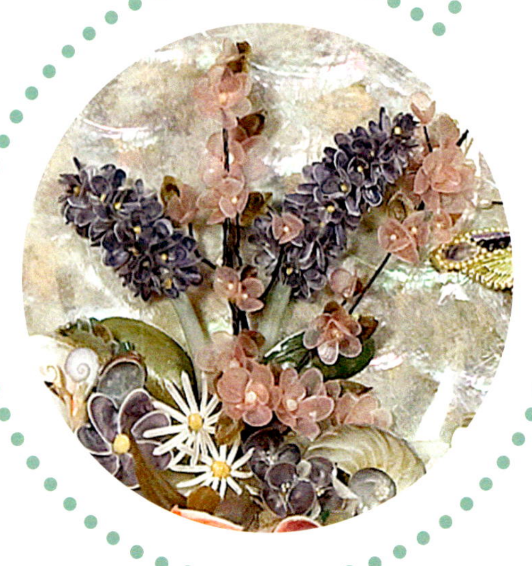

Butterfly bushes are created from miniature blue mussel shells.

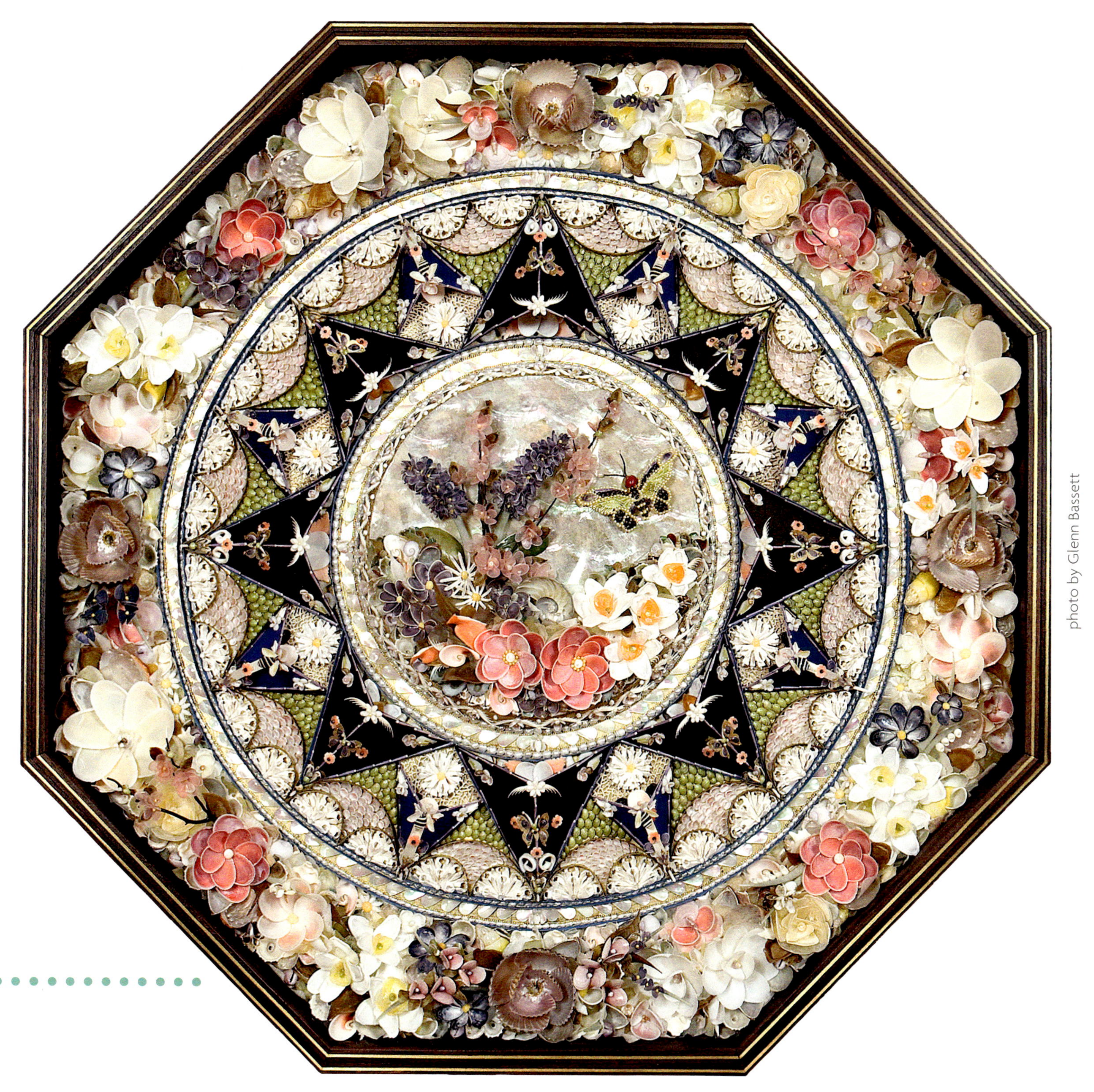

photo by Glenn Bassett

Chrysalis

In 2006 the artist planted a butterfly bush that was always visible from her studio window. Inspired by its blue flowers, she decided to interpret it for this Valentine.

24-inch mahogany case made by Bill Jordan

The braided heart is common in antique Sailors' Valentines and is difficult to master. This one is made of rose petal tellins and rosecup shells. Purple urchin spines surround the bottom and chiton pieces surround the top.

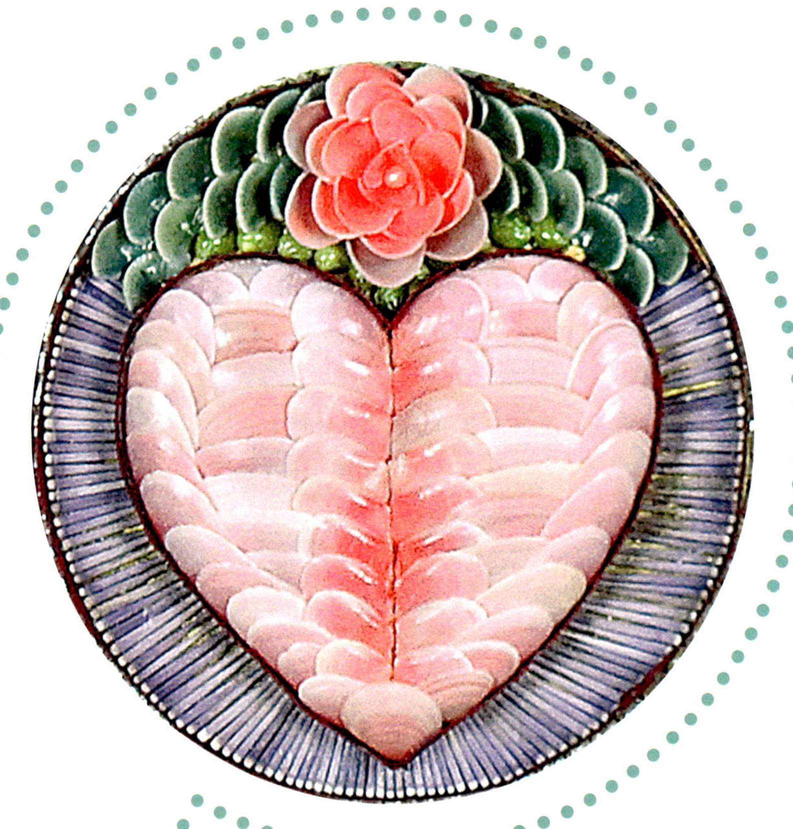

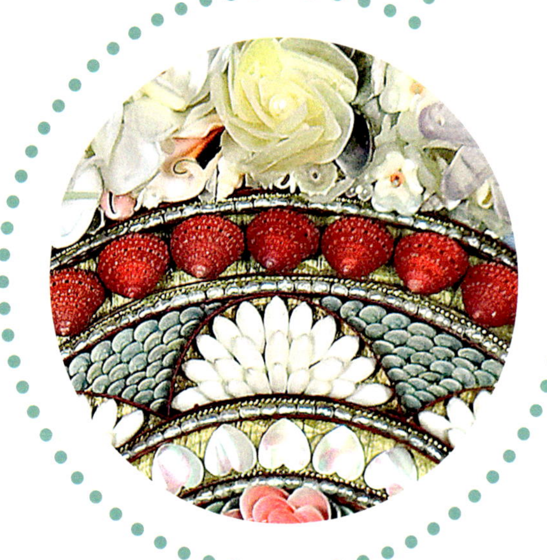

The artist searched through at least a thousand strawberry top shells to find these perfect matches.

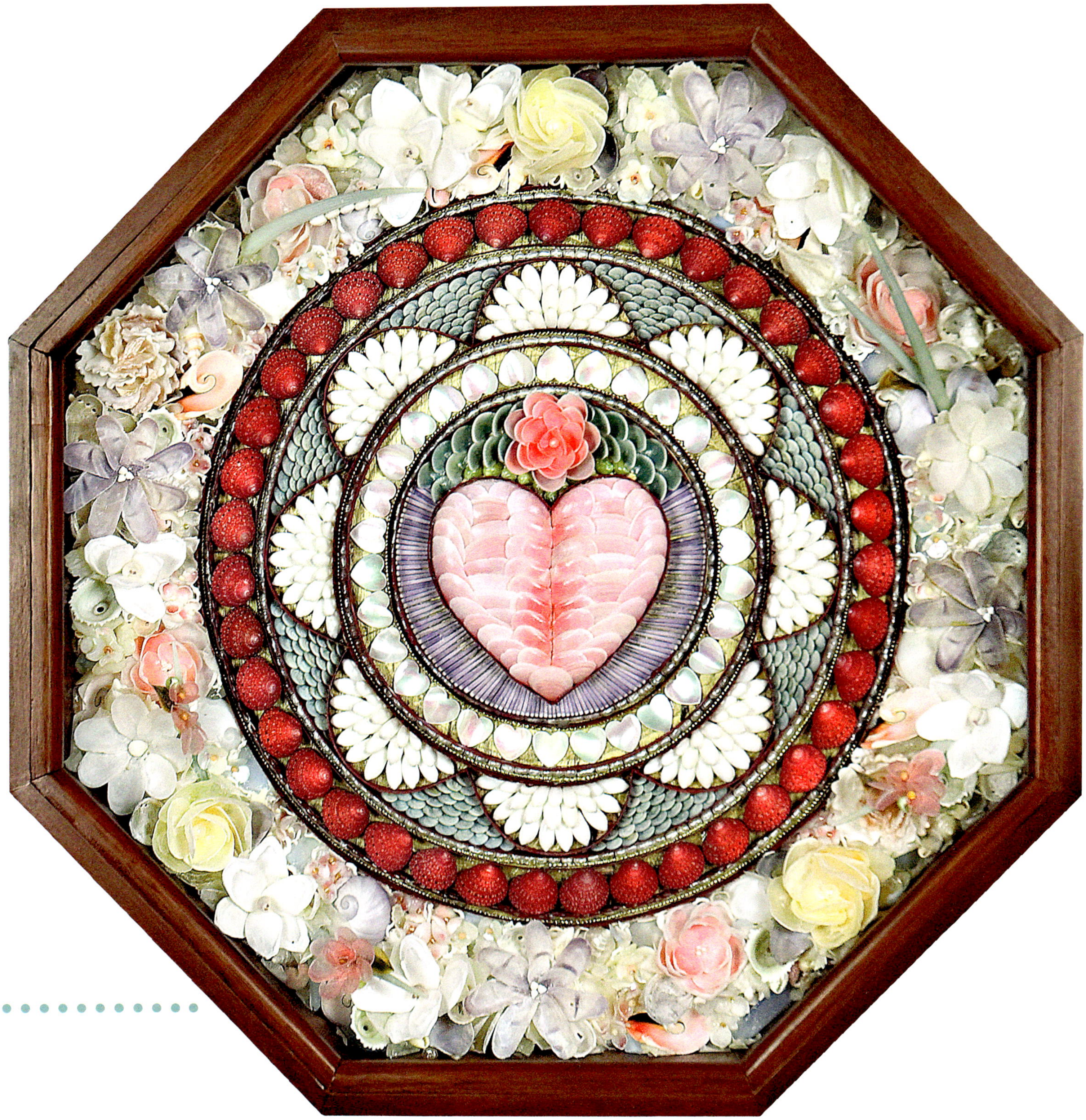

photo by Glenn Bassett

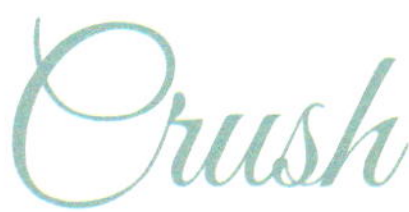

A sentimental person by nature, the artist imagined a person buying this piece for someone he or she had a secret crush on.

13-inch mahogany case made by James Perkins

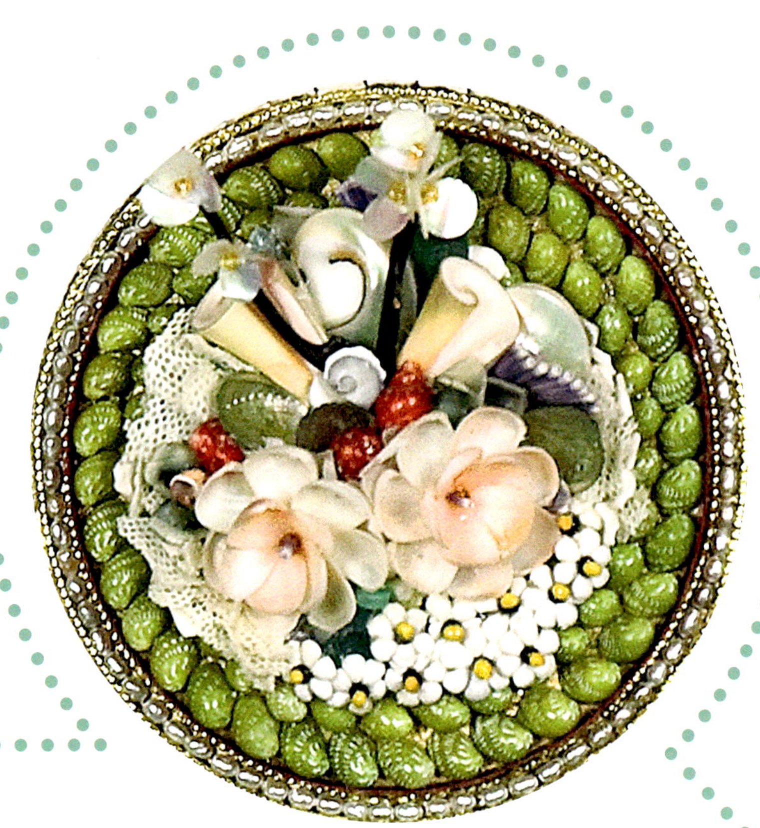

Emerald nerites encircle the center bouquet, adding great depth of color.

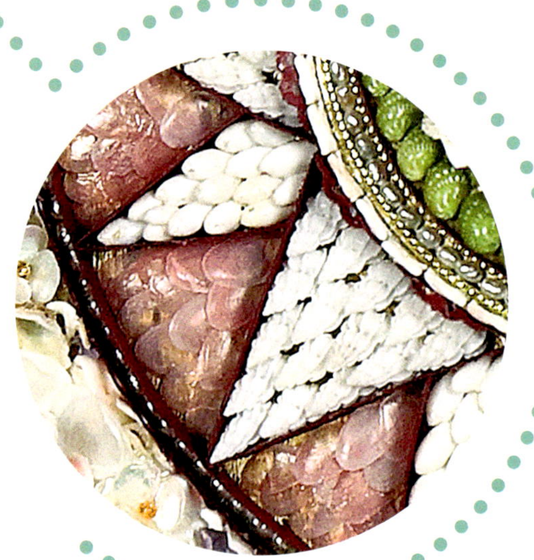

The star is filled in with pink fairy tellins, which the artist says are the most difficult shells she has ever worked with because of their delicacy. Nearly 25 percent crumbled as she placed them one by one.

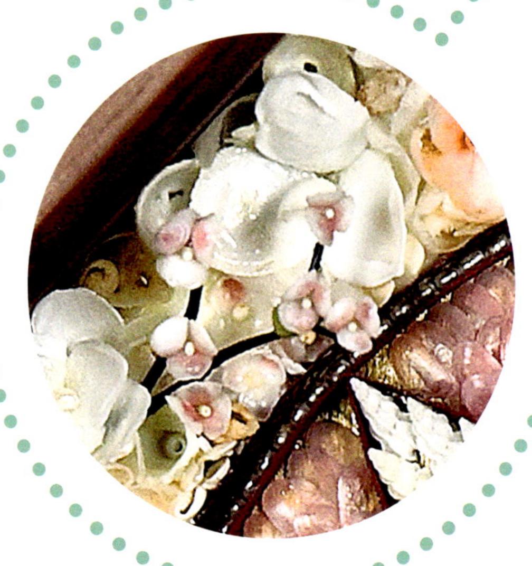

Apple blossom shells form delicate little flowers placed on branches of black coral.

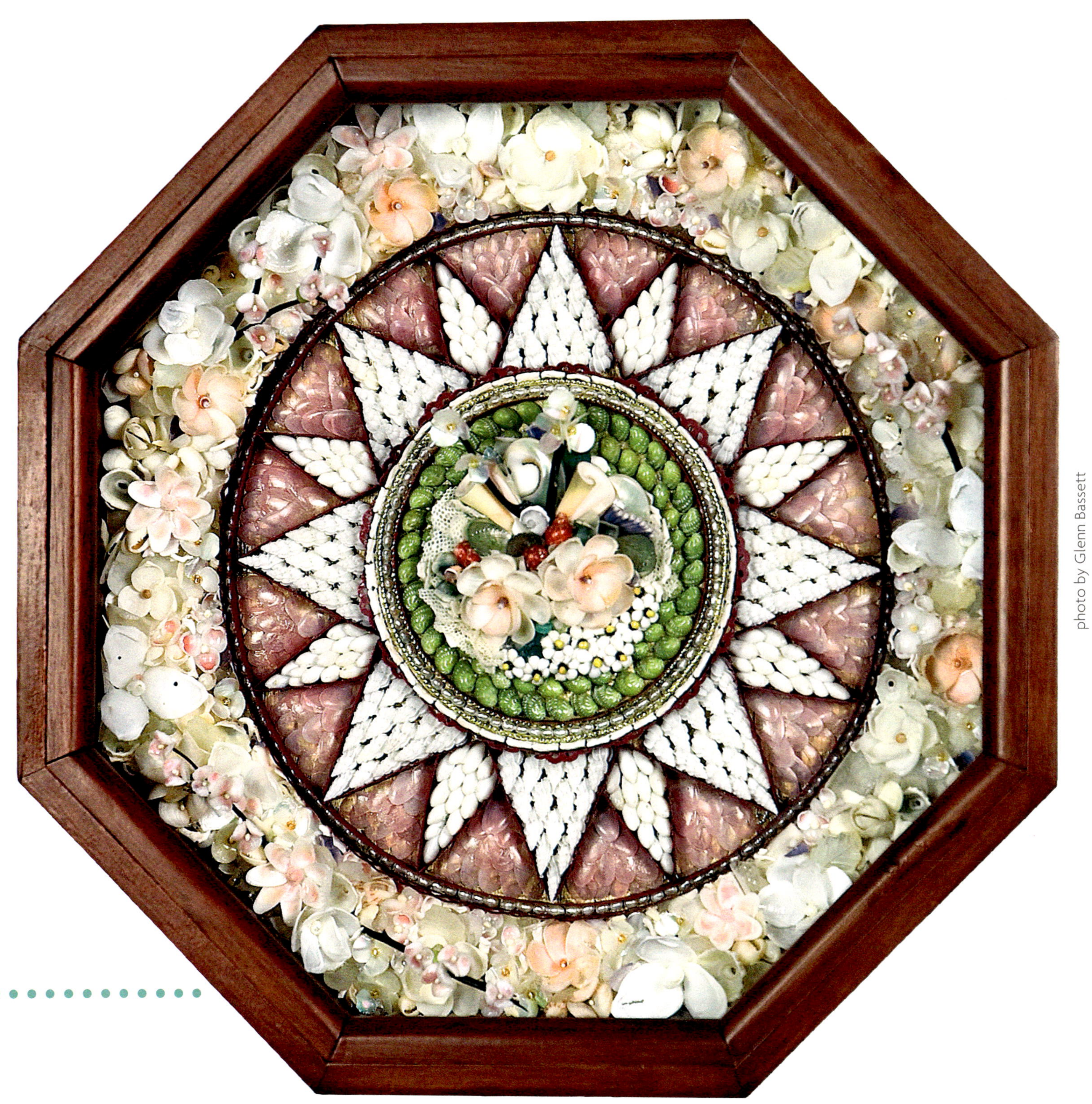

photo by Glenn Bassett

Crimson Tide

Many pieces the artist creates represent a specific season, and this portrays autumn.

10-inch mahogany case made by James Perkins

The center bouquet includes a water lily done from tiny angel wing shells, with urchin spines and yellow mustard seeds at its center.

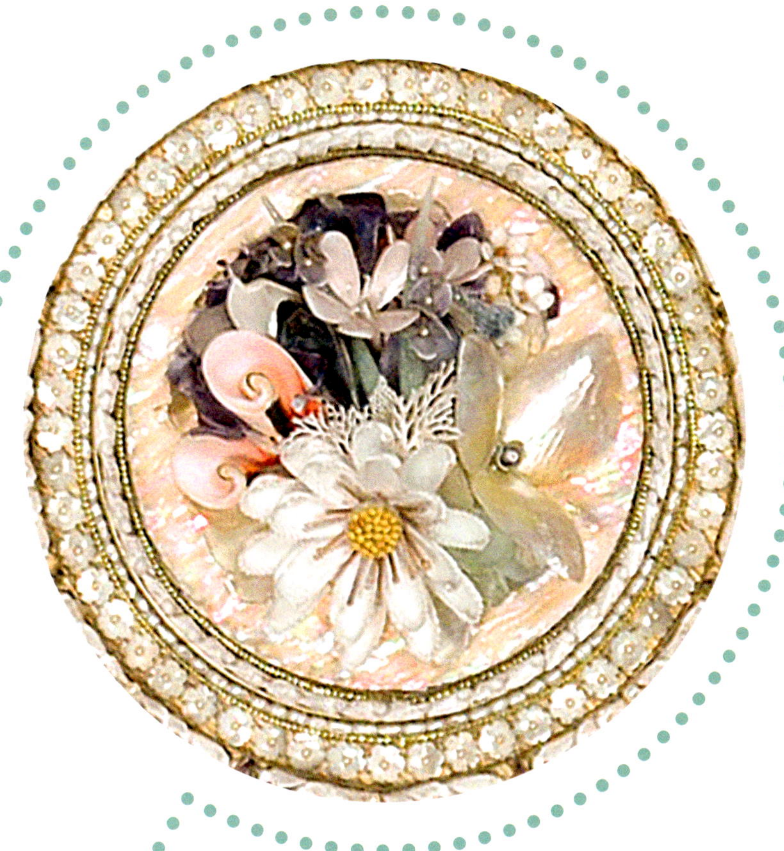

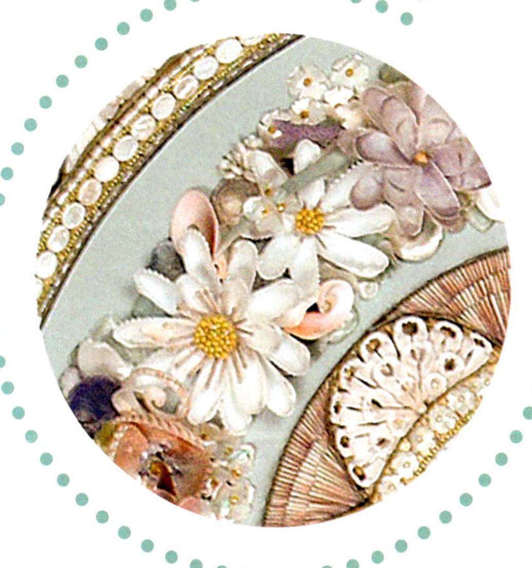

The pale blue background is silk fabric. The artist's color selection isn't usually this soft, but once she laid this out, she knew the title immediately.

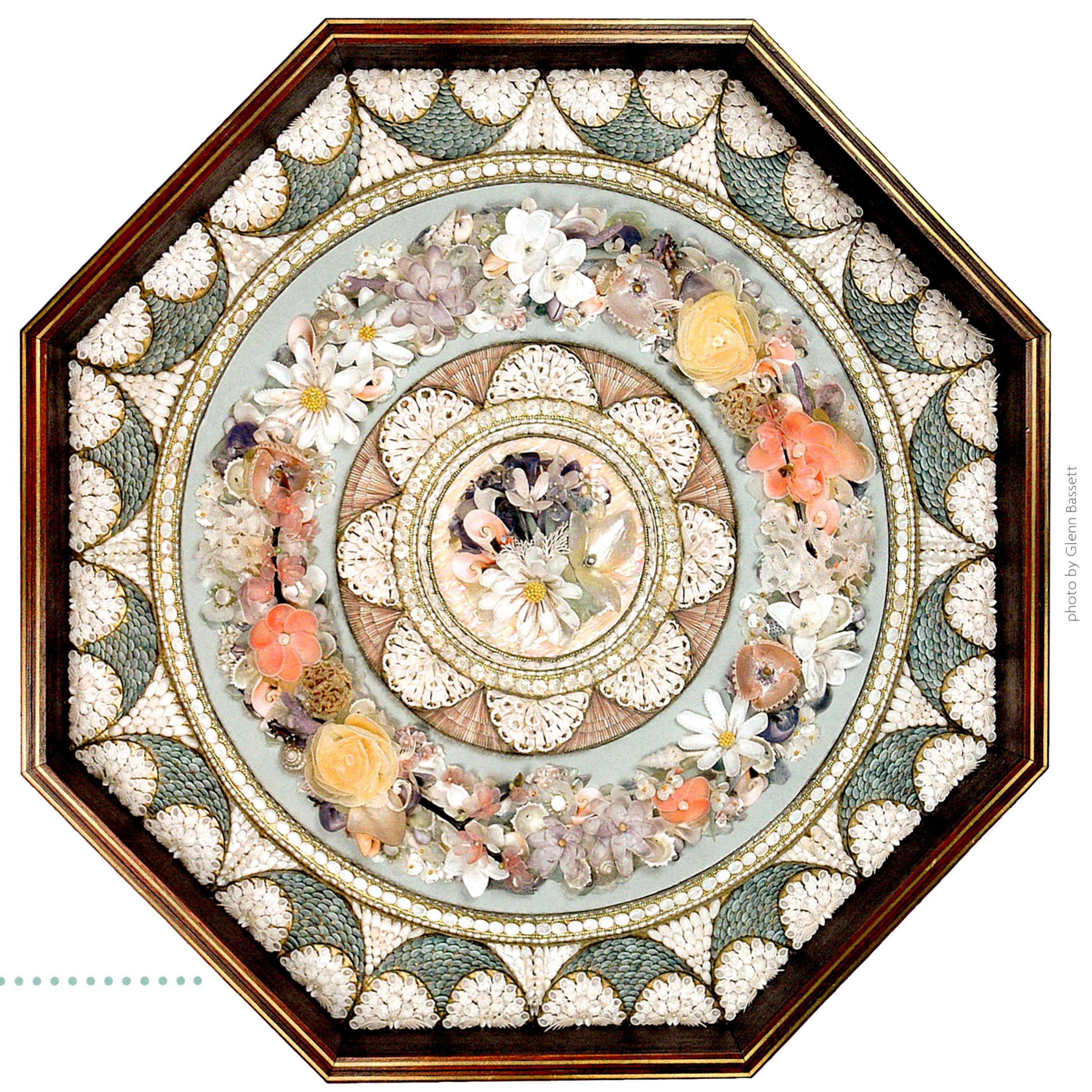

photo by Glenn Bassett

Whisper

A student challenged the artist to make a water lily. She knew immediately that it would feature baby angel wing shells, and she loved the finished product enough to incorporate them in a Sailors' Valentine done on silk. Several surviving antique pieces done on silk provided inspiration for this piece.

19-inch mahogany case made by Bill Jordan

Vibrant pink rosecup shells make up the bold flower at the bottom of the centerpiece. Surrounding it are blue flowers from micro blue mussels collected off Martha's Vineyard. Interspersed in the arrangement of flowers is lacy white coral.

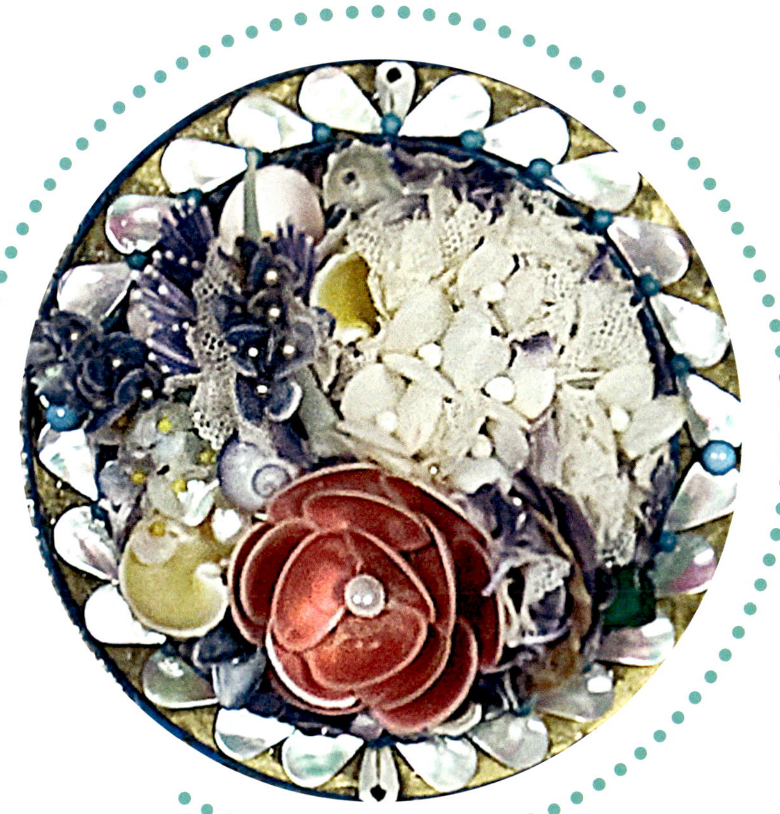

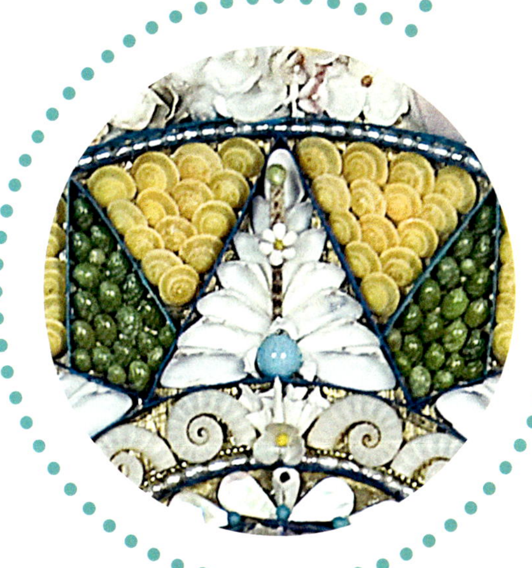

Semiprecious stones are used frequently by the artist in her work. In this piece turquoise embellishes the star. Above the turquoise sits a sea urchin spine with a lilac shell flower on top.

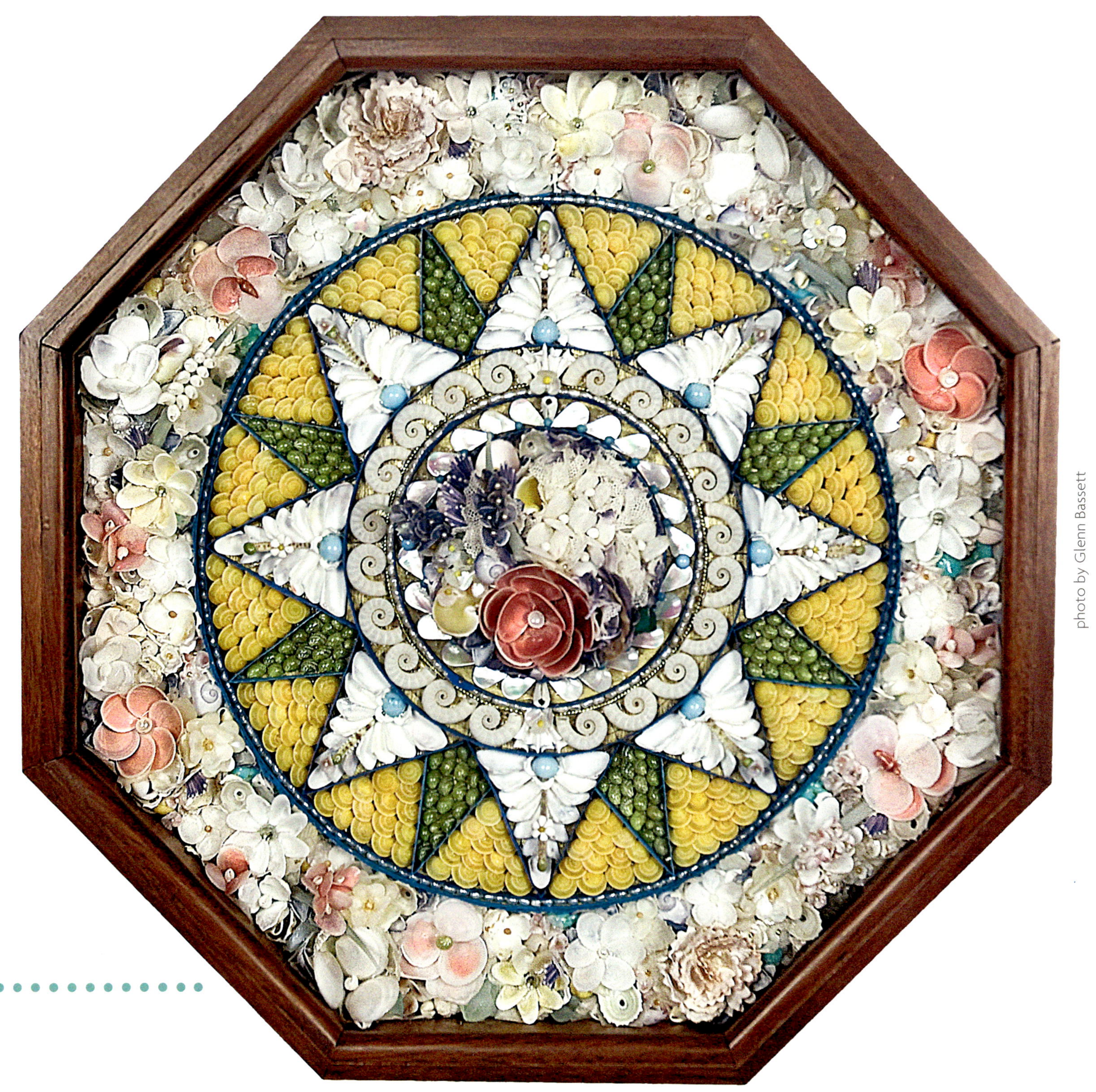

photo by Glenn Bassett

Shindig

The main living area in the artist's home is yellow, and the color is a constant source of inspiration for her.

13-inch mahogany case made by James Perkins

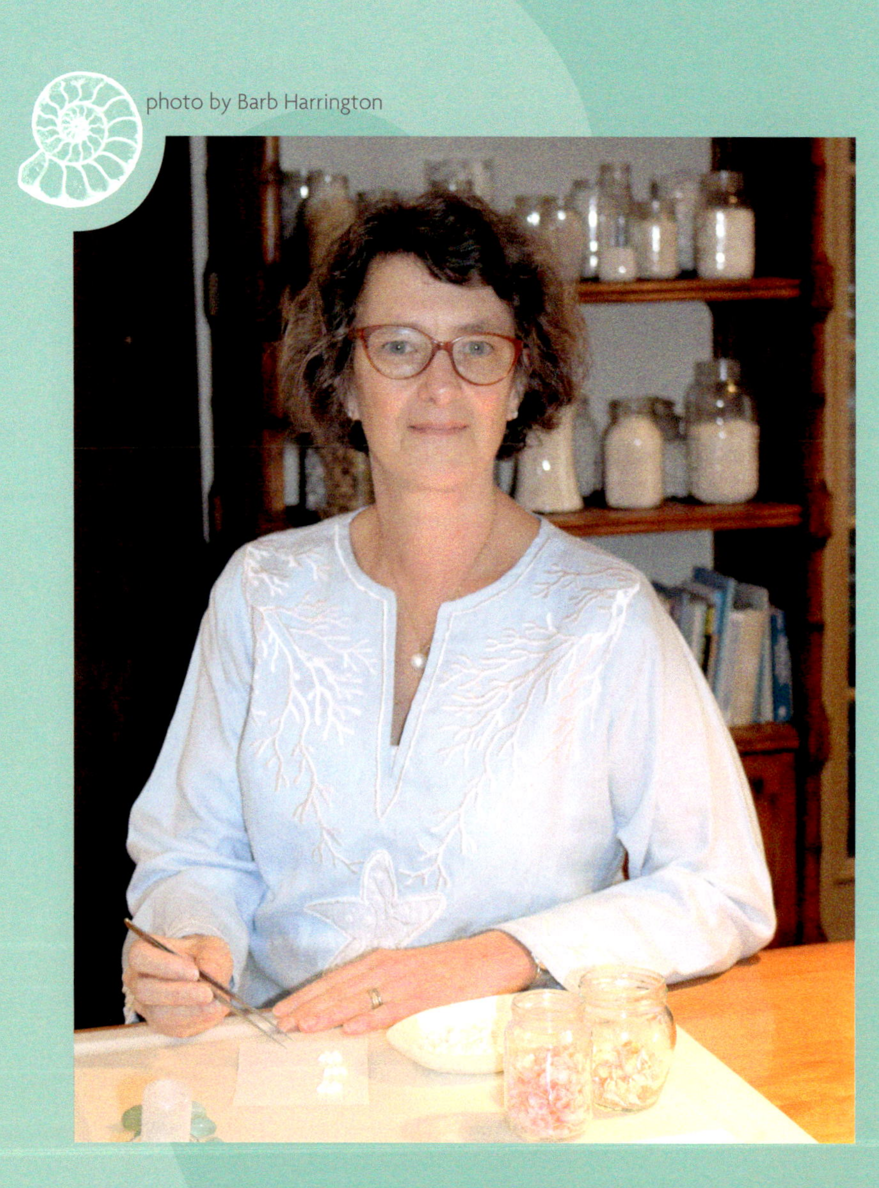
photo by Barb Harrington

Pamela Boynton

Sanibel Island, Florida

My introduction to Sailors' Valentines came about when I visited the Bailey-Matthews National Shell Museum on Sanibel Island in 1996 shortly after the museum opened. I stood before the exhibit for a long time, intrigued and mesmerized. I went on to other exhibits but kept circling back to the Sailors' Valentines, marveling at the intricacy of the shell work and the extraordinary breadth of the shells' shapes, textures, and colors. They were quite unlike anything I had ever seen. I knew then that one day I would make one myself.

A full-time job and raising children kept me busy for a few years, but in 2001 I was ready to get started. At that time there was very little information on the subject and only a handful of people making them. One of those people was Sandi Blanda*, and I called Sandi to ask for guidance. She generously shared some of her considerable knowledge, and she also directed me to Sanibel Seashell Industries, owned and operated to this day by Larry Strange and his family. They shipped me everything I needed, and so I spread out my materials and all my shells on my dining room table and began. In March of 2002 I entered three pieces in the Sanibel Shell Show, and by that summer I had work in galleries in Newport, Rhode Island, and on Cape Cod and Nantucket, Massachusetts.

In addition to making Sailors' Valentines, my husband and I have restored many pieces from the 1800s from the collections of people in both the United States and Barbados. This process has led me to a deeper understanding of and appreciation for this awe-inspiring art form.

In 2011 I became a full-time resident of Sanibel Island after having vacationed here for almost 35 years. Today, I volunteer as a docent at the Bailey-Matthews National Shell Museum. I love that I have come full-circle to the place where I discovered what is now such an integral part of who I am and what I love.

* Sandi Blanda's work can be seen on pages 22–33.

www.pfboynton.com

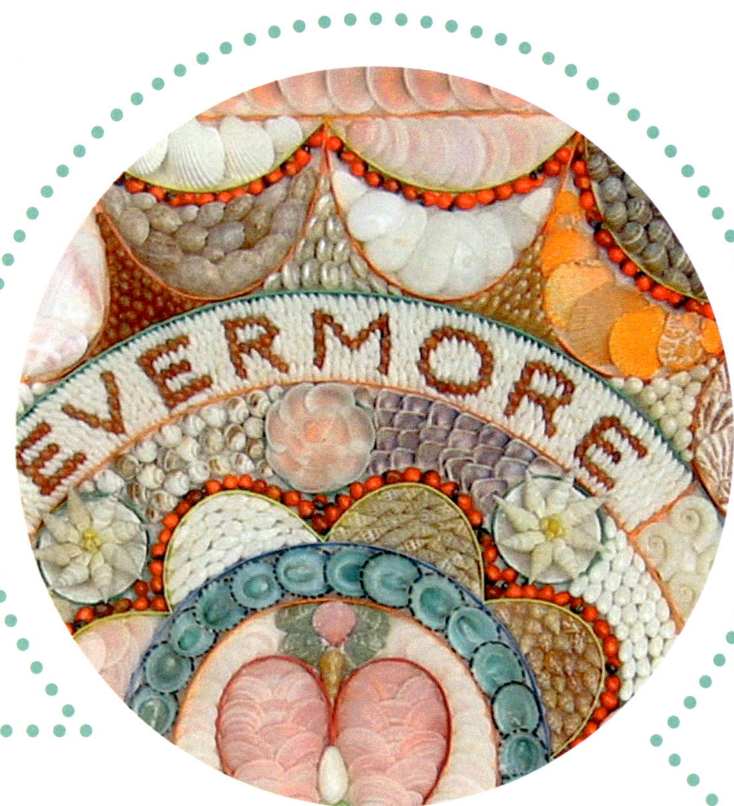

This piece is done in the traditional style of Sailors' Valentines and incorporates a number of shells that can still be found on Barbados beaches: rosecups, white rice shells, limpets, sunrise tellins, and bubble shells. Many of the original works also included red seeds called crab's eyes. Here they outline the inner and outer arches.

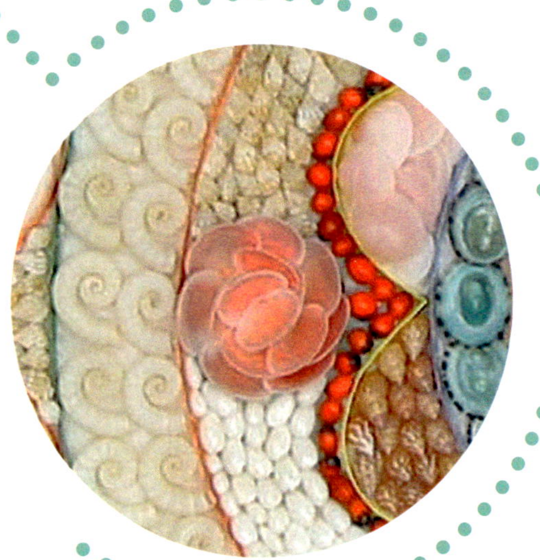

Traditional Valentines were done on cotton batting with paper dividers, as this piece is done. The curly spirula shells were frequently used in traditional pieces.

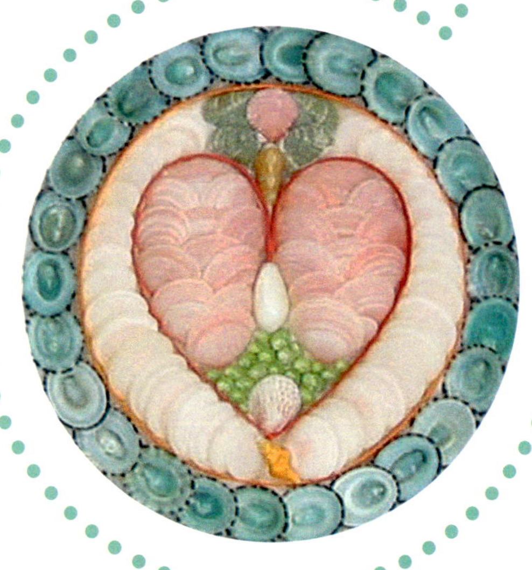

It was common in traditional pieces to find woven hearts at the center. This is done by carefully weaving rosecup shells atop one another. Blue-green limpets surround the centerpiece.

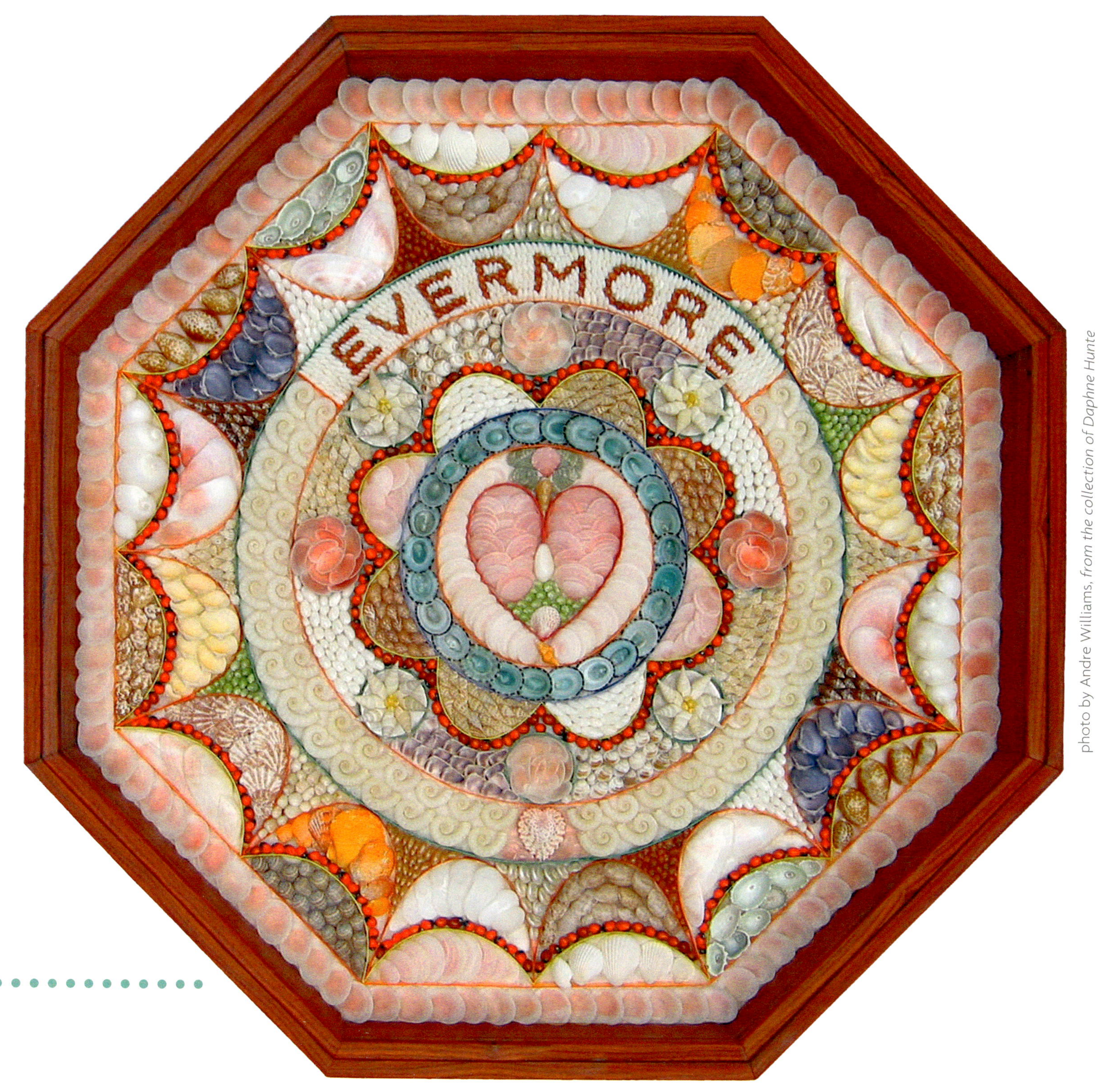

photo by Andre Williams, *from the collection of Daphne Hunte*

Evermore

Inspired by the song “Evermore,” written by the artist’s sister Sandra Boynton in memory of their sister Judy and recorded by Alison Krauss.

18-inch coco bolo case made by Jim Prestigiacomo

Larimar, with its exquisite sea-blue color, can only be found in the Dominican Republic. Larimar is called the dolphin stone; thus two little mother-of-pearl dolphins frolic above it. Encircling the heart are hundreds of tiny pinkish shells found on Barbados. In the fall of 2014 the artist was filmed over a period of several months creating this piece as part of a documentary titled *7 Sanibel Artists*, produced by David Carter.

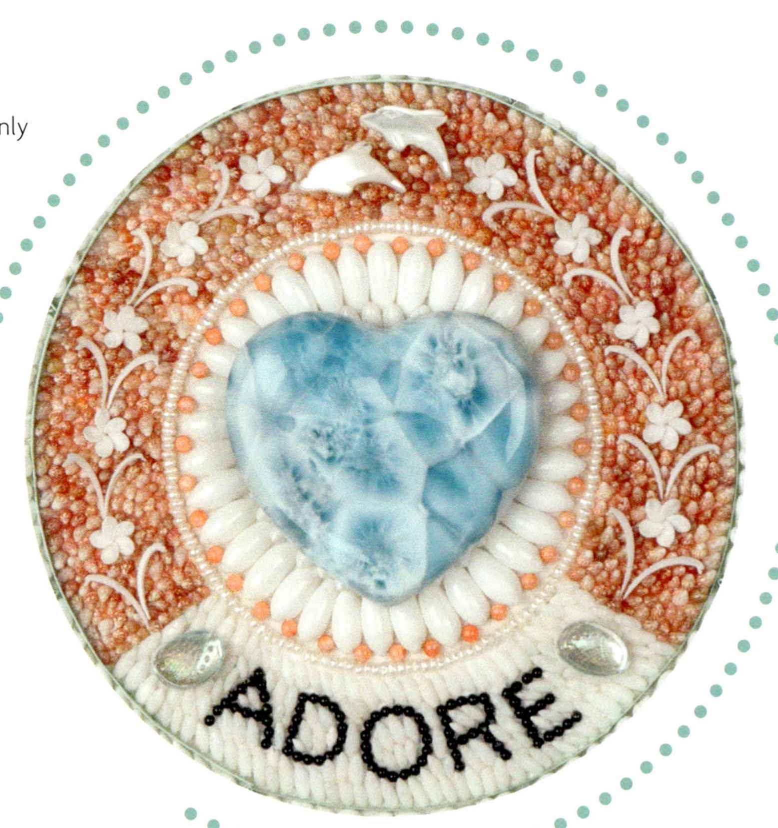

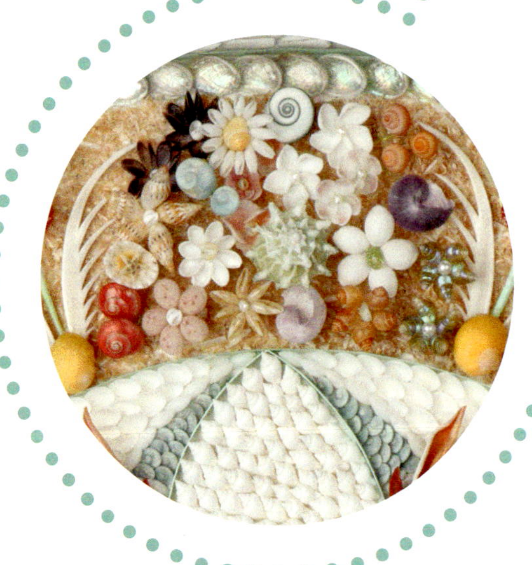

Each of the eight sides has an arrangement of shell flowers, operculums, and other sealife. They are separated by large squilla claws. Tiny green abalone shells sit inside a green paper divider.

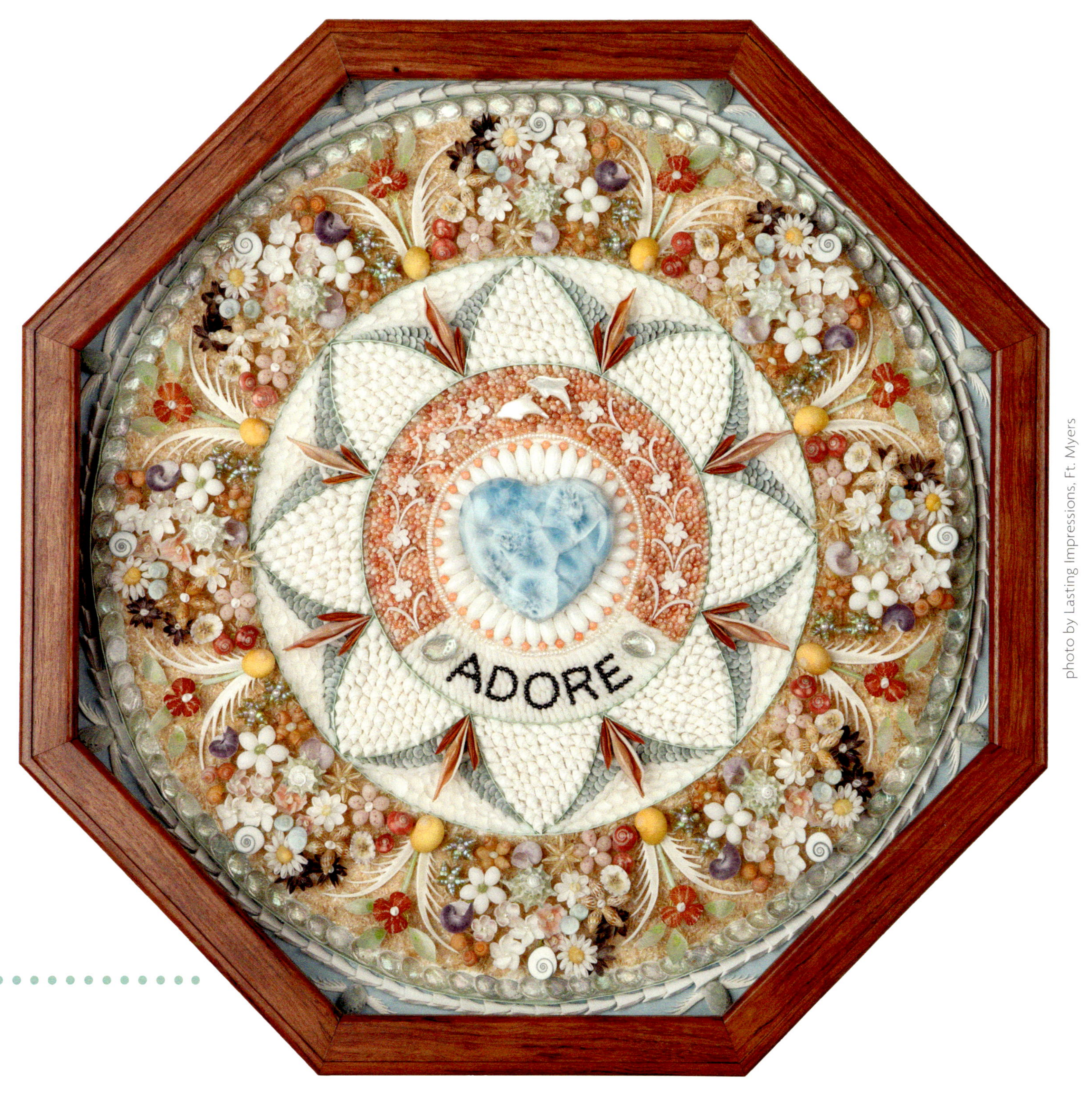

photo by Lasting Impressions, Ft. Myers

Adore

Inspired by the exquisite larimar heart at the center, which the artist ADORES.

15-inch bubinga (African rosewood) case made by Jim Prestigiacomo

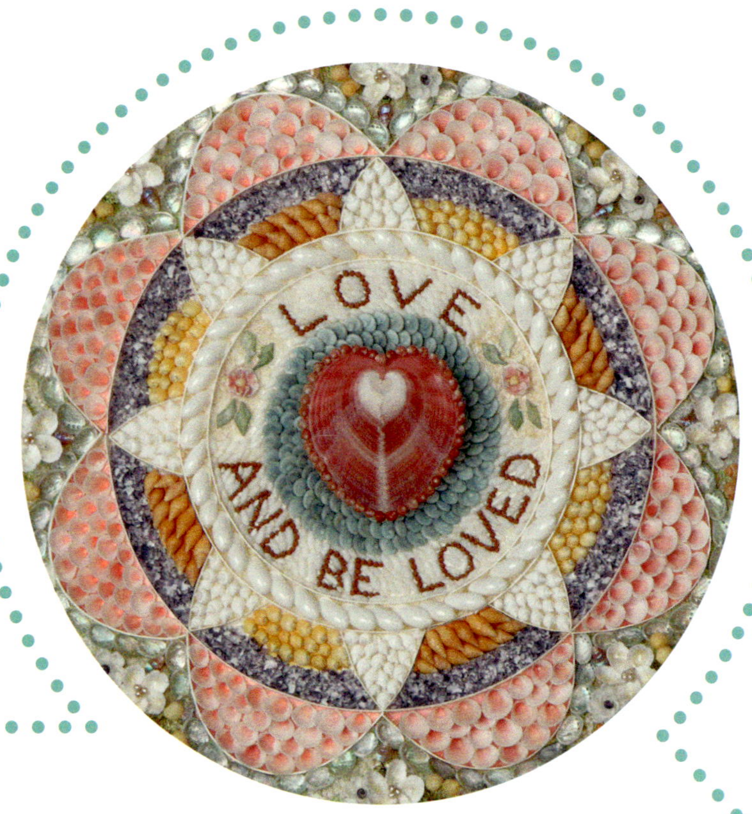

Striking pink apple blossom shells are surrounded by iridescent green abalone shells. The purple circle inside the apple blossoms is made of crushed janthinas.

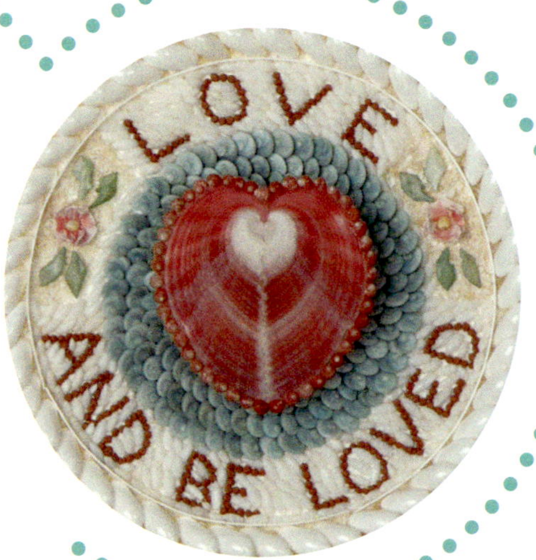

The artist frequently uses heart cockle shells in the centers of her work. At the center of this piece is one that is a stunning deep rose color in its natural state. It is surrounded by rare ni'ihau shells from Hawaii that are glued directly onto the edge of the cockle. Behind this are blue-green operculums from the astraea calcar shell.

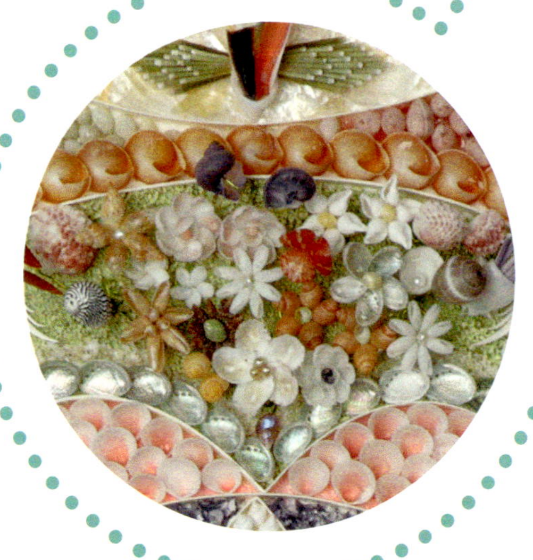

Each of the eight portions of the Valentine is filled with stemmed shell flower arrangements glued to finely sifted sand that has been dyed green.

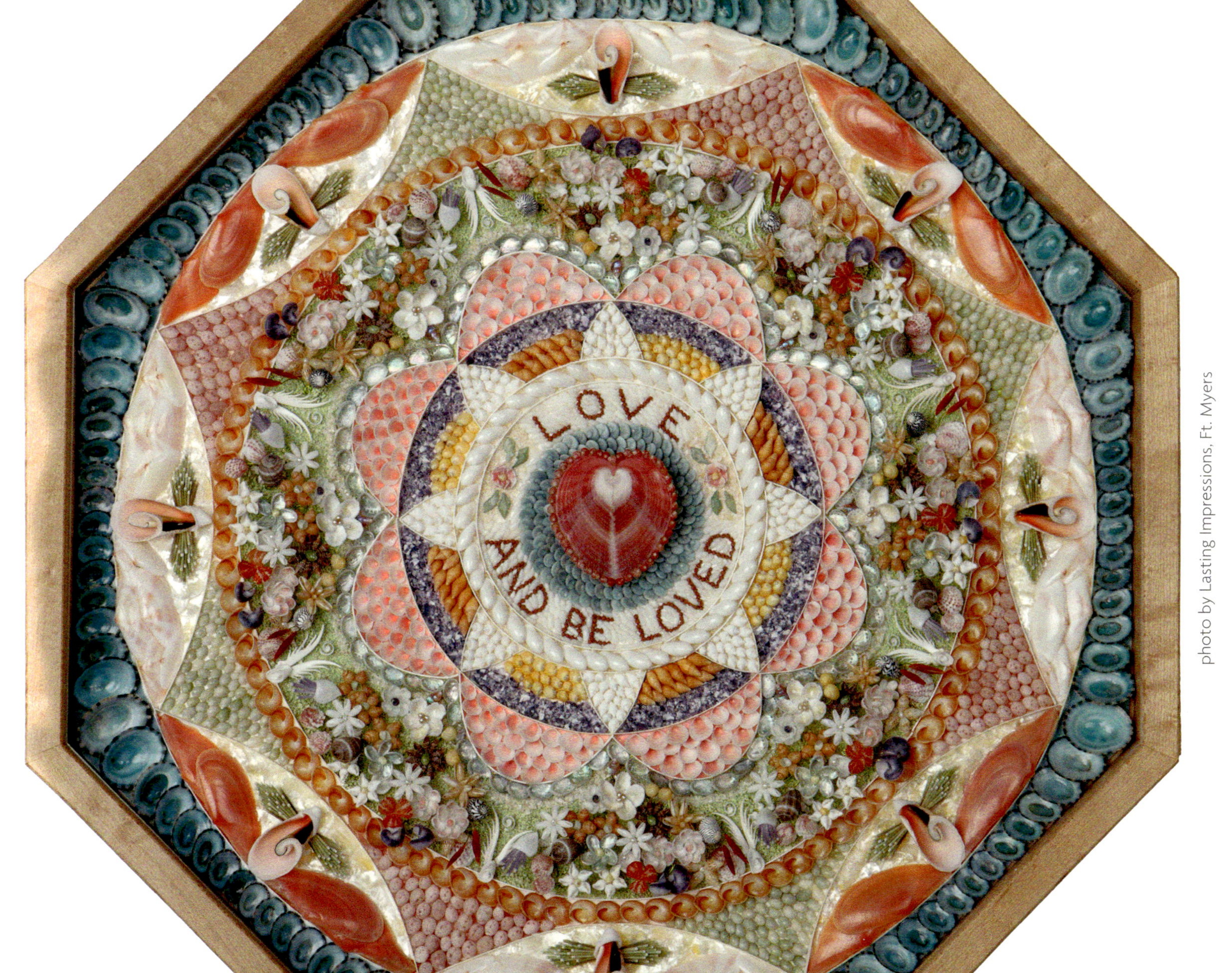

photo by Lasting Impressions, Ft. Myers

Love and Be Loved

Inspired by the song "Nature Boy," written by eden ahbez and recorded by Nat King Cole.

18-inch bird's-eye maple case made by Jim Prestigiacomo

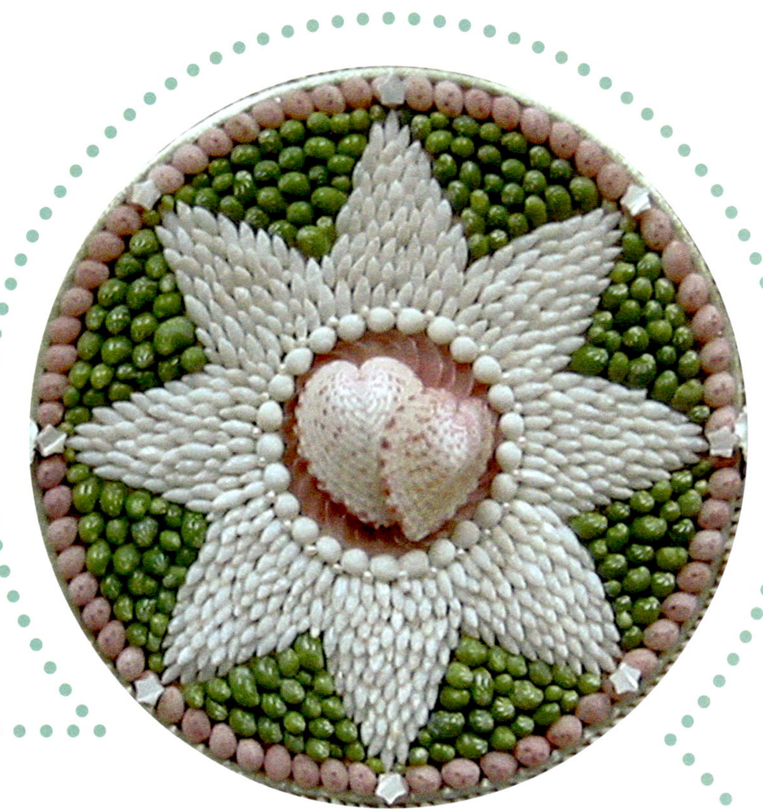

Two heart cockles are surrounded by a star of tiny white rice shells, and a mother-of-pearl star sits at each of the tips. Emerald nerites surround the star. A row of pink trivia shells collected by the artist on Barbados encircles the center.

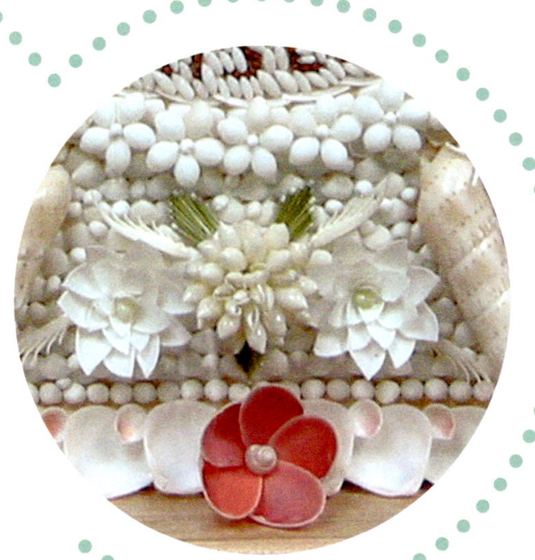

Rose petal tellins were used to create the flowers in the north, south, east, and west positions at the outer edges. Beside them sit two flowers done from triangular pieces of gooseneck barnacles and a large white flower done with white volvarina.

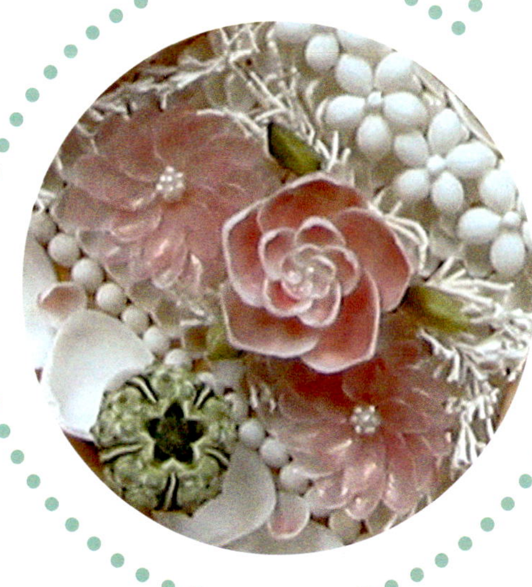

A rosecup flower sits between flowers made from translucent pink fairy tellins. Springing from this is white sea moss from Barbados beaches.

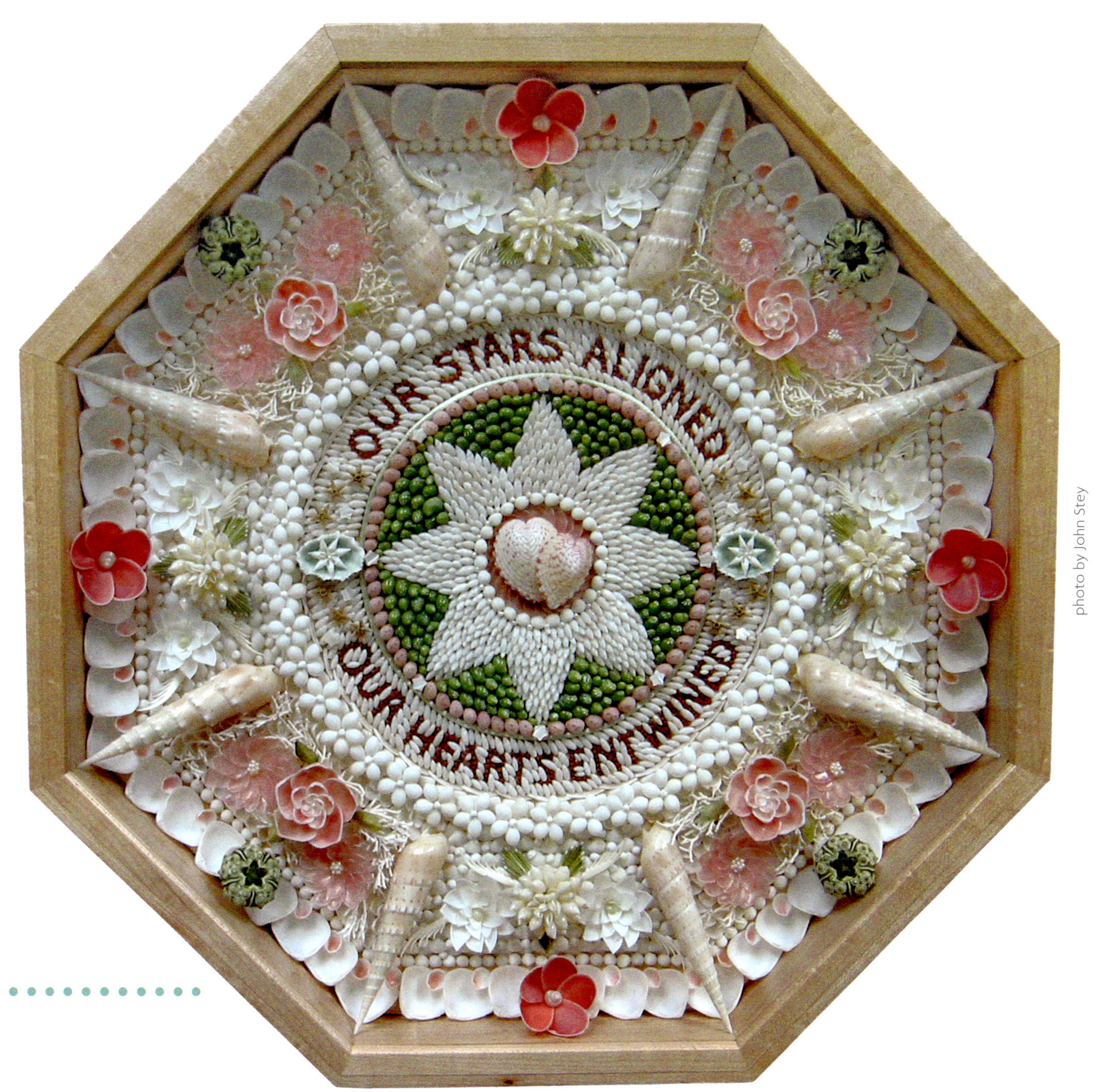

photo by John Stey

Our Stars Aligned

Inspired by the mystery of happenstance.

15-inch bird's-eye maple case made by Jim Prestigiacomo

Three of the artist's favorite gifts from the sea—a finger starfish, an abalone, and an oyster shell with a freshwater pearl inside—sit on top of crushed natural deep blue mussel shells collected on Rhode Island beaches. Surrounding this center is a circle of tiny sand dollars and pink stylaster coral.

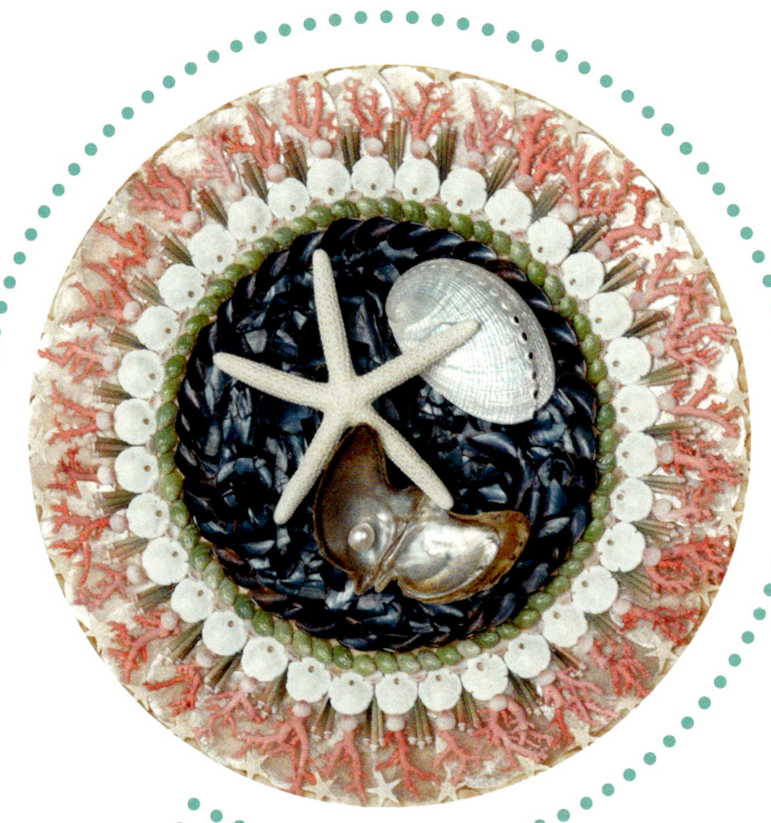

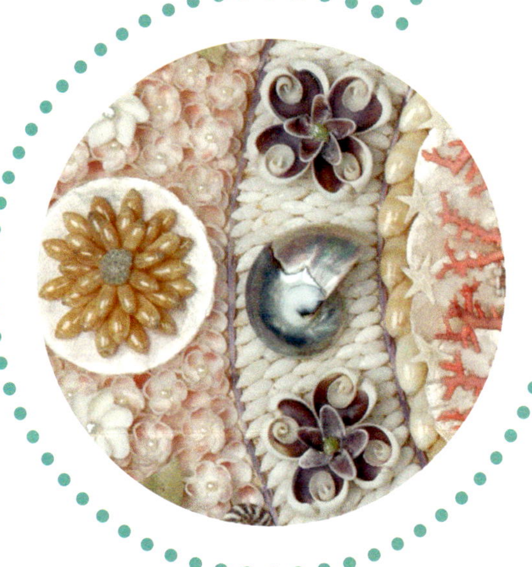

Two flowers made from sliced ringtop cowries with tiny purple coquina shells in the center frame a polished blue and white abalone shell.

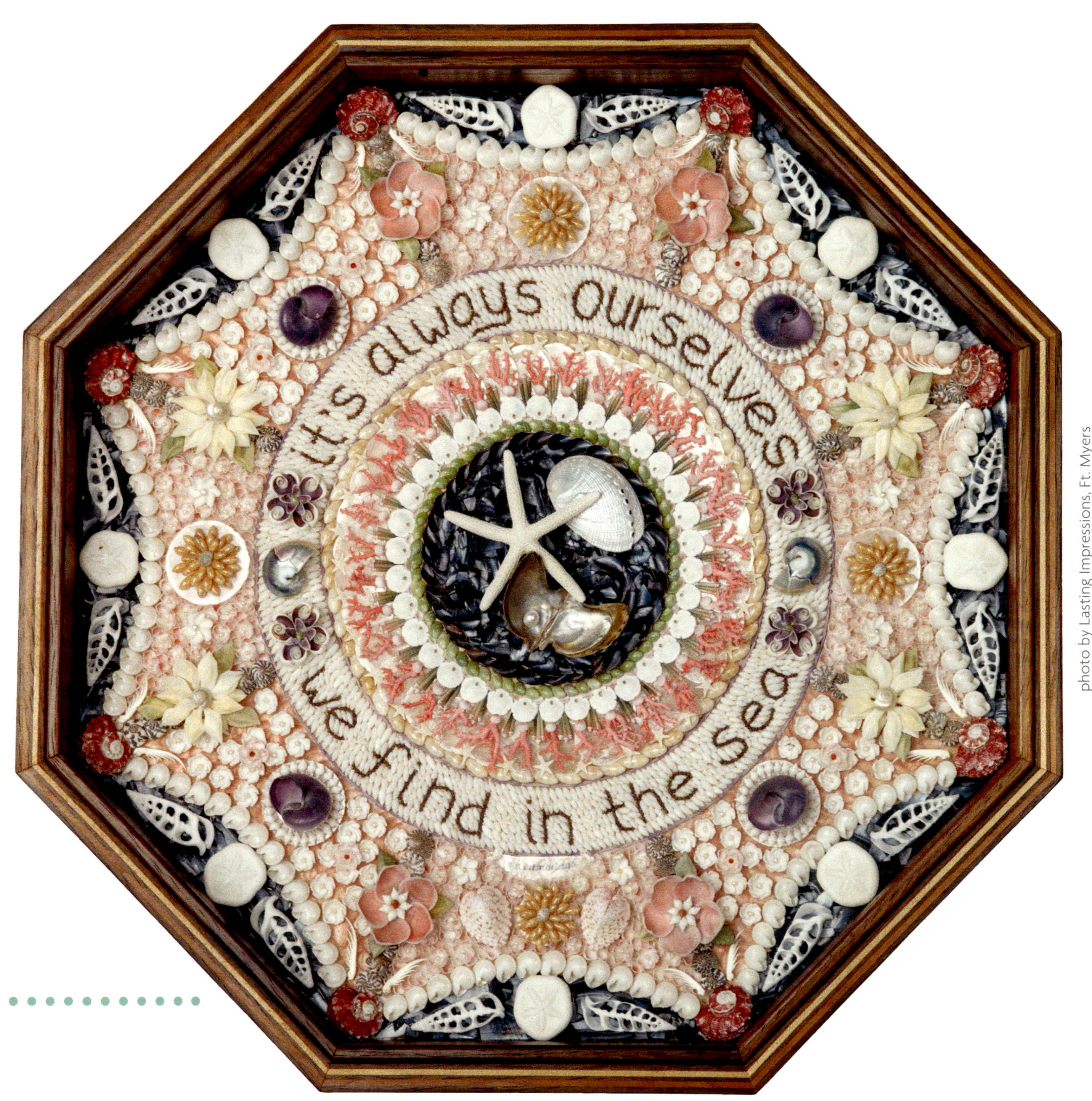

photo by Lasting Impressions, Ft. Myers

In the Sea

Inspired by the poem "maggie and milly and molly and may," by e. e. cummings.

18-inch padauk case made by Jim Prestigiacomo

photo by Robert Tucker

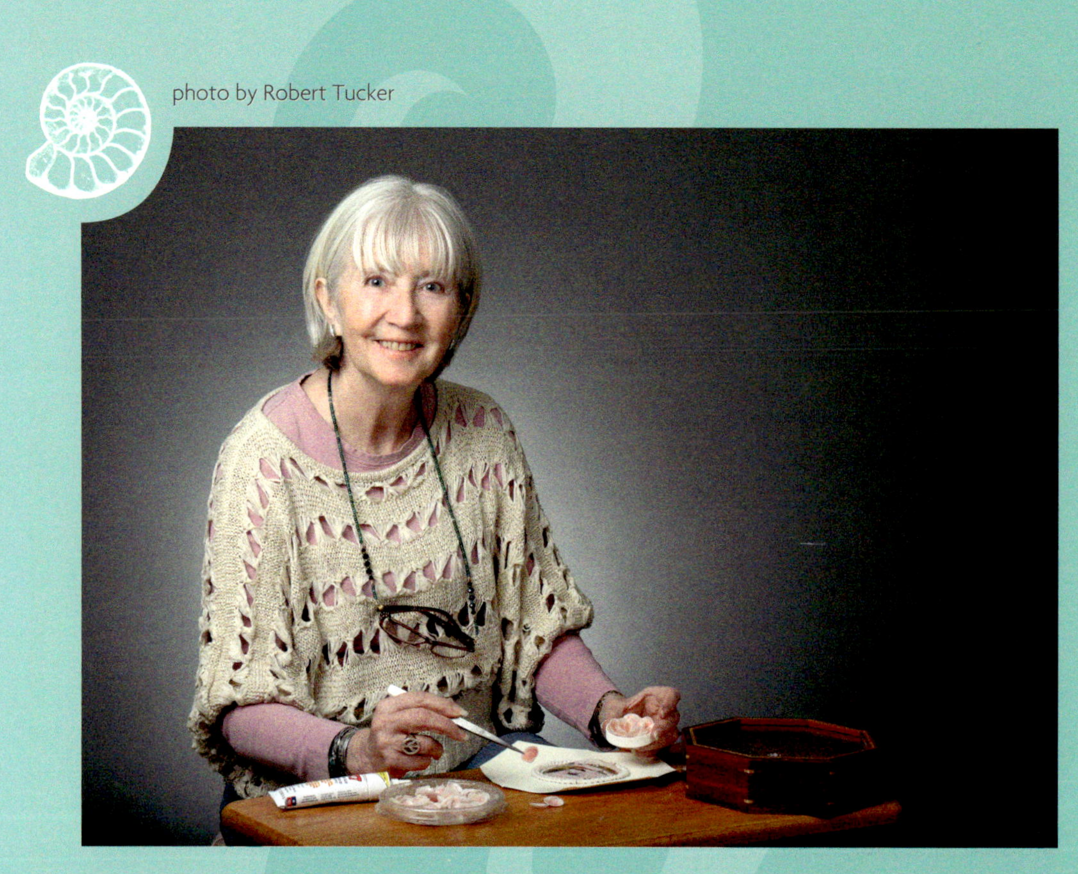

Gayle J. Condit

Brewster, Massachusetts

I was born in Colerain, Northern Ireland, raised in Toronto, Canada, and moved to Boston in 1967 and to Cape Cod the following year. I studied fashion design and construction at Ryerson Polytechnical Institute (now Ryerson University). For many years I designed and made competition figure-skating costumes; the placing of sequins and rhinestones undoubtedly taught me to use tweezers as well as I do.

I saw my first antique Sailors' Valentine about 20 years ago at the home of friends who lived in Edgartown on Martha's Vineyard. I was fascinated with the design, construction, and colors, and shortly after seeing it had to try one myself. I specialize in traditional-style Valentines and particularly enjoy creating Victorian-era pieces, as I love the delicacy of the shell work. That said, my favorite of the pieces I have done is contemporary in style. Titled *Moonhole Bequia*, it hangs in our living room and is the largest piece I have done, measuring 23 inches (see pages 52–53). I was inspired to do it to remember the many fun-filled times spent with family and friends on the island of Bequia. Moonhole* is also the first place I did an open-water scuba dive accompanied by my husband.

One of my favorite shells is the janthina. I am enthralled by its lovely purple color (my favorite color) and its fragility. It is a shell that was frequently used in the original Valentines. Most of the janthinas I use were hand-collected on one of my favorite beaches on Bequia.

My husband and I love to travel, and we have collected shells from Aruba to Alaska. When not in the Caribbean, we travel in our fifth-wheel camper. We have been to Alaska, the Canadian Maritime provinces, and to many western states. In the late '70s we also lived on St. Croix, US Virgin Islands, where we collected hundreds of shells that still remain in our ever-expanding collection.

* Moonhole is a private community on the island of Bequia in the Grenadines. Moonhole derives its name from a massive arch formed in volcanic substrate through which the setting moon is sometimes visible.

www.sailorvalentines.com

The floral arrangement grows from a flowerpot basket made of tiny mustard seeds and rice shells.

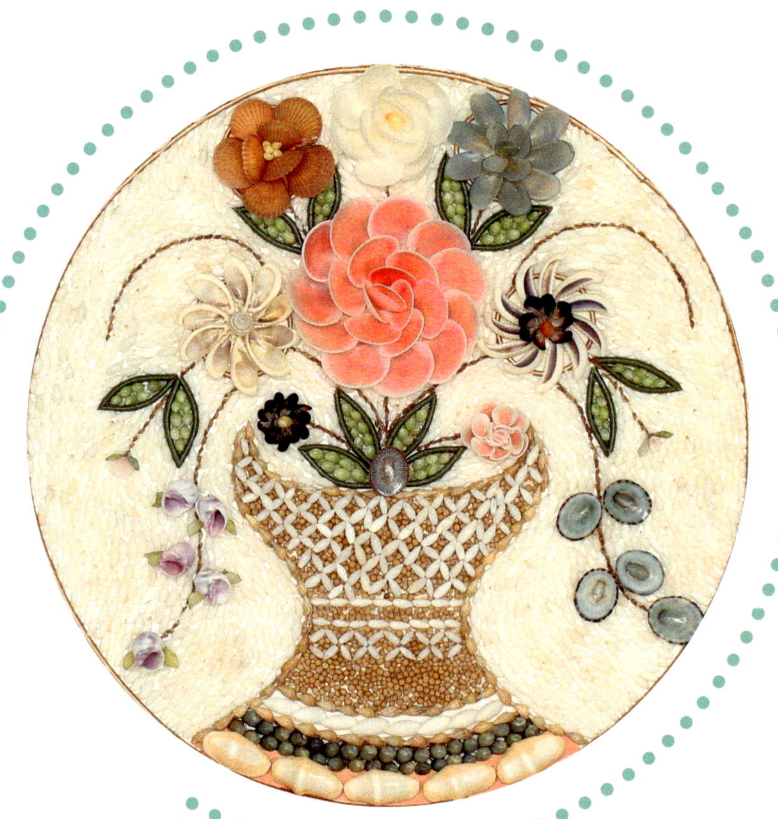

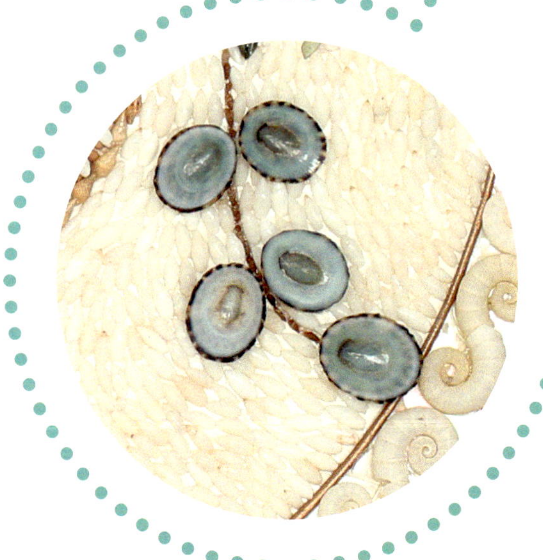

The background is made up of hundreds of tiny rice shells, in this photo with blue-green limpets atop.

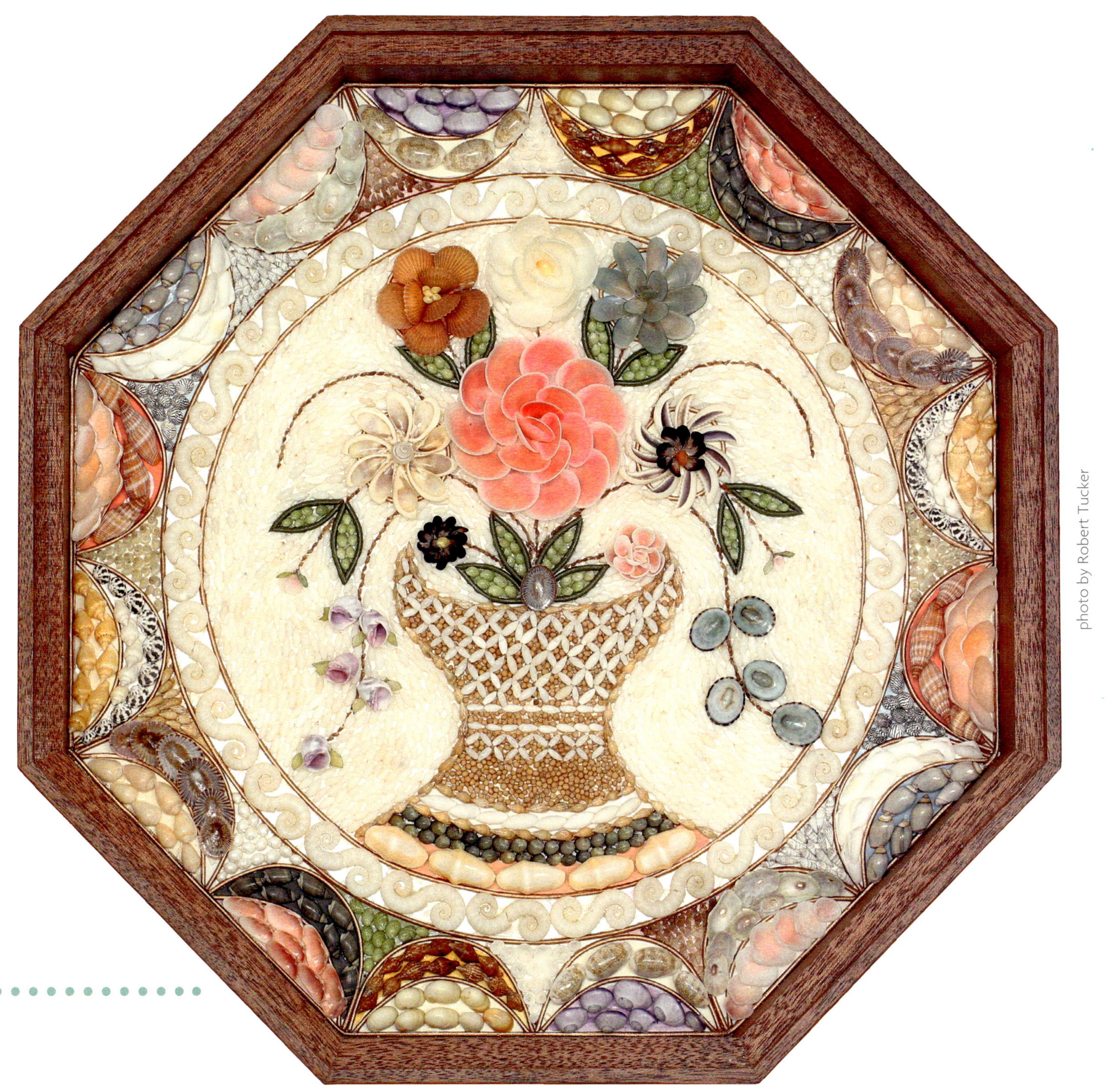

photo by Robert Tucker

Victorian Tapestry

Modeled after a Sailors' Valentine in the collection of the Strong Museum in Syracuse, New York. The museum graciously supplied the artist with photos and background information so that she could reproduce the original as closely as possible.

14-inch mahogany case made by Jim Prestigiacomo

The center cluster of roses in pink, white, and yellow reminded the artist of the roses in her English cutting garden at her home on Cape Cod.

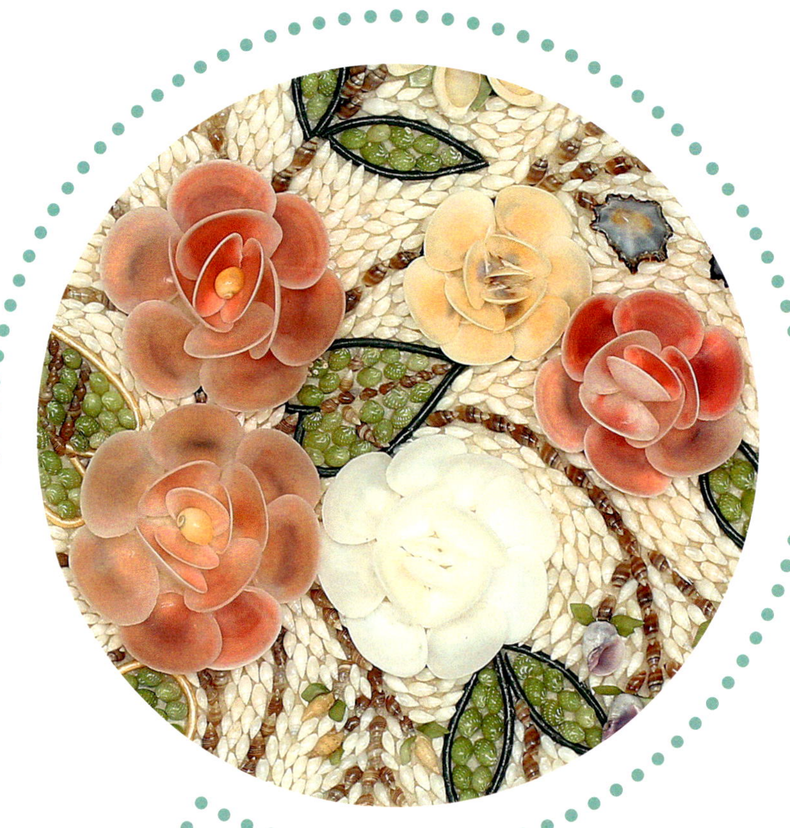

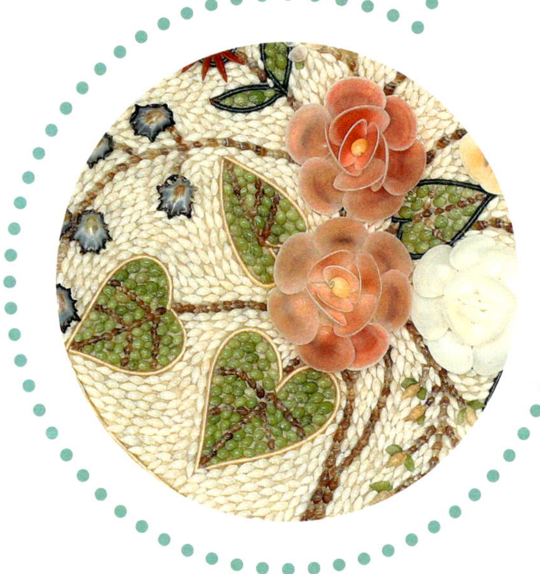

Sprigs of imaginary flowers and greenery make up the remaining center work.

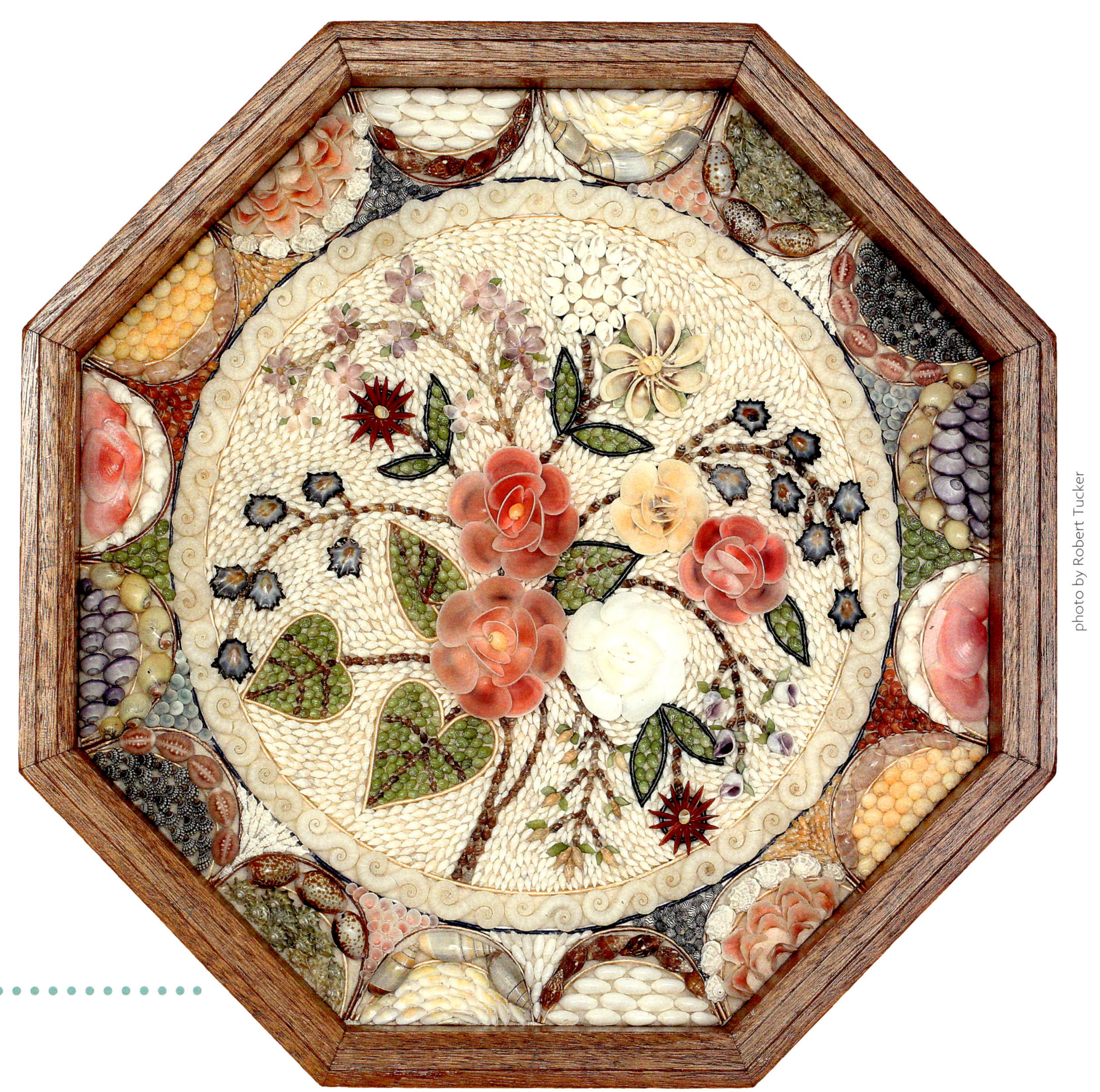

photo by Robert Tucker

My Spring Garden

Inspired by the original of this Valentine, which is pictured in the book *Under Glass: A Victorian Obsession*, by John Whitenight.

14-inch mahogany case made by Richard Hawryluk

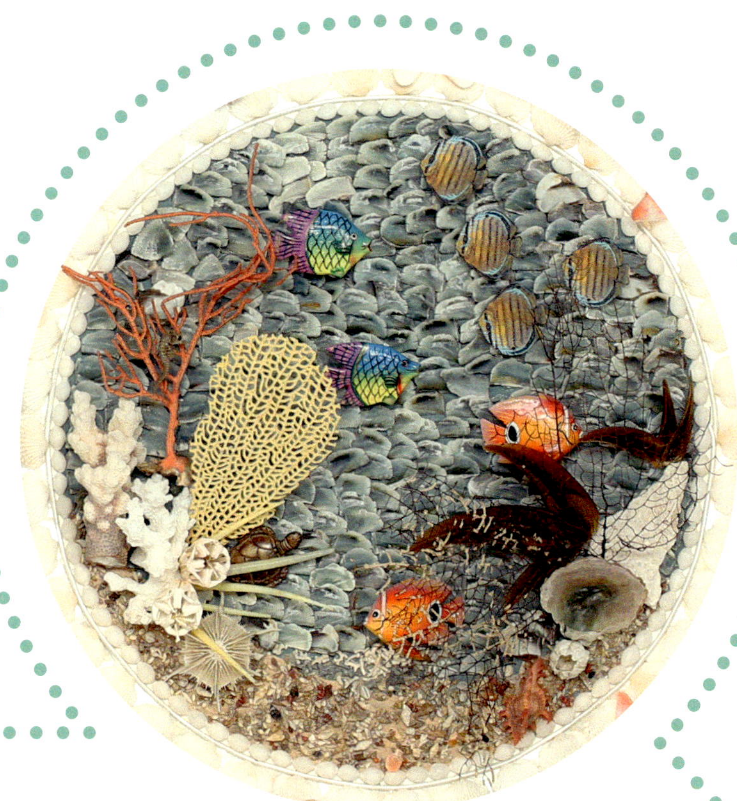

The center is an underwater mosaic representing a dive site on the island of Bequia. The water is made from cut chitons and the scene is constructed from flotsam found on Bequia beaches.

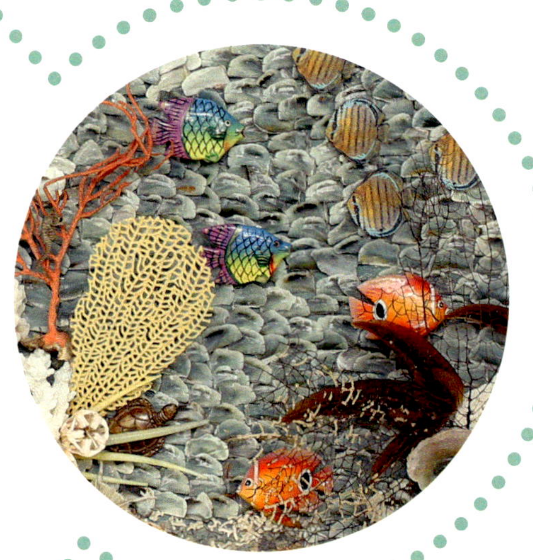

The sea creatures, carved fish, ivory turtle, and tiny seahorse were collected during numerous vacations on Bequia.

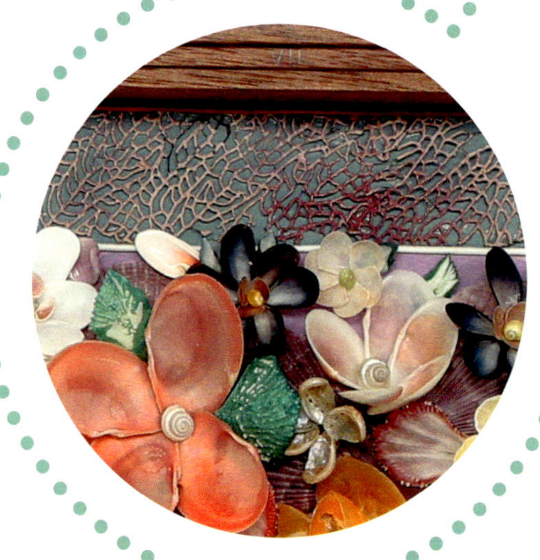

The outer ring is created with purple sea fans.

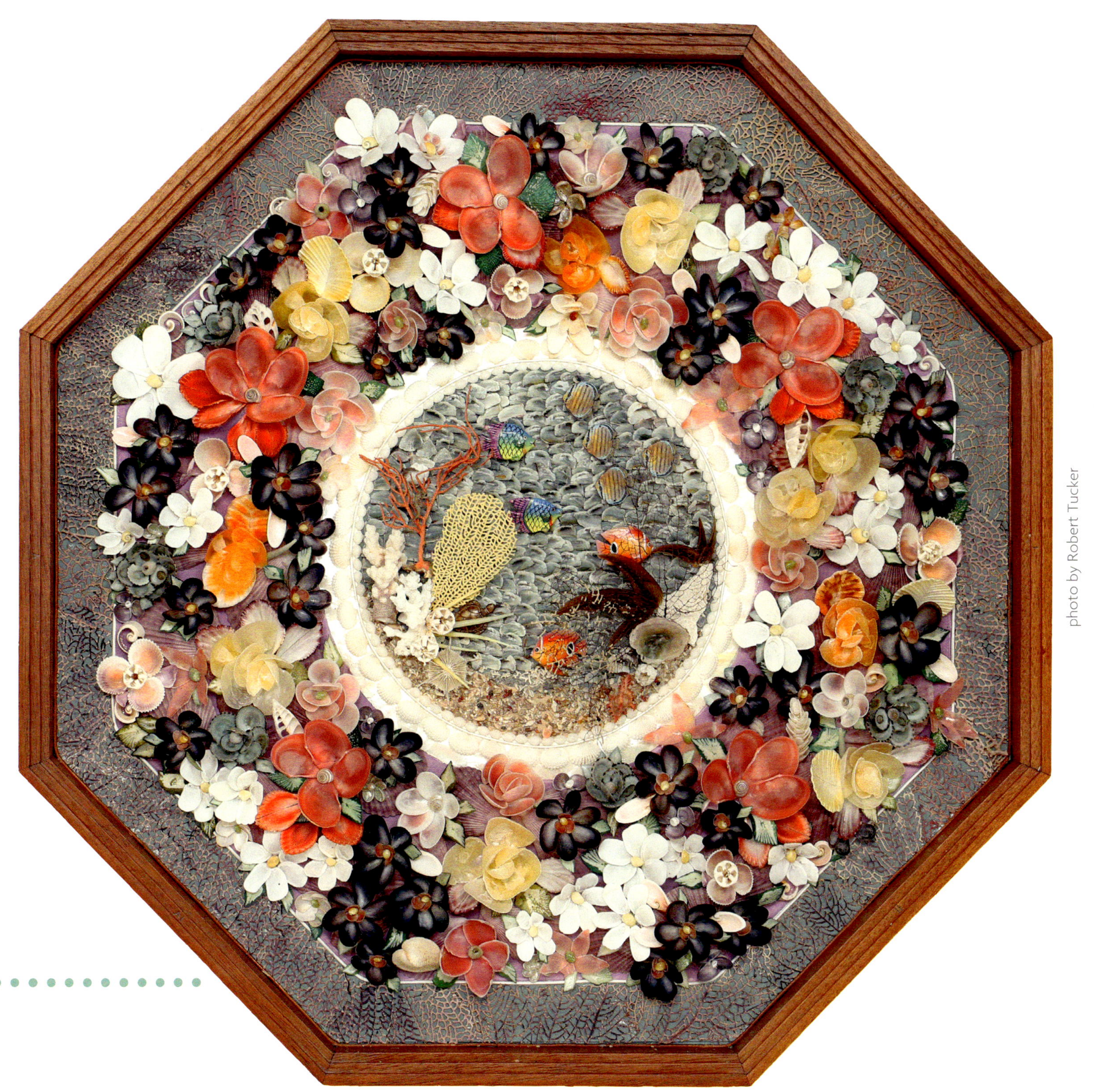

photo by Robert Tucker

Moonhole Bequia

Inspired by fun-filled times spent by the artist with family and friends at Moonhole on the island of Bequia.

23-inch mahogany case with inlay made by Richard Hawryluk

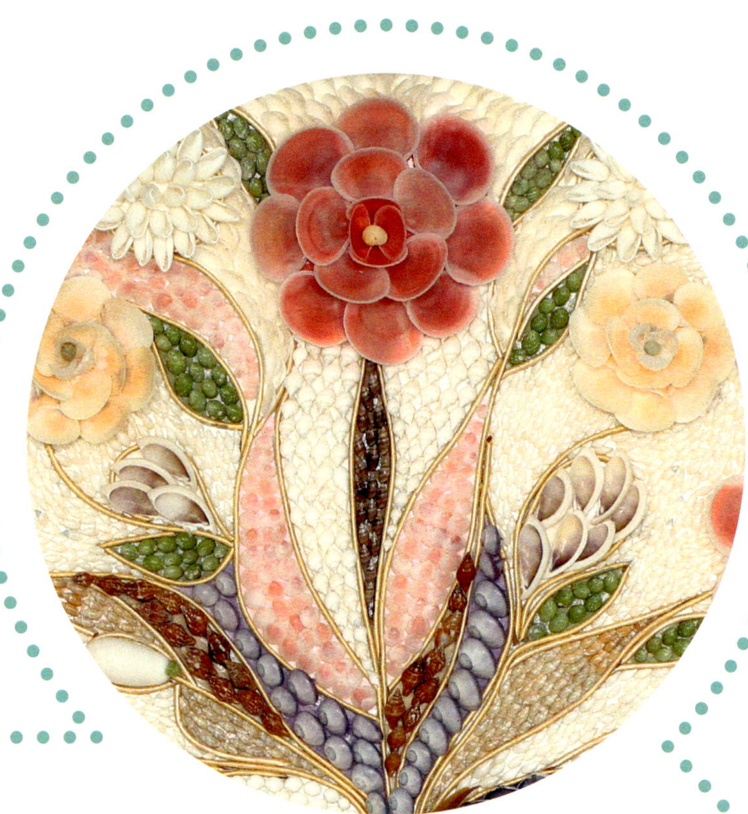

A large pink rosecup shell flower is the centerpiece for this Valentine. The leaves are made from small janthinas and pink apple blossom shells. The stem is done from miniature brown olive shells.

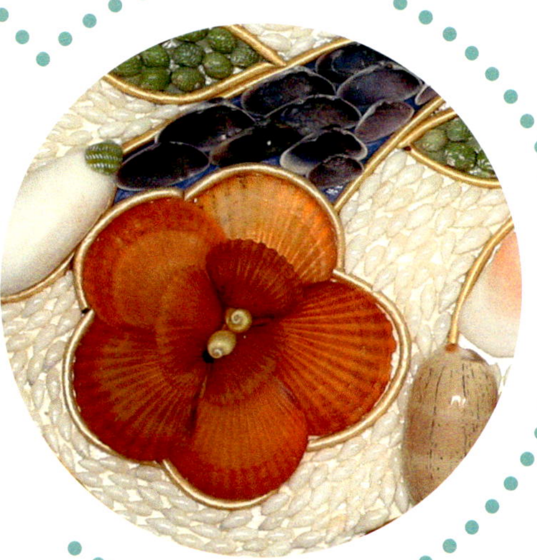

Orange scallop shell flowers sit at either side of the urn.

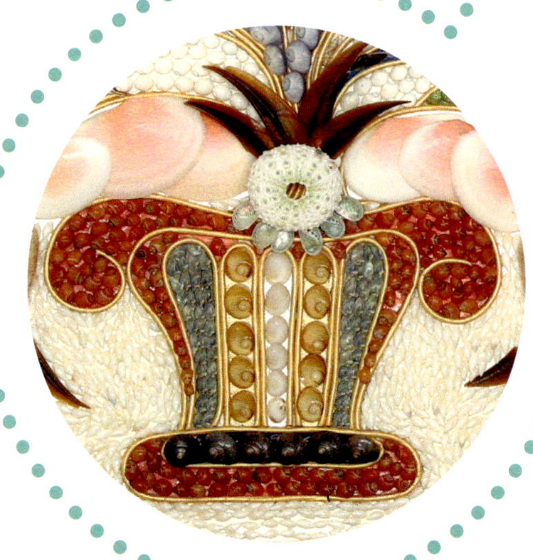

The Grecian urn is composed of black umboniums, red snails, and assorted operculums, with a tiny sea urchin.

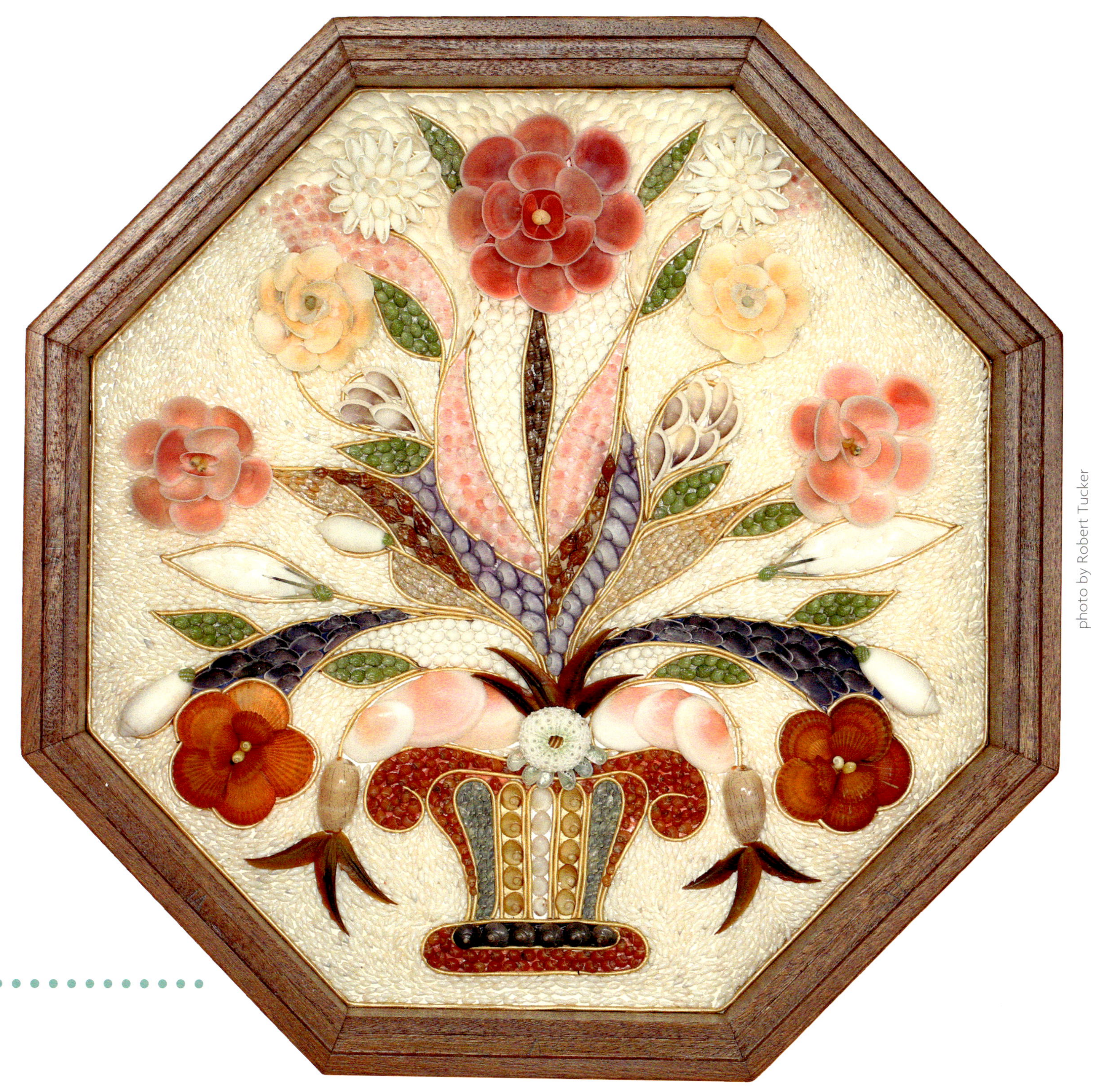

photo by Robert Tucker

A Traditional Mosaic

A Grecian urn was the inspiration for this piece. Hundreds of tiny white rice shells surround a colorful array of flowers made from rosecups, yellow clam shells, and scallop shells.

14-inch mahogany case with inlay made by Richard Hawryluk

photo by Phil Dietsch

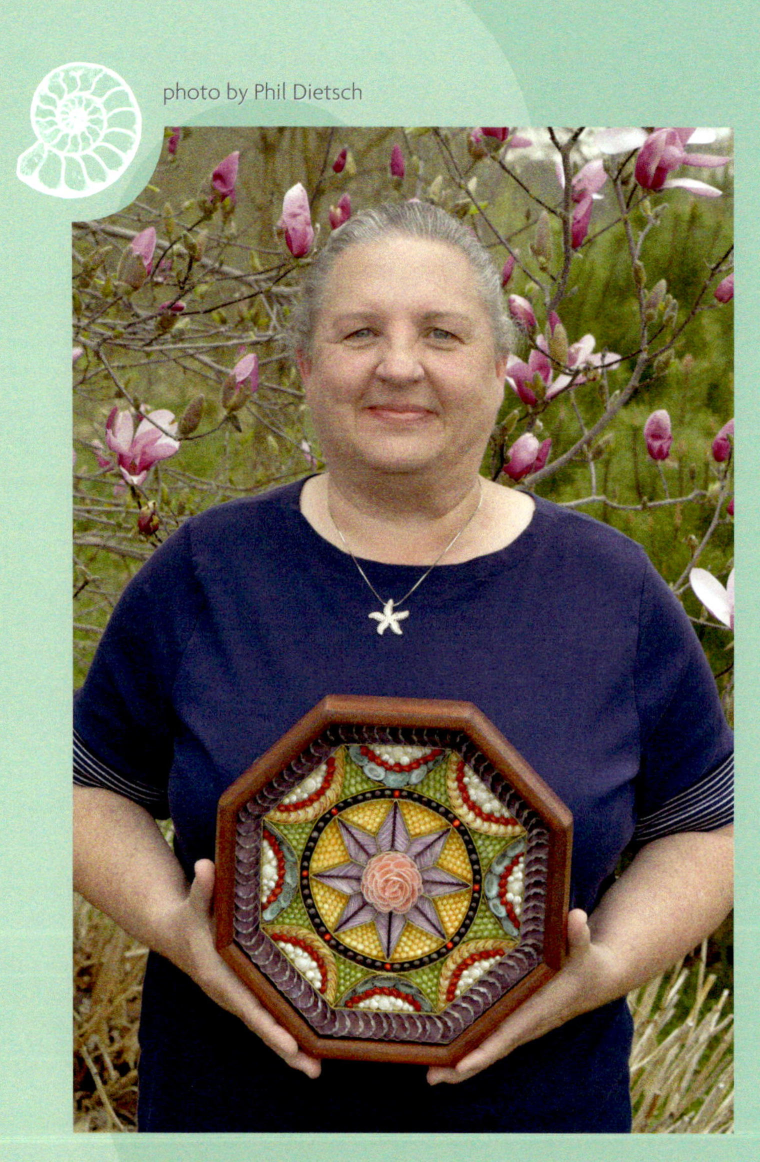

Suzanne Marie Dietsch

Wyanet, Illinois

I was first introduced to a Sailors' Valentine while researching the history of a broom maker's tools in 2004. My husband and I crafted brooms for the Living History Village of Bishop Hill, Illinois, and apparently many retired sailors took up the craft of broom making using the tools they had previously used for mending ships' sails. Upon reading further about a sailor's life, I came across the folklore of the Sailors' Valentines . . . and that's how it all began.

I made my first Valentine based on just the description in that research, not ever having seen one. In 2006, we changed our annual vacation in Florida from December to February because I had decided to enter my work in the Sarasota Shell Show, just for fun. My Valentine was displayed next to David Rhyne's* entry, which was a jaw-dropping experience for this first-timer. At the show I met Bill Jordan, who exposed me to the world of shell shows and his exquisite octagonal cases. From then on, I no longer did demonstrations of broom making or lace making; life became all about the shells.

My studio in Illinois is filled with shells and other sealife, all very delicately organized. Before beginning a beautifully constructed Valentine, one must start by devoting hours to gathering, cleaning, sorting, and sizing those little gems from the sea. Although I generally begin with a concept and perhaps a drawing, as the work progresses that original concept changes and evolves along the way.

My Valentines are designed to be one of a kind, whenever possible with the 3D effect I think adds life and interest to the patterns. Working with nature's unlimited palette of shells and sealife keeps my imagination in constant overdrive. With so many new ideas for my next pieces, there will never be time for me to duplicate my work.

By honoring skills from the past, I hope to bring the past into the present . . . with a unique twist.

* David Rhyne's work can be seen on pages 180–191.

www.seashellvalentines.com

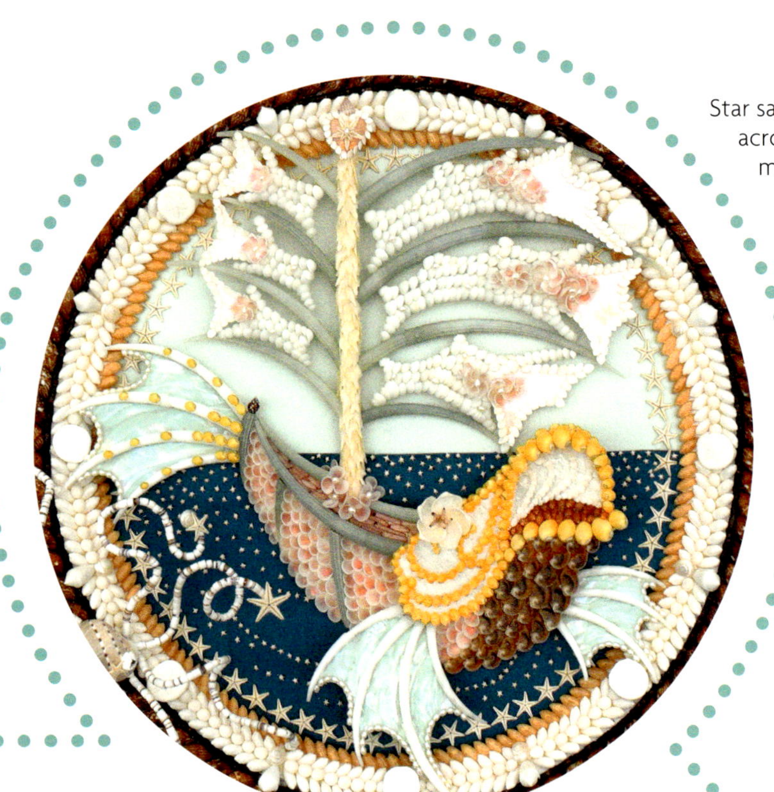

Star sand reflects the light as this stylized ship glides across a sea of satin. The ship's sails, made with mother-of-pearl inlay, are trimmed in apple blossom shell flowers. Baby cup shells, white operculums, and rice pearls add to the sails, which hang from green tusk shells on a mast of garfish scales. The mother-of-pearl oars and rudder tail are trimmed with rice pearls, white tusk shells, and yellow nerite shells.

Garlands of white volvarina shells drape the border. Yellow nerites, sliced brown and white coquinas, green tusk shells, and murex shells complete the outer ring.

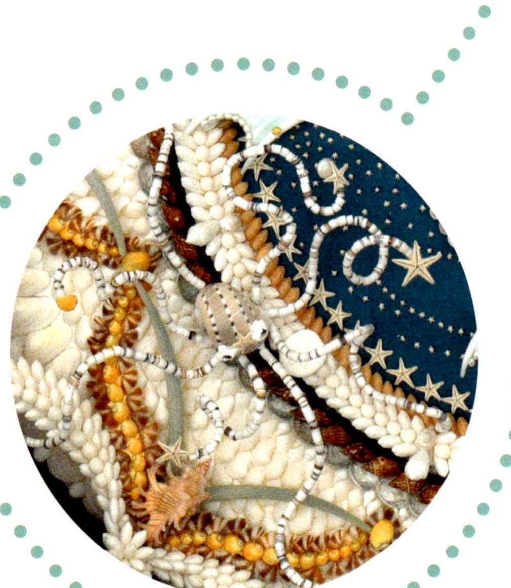

This octopus with barnacle eyes, shell body, and threaded shell bead arms adds the finishing touches.

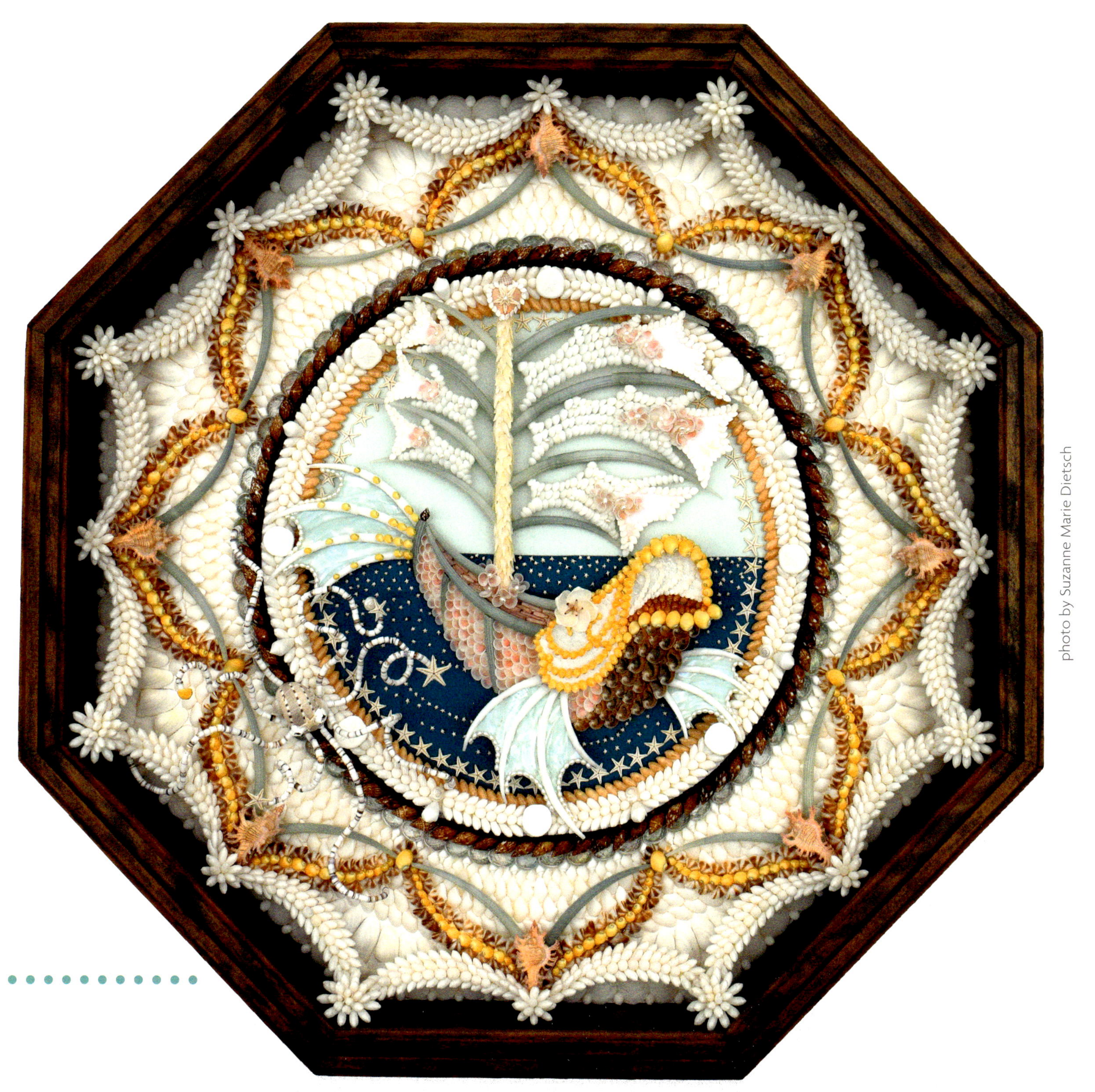

photo by Suzanne Marie Dietsch

Ship of Dreams

Inspired by a painting by Salvador Dali depicting a ship with pink gladiolus sails.

18-inch curly cherry case made by Anthony Lema

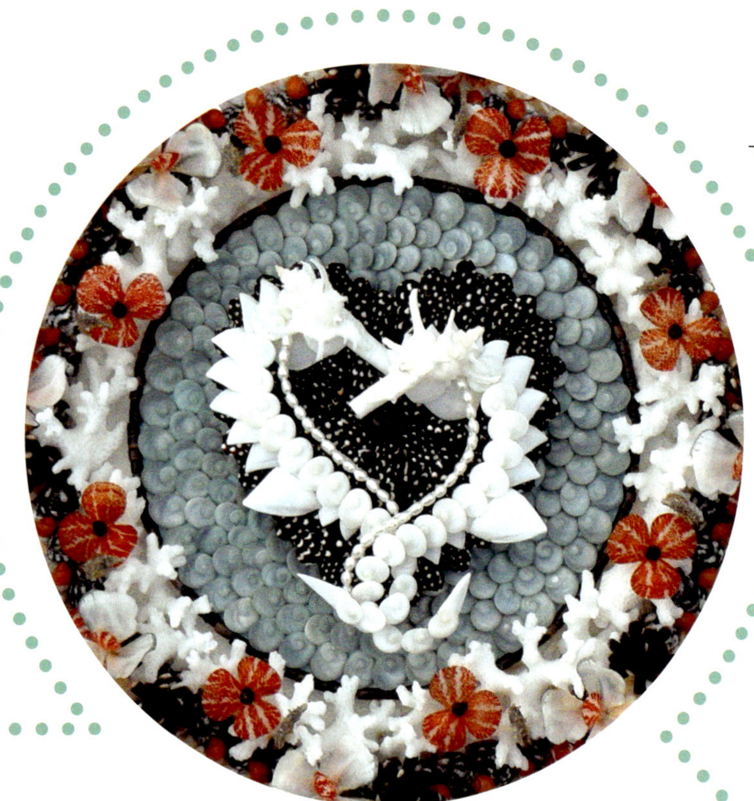

The center ring of blue operculums has an outline of pen shell beads, coral, and shell flowers made of red brachiopods, sea urchin spines, and chitons. The center heart is covered with sliced black spotted dove shells. The intertwined seahorses are constructed of white operculums and a strand of rice pearls.

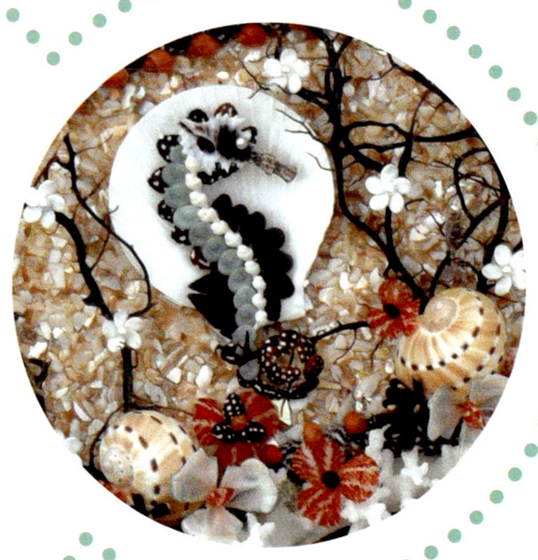

The seahorse rests on a white scallop shell. Black sea fans are in bloom with white operculum shell flowers. The seahorse is made of black spotted dove shells, operculums, baby whelks, and a pearl eye. A sea urchin spine has been used to create the snout. All are resting on a bed of mother-of-pearl chips.

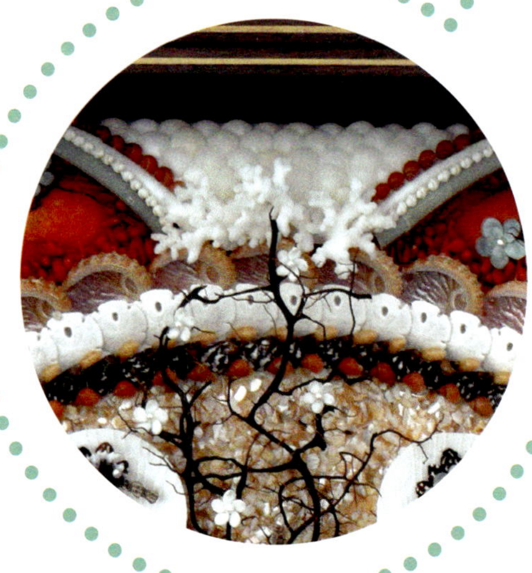

The 3D curls of white shell resemble waves crashing toward the center rings. The waves are trimmed with white coral breakers, green and white tusk shells, baby white whelks, and red snail shells.

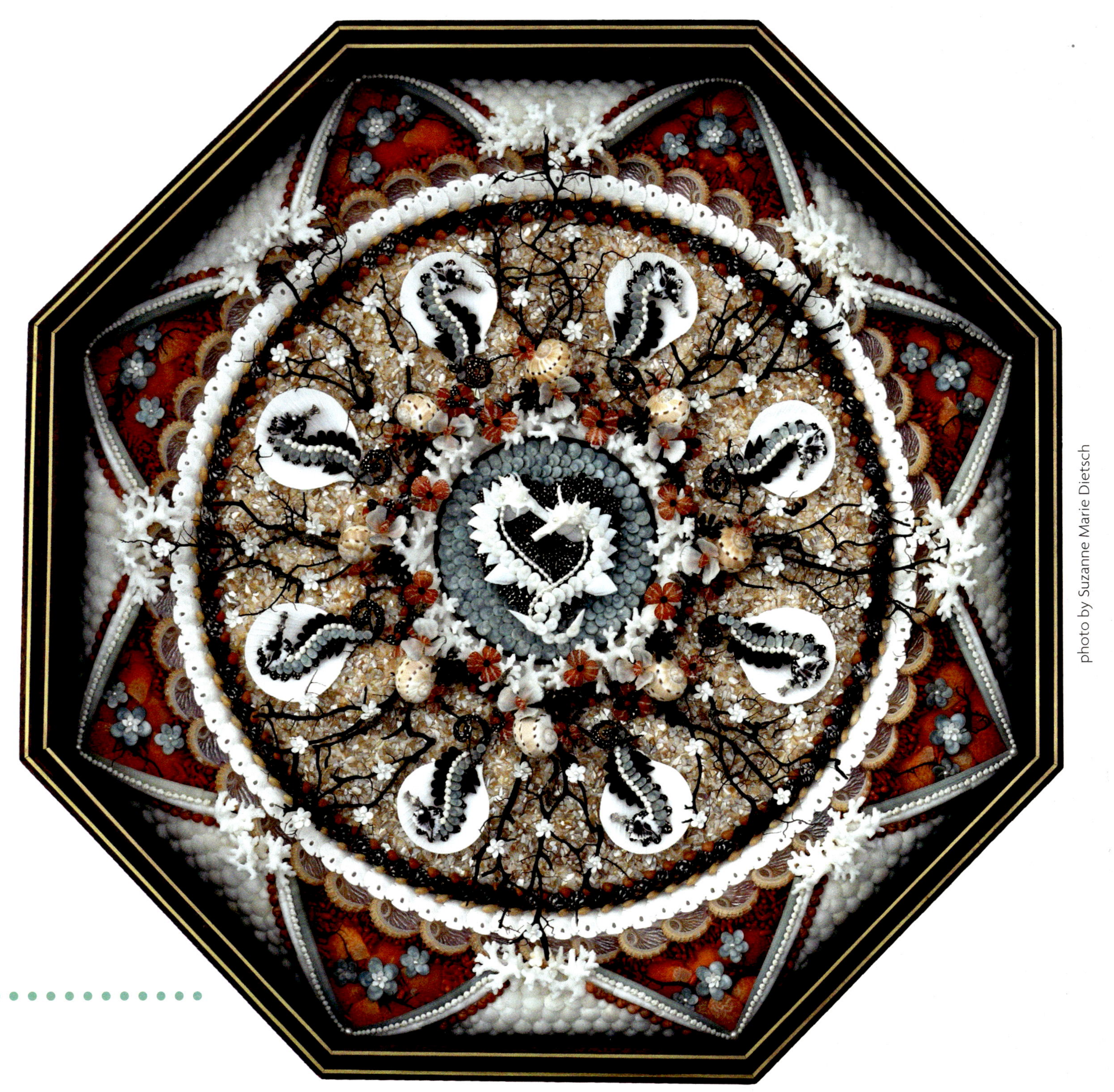

photo by Suzanne Marie Dietsch

Ocean Seahorses

Inspired by dancing seahorses in their ocean habitats.

18-inch walnut case with brass inlay made by Bill Jordan

The center attraction: A basket seastar rests on a bed of mussel and scallop shells. Pink apple blossom shells, white rice shells, tusk and dove shells, limpets, and long purple sea urchin spines create the border pattern. The basket star itself floats atop a purple sea urchin. Crushed shell has been sprinkled on a clay-covered wire frame. Sliced strawberry strombus shells make up the tips of the many curled arms.

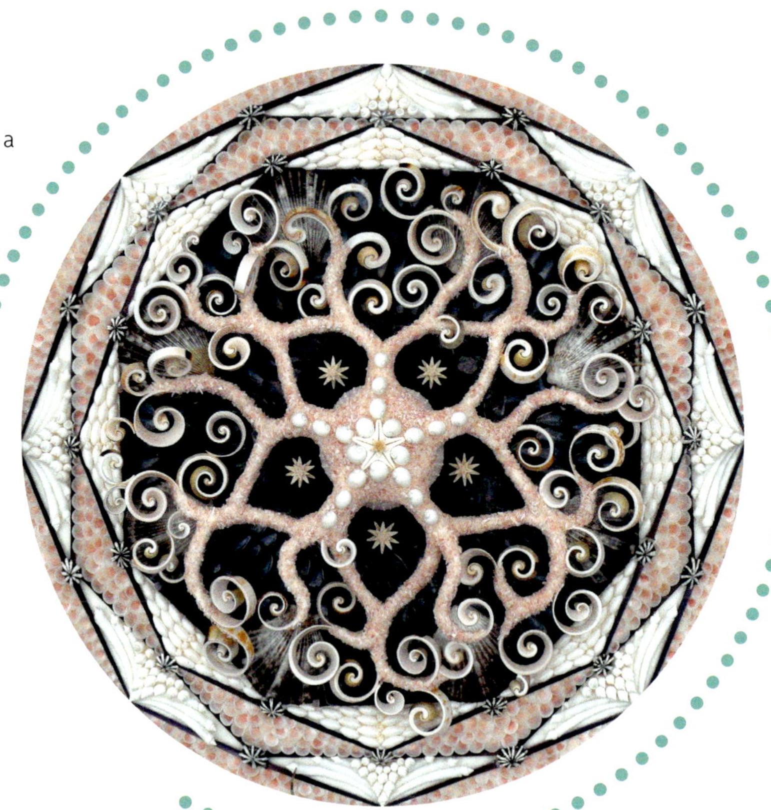

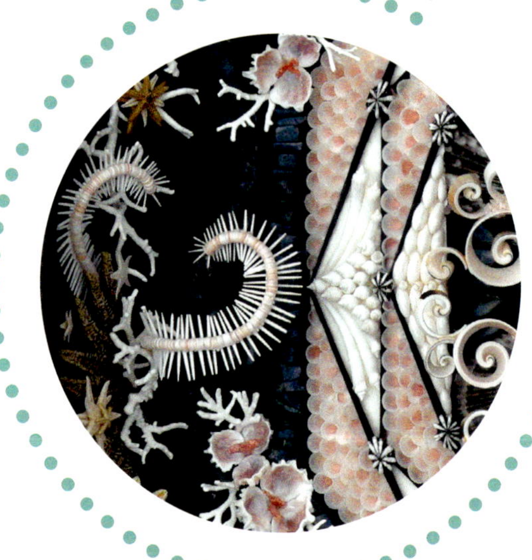

Among the natural specimens are feather seastars composed of strawberry strombus shell beads and white sea urchin spines. They are threaded to wire, which creates their free-floating arms over a bed of deep blue baby mussel shells, sea glass chips, and blue coral beads.

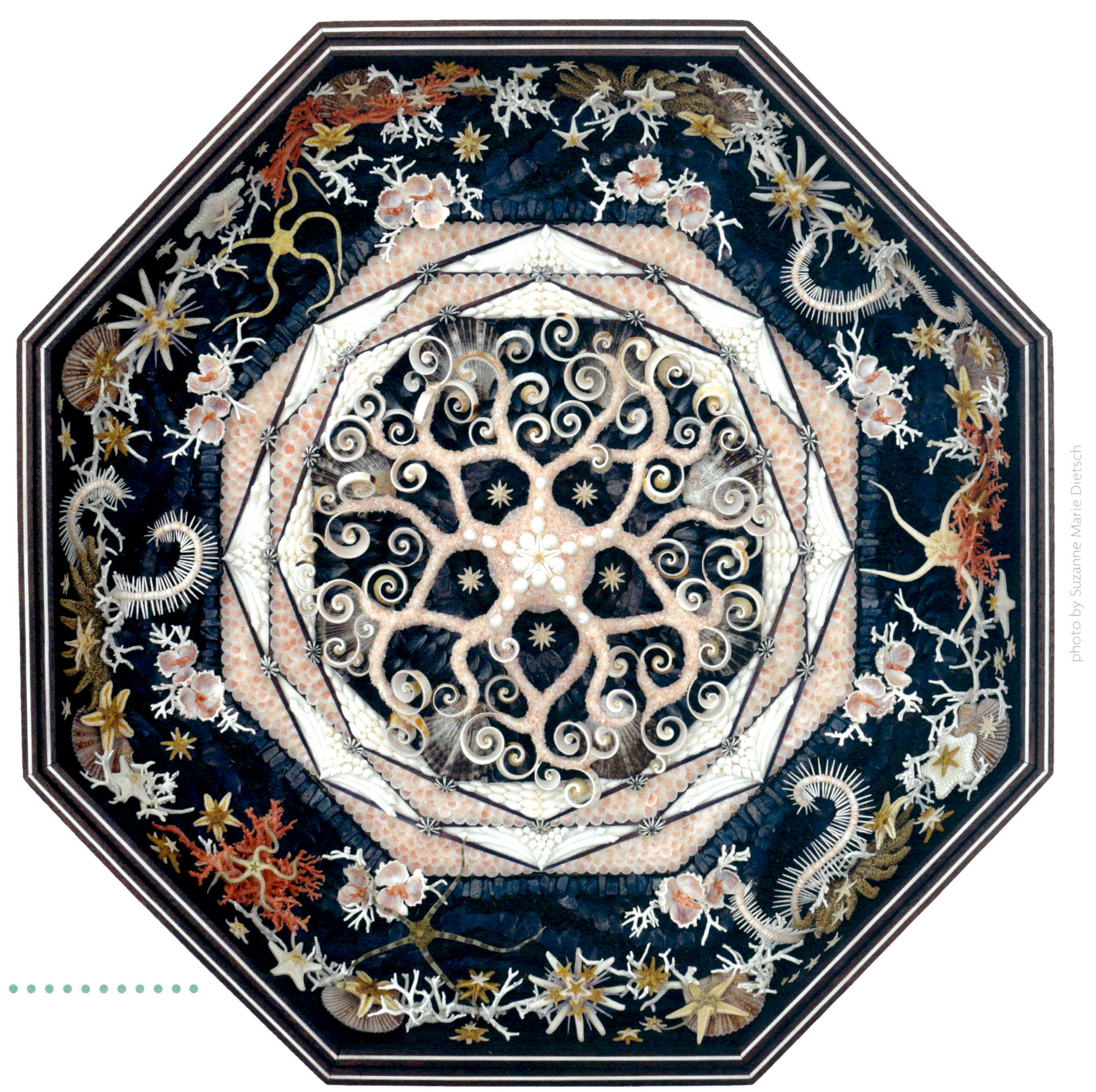

photo by Suzanne Marie Dietsch

Ocean Jeweled Seastars

Inspired by the many varieties of seastars (starfish), including the artist's favorites, the basket and feathered seastars.

18-inch mahogany case with white inlay made by Bill Jordan

The center 3D star bursts from the background layer of lavender and deep purple sea urchin spines. White rice shells, littorinas, tusk shell tips, and baby purple cowries are the base for the upward-shooting purple spines.

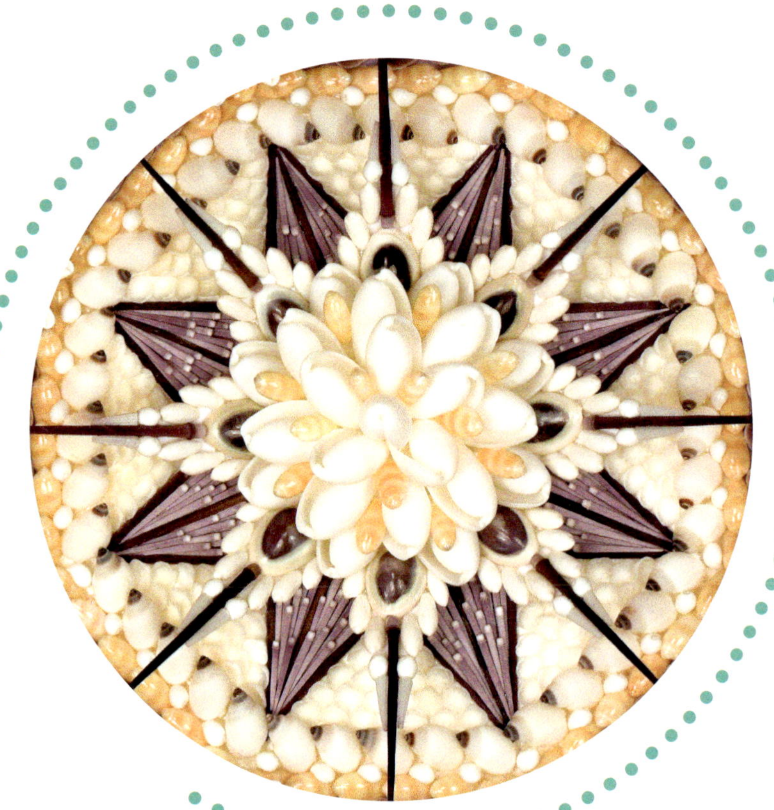

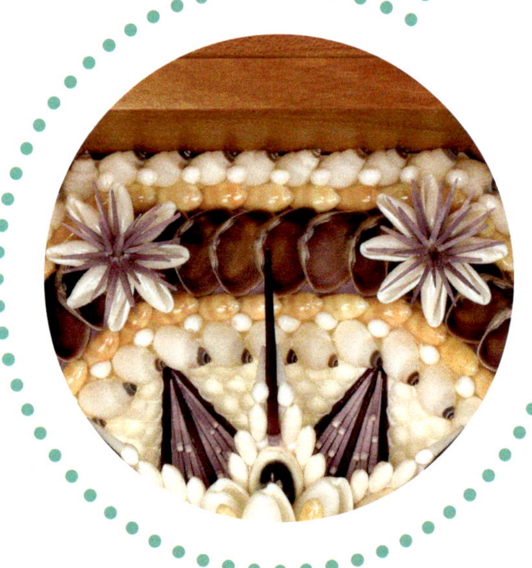

Inside the border of nipple shells sit Philippine rice shells and baby purple clams. The white volvarina shell flowers in each corner burst with lavender sea urchin spine centers.

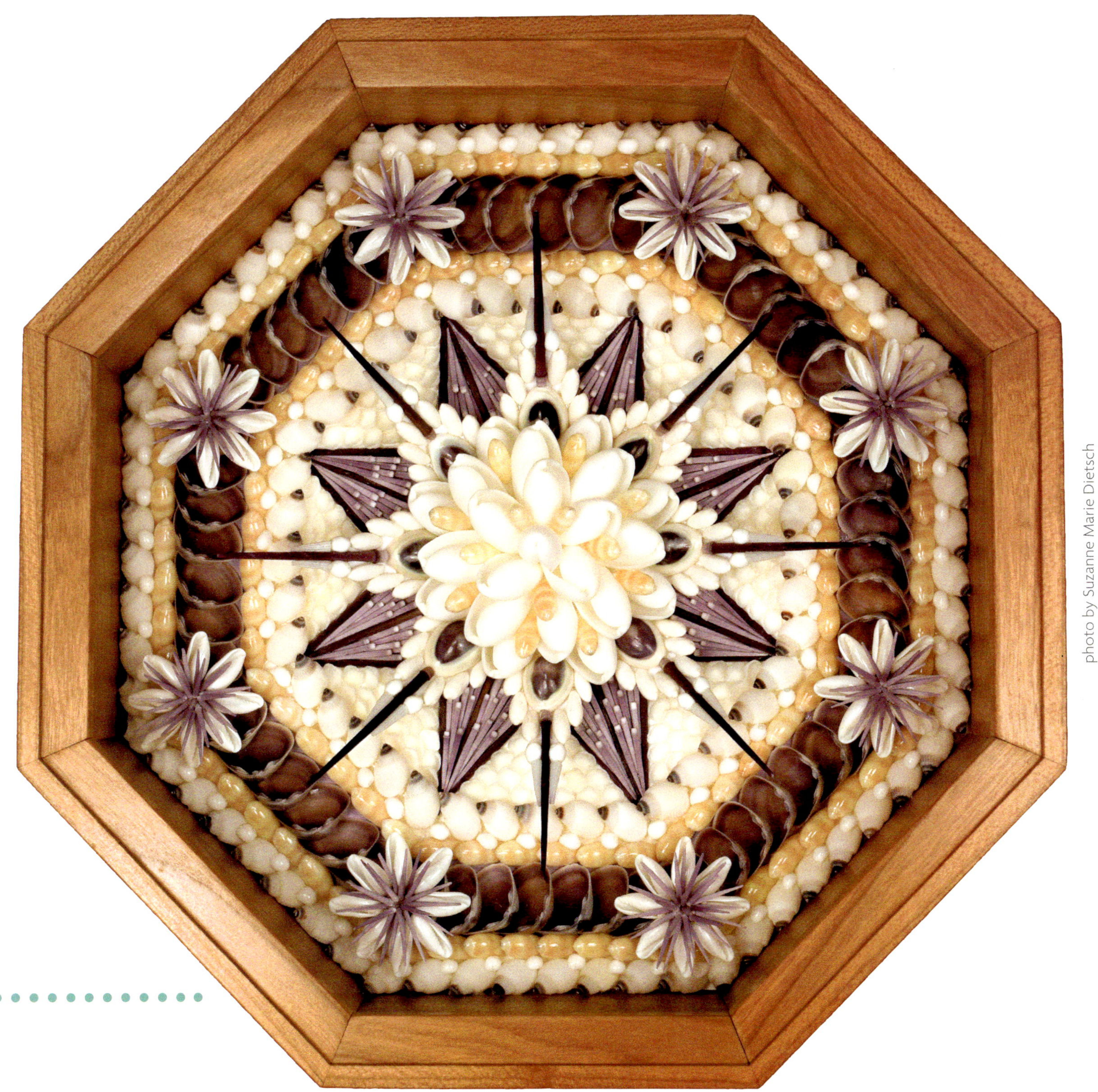

photo by Suzanne Marie Dietsch

Starlight

Inspired by our night sky, always filled with stars to wish upon.

9-inch cherry case made by Jim Prestigiacomo

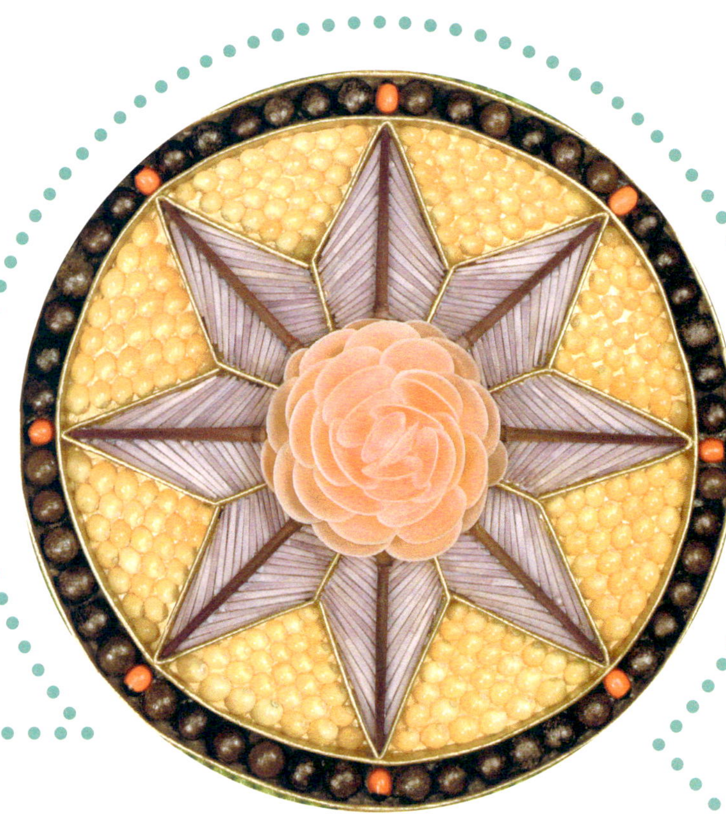

Using the traditional rosecup shell center, this cabbage rose is surrounded by a star of purple and lavender sea urchin spines. The paper dividers are brushed with gold paint. Yellow nerite shells fill in the background. The ring of seeds includes the infamous, poisonous red crab's eye seeds.

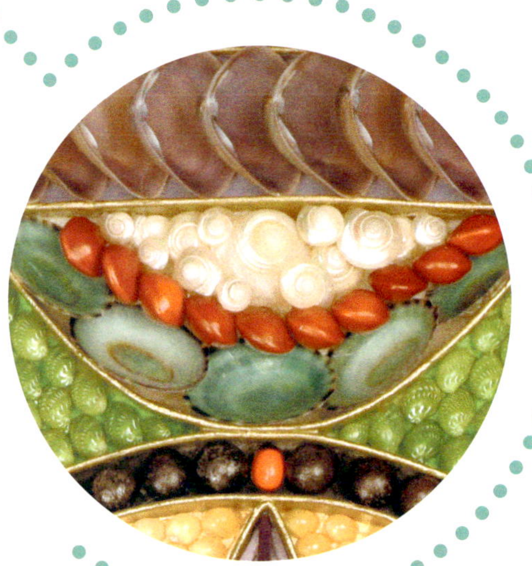

Four of the scalloped rainbows include blue-green limpets, red saga seeds, and clouds of white pearlized umboniums and malabar turbos. Emerald nerites fill the spaces toward the center ring.

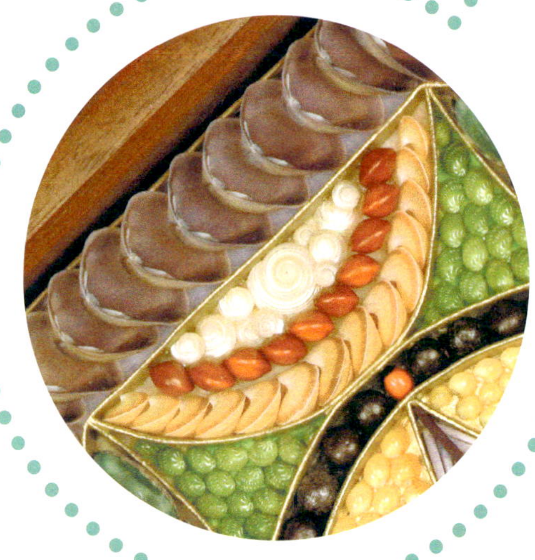

The other four scalloped rainbows include yellow snail shells, red saga seeds, and clouds of white pearlized umboniums and malabar turbo shells. Baby purple clam shells border the rainbows.

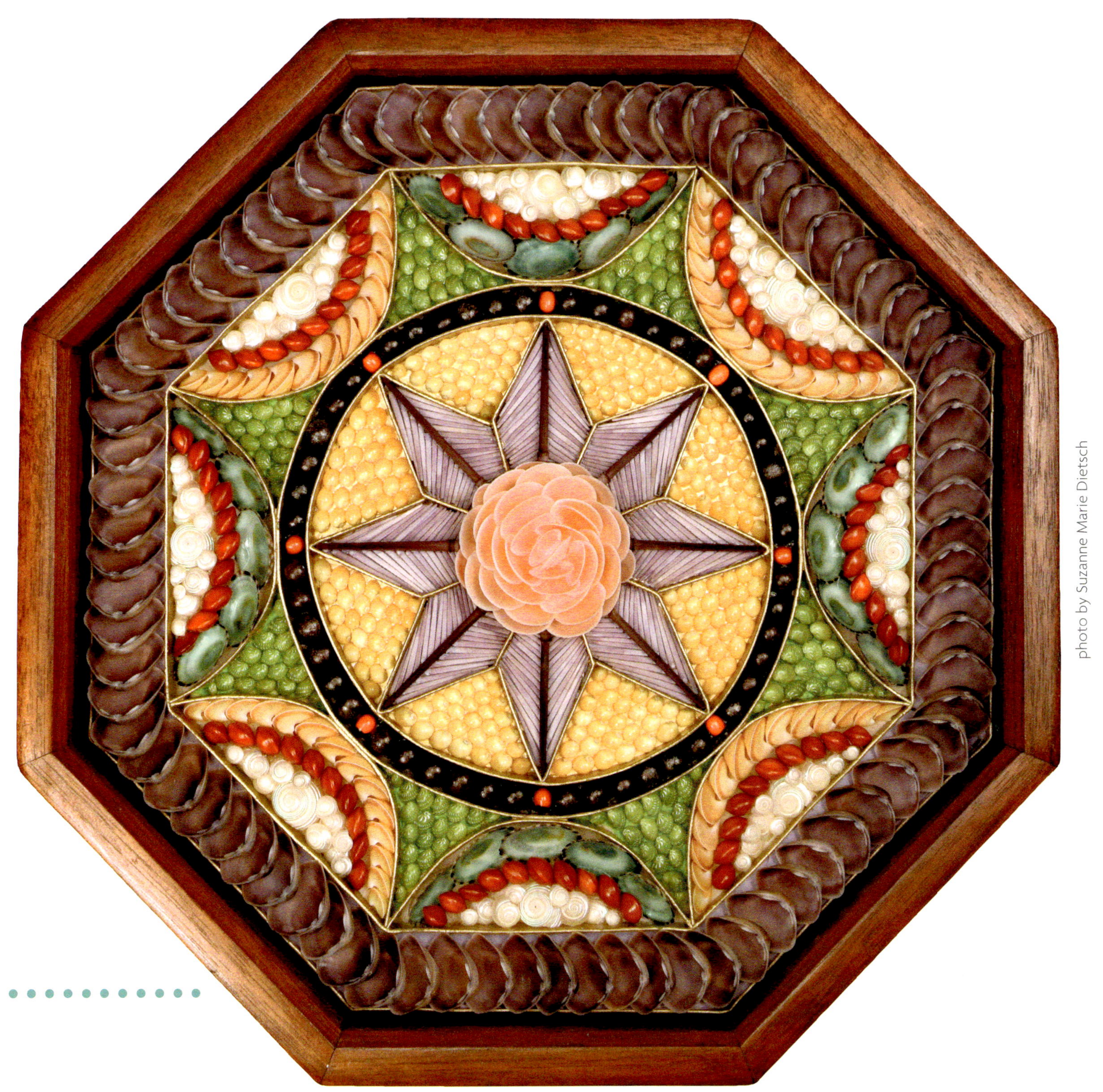

photo by Suzanne Marie Dietsch

Ocean Rainbows

The vibrant colors of nature are the inspiration for this traditional-style Valentine.

11-inch walnut case; maker unknown

photo by Heather Campbell Textiles

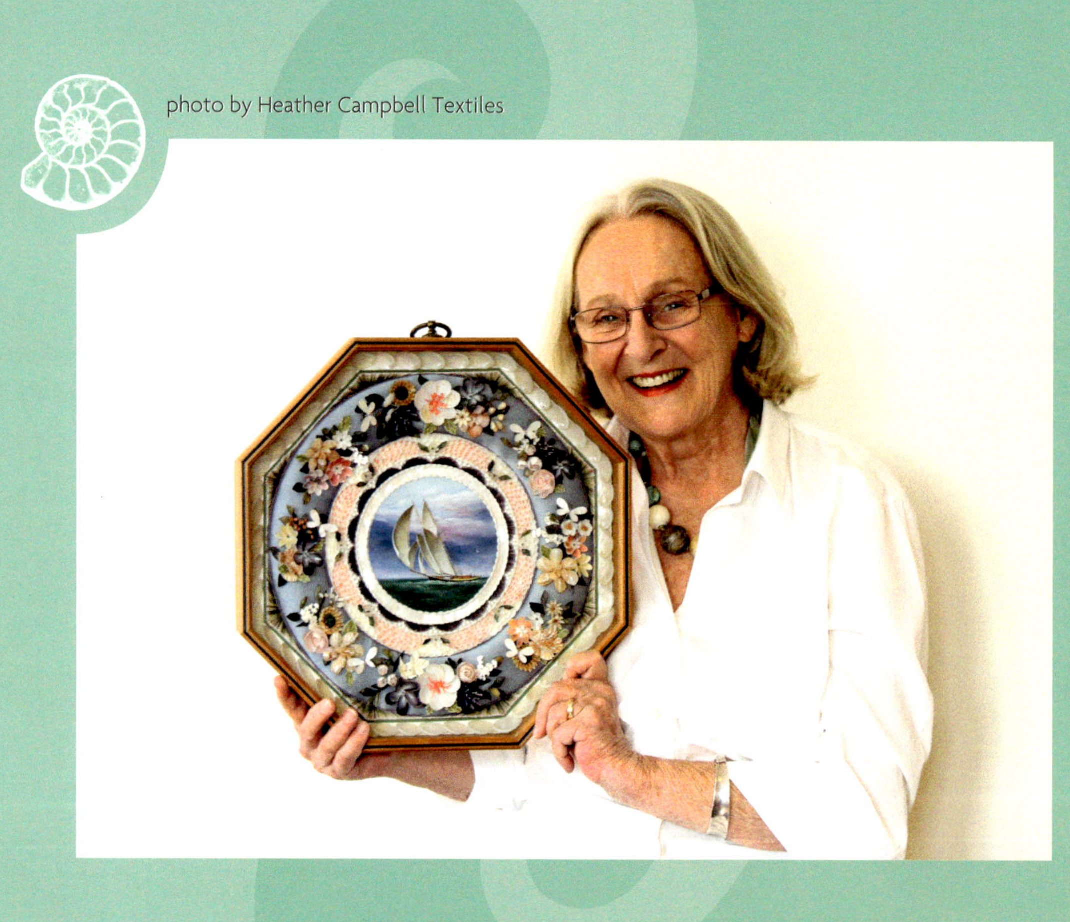

Judy Dinnick

Toronto, Ontario, Canada

I was born in Saskatoon, Saskatchewan, and raised in Toronto, Ontario, Canada, where I live today. I have drawn and painted since earliest memory. I graduated from the Ontario College of Art and also studied briefly in San Miguel, Mexico. During my marriage I lived in Nassau, Bahamas, for many years, and it was there that I first became acquainted with Sailors' Valentines, having seen an antique collection that Mr. and Mrs. Peter Vlasov had purchased from John Fondas, author of the book *Sailors' Valentines*.

Since returning to Canada in 1986, I have been involved in many aspects of the decorative arts. I have painted murals, often in trompe l'oeil style, and restored antique painted furniture. I became a tinsmith, making tôle cachepots and painting them with decorative themes. In 1991, a pair of my tôle urns was presented to the Prince and Princess of Wales during their visit to Canada.

In 2004 I turned my creative energy to making Sailors' Valentines. When I am working on a Valentine, my work space is cluttered with shells, shell flowers, paint, and numerous supplies. Somehow the most essential elements find their way into my octagonal case. I like to incorporate my love of painting into my Valentines. I almost always begin with a painting for the center and then complete the shell work with colors that are harmonious throughout the entire design. Often my table appears like a little garden of shell flowers, ready to be picked for use in my Valentine.

I have met many Valentine artists at the Sanibel Shell Show in Florida. It is wonderful to see their extraordinary and varied work and to share my interest in Valentines. The aesthetic beauty of shells from around the world is an inspiration to all of us involved in this rewarding art form.

www.sailorsvalentineart.com

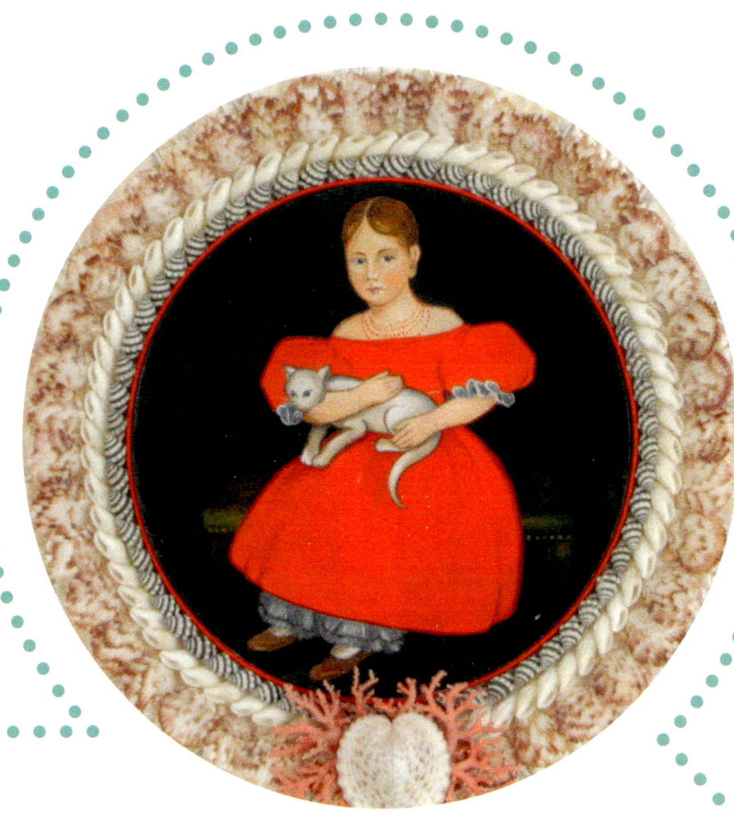

The artist's miniature oil painting is framed with three rows of shells including little pink scallops, complementing the colors in the painting. Surrounding these are white cup shells, rice shells, and strombus shells.

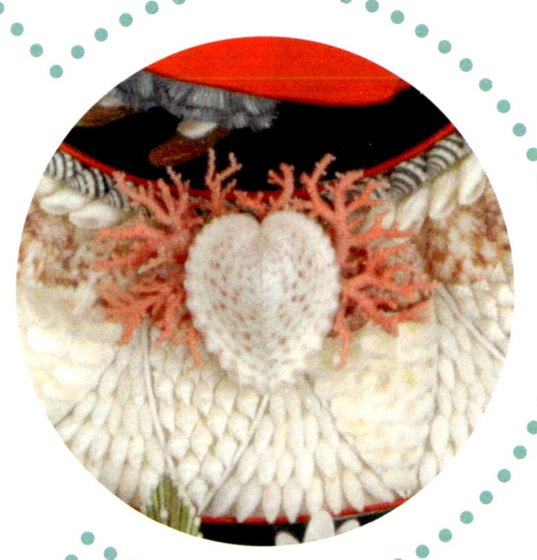

A heart cockle rests at the base of the painting along with rare pink stylaster coral, sometimes called lace coral. This slow-growing coral is found in shaded areas of reefs, often in caves and crevices.

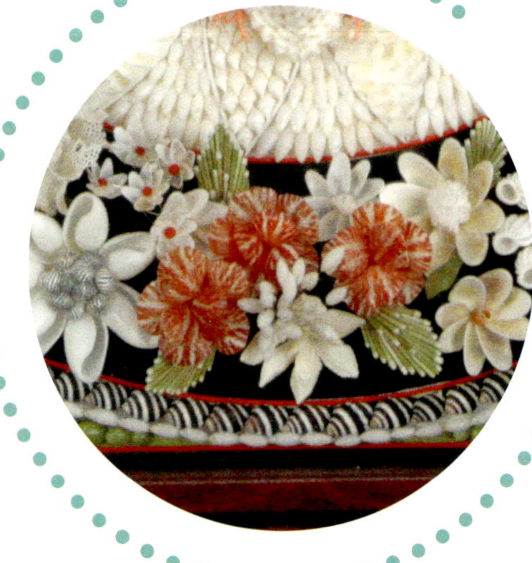

The ring of shell flowers lies on a black silk cushion. The reddish flowers are made from brachiopod shells from the Philippines. Around them are a spray of wired white rice shells and leaves made with green urchin spines.

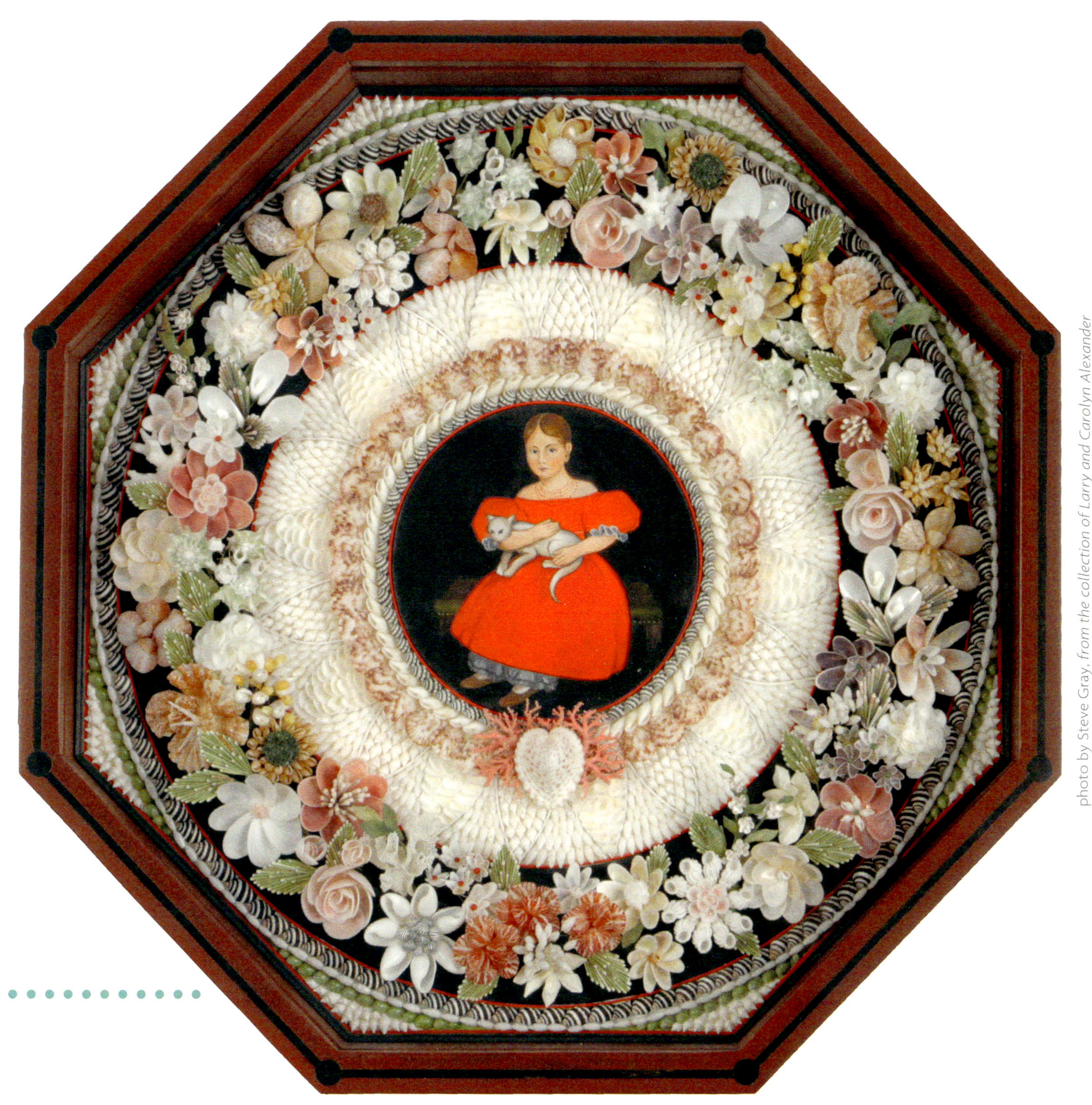

photo by Steve Gray, from the collection of Larry and Carolyn Alexander

Girl in Red

Inspired by a painting by American folk artist Ammi Phillips (1788–1865), an itinerant portrait painter who painted over a period of five decades.

16-inch rosewood case made by Jim Prestigiacomo

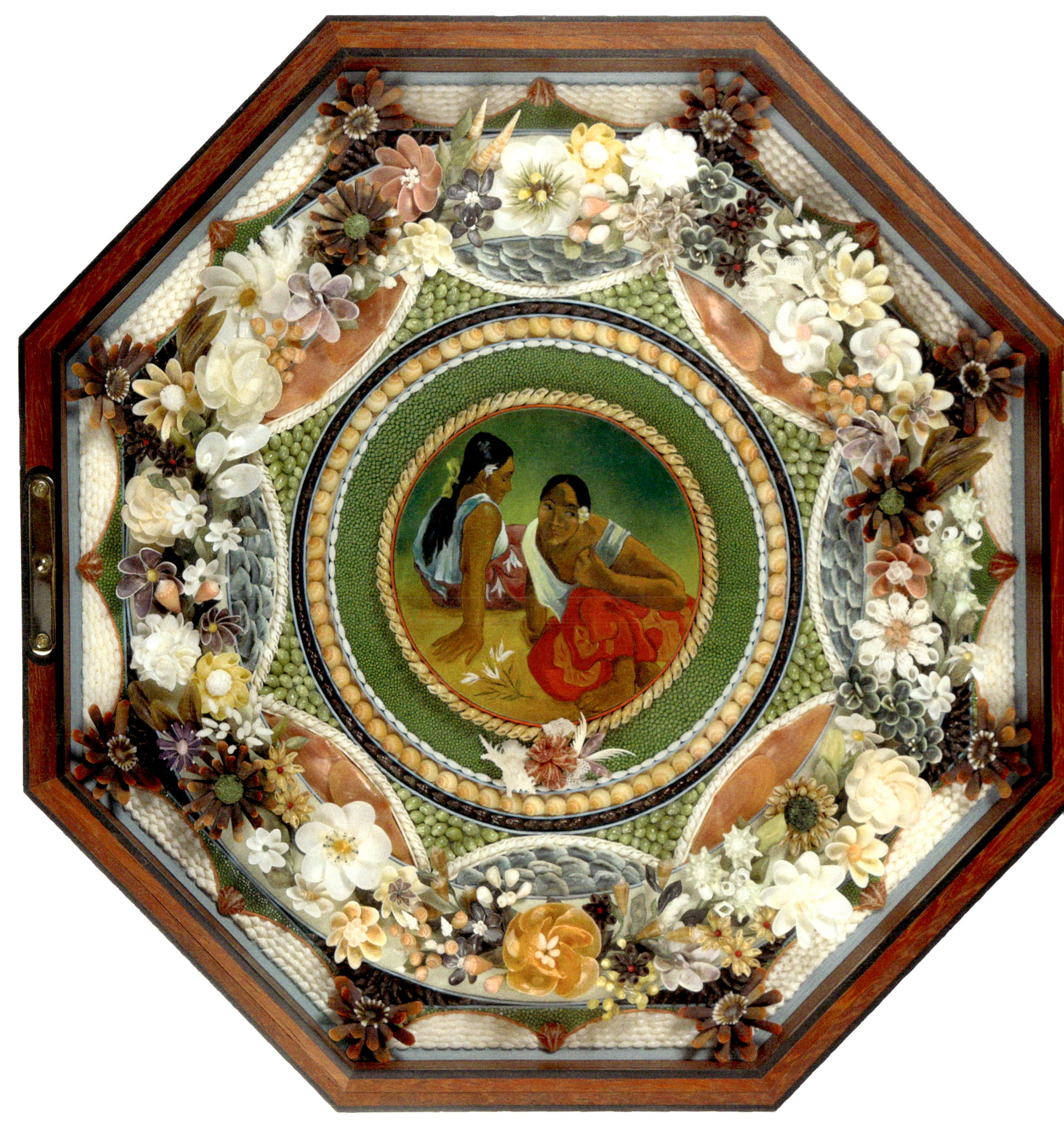

Inspired by the art of French post-impressionist artist Paul Gauguin (1848–1903).

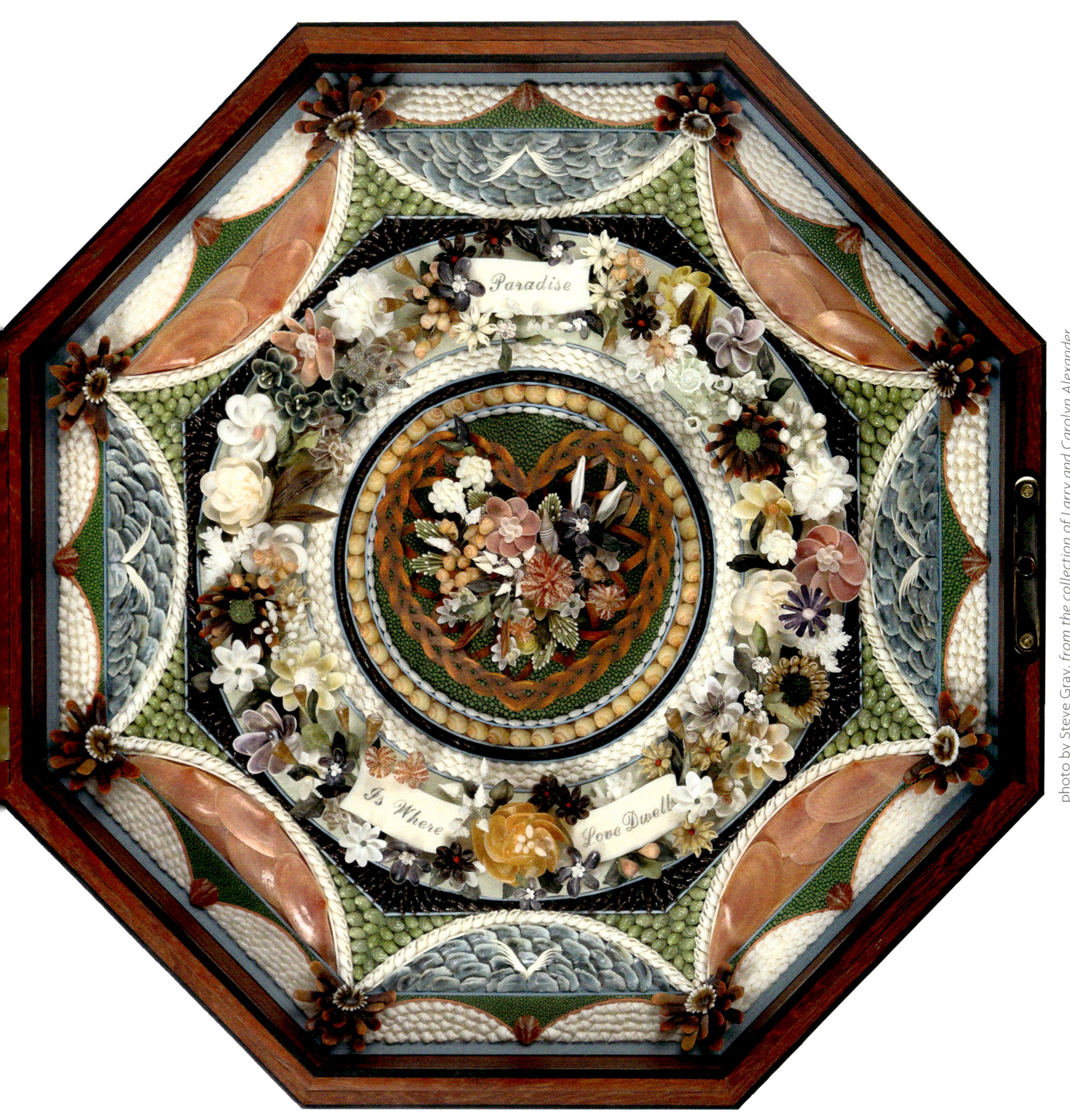

photo by Steve Gray, from the collection of Larry and Carolyn Alexander

Paradise Is Where Love Dwells

16-inch (each side) rosewood case made by Jim Prestigiacomo

The miniature oil painting reflects the colorful life in the South Seas. The outer circle is done with Polynesian land snails. The emerald green shagreen (the dyed skin of stingrays) has been used for centuries on objets d'art.

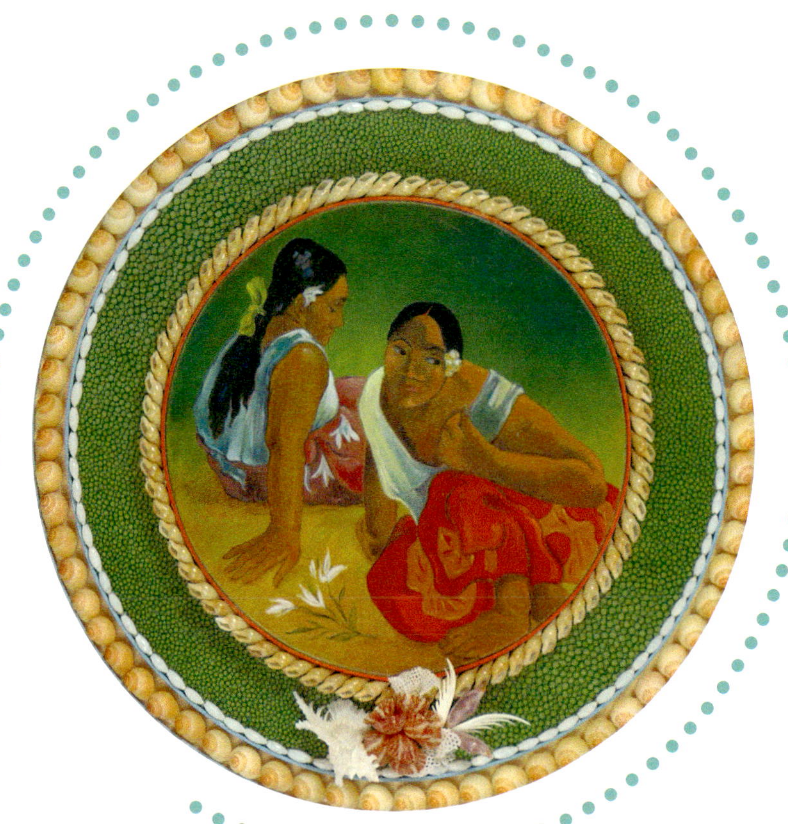

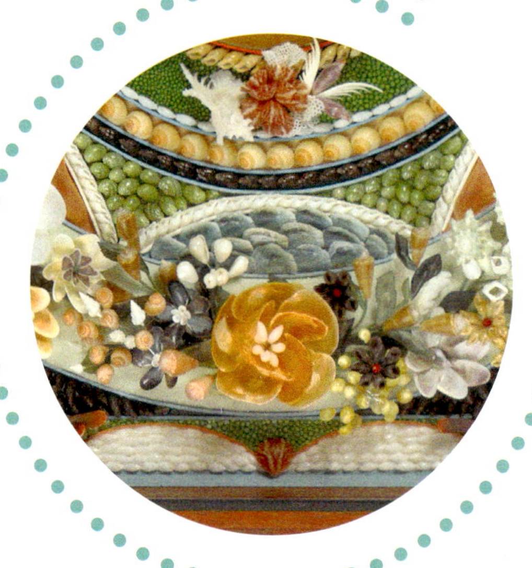

The orange center flower is created from jingle shells. All eight sections include blue chitons and tellins from the Philippines. The shell flowers lie on a ring of pale green silk, and the flowers and individual shells are wired and glued to the silk.

The heart-shaped basket was created by the artist from paper that she painted. It sits on a background of shagreen. The basket holds flowers made from small rose petal tellins, orange Polynesian land snails, blue mussel shells, and coquinas.

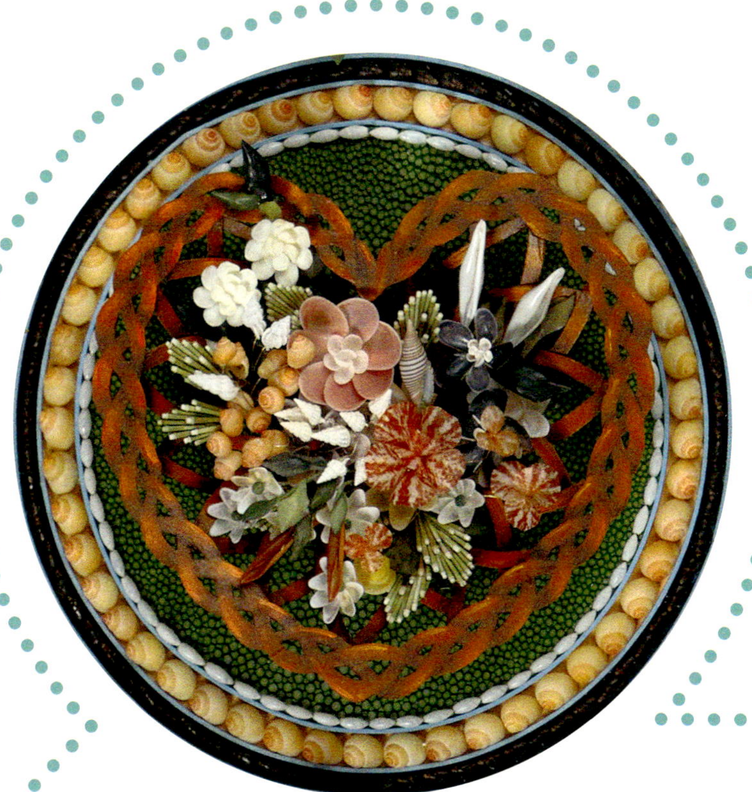

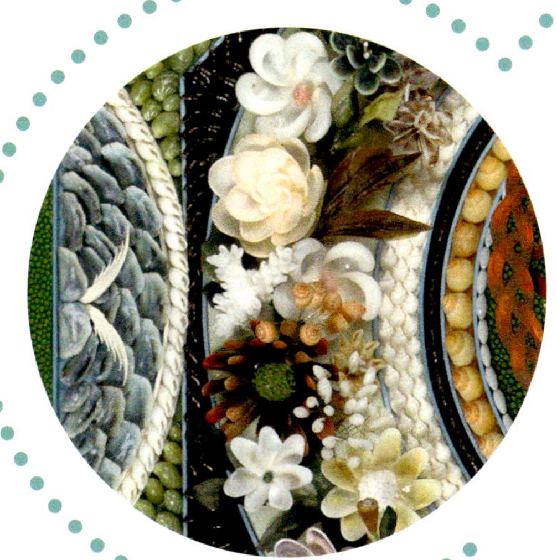

A grouping of shell flowers includes a flower made of Tampa tellins with two brown operculums as leaves. Above that is a flower of baby's ear shells, and below is a flower of orange-tipped sea urchin spines beside wired rice shells. The artist used strong colors in this double Valentine, trying to show the vibrance of flora and fauna in the South Seas.

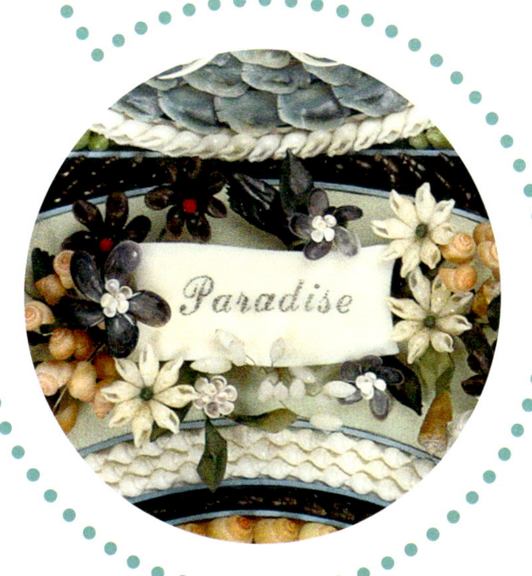

"Paradise" is written in scrimshaw on an old ivory piano key, as is the other lettering in the piece.

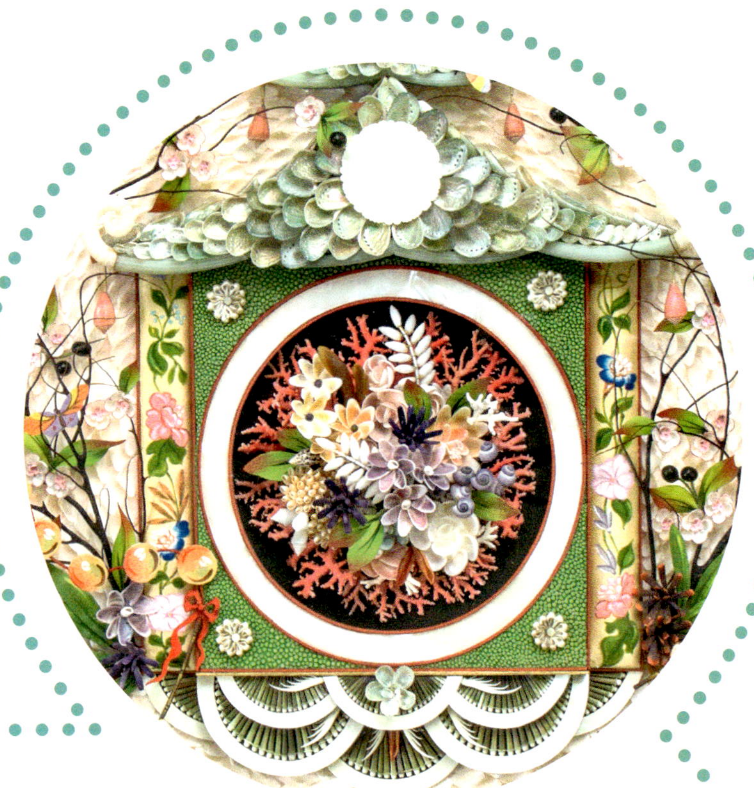

The center pagoda has a recessed window displaying shell flowers and pink stylaster coral. Green shagreen is behind the centerpiece, and leading up to it are mother-of-pearl circles, green sea urchin spines, and squilla claws.

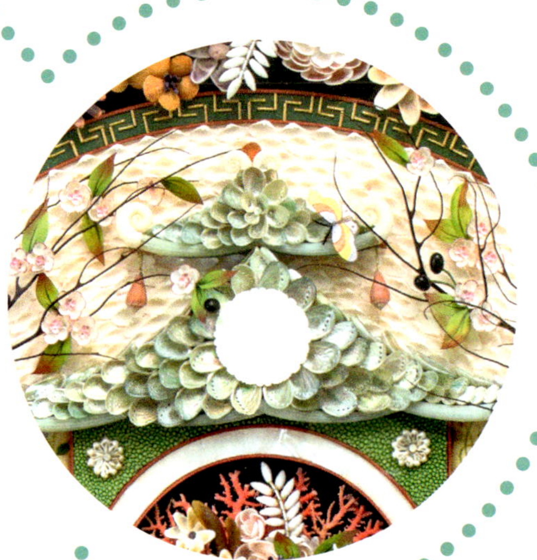

The pagoda is surrounded by cherry blossoms and butterflies made from fish scales. The roof is created from abalone shells and features an antique mother-of-pearl gaming counter. Branches from black coral with painted fish-scale leaves sit to the sides.

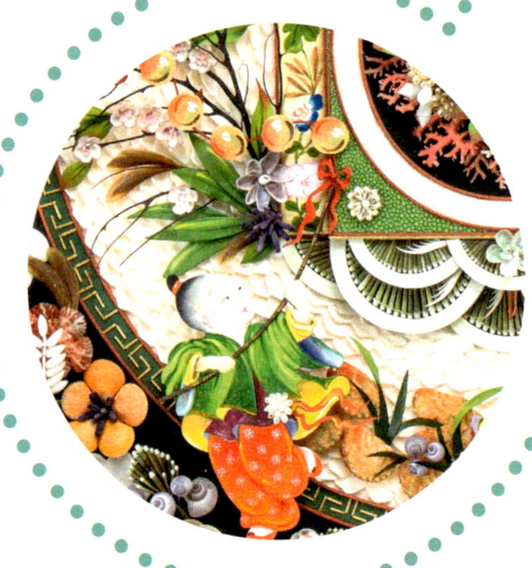

The artist made children from wood that she then painted. They are flying kites in the garden. Painted gold sea urchin spines sit on a narrow border of deep green, reflecting oriental design.

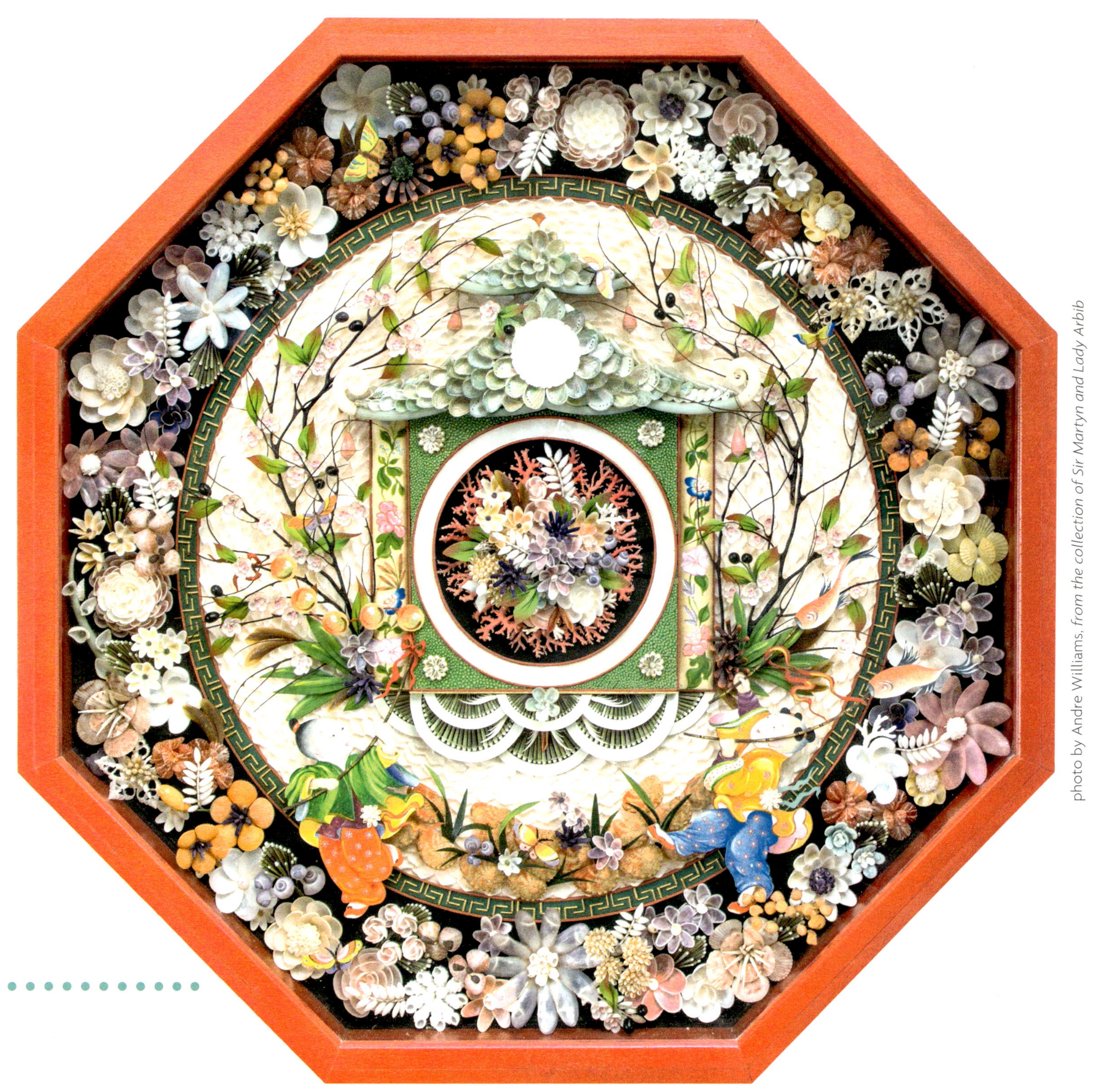

photo by Andre Williams, *from the collection of Sir Martyn and Lady Arbib*

Garden of Joy

Inspired by the numerous beautiful elements of Chinese art.

18-inch case made by Jim Prestigiacomo and painted by the artist

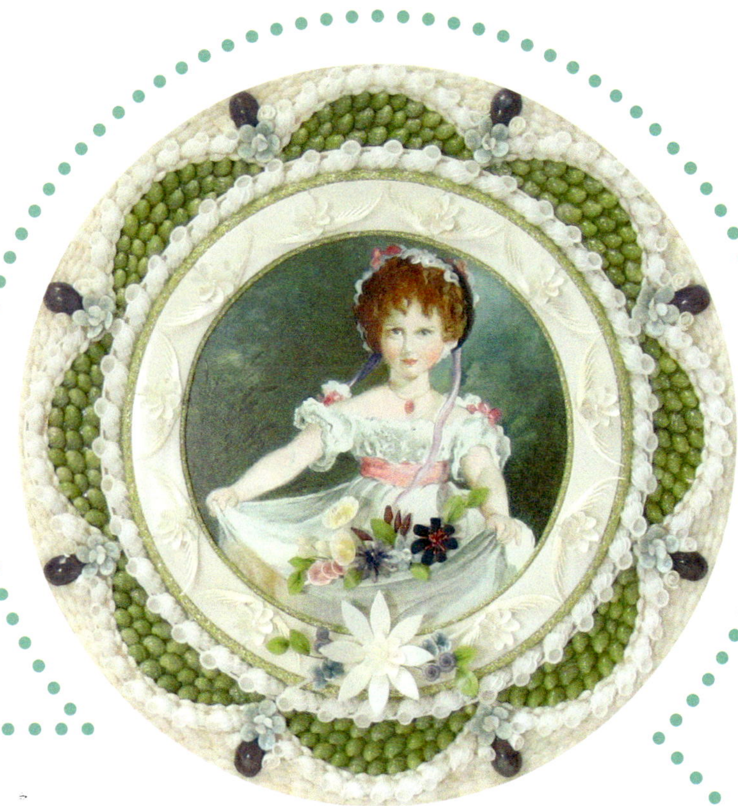

The miniature oil painting, done by the artist, features a child holding shell flowers in her apron. Her necklace boasts a real conch pearl. The ivory frame around the painting is made from old ivory piano keys.

Tiny white rice shells form the background for eight bouquets of pink fairy tellin flowers with little janthinas at the sides. Blue morning glories are made with crushed blue coral, and rice shell daisies abound.

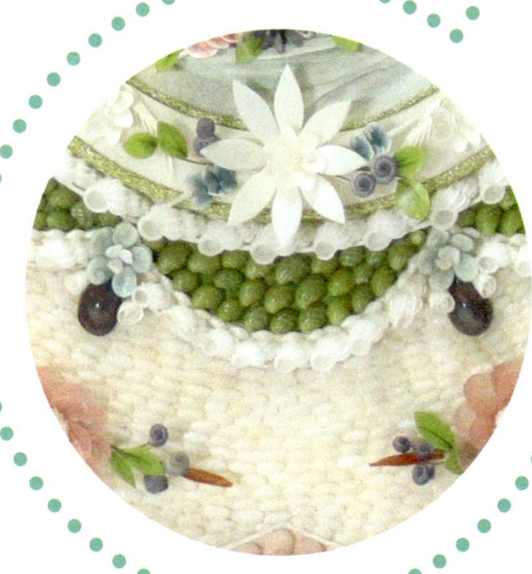

At the base of the painting is an ivory flower enhanced with purple janthinas and tiny blue chitons. The deep purple accents are the tops of cowry shells, and the small blue flowers are done from the operculums of astraea calcar shells.

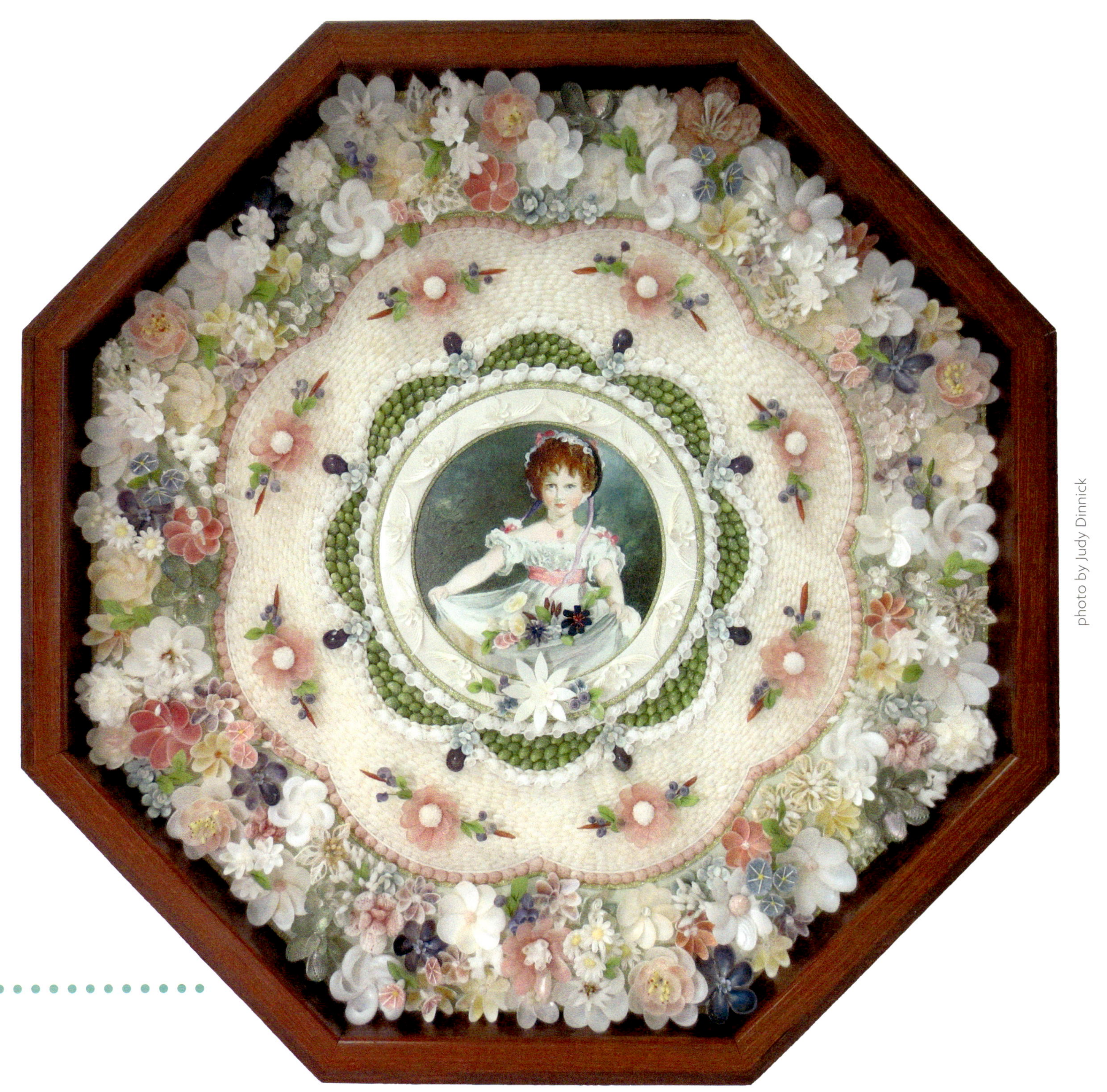

photo by Judy Dinnick

Ocean Spring

A celebration of youth and the many glorious gifts from the sea.

18-inch mahogany case made by Jim Prestigiacomo

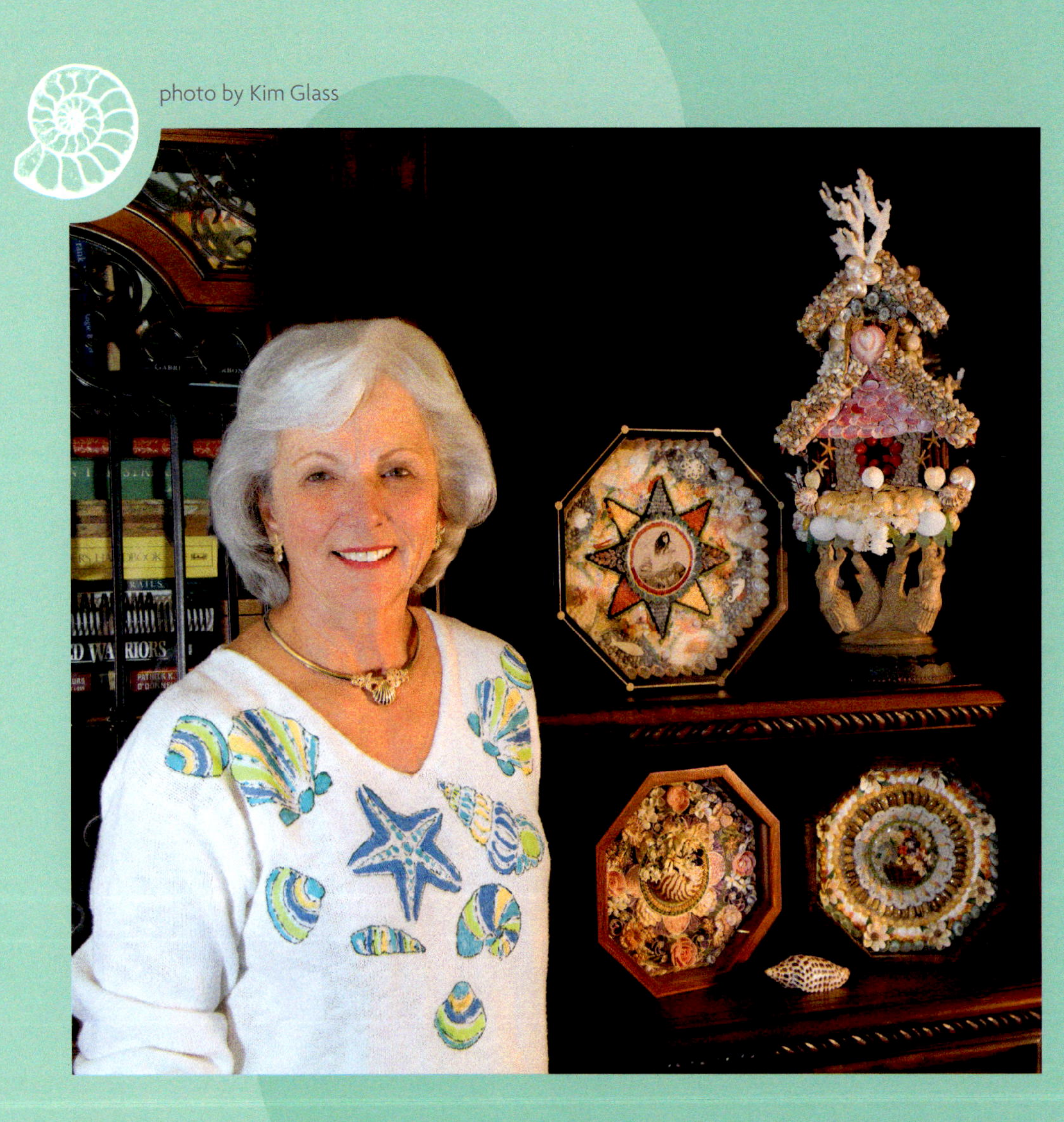

photo by Kim Glass

Joy Henderson

Lacey's Spring, Alabama

On a visit to Daytona Beach as a child, I gathered seashells in a pail that I left on the balcony for the night. Imagine my surprise the following morning when I found that my shells were no longer in the bucket but crawling all over the balcony. Thus began my fascination with these incredible wonders of nature.

After reading about the Sanibel Shell Show on a calendar of Southern art events, my daughter Rhonda and I attended it in 2000. We were astounded by the variety and quality of the artistic entries made from seashells and other sealife. We went directly to a shell shop and bought seashells to encrust a triple valance in our home. The next project was to encrust a birdhouse, and that was my first entry in the Sanibel Shell Show. While at this show I was particularly enthralled with the Sailors' Valentines, which I had never seen before. Soon after, I took classes from Sailors' Valentine artists Judy Dinnick* and Sandy Moran.**

When I begin a piece I start by deciding on a theme and a centerpiece. Once I create the centerpiece, I work from the center outward. I love to include rare and unusual shells and sea-related items in my Valentines. Among these are Hawaiian ni'ihau shells, Aboriginal maireener shells, sharks' teeth, and Tahitian pearls. Though I have a studio in our home, I often work at the dining room table so my husband, Rod, and I can enjoy the vast array of shells spread out before us as we eat our meals.

I am a member of the North Alabama Shell Club, where I am privileged to meet with seashell experts and enthusiasts. Through the shell club I heard about Conchologists of America, an international malacological organization, and now I go each year to their annual convention to purchase new shells from vendors whose tables are laden with specimen seashells from all over the world. I am always in awe of what mollusks create.

Several times each year I travel to Sanibel Island, where in addition to entering my Sailors' Valentines in the annual Shell Festival in March, I spend many hours on the beaches collecting shells for my Valentines and photographing birds at J. N. Ding Darling National Wildlife Refuge.

* Judy Dinnick's work can be seen on pages 68–79.
** Sandy Moran's work can be seen on pages 146–155.

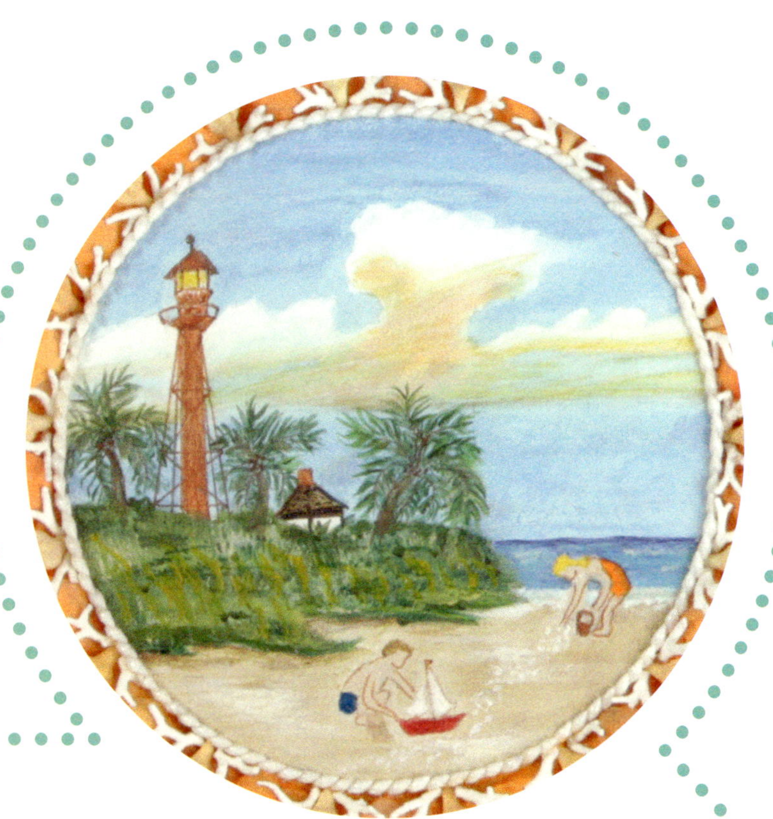

The center depicts the Sanibel Lighthouse, a favorite destination for visitors and residents alike.

This Valentine features Sanibel's many natural treasures. At the center is a roseate spoonbill made by Judy Dinnick (who also made the great blue heron and white pelican in this piece). The shells in the scallop shapes are an immature fighting conch (left) and an immature junonia (right), both found on Sanibel beaches.

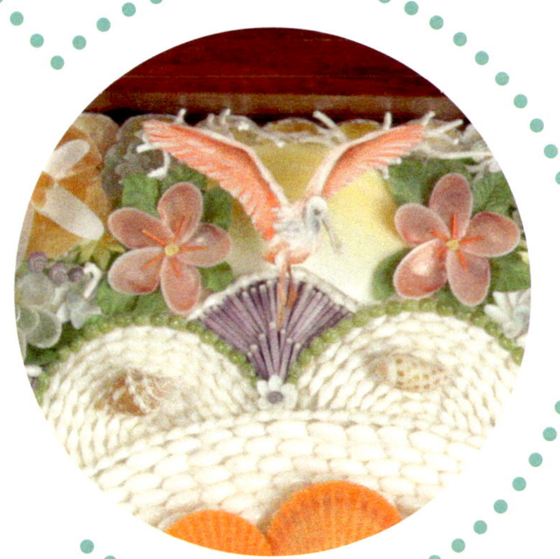

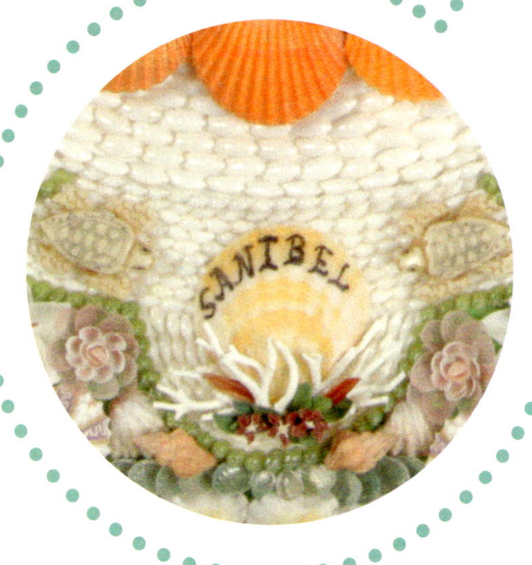

Sea turtles are a protected species on Sanibel Island and appear in this piece because they are such an integral part of the island's culture.

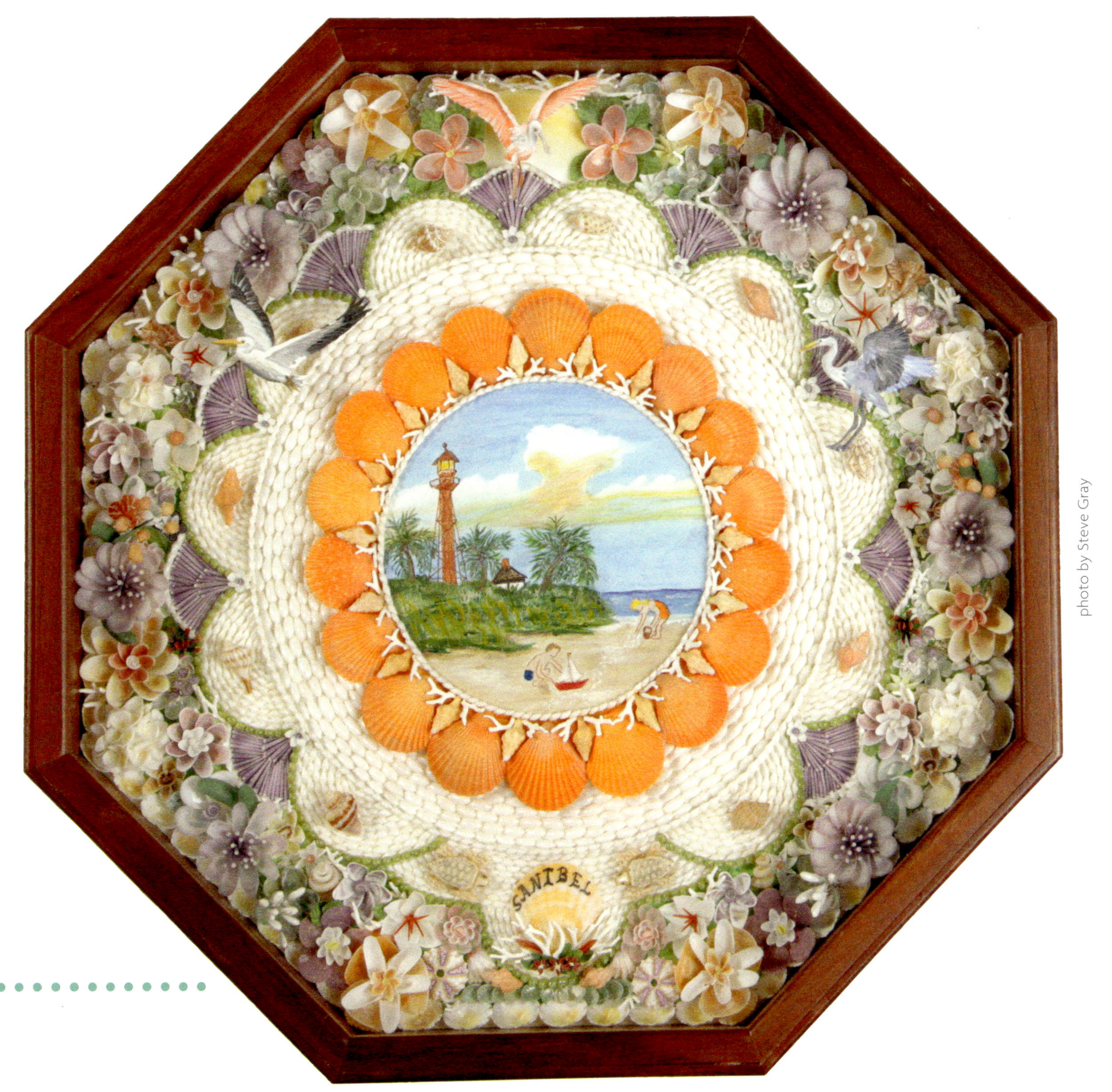

photo by Steve Gray

Sanibel

Inspired by the many natural beauties of Sanibel: seashells, the lighthouse, birds, turtles, and people enjoying these treasures.

15-inch red mangrove case made by Jim Prestigiacomo

In the center are dolphins at sea, carved from ivory. The waves are cut from capiz shells. Operculums with dazzling blue spirals surround the centerpiece, and white coralized algae sits along the bottom edge.

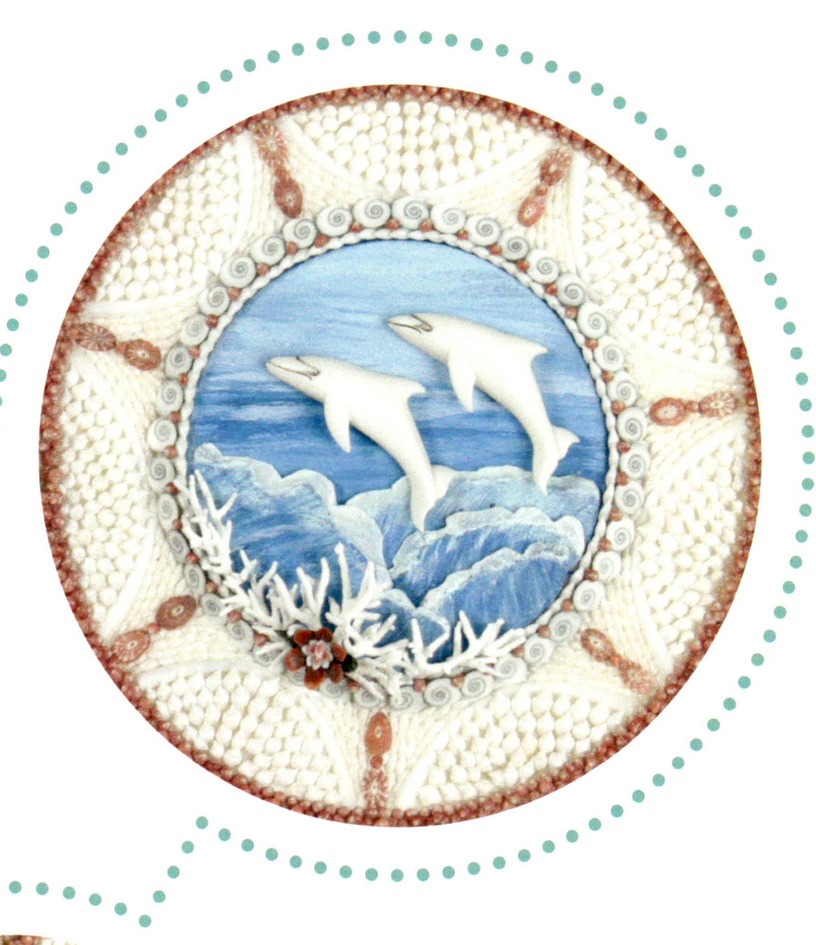

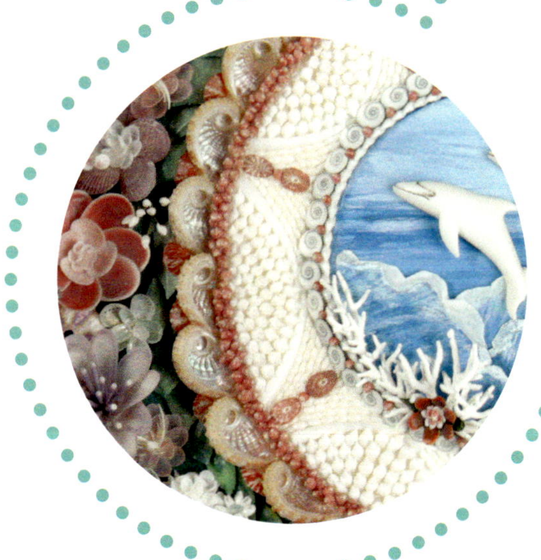

The centerpiece is surrounded by a lei of rare tiny ni'ihau shells from Hawaii. Surrounding the lei is a circle of red abalone shells. The lush green circle is done with dyed garfish scales.

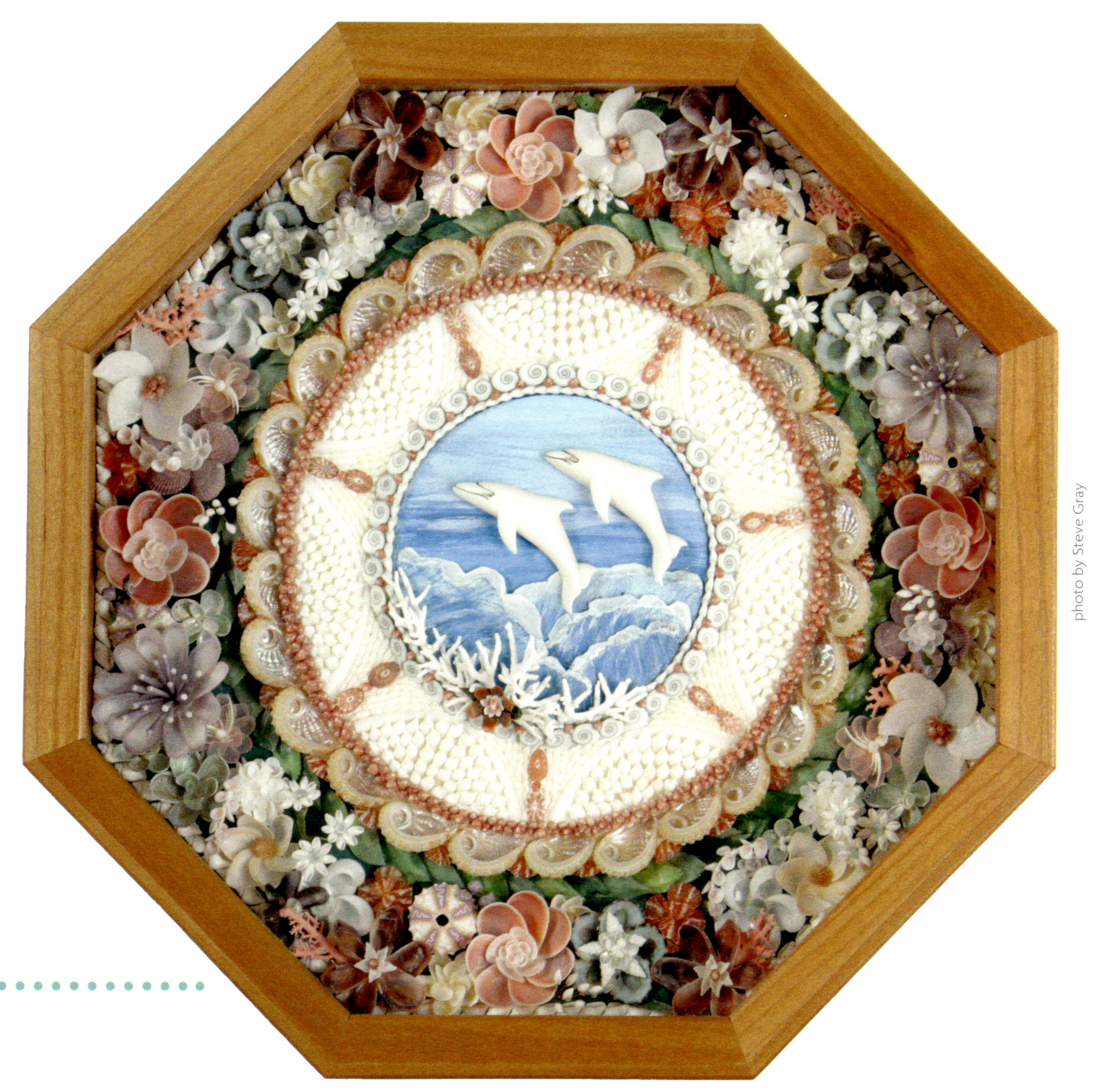

photo by Steve Gray

Dolphin Dream

Inspired by dolphins at sea . . . a magical sight treasured by lovers of the sea for centuries.

12-inch cherry case made by Jim Prestigiacomo

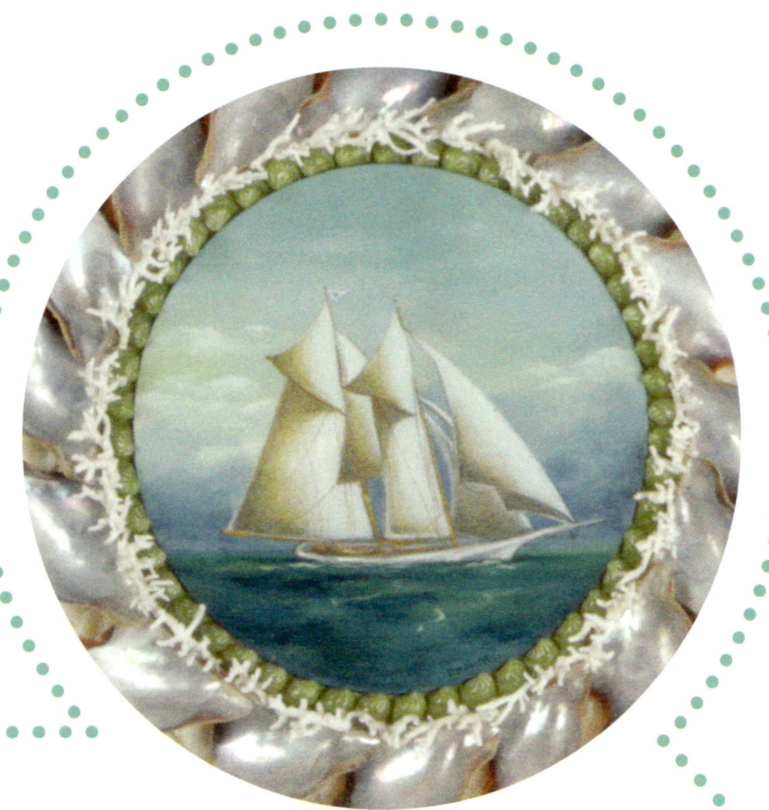

The centerpiece is an oil painting of the *Madeleine* done by Judy Dinnick.

Tiny white strombus shells create interesting texture in the star pattern.

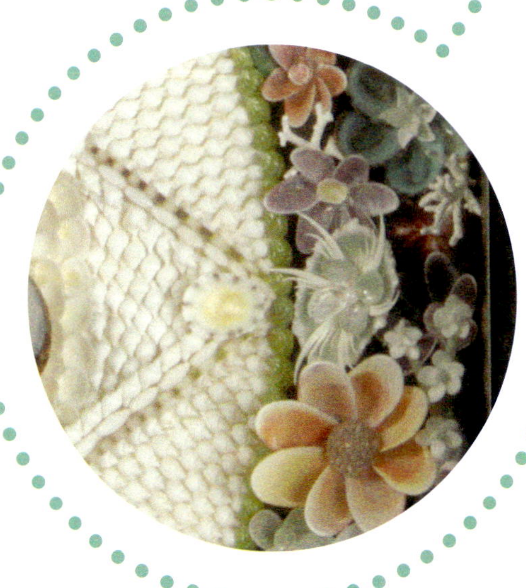

The outer edge of this Valentine is encased with seashell flowers made from coquina shells, blue-green limpets, Job's tear shells, operculums, and squilla claws. White coralized algae pieces sit among the flowers.

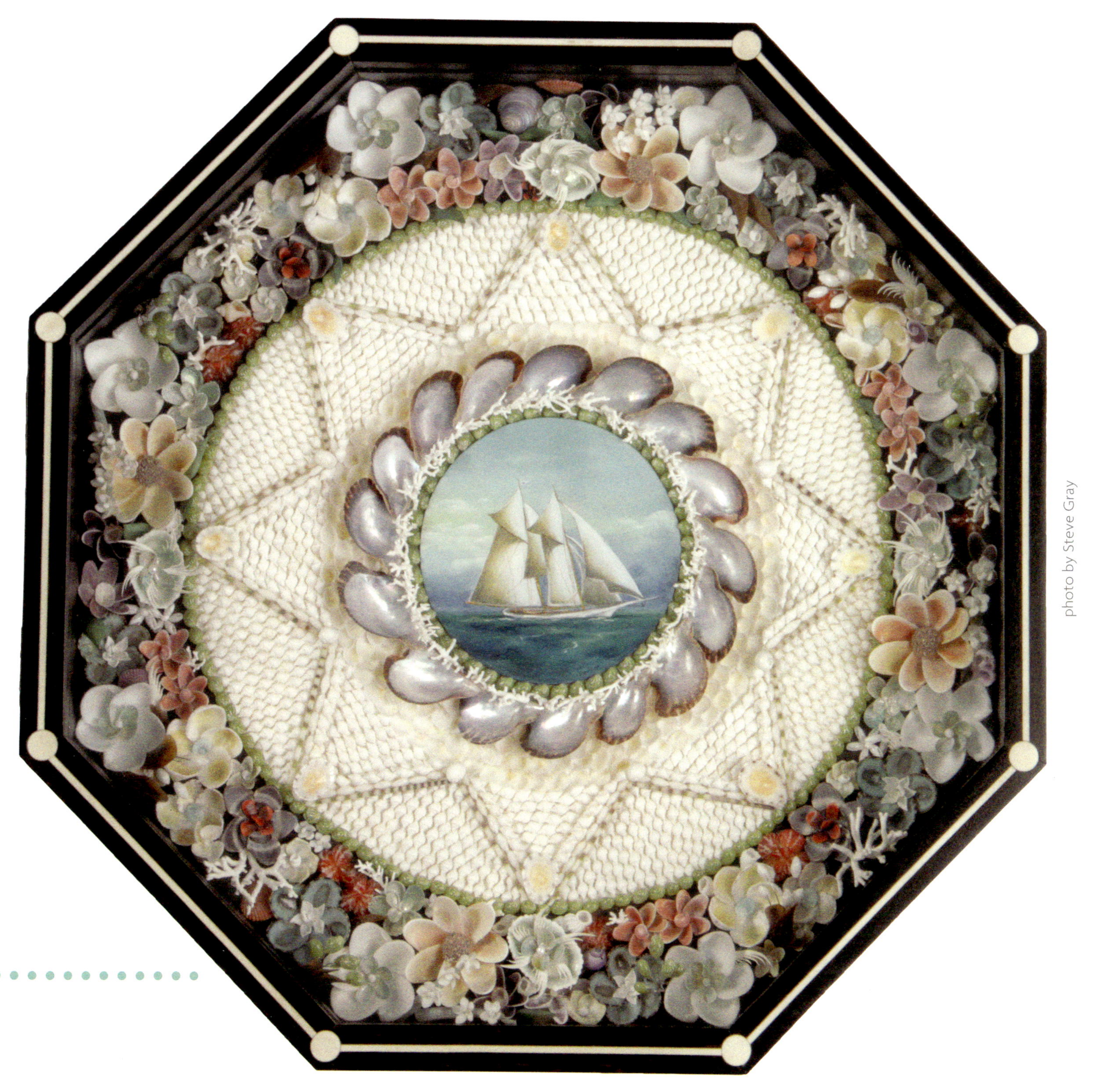

photo by Steve Gray

Sailing

Inspired by the *Madeleine*, defender of the 1876 America's Cup race.

13-inch ebony case with ivory inlay made by Jim Prestigiacomo

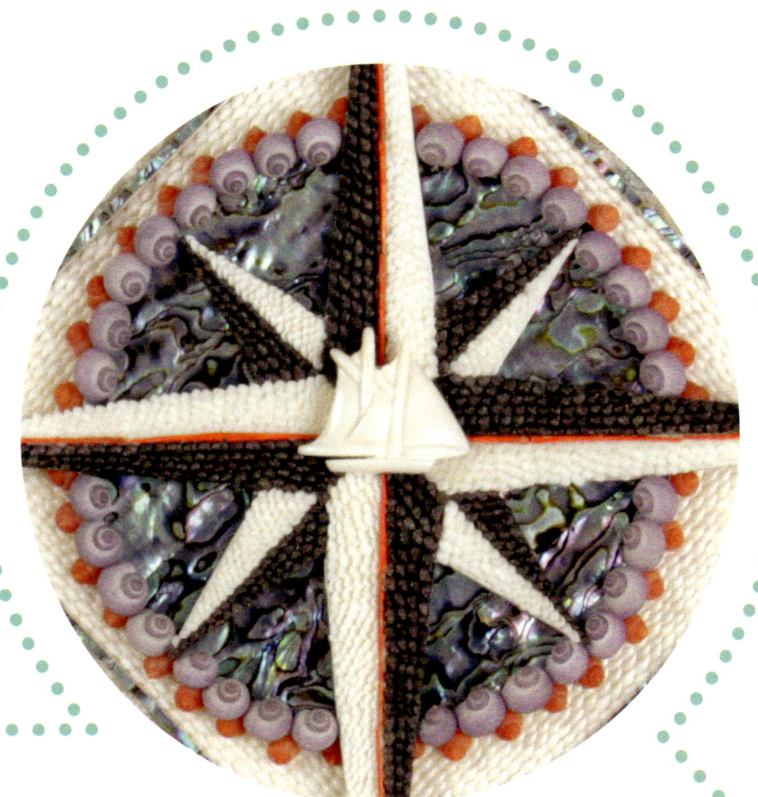

The black and white of the points are divided by orange sea urchin spines. Purple janthina shells form the circle around the star shape. Blue abalone is used for the background and also to outline the square edges around the centerpiece.

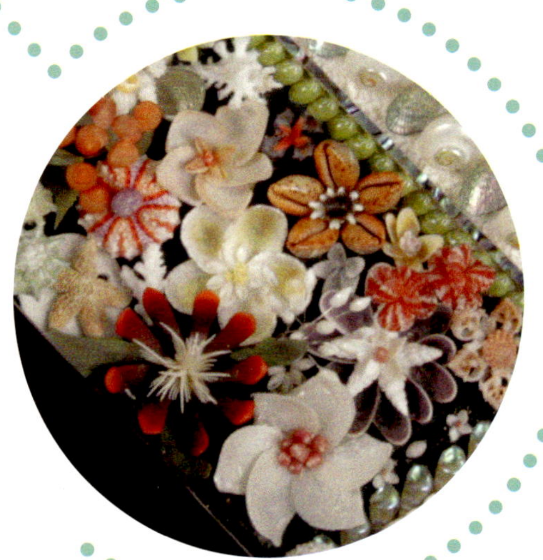

Beautiful, colorful flowers made from red urchin spines, Tampa tellins, red brachiopods, yellow coquina shells, and rust-colored cowries add vibrance to the work.

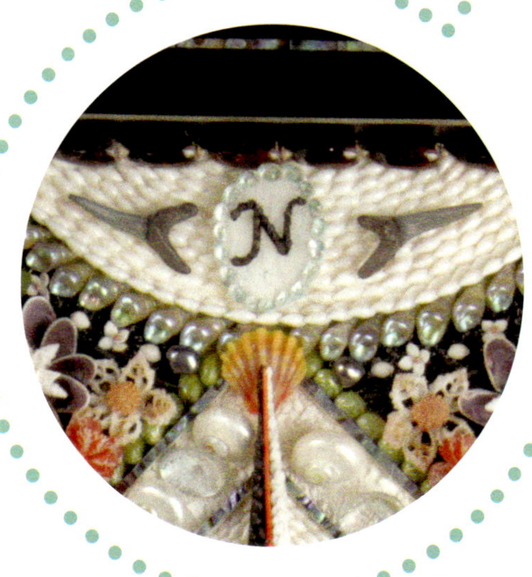

The shells around the oval with the letter "N" are blue abalone, and sharks' teeth sit to either side of the letter. The greenish iridescent shells forming a border for the scallop are rare Tasmanian maireener shells.

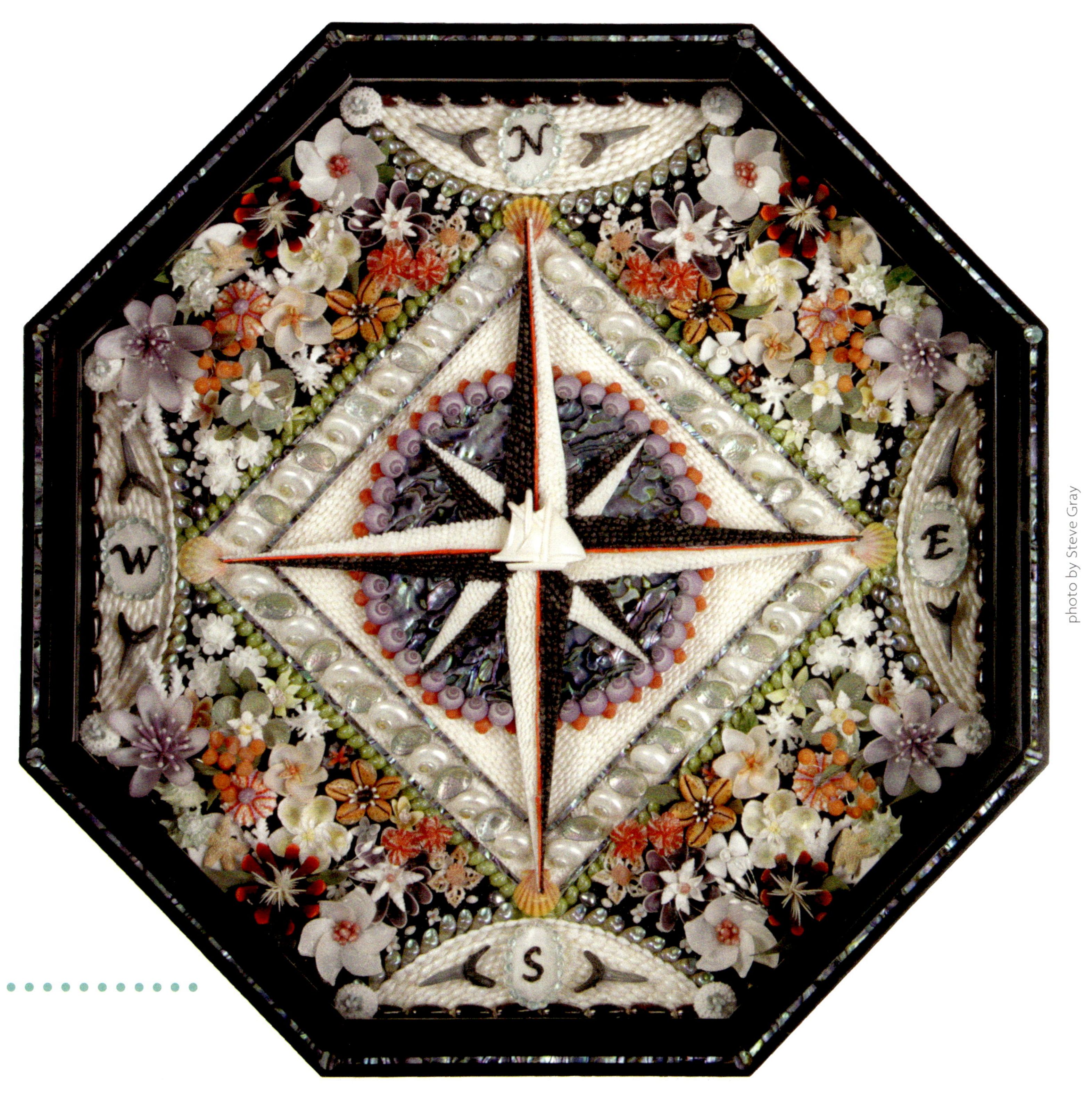

photo by Steve Gray

Compass Rose

Inspired by the compass rose,
which evokes images of centuries of seafaring adventurers.

14-inch ebony case with paua shell inlay made by Jim Prestigiacomo

photo by Andre Williams

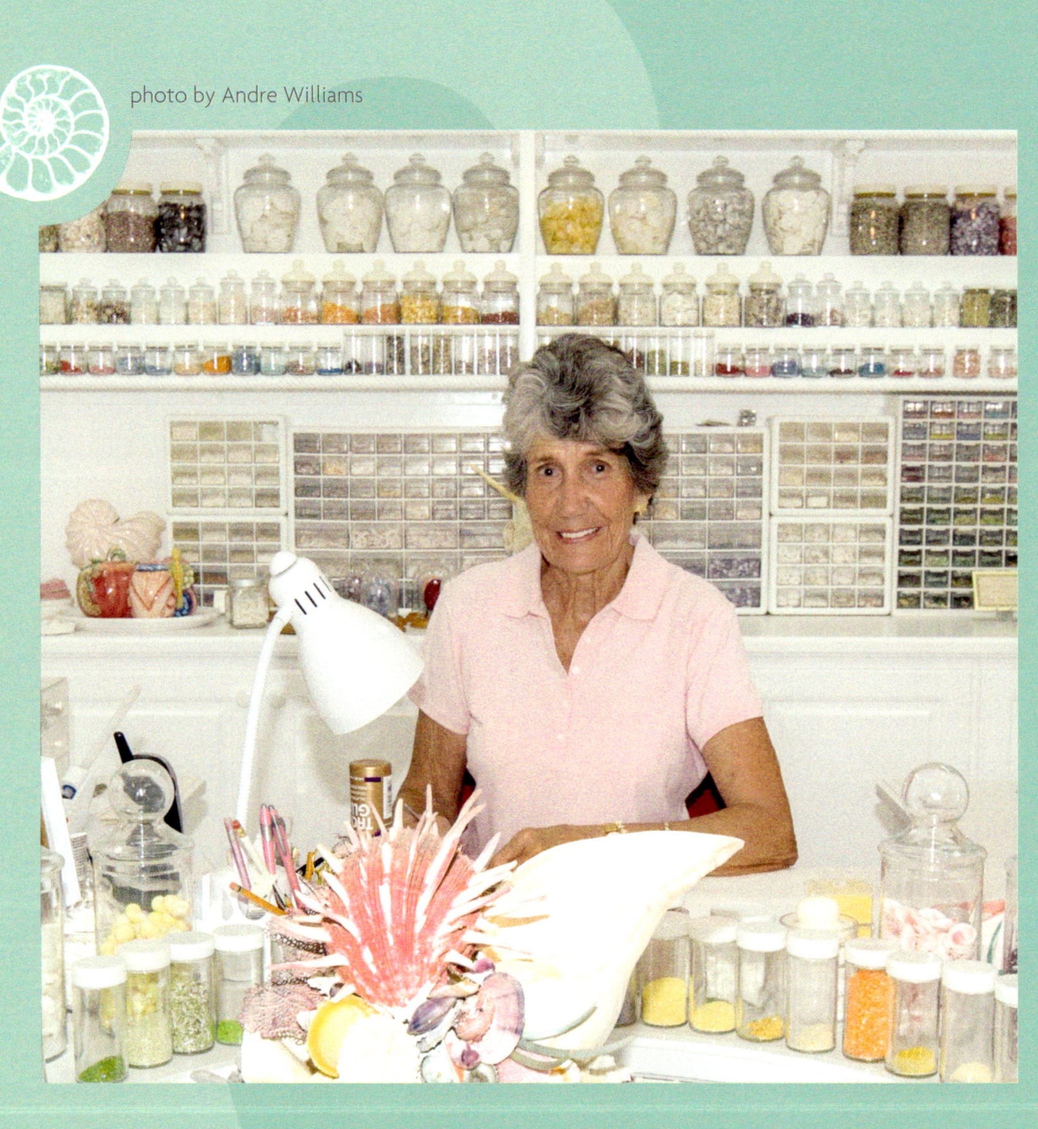

Daphne Hunte

Barbados, West Indies

I had the good fortune to be born on the island of Barbados in the Caribbean and was raised on the most breathtaking part of the island—Bathsheba, situated along the rugged, unspoiled east coast. It was in this setting, amid the awesome beauty of nature in its purest form, that I began my collection of seashells. I took an interest in painting and drawing at an early age, but then began using the shells I had collected to create pictures and jewelry that I gave to friends and family.

It was not until after I was married and had a family that I made time to pursue my shell art. I had read that Sanibel Island was an ideal place to find shells and also that a shell show was hosted there every March. So I set out to create a freestanding floral arrangement to enter in the 1980 show. The following year, I entered the show again, and it was at that show that I first encountered Sailors' Valentines. I was so intrigued by their geometrical designs and to learn of their linkage to Barbadian history. I returned home knowing I needed to design one of my own. Although I preferred the freedom of the three-dimensional floral arrangements, even following the traditional design my heart came alive for this unique art form. For several years I entered my Sailors' Valentines and floral arrangements in the Sanibel Show, and in 1991 I was asked to be an artistic judge. It was a great honor, and I have judged the show several times since.

In 2003 I saw an article in the February edition of *Martha Stewart Living* featuring a Sailors' Valentine and decided it was time to return to the Sanibel Shell Show. I was totally in awe of the contemporary artists and their work, and I was elated to purchase the Valentine by Sandy Moran* that had been featured in the magazine. When I returned home I decided to create a second Valentine, this time incorporating flower displays with movement and three dimensions, as I did in my shell floral arrangements. My husband Robin was about to celebrate an important birthday, so I made him a double Valentine. It remains one of his, and my, favorite pieces. I have since done many more Valentines, most given as gifts, and on the following pages you will see those created for my three daughters.

I am as passionate about Sailors' Valentines in 2015 as I was the first day they caught my eye. Fortunately, we live only a short distance from Bathsheba Beach. I remember clearly when the Nina & Frederik song "Listen to the Ocean" was released in 1960, and shortly thereafter recorded by The Merrymen, with whom my husband Robin played. I would walk along the beach singing the words, "Listen to the ocean, echoes of a million seashells." To this day, as I walk the beach I sing those words again, and I find new inspiration for my art.

*Sandy Moran's work can be seen on pages 146–155.

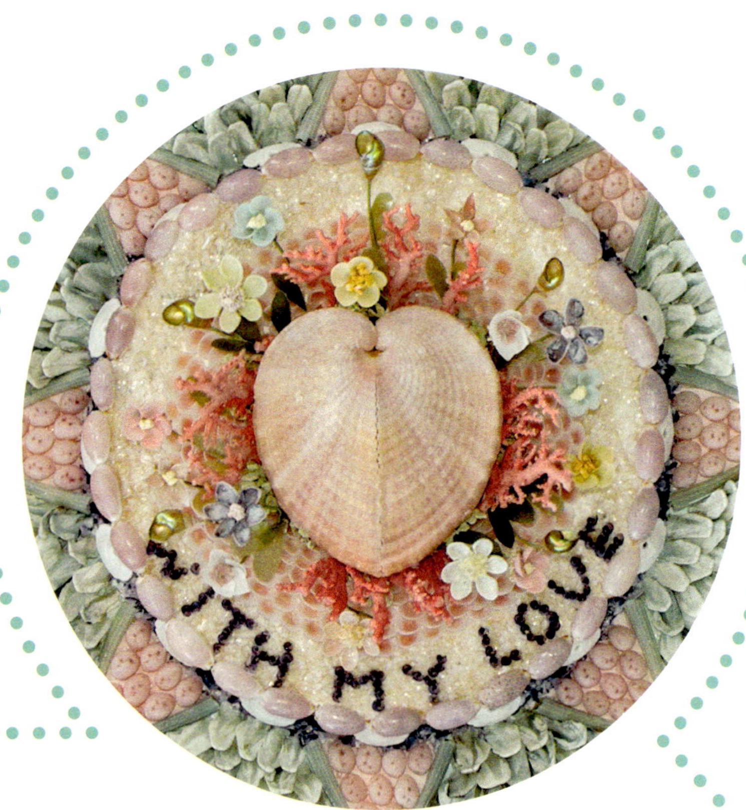

A pink-tinted heart cockle is surrounded by natural pink stylaster coral, interspersed with tiny stemmed shell flowers and iridescent green snail shells. These all emerge from a background of crushed spirula, surrounded by pale lilac marginella shells. "With My Love" is written in tiny purple janthinas.

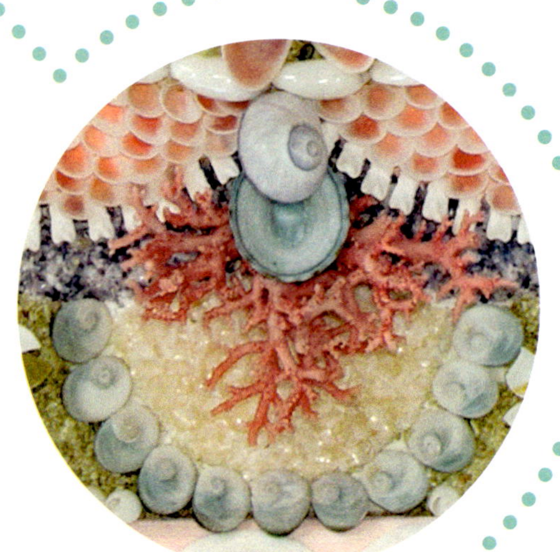

Each of the eight sides has an arch where more pink coral springs from a bed of crushed spirula surrounded by tiny blue operculums.

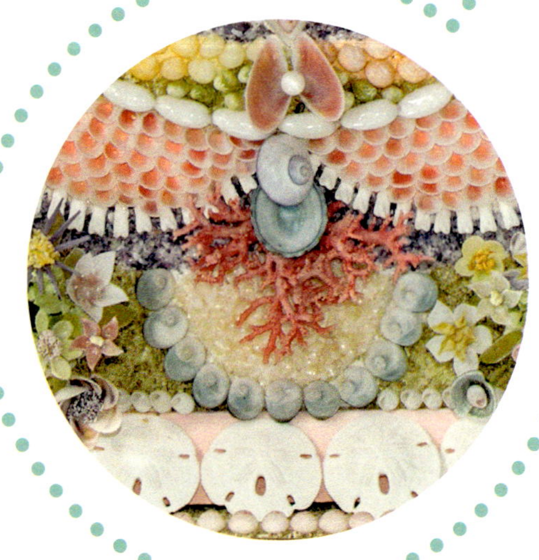

Rose petal tellin shells are used to make the little butterflies with a pearl in the center (seen here at the top). Pink apple blossom shells are outlined with pieces of a sea urchin. Around the entire edge sit delicate baby sand dollars and tiny pink trivia shells collected on Barbados.

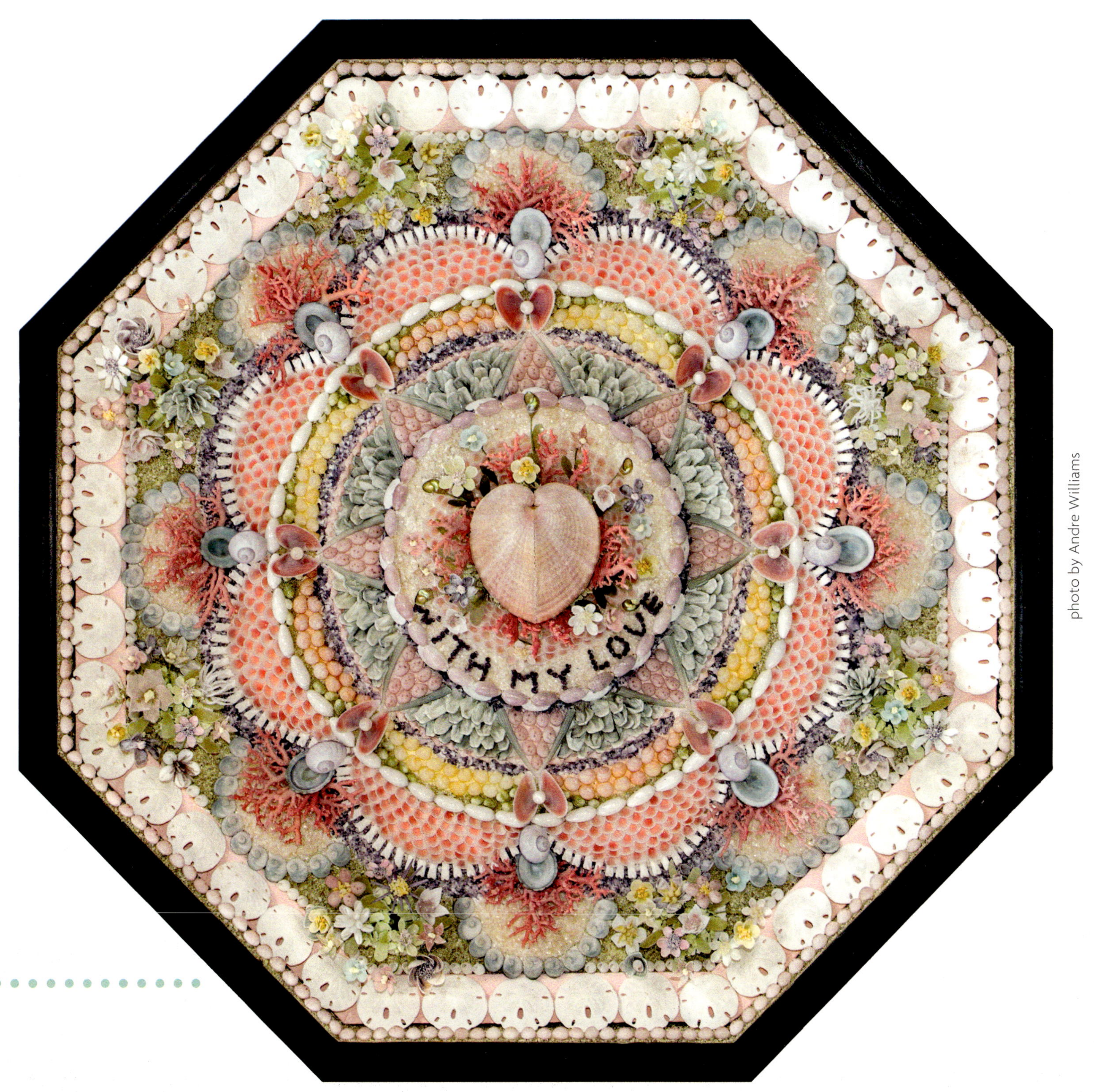

photo by Andre Williams

With My Love

Inspired by the artist's love of the stunning pink stylaster coral that bursts with color in this Valentine, made "with love" for her daughter Roberta.

16-inch mahogany case made by Jim Prestigiacomo

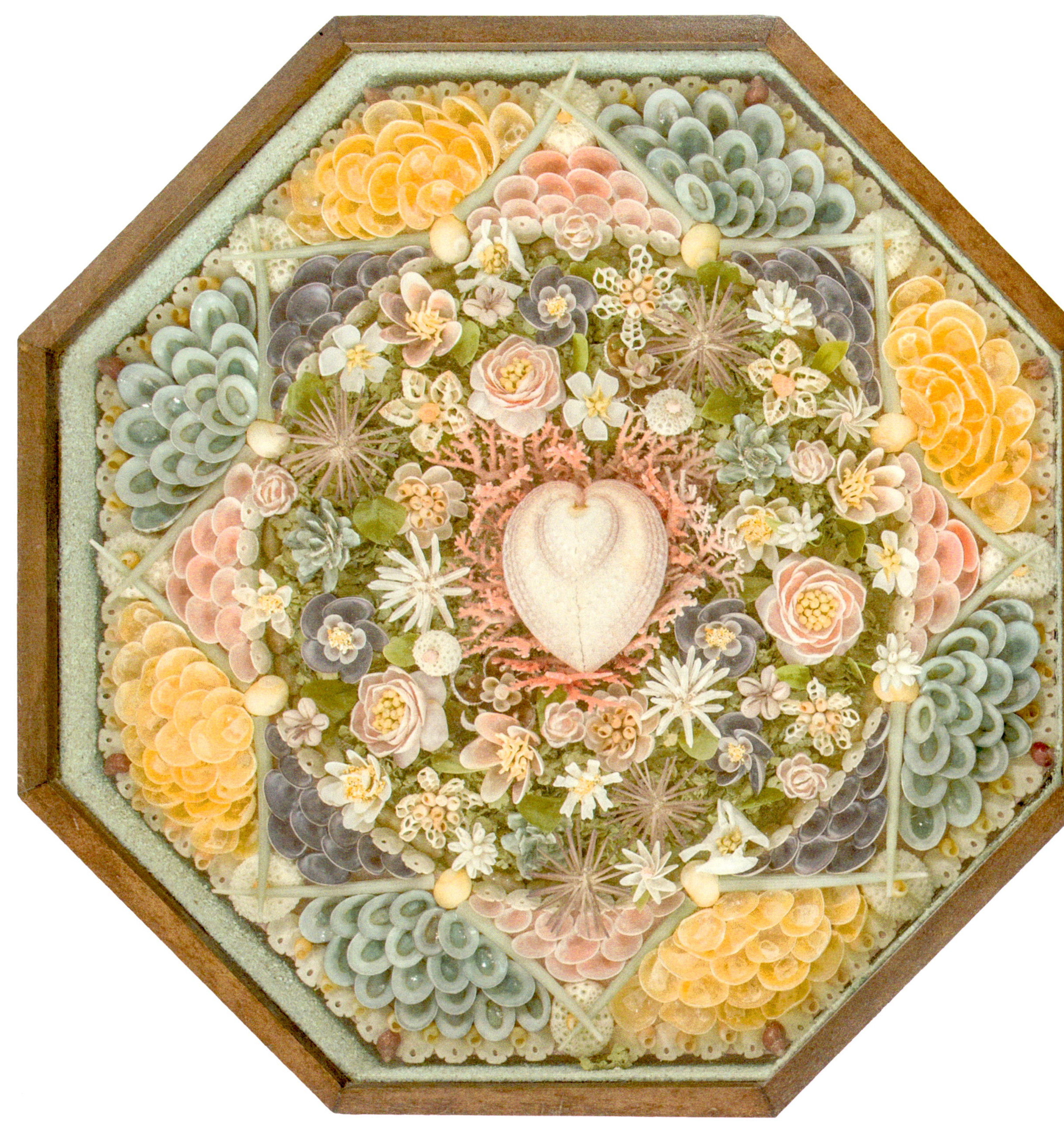

Inspired by the garden of the artist's daughter Carolyn. The little girl is making her way home after picking a bouquet of flowers from her "Garden of Love." The exquisite Barbadian background scenery was hand-painted by Carolyn.

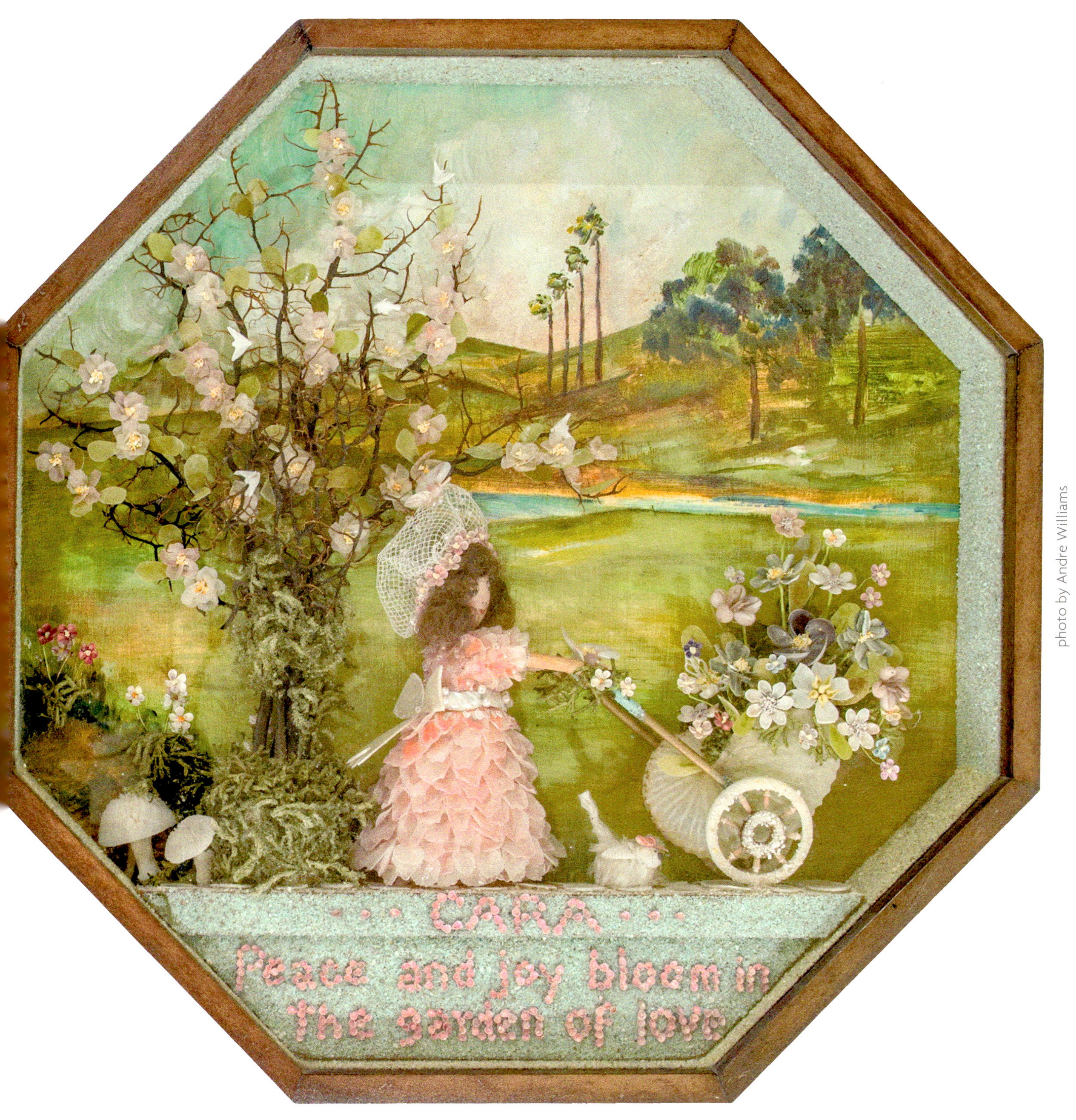

photo by Andre Williams

Garden of Love

12-inch (each side) Barbados mahogany case made by Hall Ward

Surrounding the heart cockle is a spray of pink stylaster coral and a garden of individually stemmed flowers made from pink cup shells, pieces of gooseneck barnacles, and pieces of sea urchins, all found on Barbados beaches. This is accented with foliage of sea moss and fish scales.

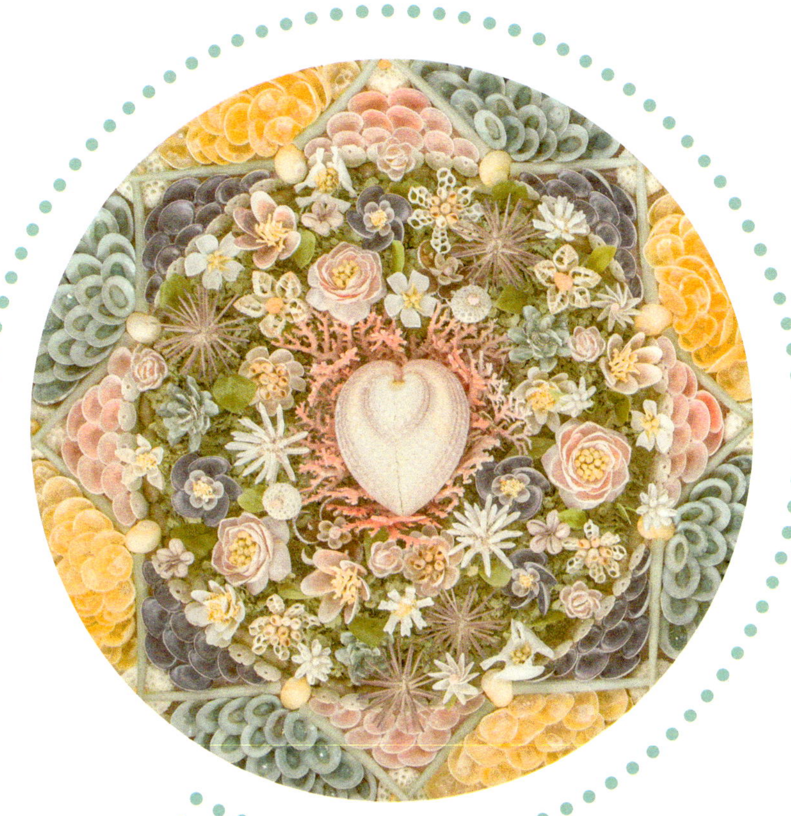

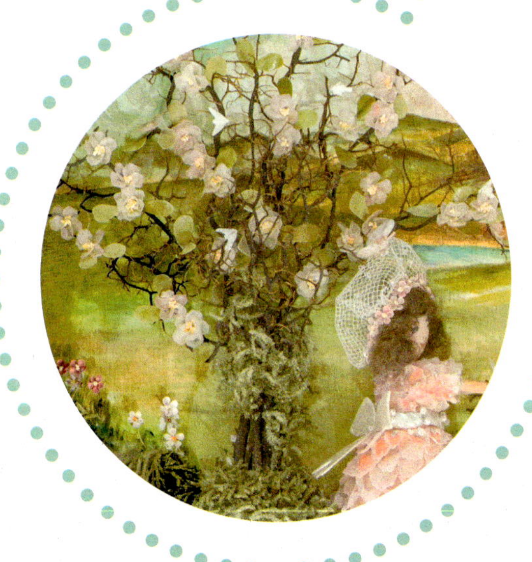

An apple blossom tree is in full bloom, fashioned from sea fans and pink dyed barracuda scales. It is accented with peace doves (sections made from pieces found in the center of sand dollars). The leaves are made from dyed fish scales.

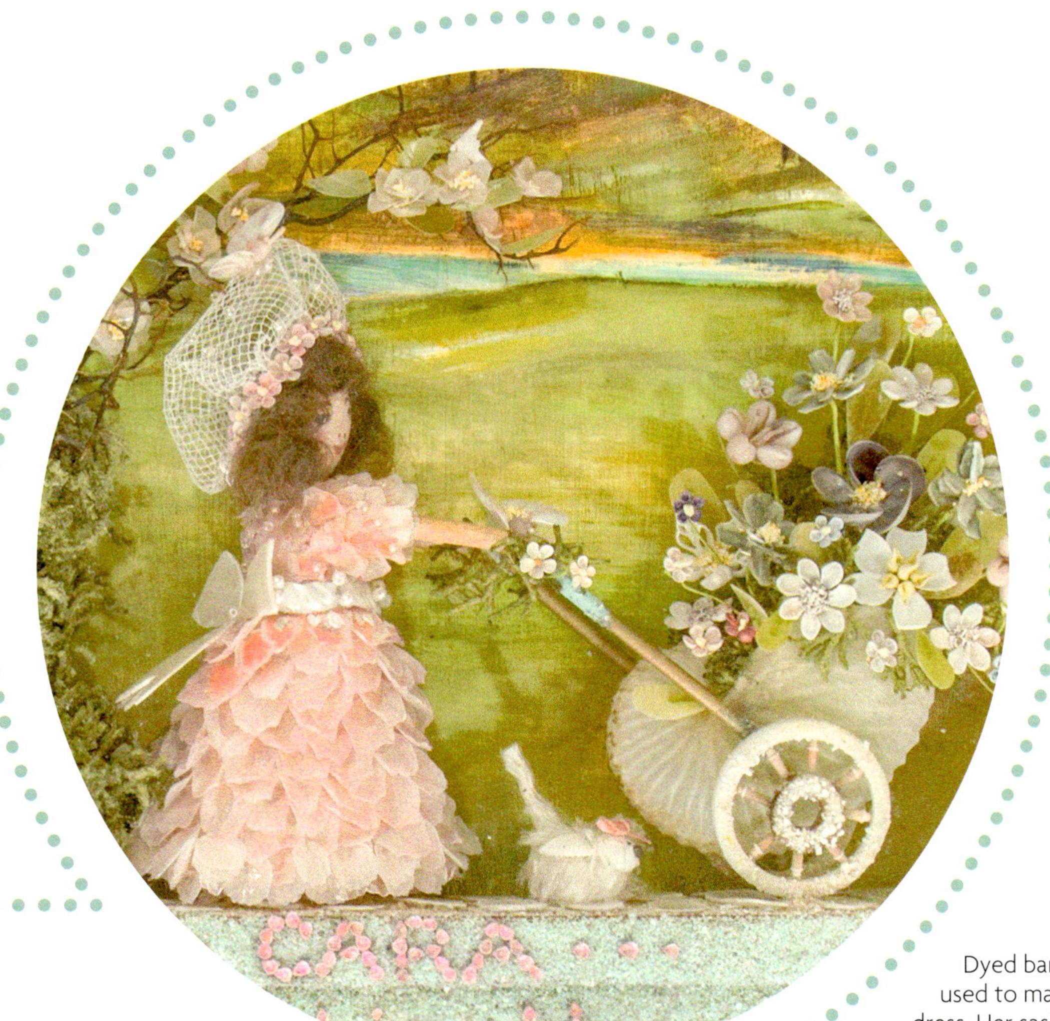

Dyed barracuda scales were used to make the little girl's dress. Her sash and bow are cut from a nautilus shell and her face is a hand-painted shell. Little pearls adorn her bonnet and blouse, and tiny dyed cup shell flowers surround her hair.

A baby paper nautilus shell holds a bouquet of shell flowers done from blue chitons, pieces of gooseneck barnacles, pink trivia shells, and dyed lilac shells, with leaves of dyed fish scales. The wheel is cut from a shell and covered in crushed shell, and the spokes are made from sea urchin spines.

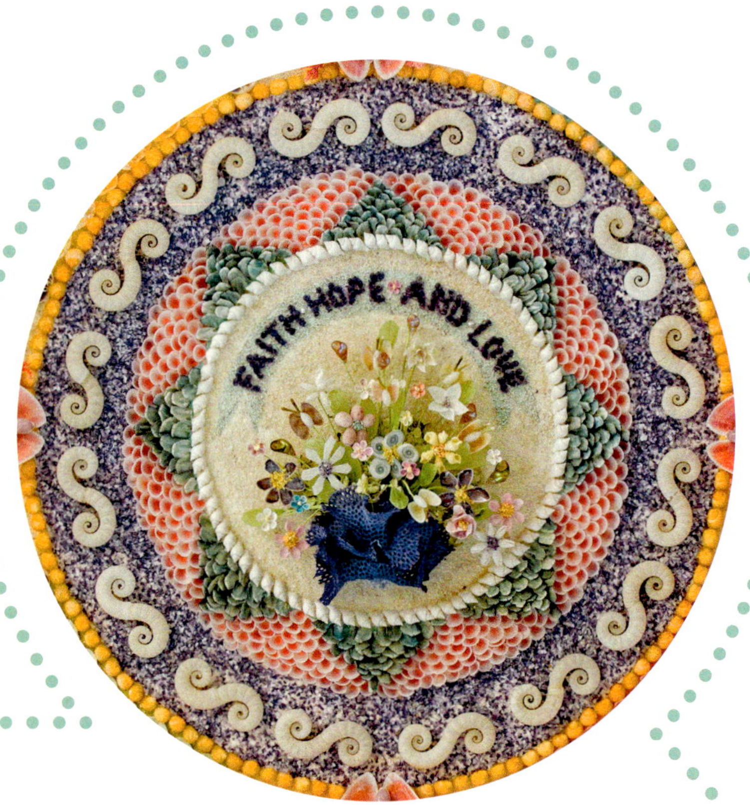

Exotic natural purple bryozoa adds drama to the centerpiece and is complemented by the outer crushed janthina circle that holds spirula shells. The words are written in baby purple janthinas. Surrounding the outer circle are brilliant yellow nerites.

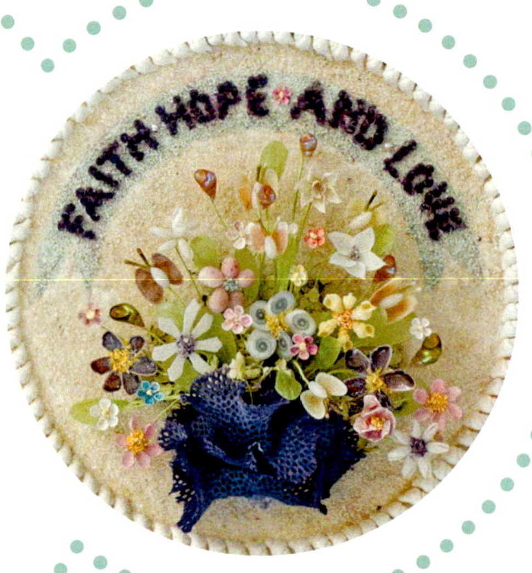

An intricate bouquet of individually stemmed shell flowers and butterflies is painstakingly arranged in the purple bryozoa vase. Crushed spirula form the background for this centerpiece.

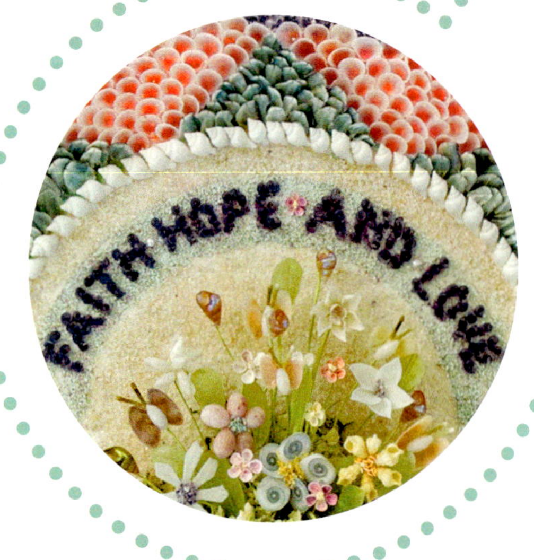

Blue chitons form the star around the center, with pink apple blossom shells interspersed.

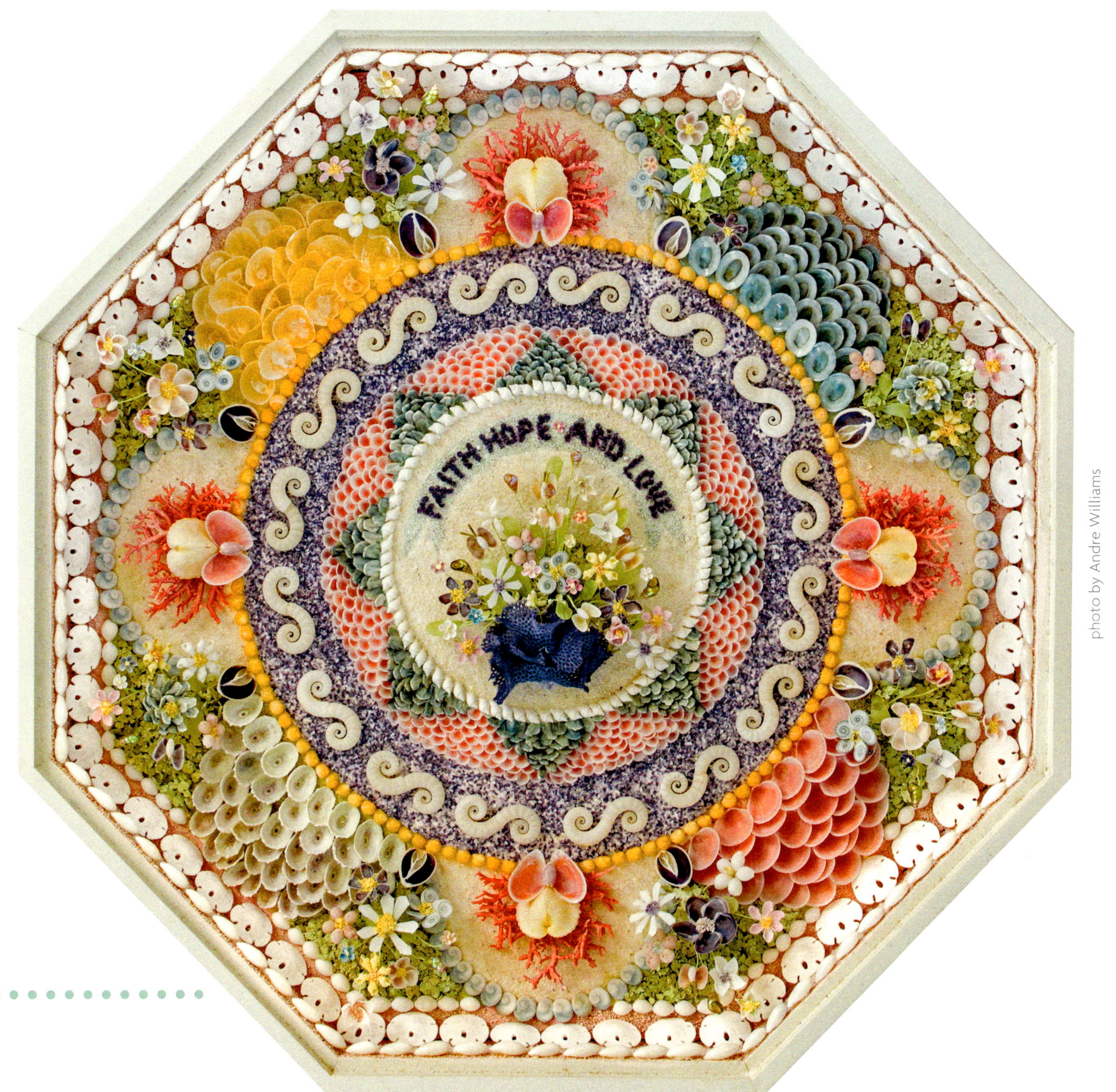

photo by Andre Williams

Faith, Hope and Love

Inspired by the stunning piece of beautiful purple bryozoa that holds a bouquet of delicate stemmed shell flowers. Made by the artist for her daughter Gina.

16-inch cedar case (painted white) made by Gerda Reid

Painted by the artist's daughter Carolyn, the mermaid is enhanced with a crushed abalone tail. She is surrounded by vibrant blue operculums and triangles of pink trivia shells. Purple sea urchin spines and white pieces from the sea urchin encircle the soothing centerpiece.

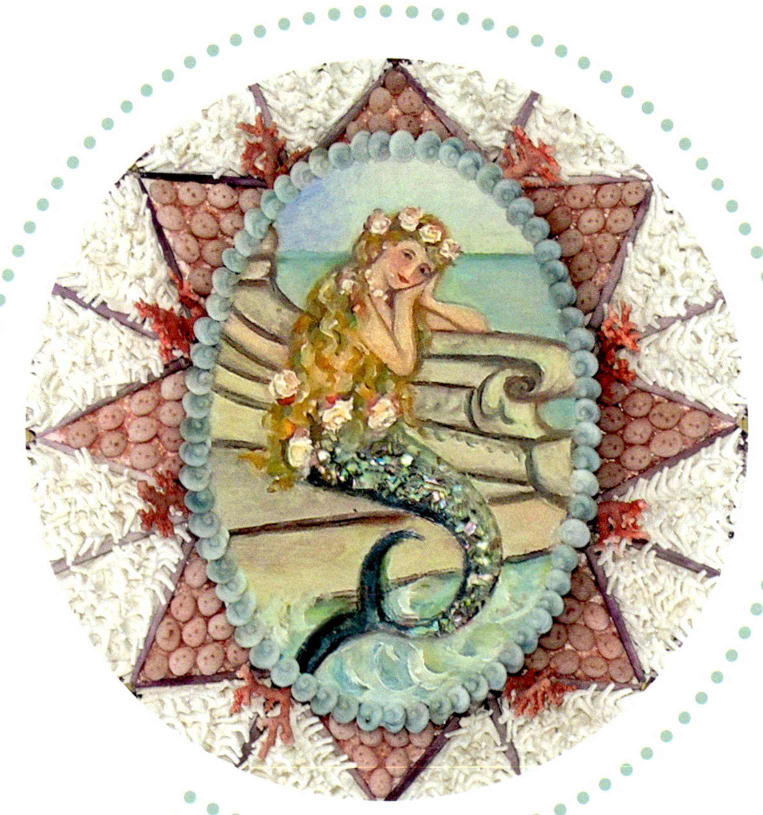

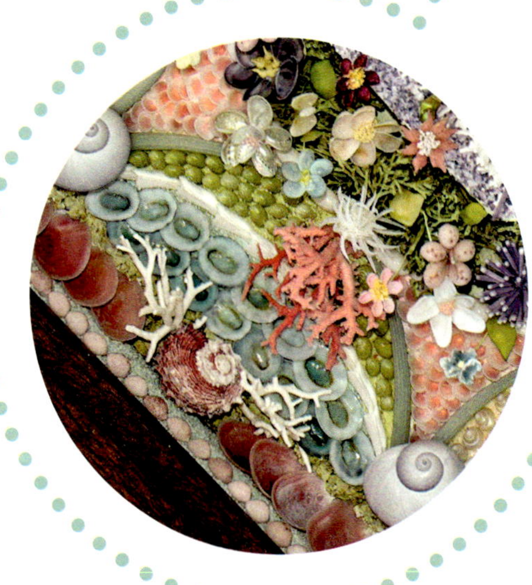

Clusters of individually stemmed flowers sit on a bed of dyed sea moss. Bunches of bright pink stylaster coral and flowers made of blue-green limpets, purple janthinas, and strawberry top shells create a colorful garden that envelops the pensive mermaid.

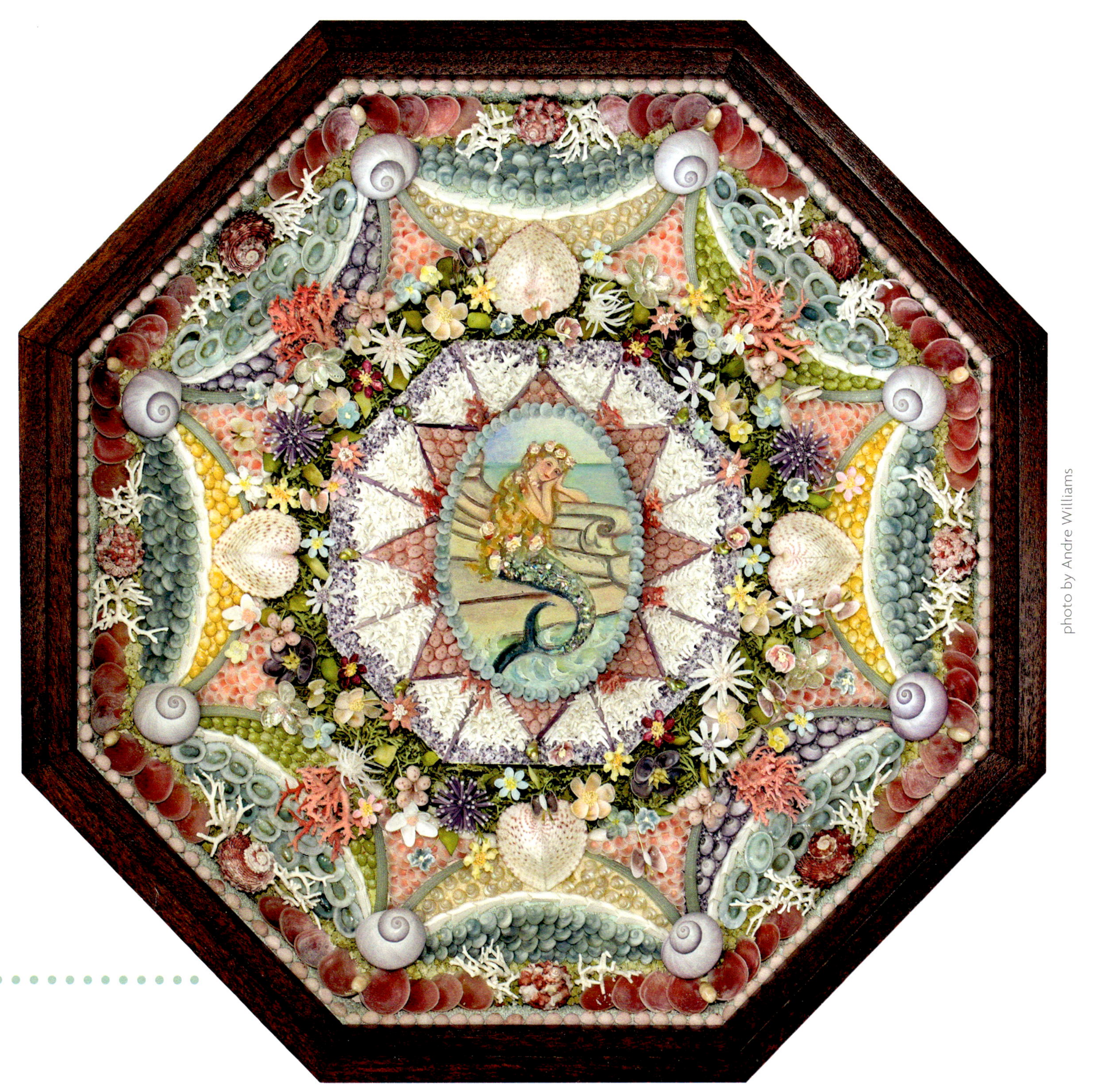

photo by Andre Williams

A Mermaid's Garden

Inspired by the mermaid at the center of this Valentine, painted by the artist's daughter Carolyn.

16-inch mahogany case made by Gerda Reid

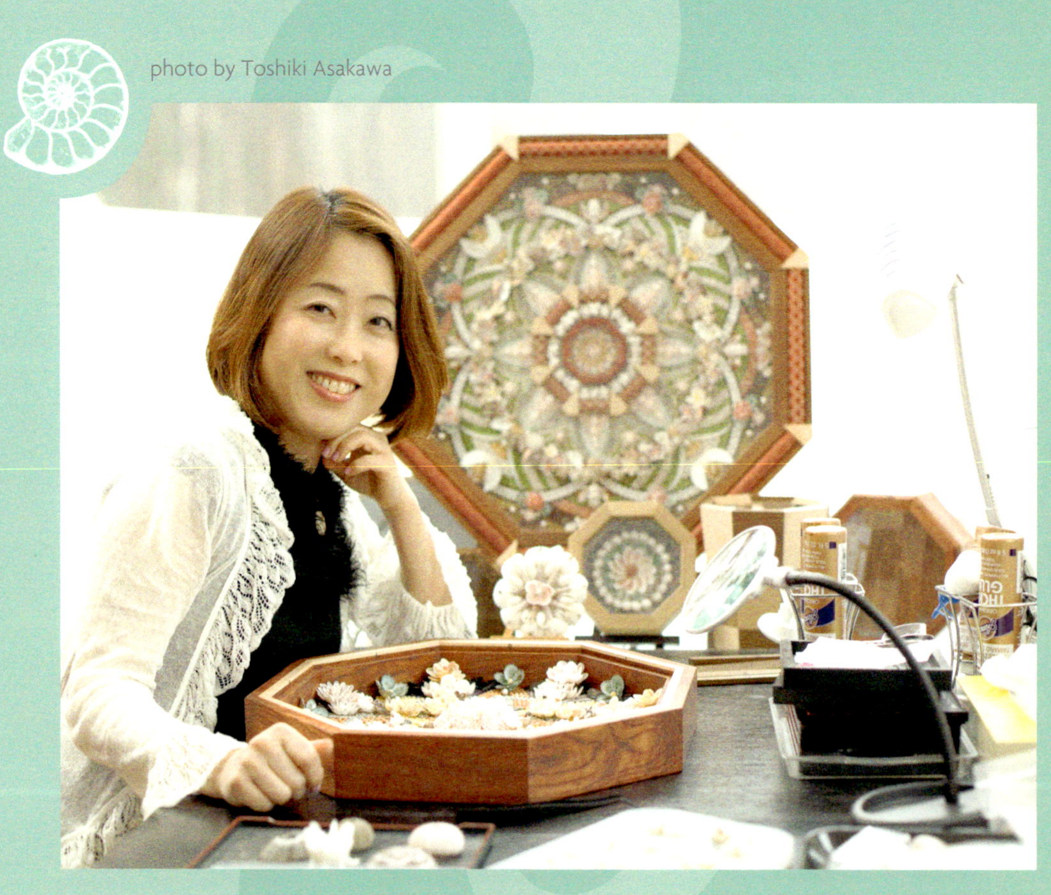

photo by Toshiki Asakawa

Hatsue Iimuro

Hokuto, Yamanashi, Japan

I saw Sailors' Valentines for the first time in a shop on Cape Cod, Massachusetts, in 2006. At the time I was living in Boston with my family because of my Japanese husband's job; we lived there from 2005 to 2009. I thought they were such superb masterpieces of shell art and unlike anything I had ever seen in Japan. I located a teacher who helped me find shells and a case and showed me how to get started, and I began my first Sailors' Valentines that year. I was intrigued by arranging shells, all different in color, size, shape, and texture, in the limited space of an octagonal box.

Since 2010 I have held an annual event at the resort facility Risonare Yatsugatake in Hokuto to introduce this shell art to children. In autumn of 2011 I established the Japan Sailors' Valentine Association to promote this art form in my country.

My studio in Hokuto is in the woods, and I attempt to harmonize the shells, a natural product of the sea, and the wood frame, a natural product of the forest. I've been trying to combine the art of Sailors' Valentines with various Japanese art forms since my first piece. I am determined to continue doing this in my future work creating Sailors' Valentines.

My favorite piece is *Japan Rise Again*, which you will see on the following pages. It was created following the 2011 Great East Japan Earthquake and was my first entry into a shell show, the 2012 Sanibel Shell Show. This was also the first piece I created with the idea of trying to combine the spirit of Japanese art with the art of Sailors' Valentines—the first piece sent out from Japan to the world.

I have entered the Sanibel Shell Show each year since 2012, and in 2015 I took five of my students to the show, two of whom entered Sailors' Valentines of their own.

My passion is to build a bridge between America and Japan as a Sailors' Valentine "preacher." I would be thrilled to see the two countries become One World someday through my work among people in two different worlds.

www.japan-sva.com

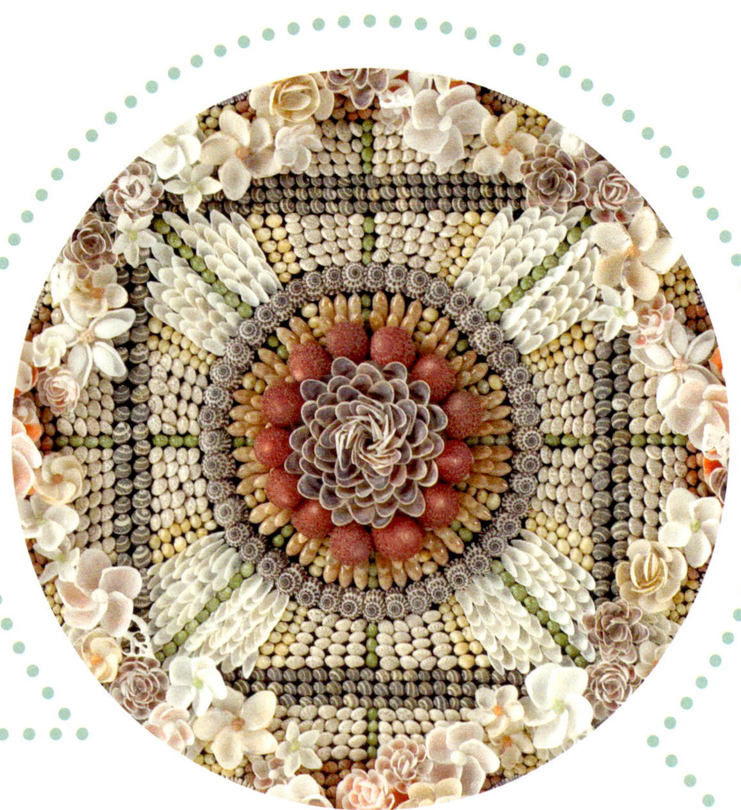

A flower of baby purple clams blooms from the center. This is surrounded by a circle of strawberry tops and tan Philippine rice shells. Radiating lines done with emerald nerites, yellow nerites, and white nut clams stream outward. This symbolized to the artist the energy and power of fireworks.

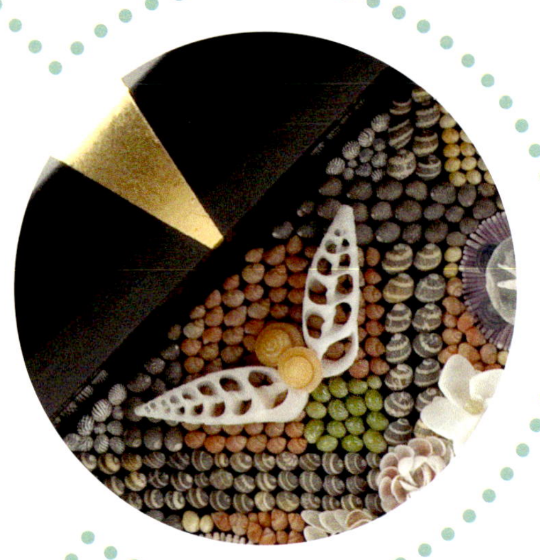

The center-cut white cerith shells and flat yellow button snails express birds flying and coordinate with the triangle-shaped gold on the frame.

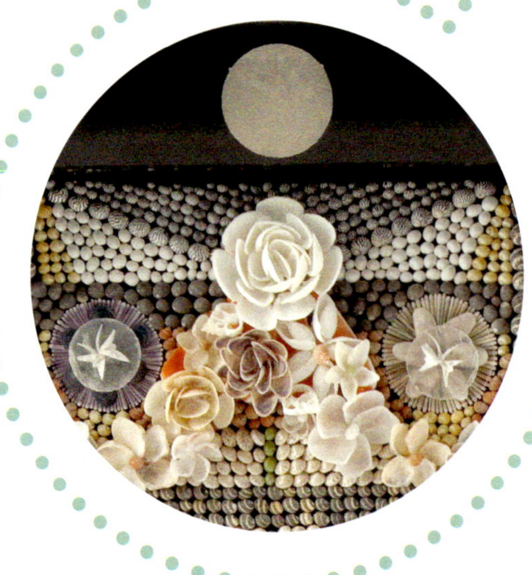

The white cay cay shell flower at the top center coordinates with the silver circles of the frame. To either side a butterfly made from sand dollar doves with barnacle pieces as antennae sits atop a capiz circle. They are surrounded by purple and green sea urchin spines.

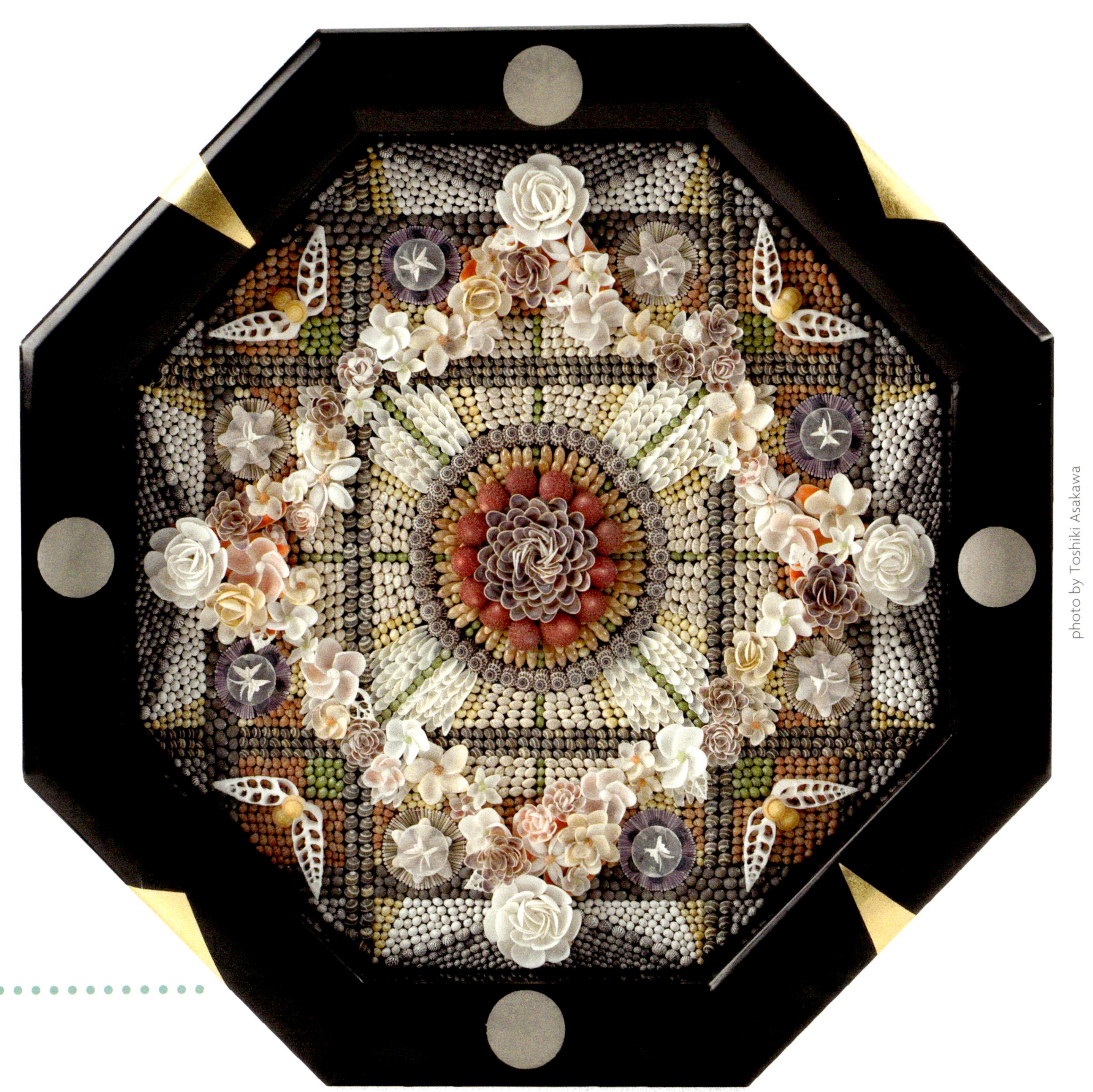

Japan Rise Again

Inspired by the artist's wish to encourage the Japanese people to rise up from the tragedy of the Great East Japan Earthquake.

20-inch urushi (traditional Japanese lacquer made from tree sap) case with gold and tin inlay, lacquered in black, made by Kazuo Saito

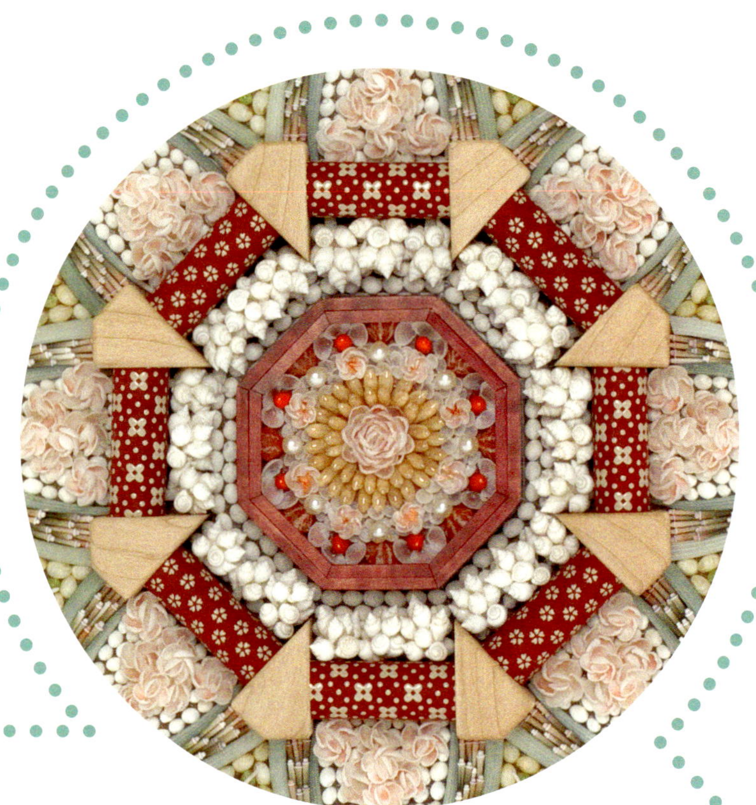

White nassa shells depict the flower buds. Inside these is a 3-inch octagonal case (made by Bill Jordan) filled with apple blossom shells, rice shells, and crab's eye seeds. The nassas are surrounded by a miniature *inden* frame. (Inden provided by Indenya Uehara Yushichi Co. Ltd.)

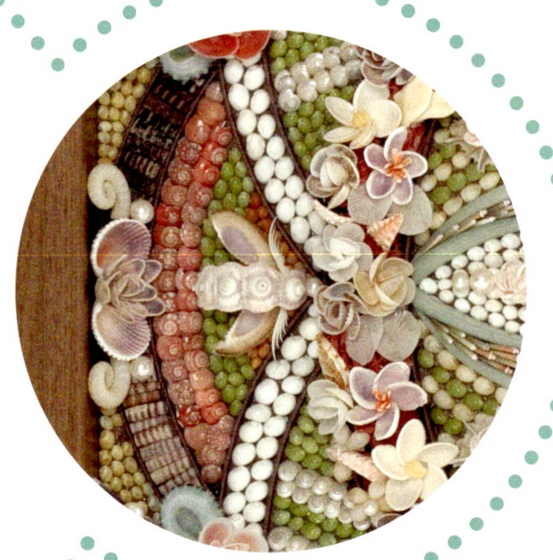

Using cut purple cowry shells, cut sea urchins, and squilla claws, the artist expresses a shower of falling cherry blossoms. The emerald nerites as leaves represent cherry blossoms after the flowers have fallen from the trees.

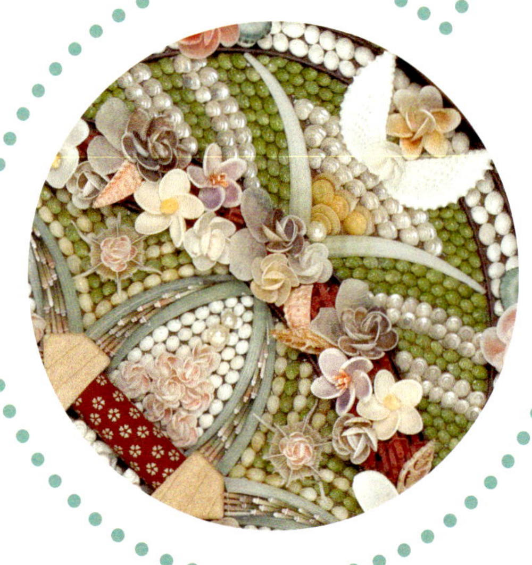

Flower petals are made with green tusk shells with white littorinas encasing apple blossom flowers representing cherry blossoms.

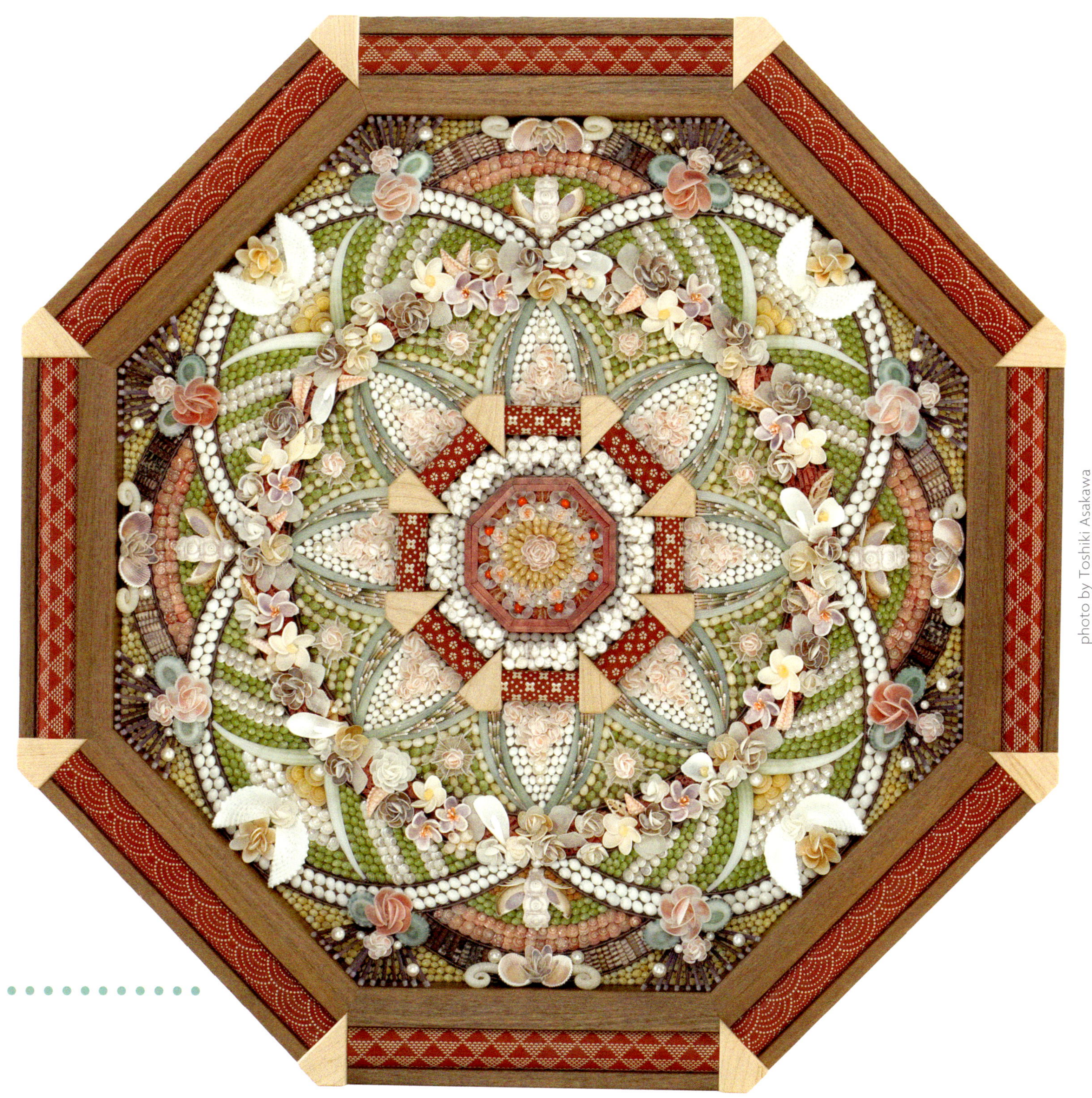

photo by Toshiki Asakawa

Floral Breeze

Inspired by falling cherry blossoms.
Spring is the season for cherry blossoms in Japan.
The Japanese think cherry blossoms are beautiful not only when blooming, but also when the flowers are falling.

22-inch walnut, maple, and inden (the traditional Japanese craft of applying decorative lacquer patterns on deerskin by hand) case made by Hiroyuki Akaishi

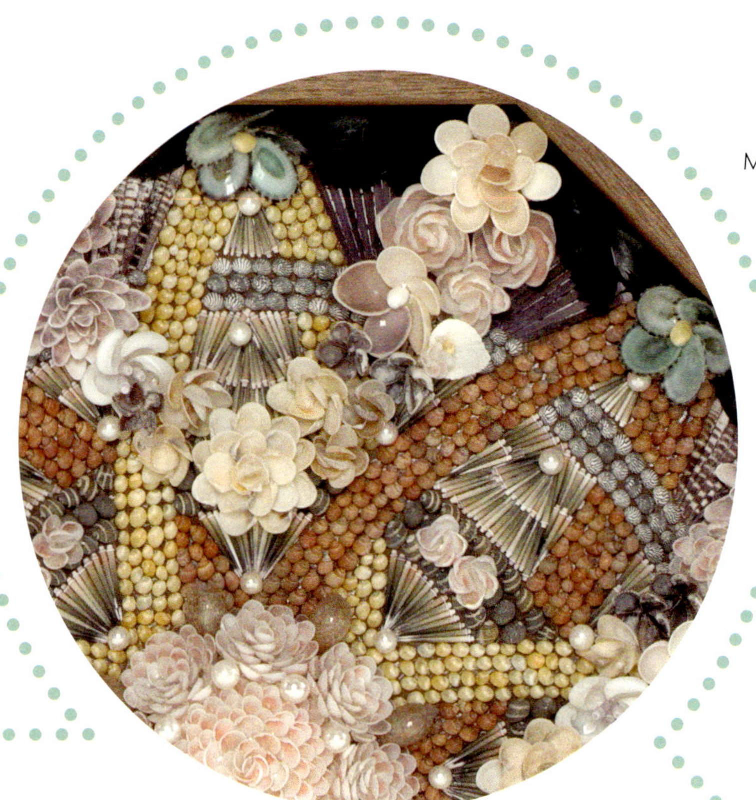

Many small shells create strongly defined lines for this piece. Yellow nerites and red mongo snails form tall arched lines; zebra nerites and black littorinas form a circle toward the outer edge. This piece combines the spirit of mandara and Japan; the lines represent the pattern of a mandara and the flowers represent Japan.

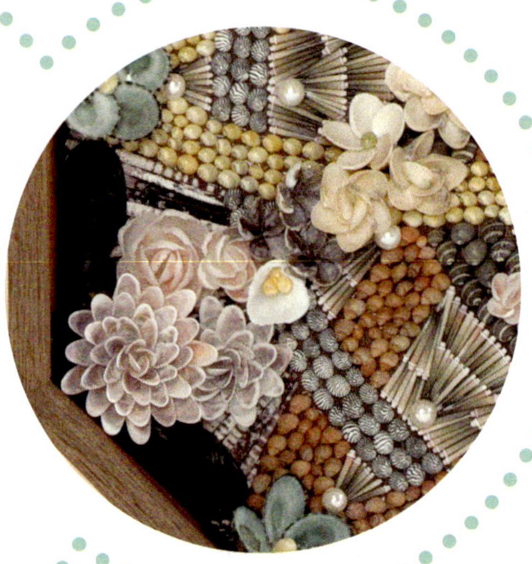

The base is covered with purple sea urchin spines, and blue mussel shells are placed in each corner. The artist's intention is to express the feeling of Japanese flowers through her color choices.

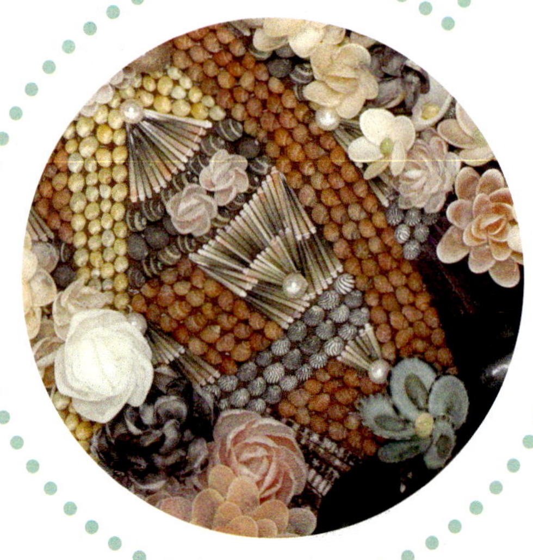

The artist frequently uses sea urchin spines in her work. They come in many colors and shapes: purple, pink, lavender, green; thick or thin; long or short. Here pink-tipped green urchin spines form varied layers. Freshwater pearls appear throughout the piece.

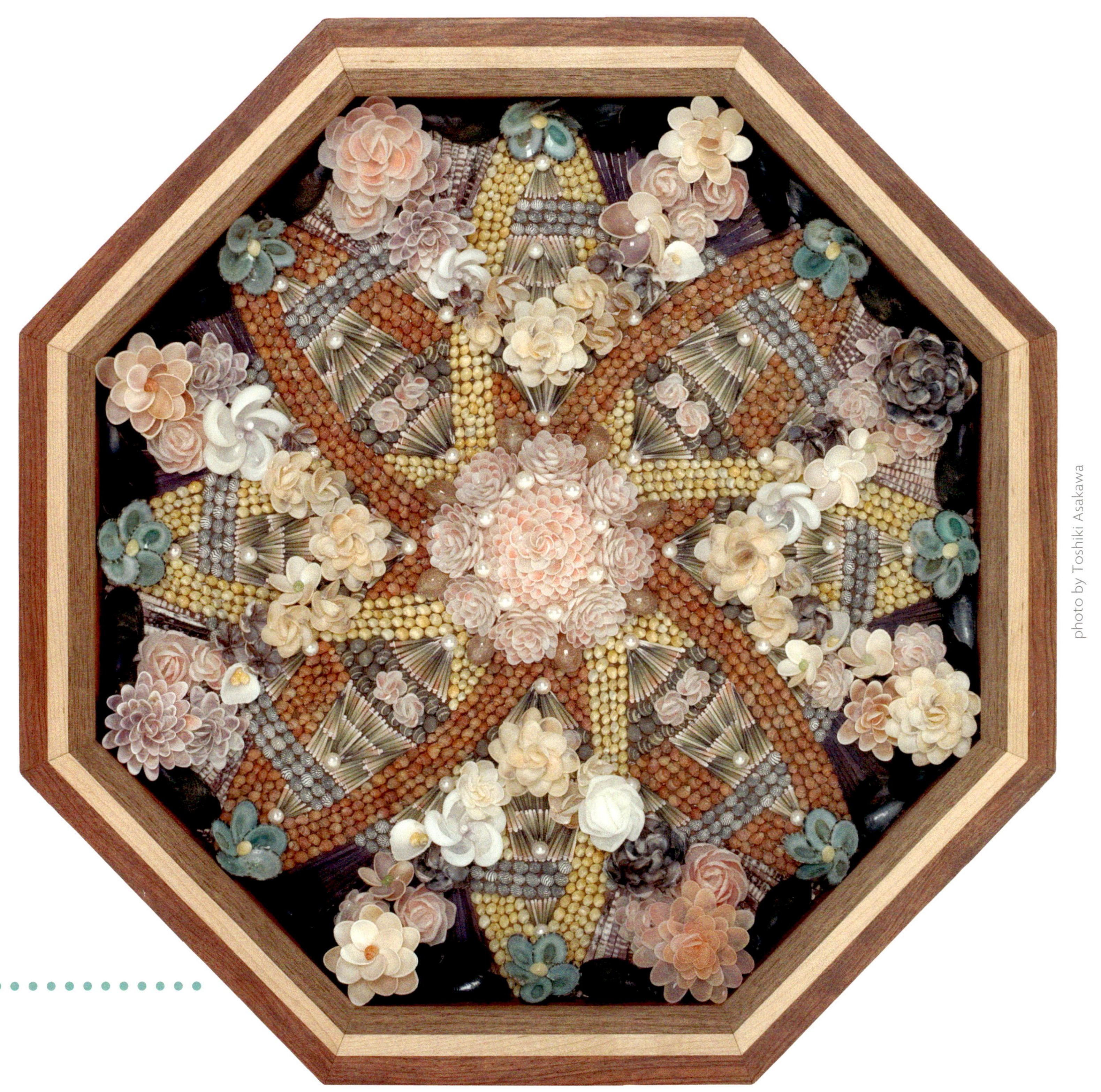

photo by Toshiki Asakawa

Mandara

Inspired by the *mandara* (the Japanese word for mandala). Mandara literally means "circle" and symbolizes the notion that life is never-ending.

16-inch bubinga, maple, and walnut case made by Hiroyuki Akaishi

At the center, apple blossom shells shaped into small flowers are placed outside by crab shells. Eight striking purple janthina shells atop emerald nerites surround this. Tiny apple blossom flowers sit on green chiton pieces just outside.

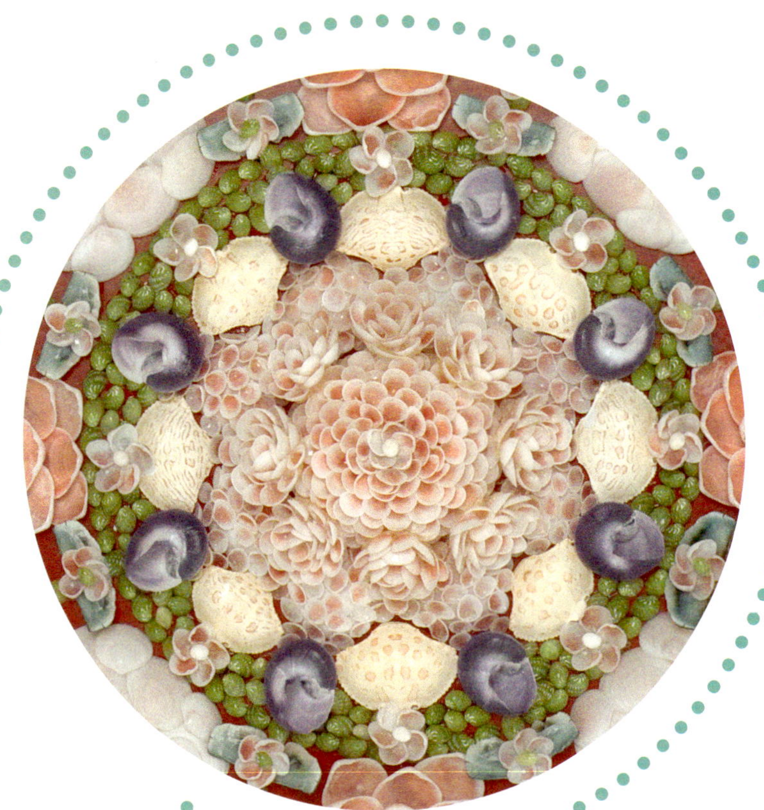

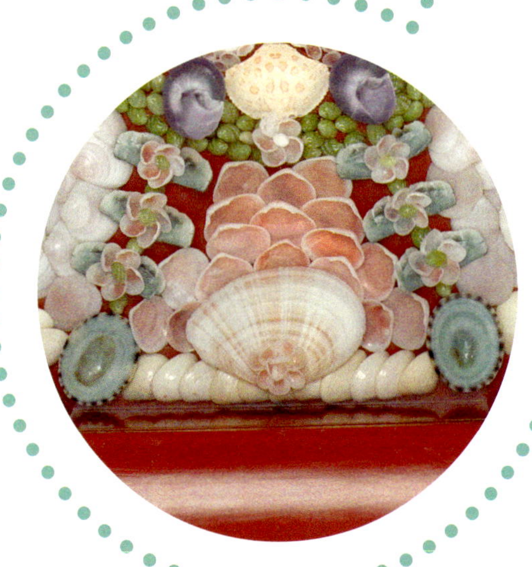

Blue-green limpets sit at each corner, complemented by the color of green chiton pieces with apple blossom flowers on top. A tellin sits between the limpets, and rosecup shells trickle toward the center.

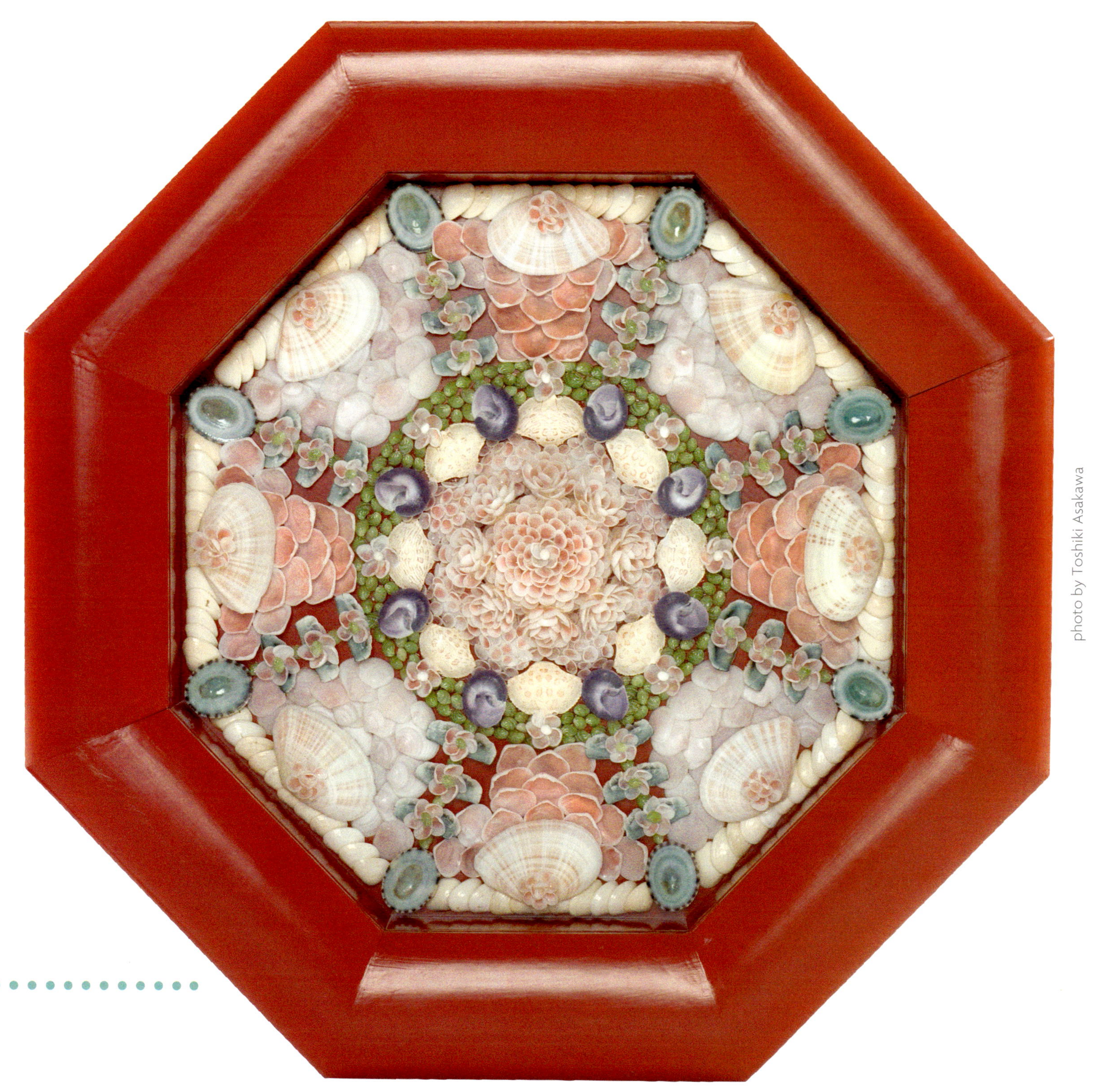

photo by Toshiki Asakawa

Japanese Blossom

Inspired by Japanese cherry blossom trees in full bloom.

14-inch *urushi* (traditional Japanese lacquer made from tree sap) case lacquered in red made by Kazuo Saito

photo by Melanie Moraga

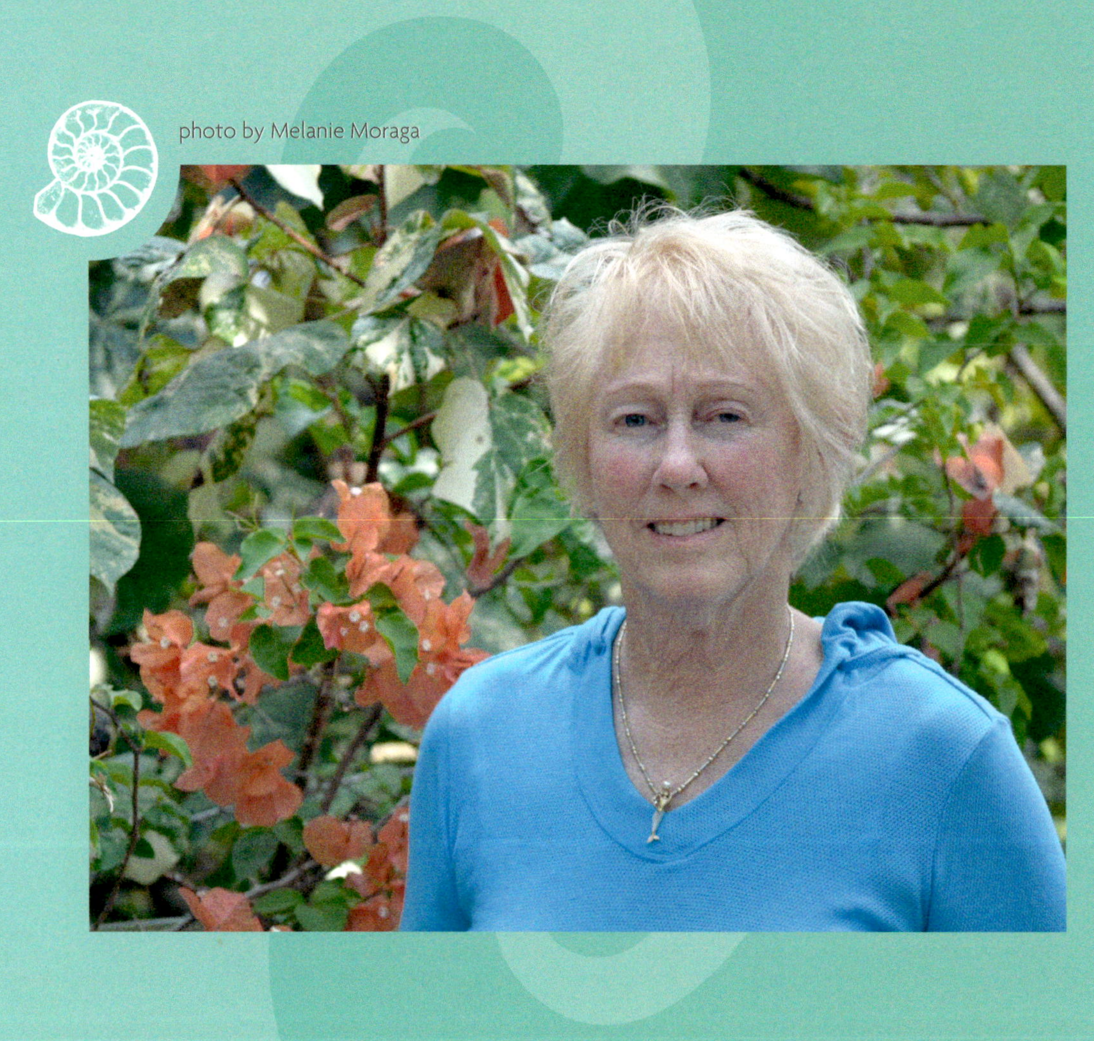

Brandy Llewellyn

Evergreen, Colorado

My creative ability surfaced as a young adult and expressed itself in various mediums. I painted in watercolor and oils, sewed, and did needlepoint and cross-stitch as well as beading and leather work. As an adult I became interested in medium-format photography, including developing and hand-coloring black and white prints.

I saw my first Sailors' Valentine in 1999 at the annual Sanibel Shell Show after my husband, Rhys, and I purchased a home on Sanibel. I was totally in awe of their colors and complexity and could not imagine the work that went into creating such art. I have had a fascination with seashells from an early age, and after being a spectator at the Sanibel Shell Show for nine consecutive years, I decided it was time to make my first Valentine and enter the show. It was inspiring to see the culmination of my efforts when I competed in the 2008 show with artists whose work I had admired for so long.

I love creating small, intricate pieces and am very comfortable with the process, having worked in the dental profession for 22 years. Color and texture are important to me, and with so many beautiful shells available from all over the world, it is an education and a wonder each time I use a different shell. I am fortunate to be able to personally collect many of my shells from Sanibel beaches. My studio in Colorado is spacious, and living in the mountains provides a quiet atmosphere in which I can work out a design, which might include a center painting or intricate work that catches the eye.

Making Nantucket-style baskets with a tapestry thread design has been a passion for many years as well. I have taught classes on making both Sailors' Valentines and Nantucket baskets. Sharing my ideas and techniques with others brings me enormous pleasure. I love helping others discover and develop their creative abilities and seeing the satisfaction that comes from realizing their talents and dreams.

www.basketstudio.com

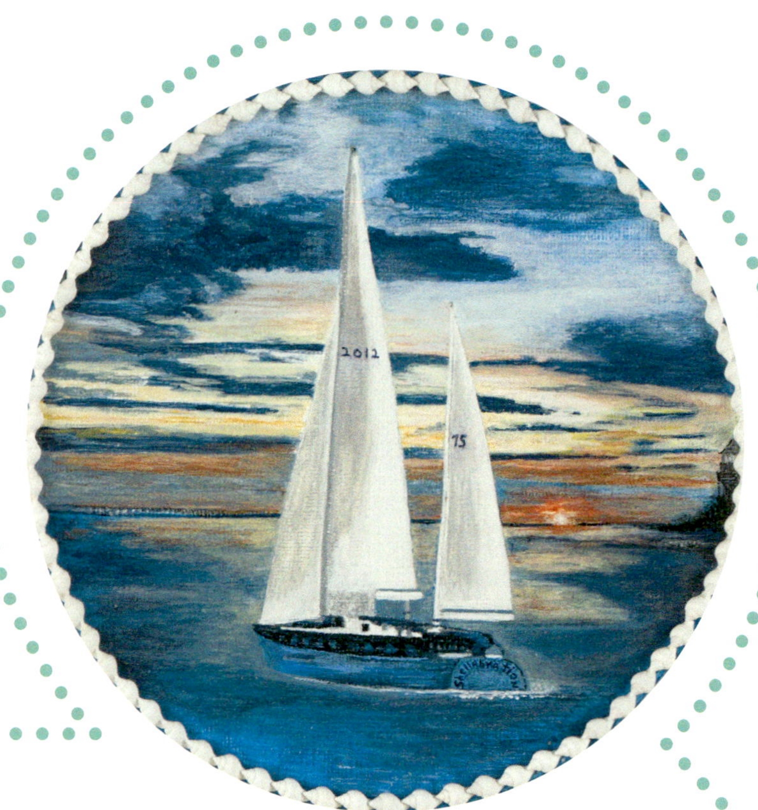

To reflect the 75th Sanibel Shell Show in 2012, the artist painted a sailboat in the center of the Valentine with the year on one sail and the number 75 on the other. The theme of that year's show was "Shellabration," which is added to the boat's transom.

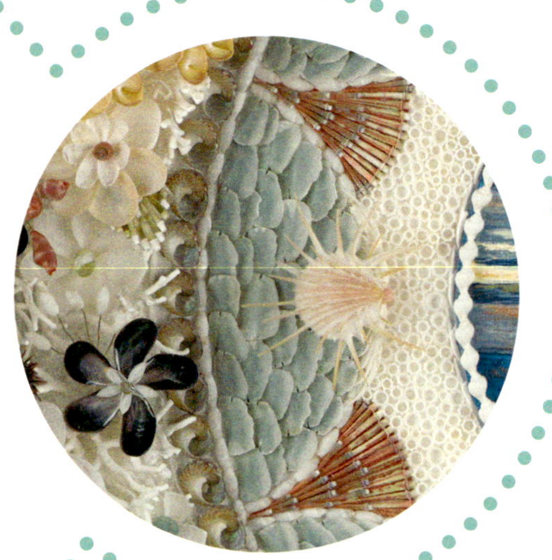

A thorny oyster shell, representing West on a compass, sits atop beautiful blue-green chiton pieces collected on Barbados. To the left lies a flower made of blue mussel shells.

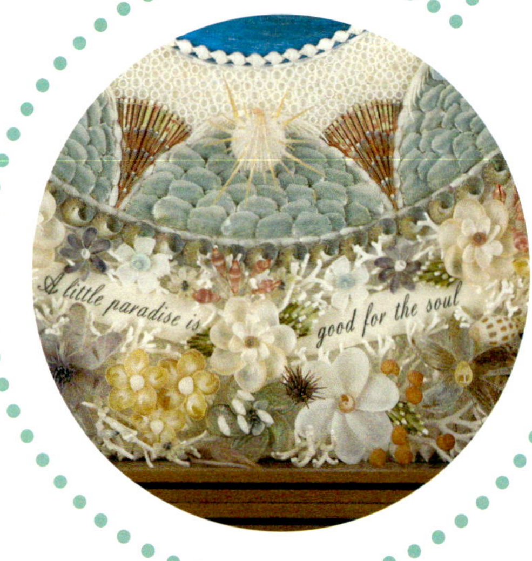

A favorite saying of the artist's, "A little paradise is good for the soul," is scrimshawed on fossil ivory plates among delicate shell flowers. Offset beneath the word "soul" sits a baby junonia shell found on Sanibel.

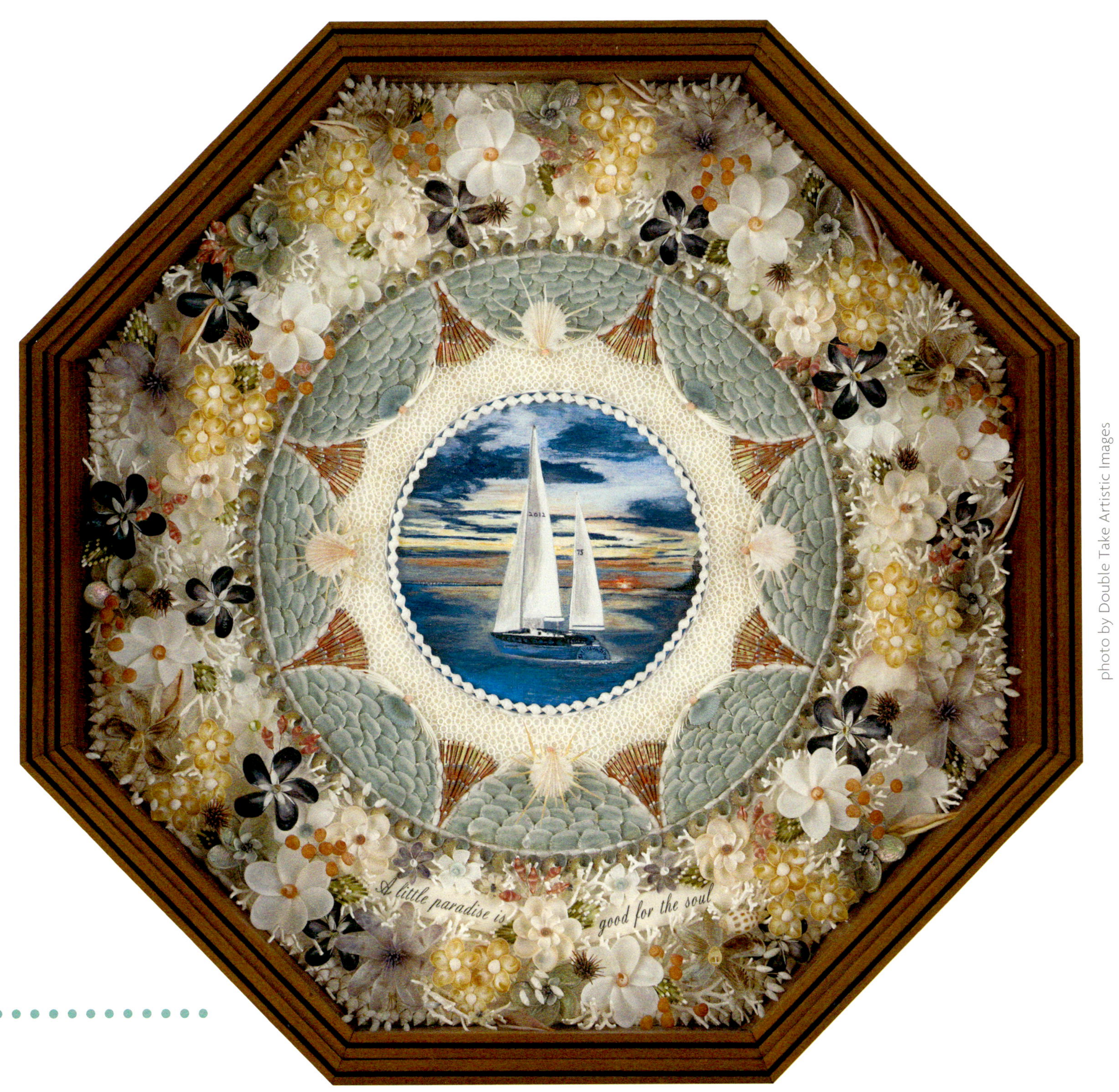

photo by Double Take Artistic Images

Another Day in Paradise

Inspired by the artist's love of Sanibel Island and the serenity of sailing vessels.

15-inch cherry case made by Bill Jordan

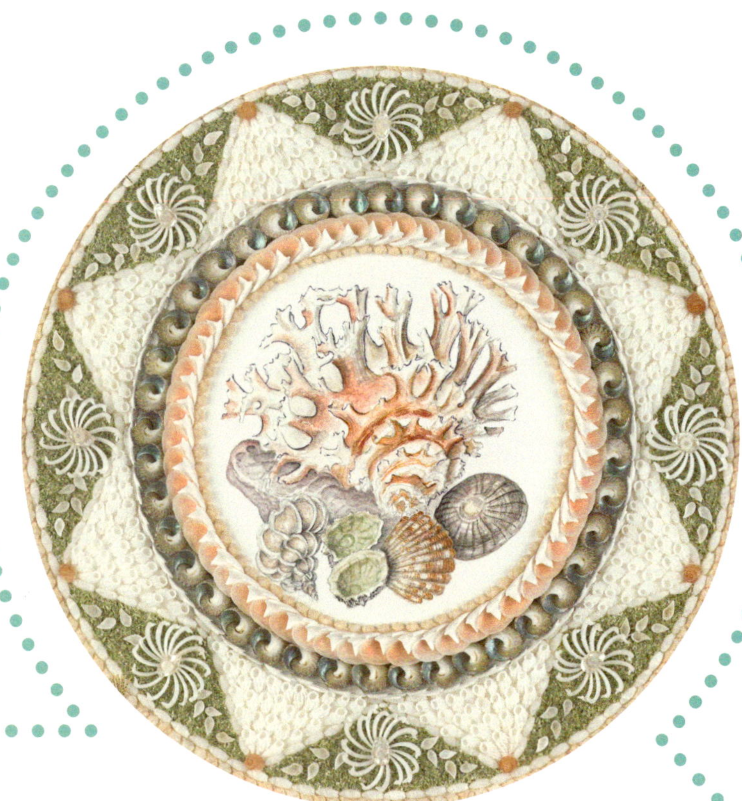

Shells chosen by the artist were painted by botanical artist Lois Jackson for this center. They include a spondylus oyster, keyhole limpets, a specious scallop, and the precious wentletrap that, so exquisitely formed, was valued above rubies in the early 18th century.

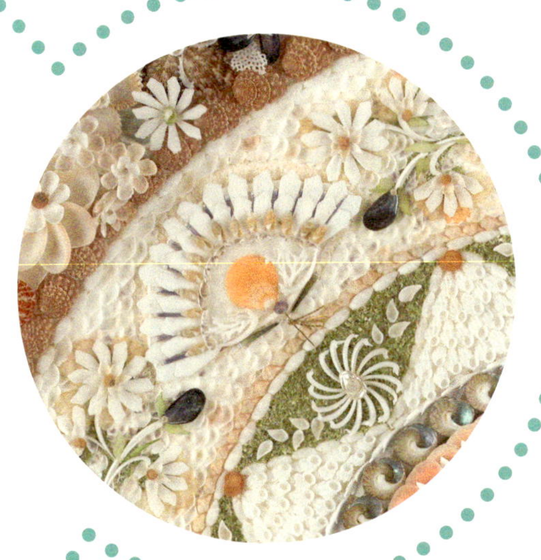

The fan gives this Valentine a Victorian feeling. It was created from capiz shell, sections of gooseneck barnacles, purple sea urchin spines, Philippine rice shells, tiny janthinas, and baby orange scallop shells.

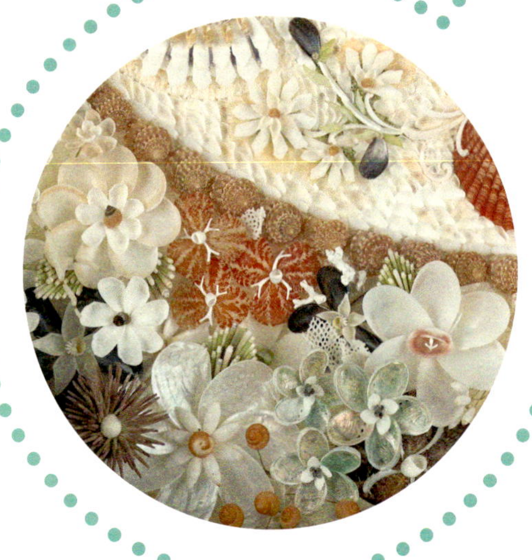

Delicate flowers are reminiscent of a Victorian garden. They are made from red brachiopods, pearlescent pandora shells, green abalone, white tellins, gooseneck barnacles, and sea urchin spines.

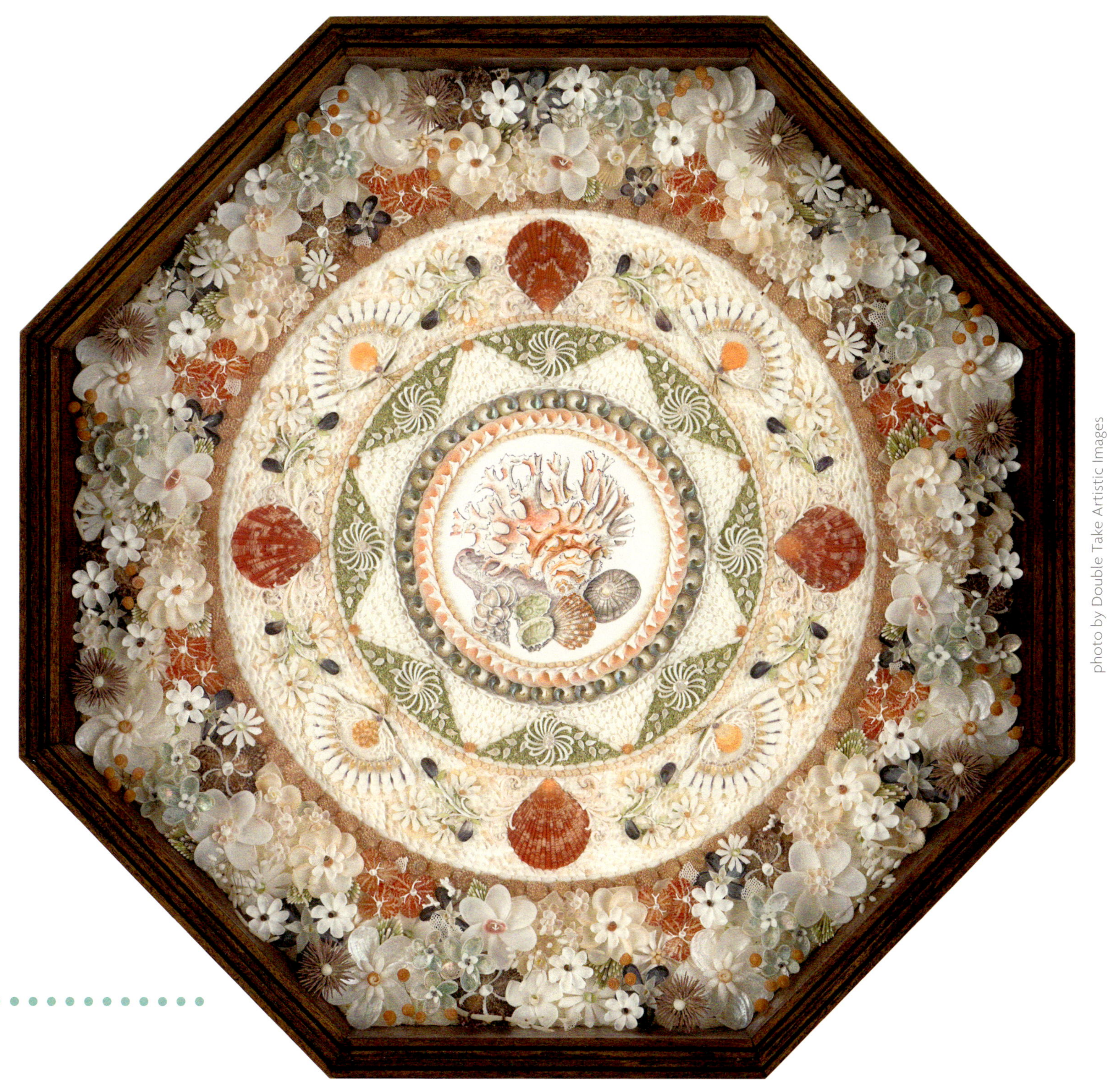

photo by Double Take Artistic Images

Victorian Fantasia

Inspired by the artist's desire to create a Valentine with a brighter palette and a Victorian perspective.

17-inch cherry stained case with ebony inlay made by Bill Jordan

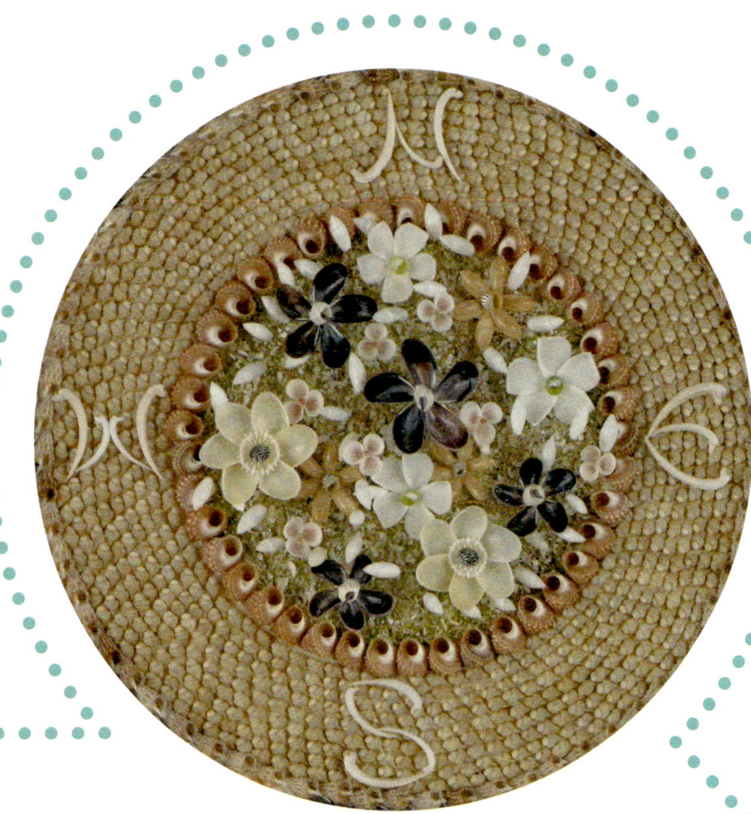

Baby lightning whelks are used behind the letters in the center to give the appearance of needlework. Directional letters of the compass points were made from pieces of gooseneck barnacles. A row of upside-down strawberry cumingi shells surrounds the delicate flowers.

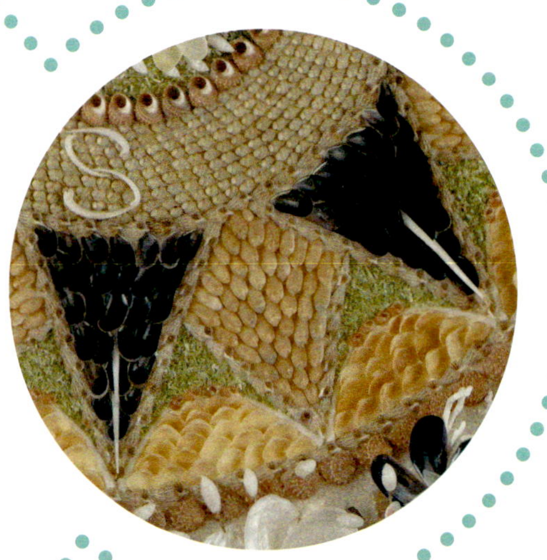

The 16 points of the compass are made from blue mussel shells and Philippine rice shells, with crushed green sea urchin spines between each point.

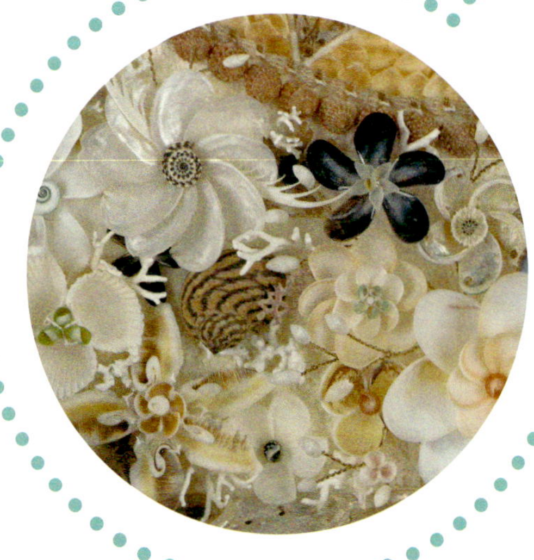

Pearlescent pandora shells were used for the dominant flowers in this Valentine. Blue Atlantic wing oyster shells form leaves, and white rice shells glued on 24-carat gold–filled wire create delicate sprays.

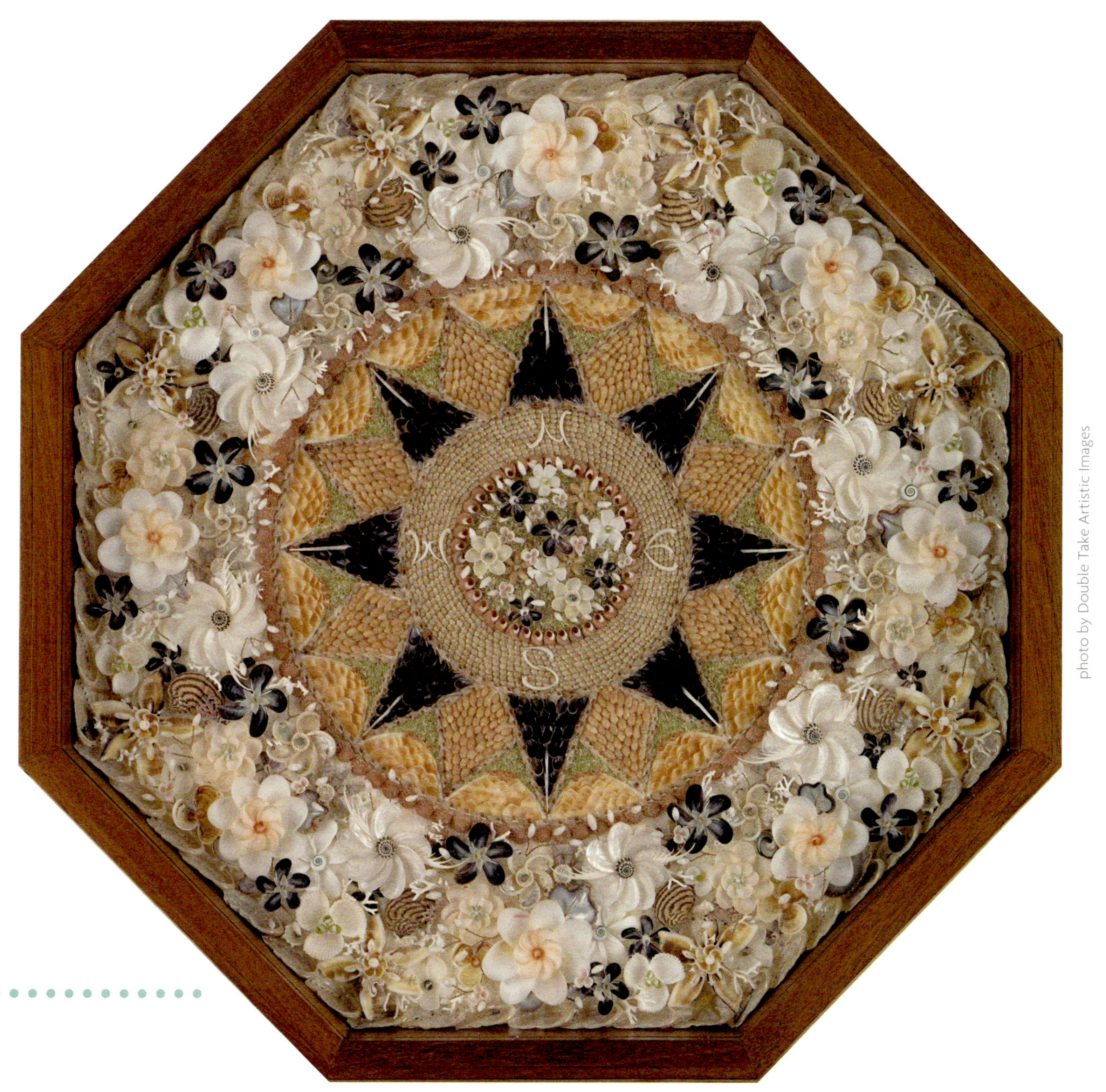

photo by Double Take Artistic Images

Homeward Bound

Inspired by the 16-point ship's compass rose.

20-inch mahogany case made by Jim Prestigiacomo

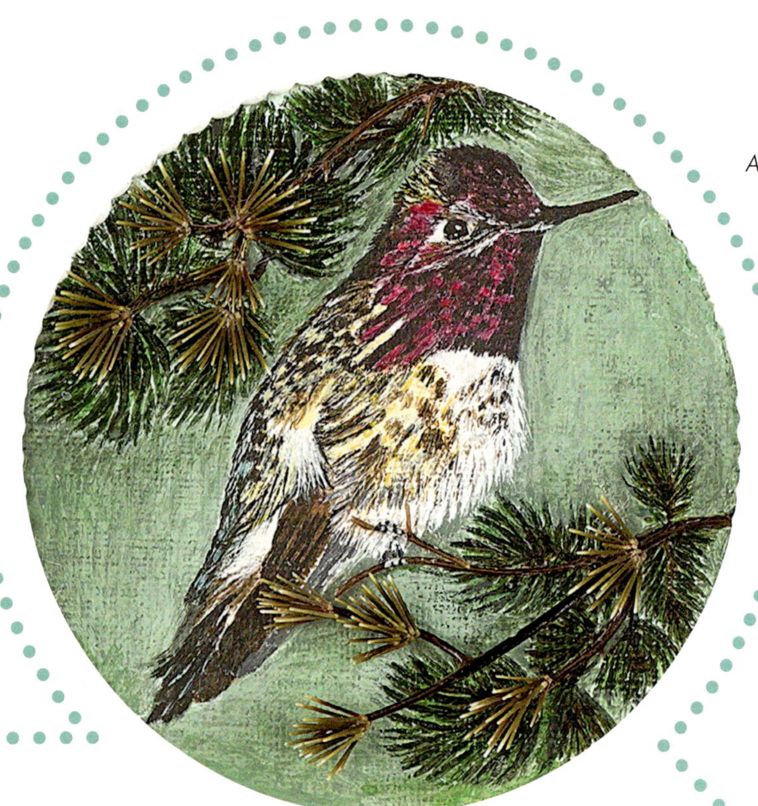

Anna's Hummingbird, an acrylic painting by the artist, draws one's eye immediately to the center of this Valentine. Spending summers in Colorado, she has many occasions to watch the hummingbirds sitting still in the pine trees. Sea fans and sea urchin spines are placed to give a three-dimensional feel to the branches.

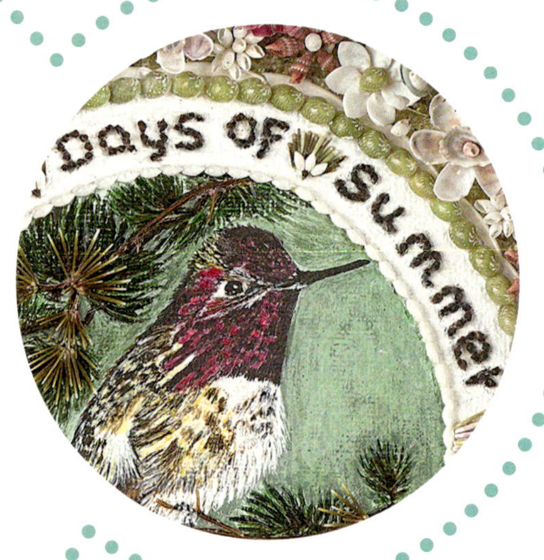

Very tiny black top shells were used to create the lettering in this piece . . . painstaking work.

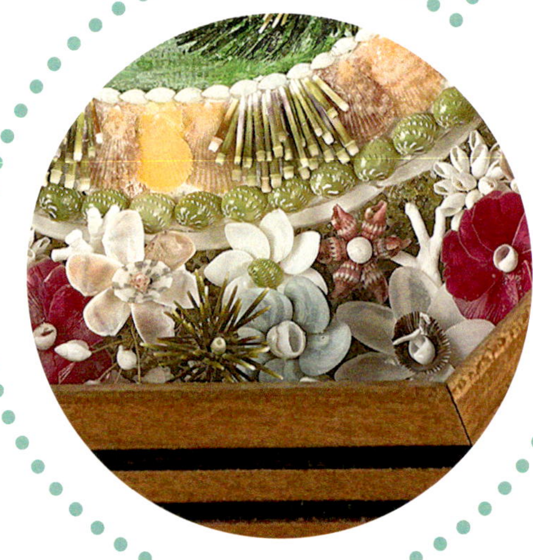

Delicate, colorful miniature flowers are a defining element of the artist's work. The flowers around the edges of this piece were made from blue operculums, vintage dyed fuchsia fish scales, white operculums, and green sea urchin spines, with pieces of coralized algae interspersed.

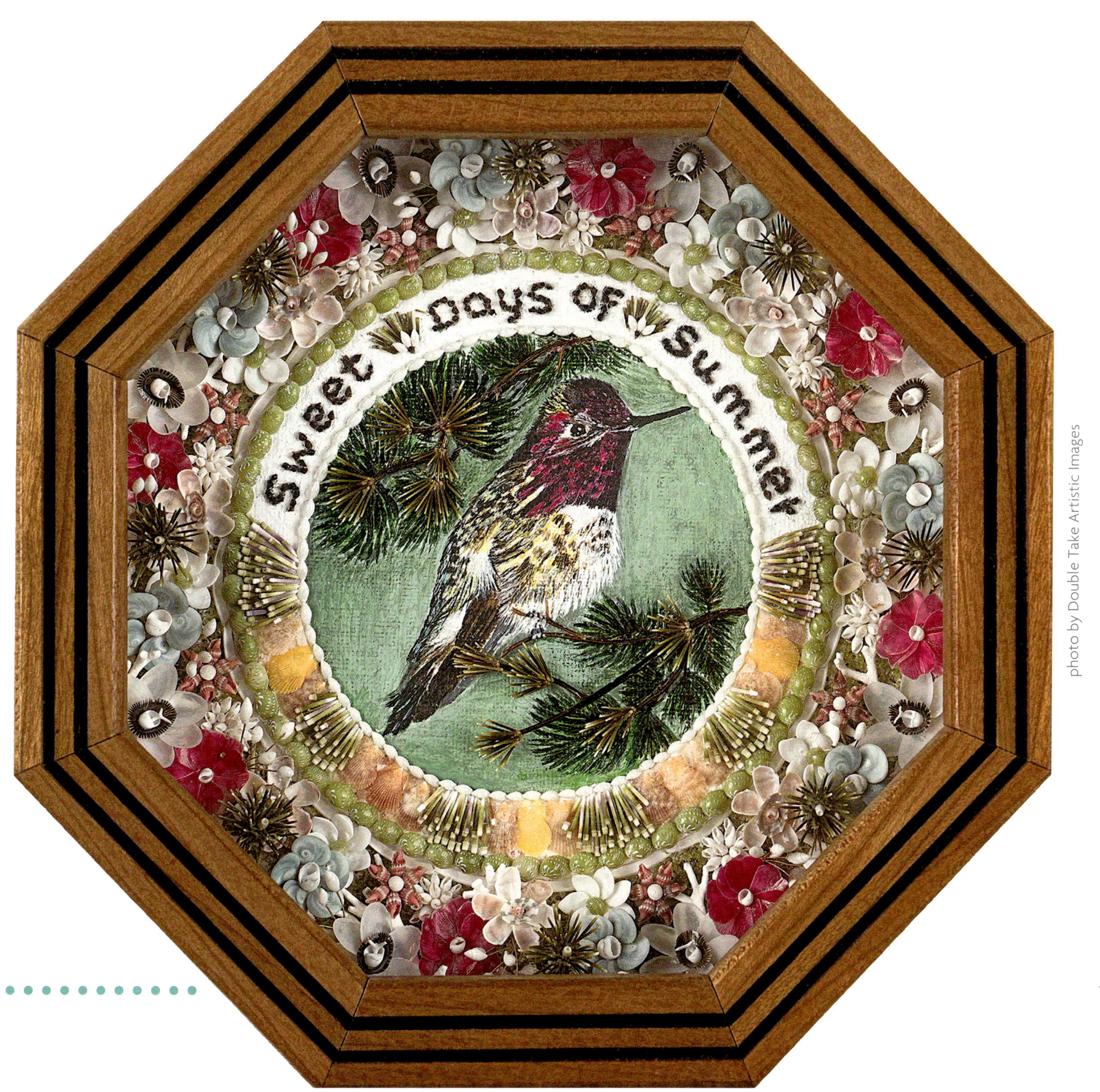

photo by Double Take Artistic Images

Sweet Days of Summer

Inspired by the artist's love of hummingbirds.

6-inch cherry case with ebony inlay made by Jim Prestigiacomo

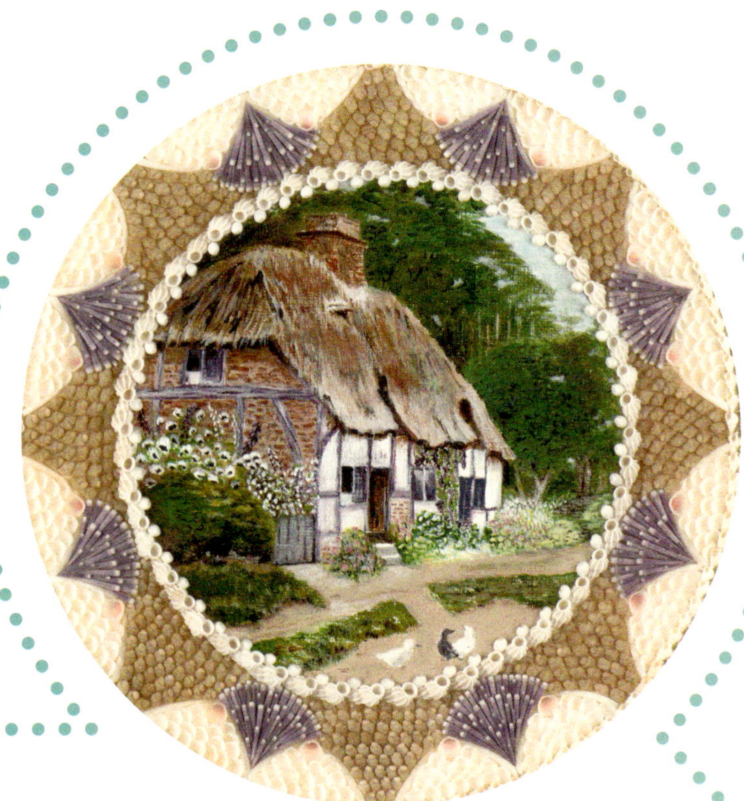

The acrylic painting of the thatched cottage, done by the artist, is one of her favorites. It is encircled by wentletraps and white snail shells. White cup shells provide the background for alternating triangles of baby lightning whelks and purple sea urchin spines, complementing the colors of the painting.

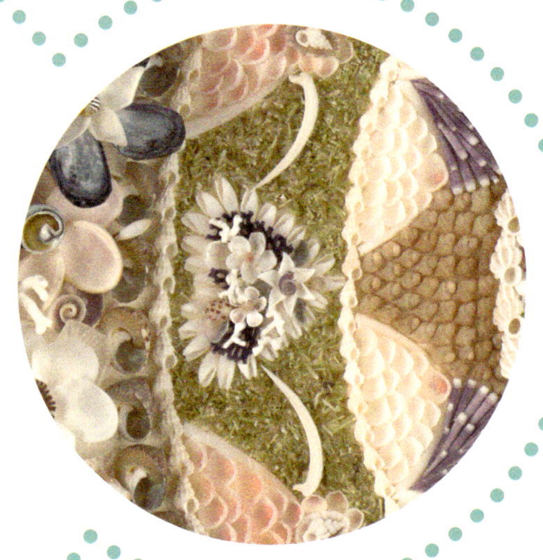

Rice shells outline a heart comprised of baby coquinas, Job's tears, and purple bryozoa resting on a bed of crushed green sea urchin spines bordered by pink apple blossom shells. Curved pieces of gooseneck barnacles emanate outward.

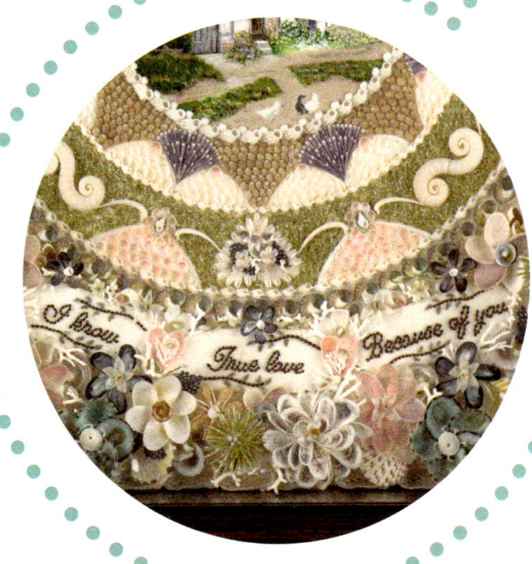

An English flower garden has been fashioned of pink and white tellins, blue mussel shells, coralized algae, California limpets, green sea urchin spines, and the rare pecten imbricata. Three capiz shells serve as background for the inscription done with tiny top shells.

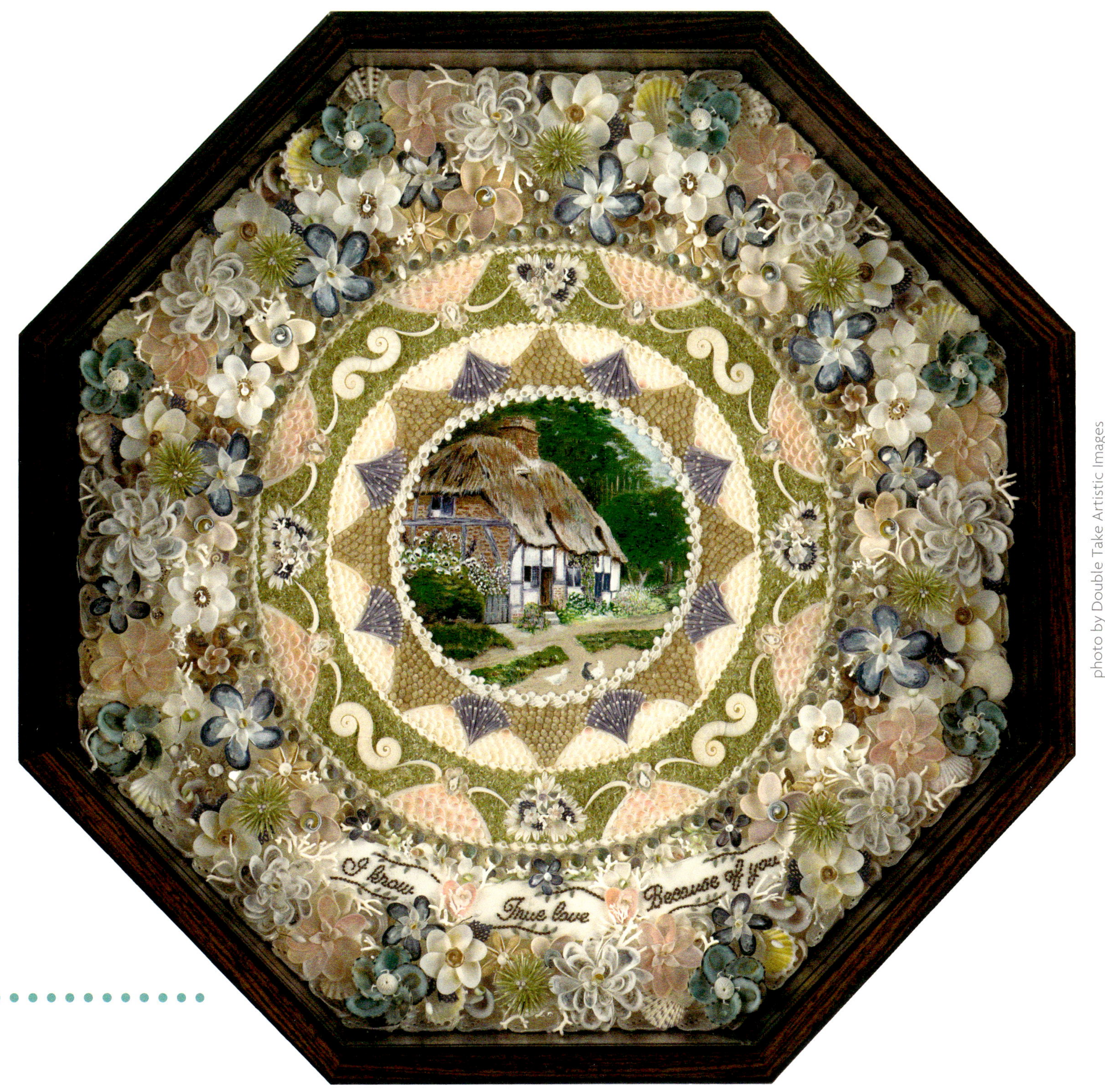

photo by Double Take Artistic Images

Yesteryears

Inspired by a nostalgic visit to the English Cotswold villages and gardens.

16-inch mahogany case made by Jim Prestigiacomo

photo by Martha Madeira

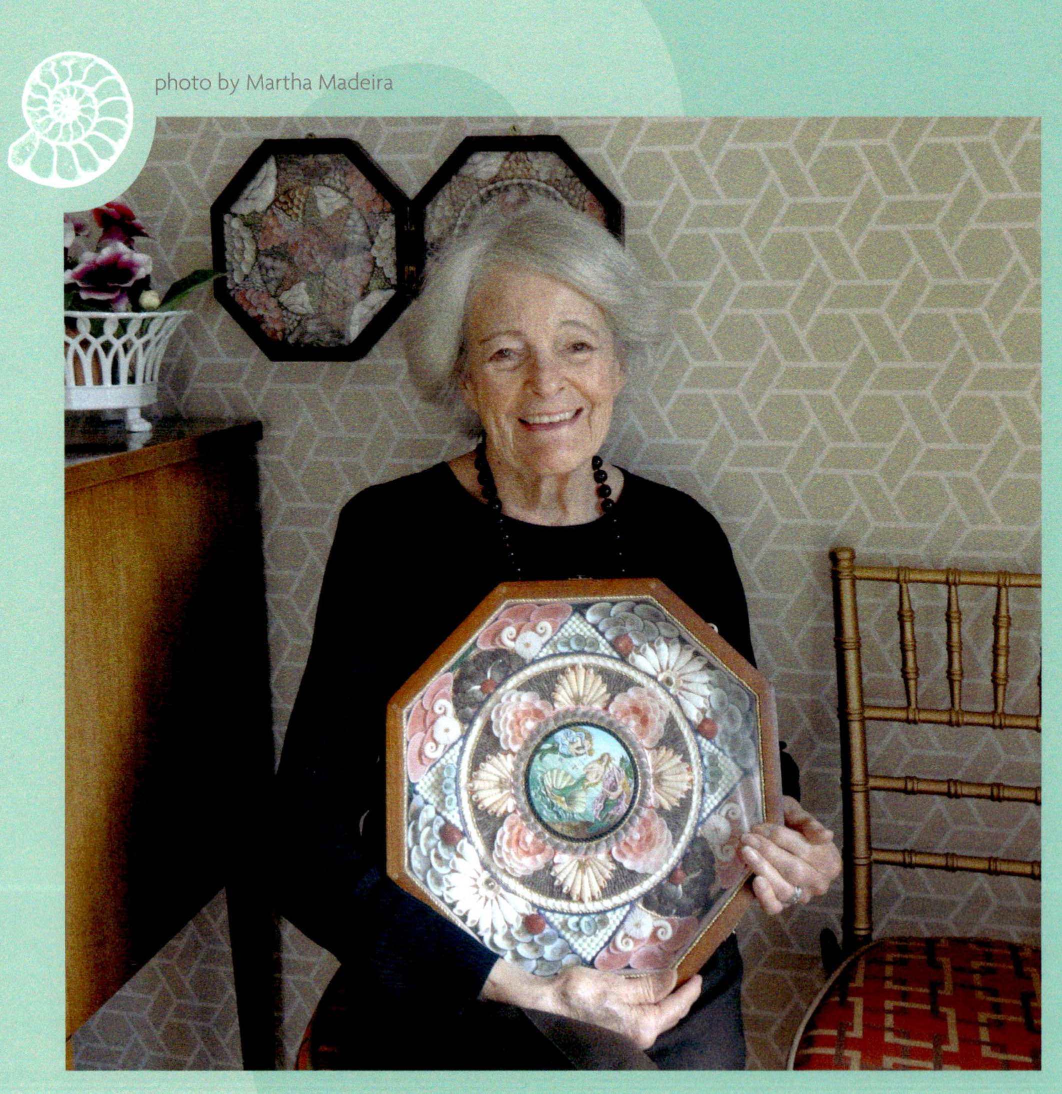

Grace L. Madeira

Bryn Mawr, Pennsylvania

When I was a small girl, I spent hours picking up shells on our Cape Cod beach. My mother nicknamed me "Fanny" because that was all that could be seen of me . . . upended, gleaning shells and the endless beach detritus of childhood fascination.

Later on, I became an honors graduate of Garland Art School in Boston, Massachusetts, and for a while I had my own studio in Cotuit on Cape Cod. I was refinishing portraits, bronze-stenciling Hitchcock chairs, and experimenting with other mediums. I married, and once past the era of three girls in diapers, I began making collages using antique bird prints, which I surrounded with shells, dried seaweeds, and other dried materials.

In the 1960s a friend gave me an octagonal frame and persuaded me to fill it with a shell design. I had long ago admired two double antique Sailors' Valentines belonging to friends, so I was familiar with the craft. I was hooked then and there, and set about making a few of my own, at first using octagonal clock boxes.

I soon became acquainted with Bernard Woodman, a nearby Cape Cod neighbor and one of the early contemporary Sailors' Valentine makers. He became a friend and mentor, generously sharing techniques and sage advice as well as shell sources and information. When he passed away, by good fortune I was able to buy the entire contents of his studio at auction with two friends.

By 2014 I had made more than 145 Sailors' Valentines, in addition to numerous flower baskets, bird designs, and various other subjects. My signature mark on all my frames is a thin gold cording that runs along the edge of the glass and the cap. My Woodman training taught me to lay out my complete design in cording. Then the challenge came to fill those spaces with appropriate shells, to put light next to dark for contrast, and to create interesting designs.

I always line my cases with cardboard and use a water-based glue, which enables me to retrieve any mistakes and save a precious shell if need be. I have no favorite shell; the chase for something different is always my quest.

Little did young "Fanny" know what she was getting herself into when she picked up that very first shell!

*Grace Madeira is one of the authors of *Sailors' Valentines: Their Journey Through Time*, Schiffer Publishing, 2006.

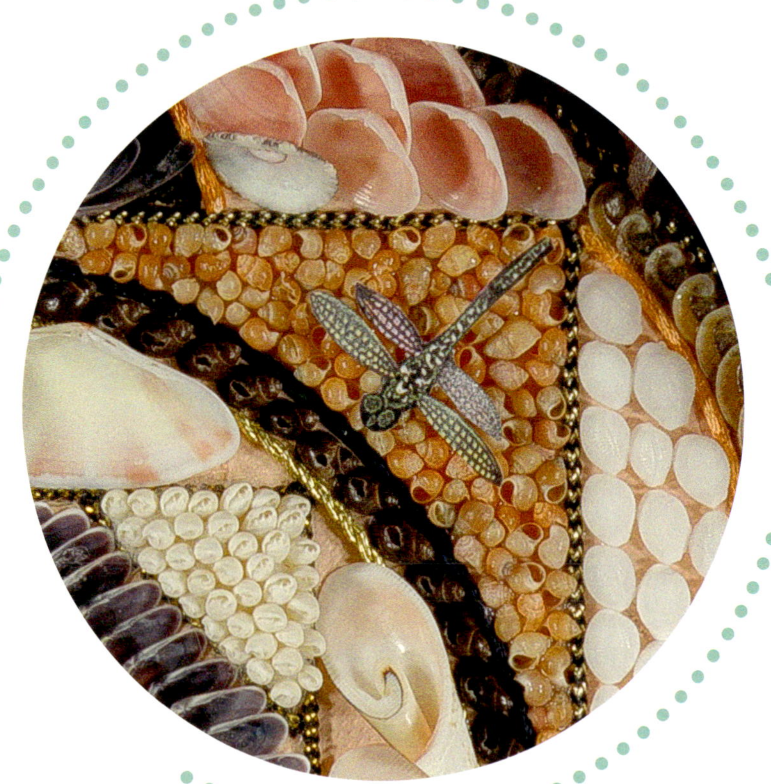

The artist created the delicate dragonflies in each corner from paper that she then painted.

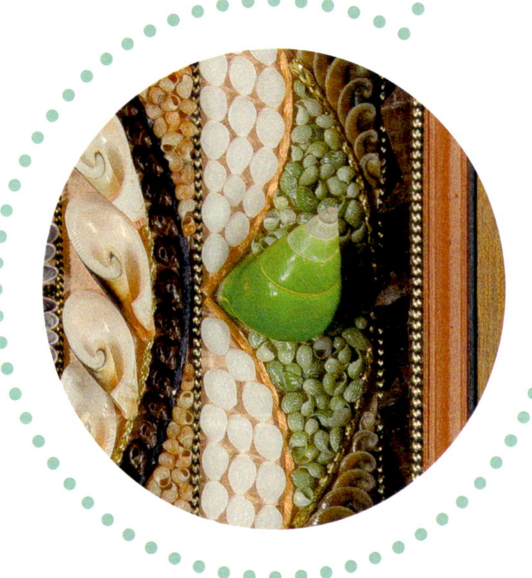

This rare and magnificent green shell is a tree snail called Papuina pulcherrima, found on Manus Island, Papua New Guinea.

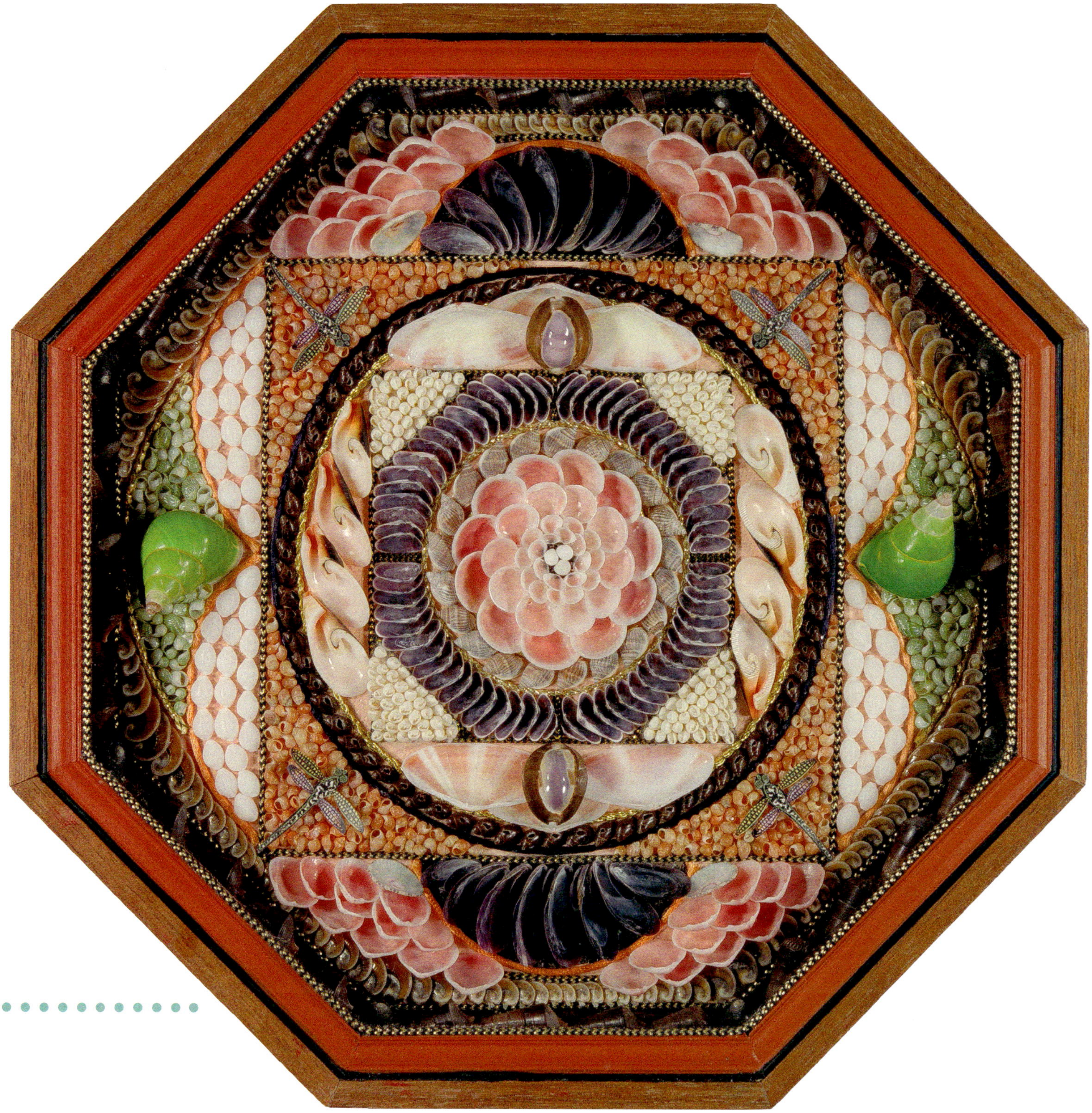

photo by The Camera Shop, Bryn Mawr

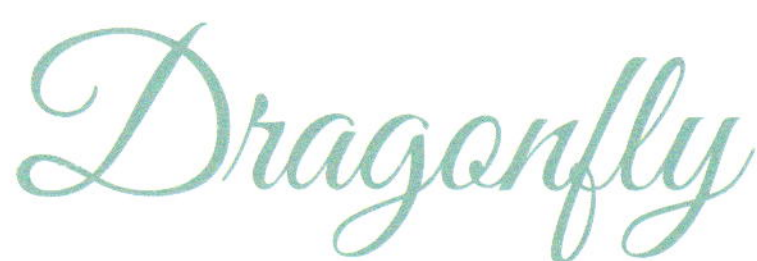

Dragonfly

Inspired by the beauty and intrigue of dragonflies.

12-inch case made by the artist; wood unknown

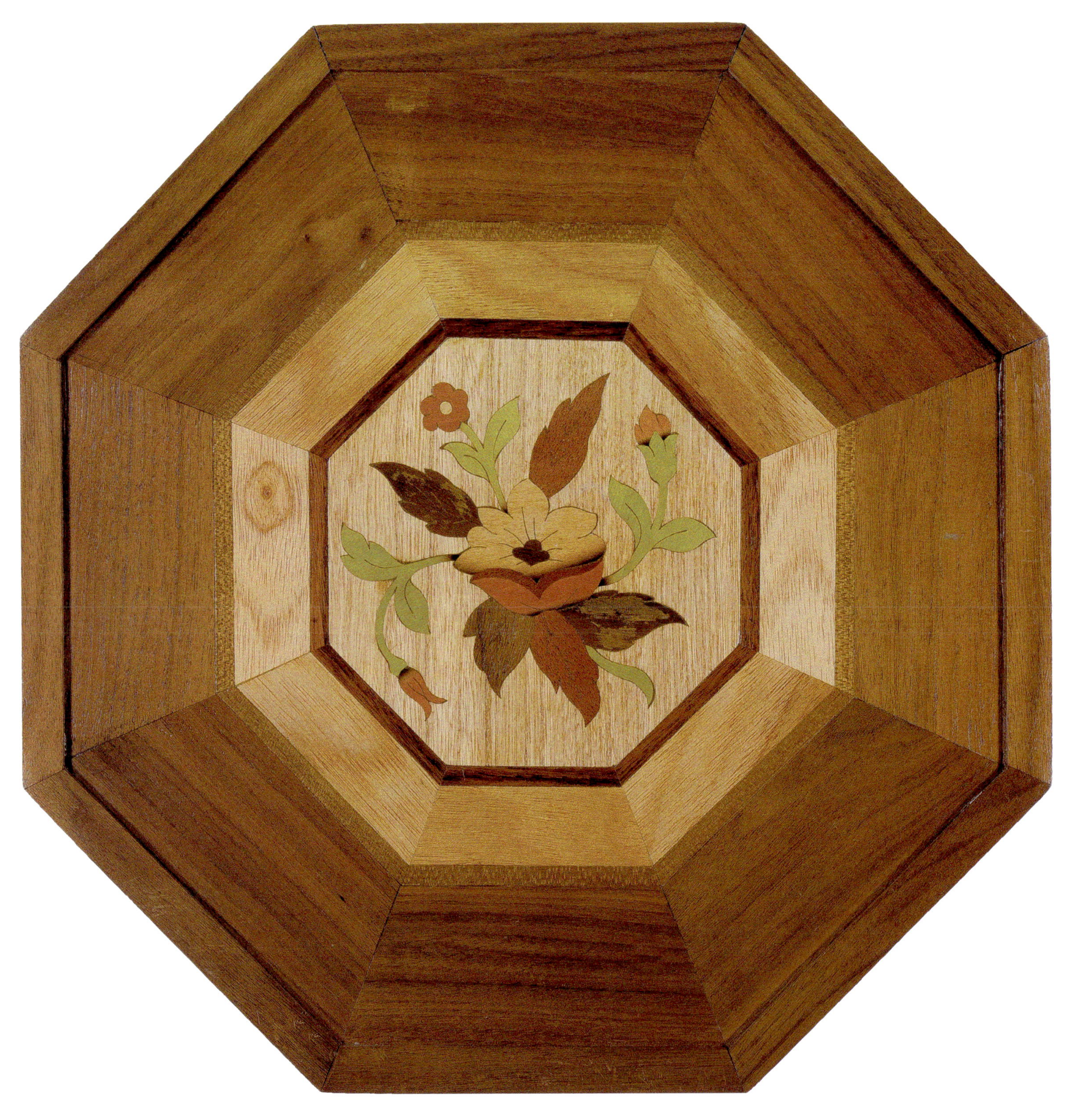

back of case

inlay work by L. Rodman Page

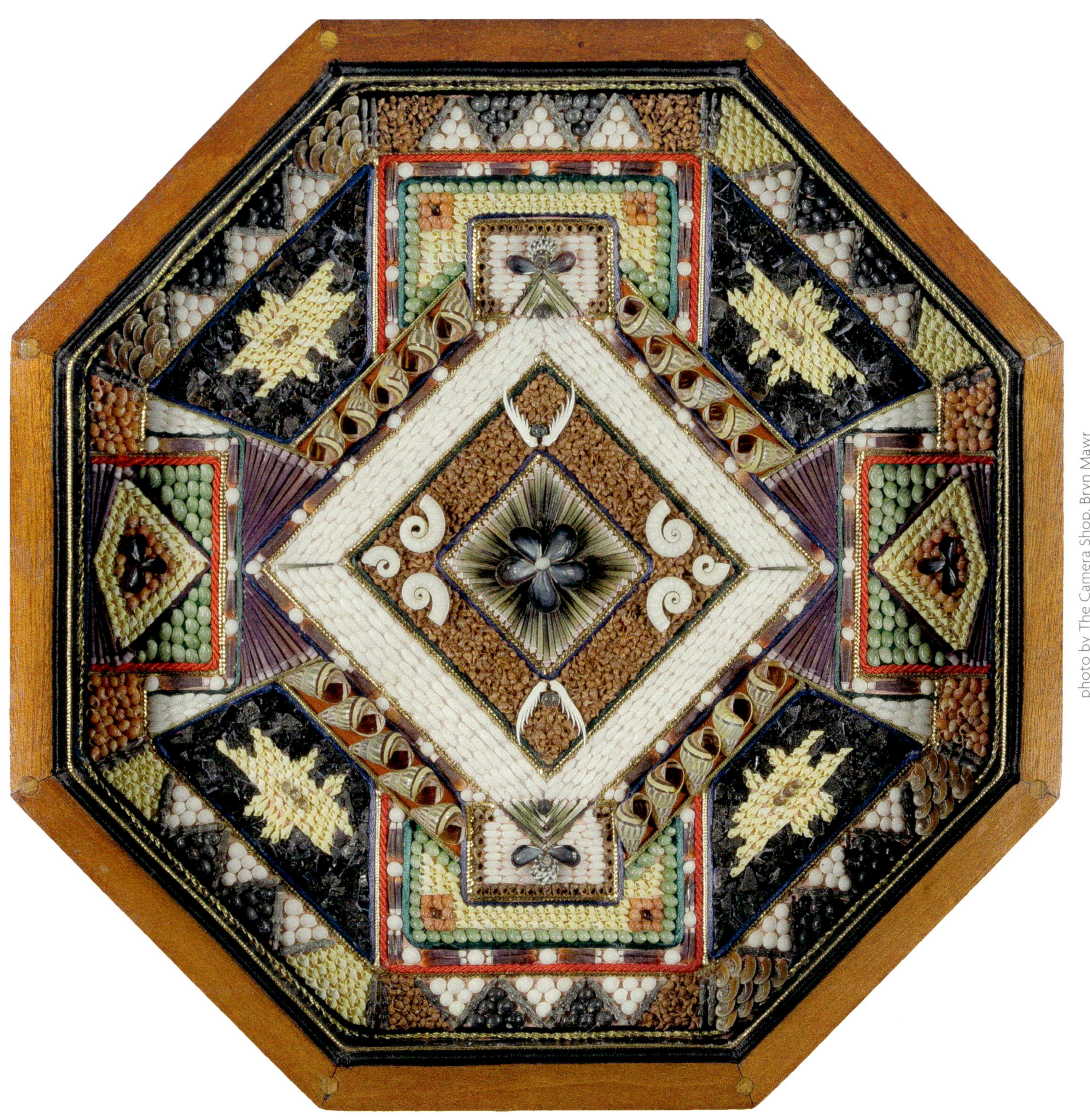

photo by The Camera Shop, Bryn Mawr

Persian Carpet

Influenced by the magnificent abstract patterns of Oriental rugs.

14-inch case made by L. Rodman Page, husband of Sailors' Valentine maker and friend of the artist Mary S. Page; wood unknown

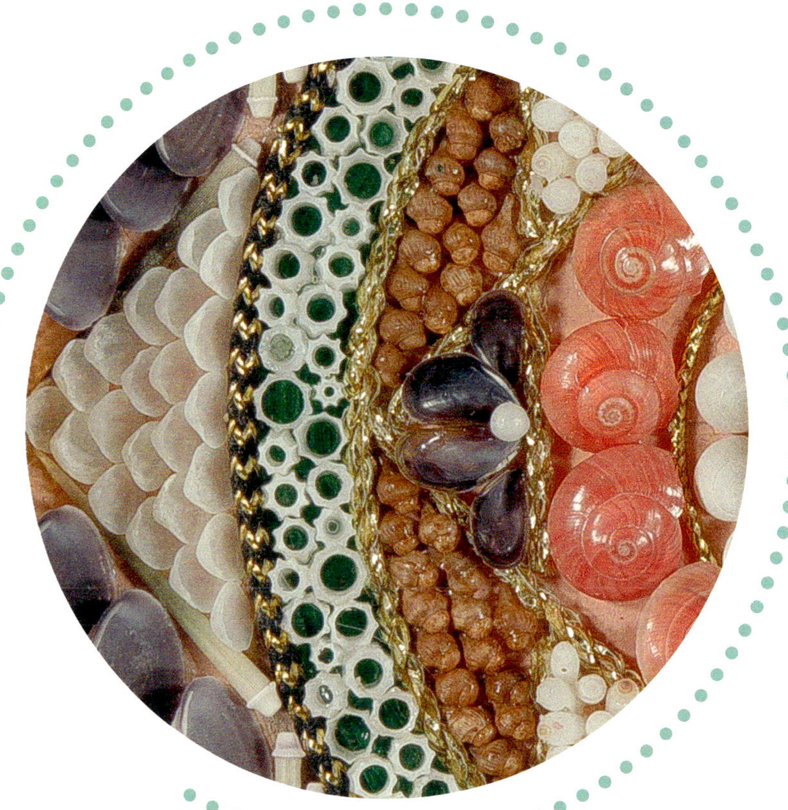

The circular white shells are cut tusk shells placed upright on a painted dark green background, creating a distinctive and textured appearance.

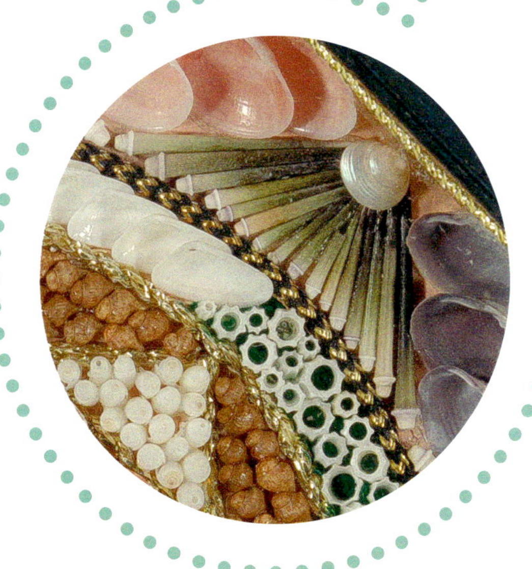

Green sea urchin spines create a sunburst effect in the corners.

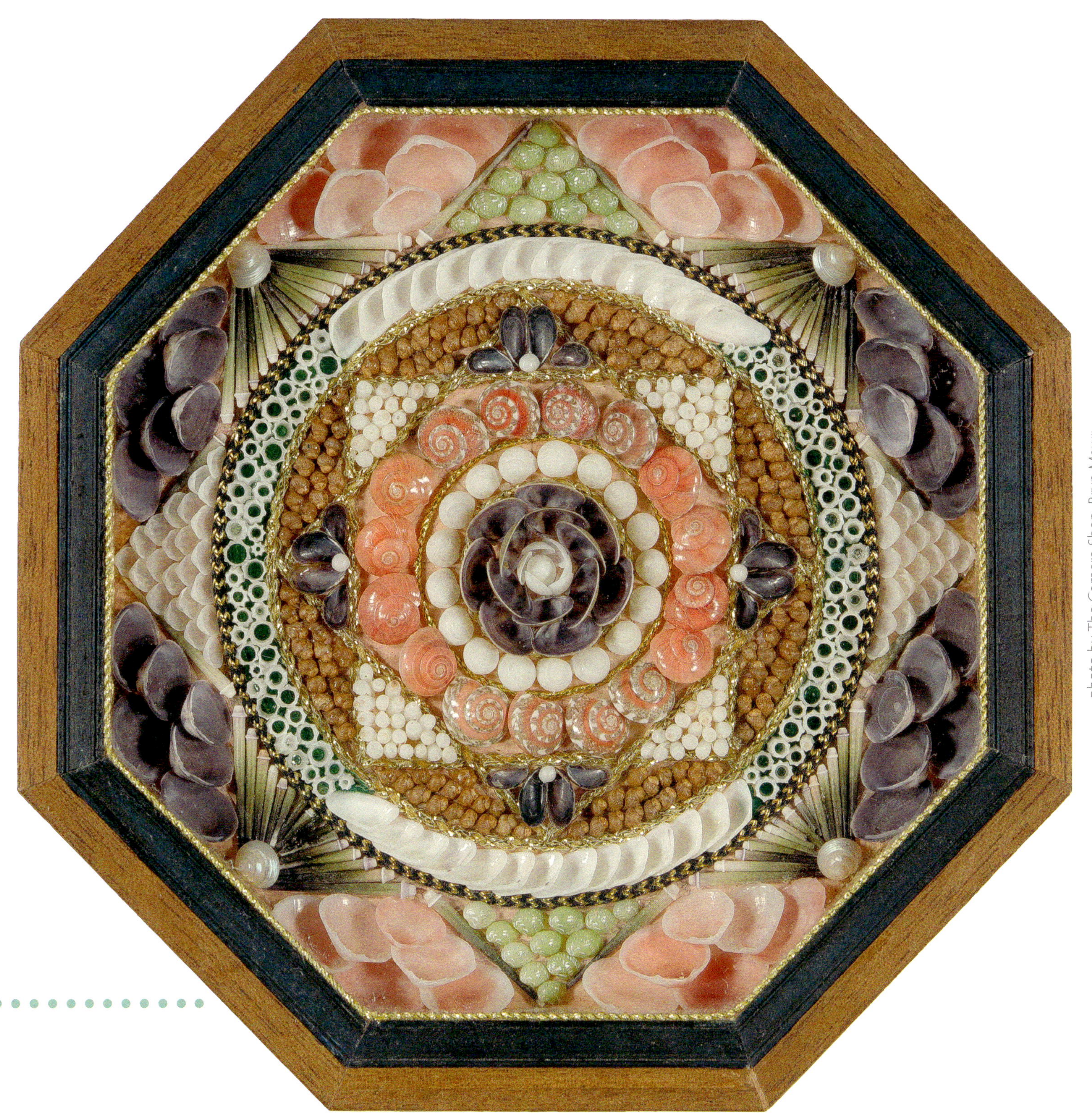

photo by The Camera Shop, Bryn Mawr

Martha

A 50th birthday gift from the artist to her daughter Martha.

6-inch case; wood and maker unknown

Light and dark purple sea urchin spines placed in varied directions surround the onion domes.

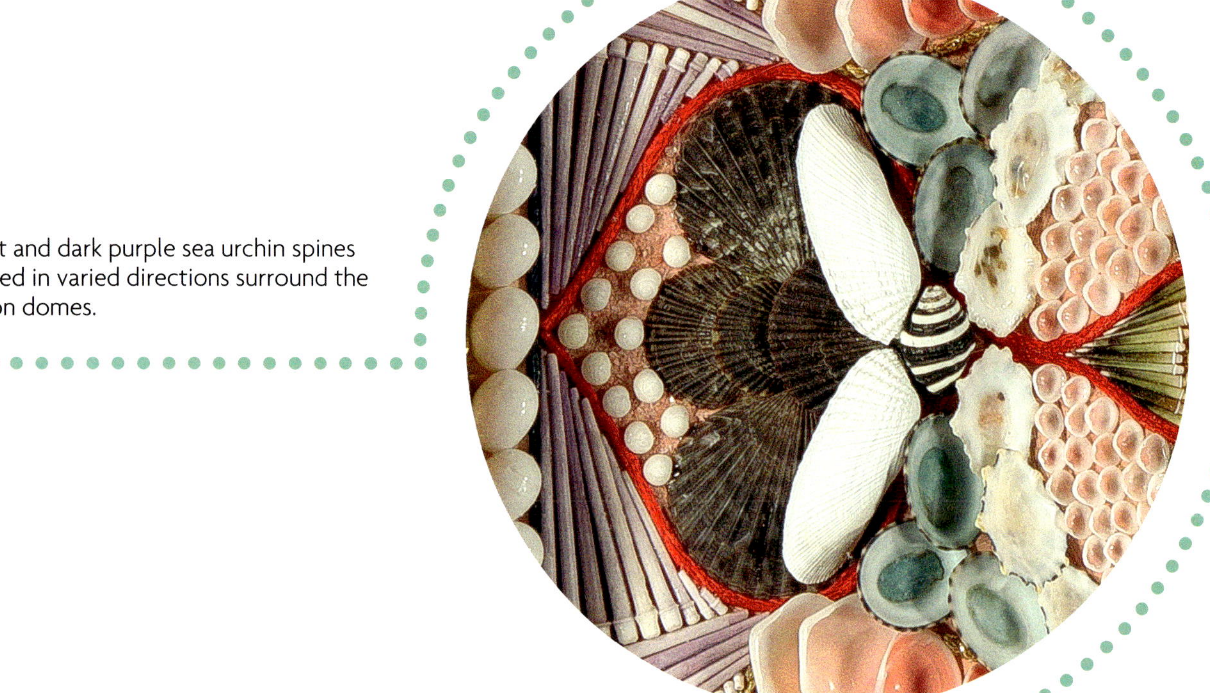

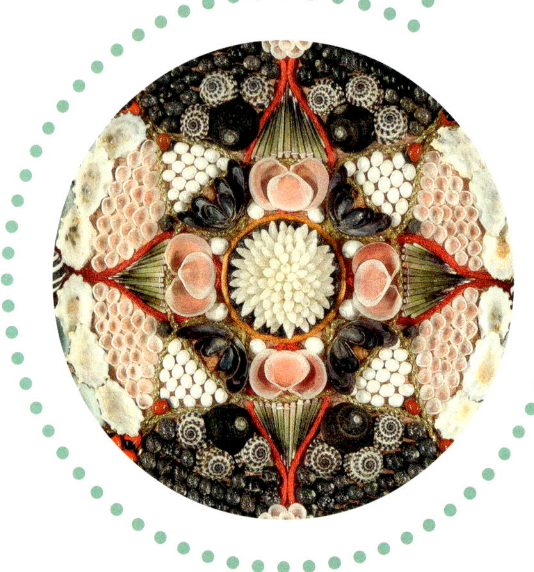

Red cord dividers filled with green urchin spines surround a flower made of white rice shells, creating a striking centerpiece.

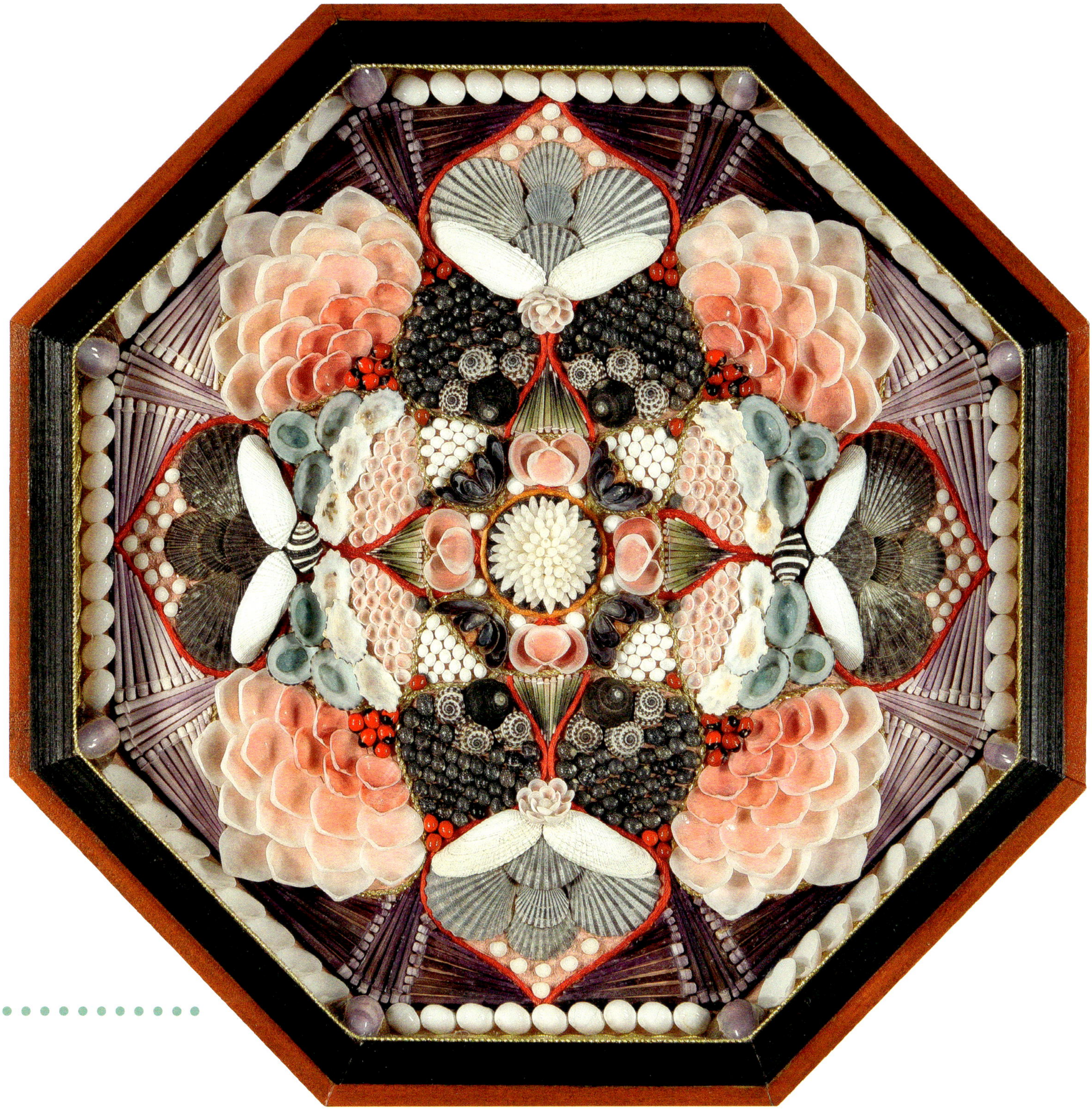

photo by The Camera Shop, Bryn Mawr

Study #66

Inspired by the artist's desire to create a piece with great contrast and depth of color.

13-inch case made by the artist; wood unknown

photo by Dan Cook

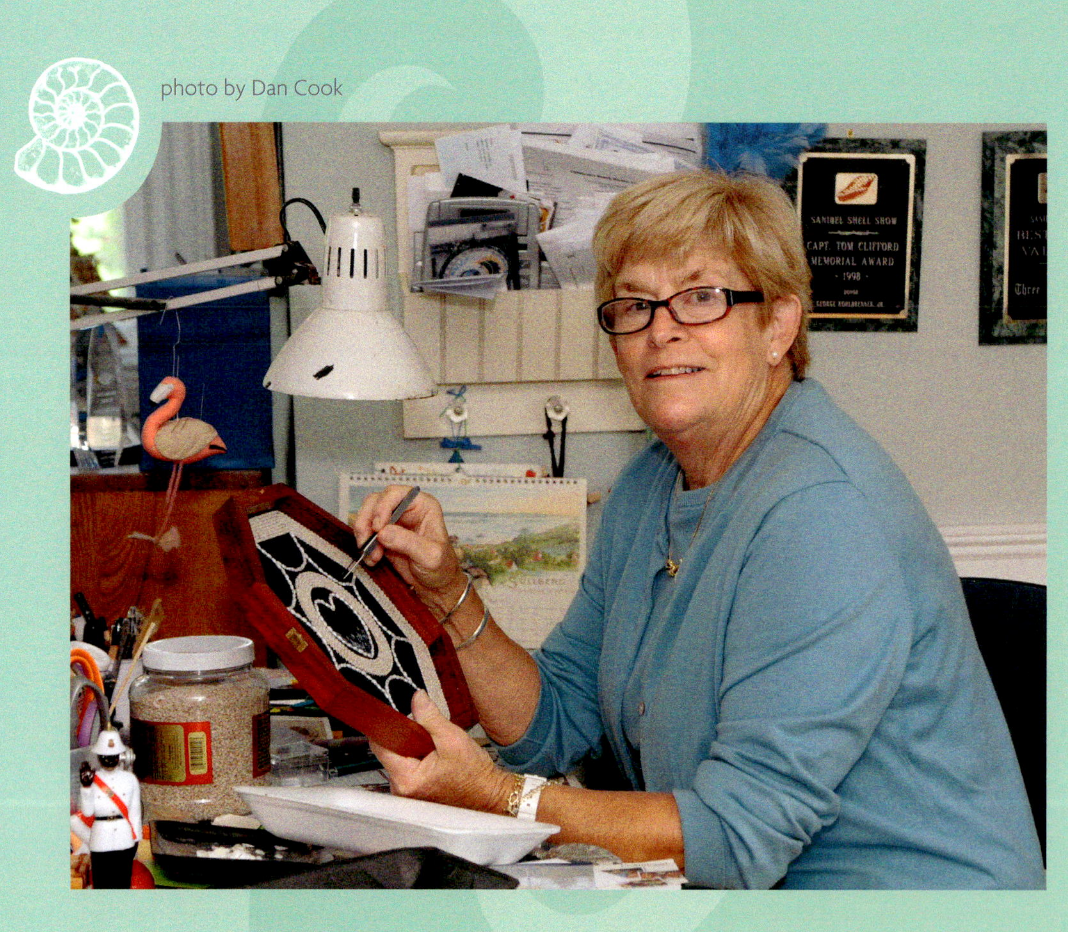

Constance Marshall Miller

Lewes, Delaware

While counting my credits for graduation from the University of Delaware, the woman doing so misunderstood me when I said I was still undecided about a major and told me that as an art major I needed to take art classes. As a junior that's what I did, because in those days we listened to our elders. I have a BA in art and an MA in printmaking. Once I got into art I knew it was just where I belonged. I spent my entire career as an art teacher, the last 17 years teaching students at Cape Henlopen High School in Lewes.

I began collecting seashells when I was four years old, and it's been a passion ever since. While vacationing on Sanibel Island in 1986, I saw my first Valentine on an advertisement for the opening of what is now the Bailey-Matthews National Shell Museum. The Valentine had been made by a man named Bert Porreca. I knew of Mr. Porreca, who could be found searching for wentletraps every afternoon on the beach. I spoke with him about his Valentine, and as soon as I got home from that vacation I made a box and created my first Valentine. That was more than 60 Sailors' Valentines ago.

I generally begin my work with the wording, and I am known to use a lot of words. I like song titles and lyrics. Fashioning animals from shells is a real challenge, and many of my Valentines include animals, particularly birds. I also use the compass rose frequently, as it reminds me of sailing and the sea, two of my passions. The piece I most enjoyed making is *Octopus's Garden* (see pages 136–137). *Silver Swan* is another favorite, as it contains 31 words and the centerpiece took a record 100 hours to create.

In addition to Valentines, I create other shell-related art. I also paint, do pen-and-ink and scratchboard drawings, and make ceramics in my studio, a perfect space with the northern light that is good for drawing, painting, and shell art. I am a doting grandmother to five grandchildren, and this year my two granddaughters made their first Sailors' Valentines, which pleased me greatly.

*Constance Marshall Miller is one of the authors of *Sailors' Valentines: Their Journey Through Time*, Schiffer Publishing, 2006.

www.cmmshellart.com

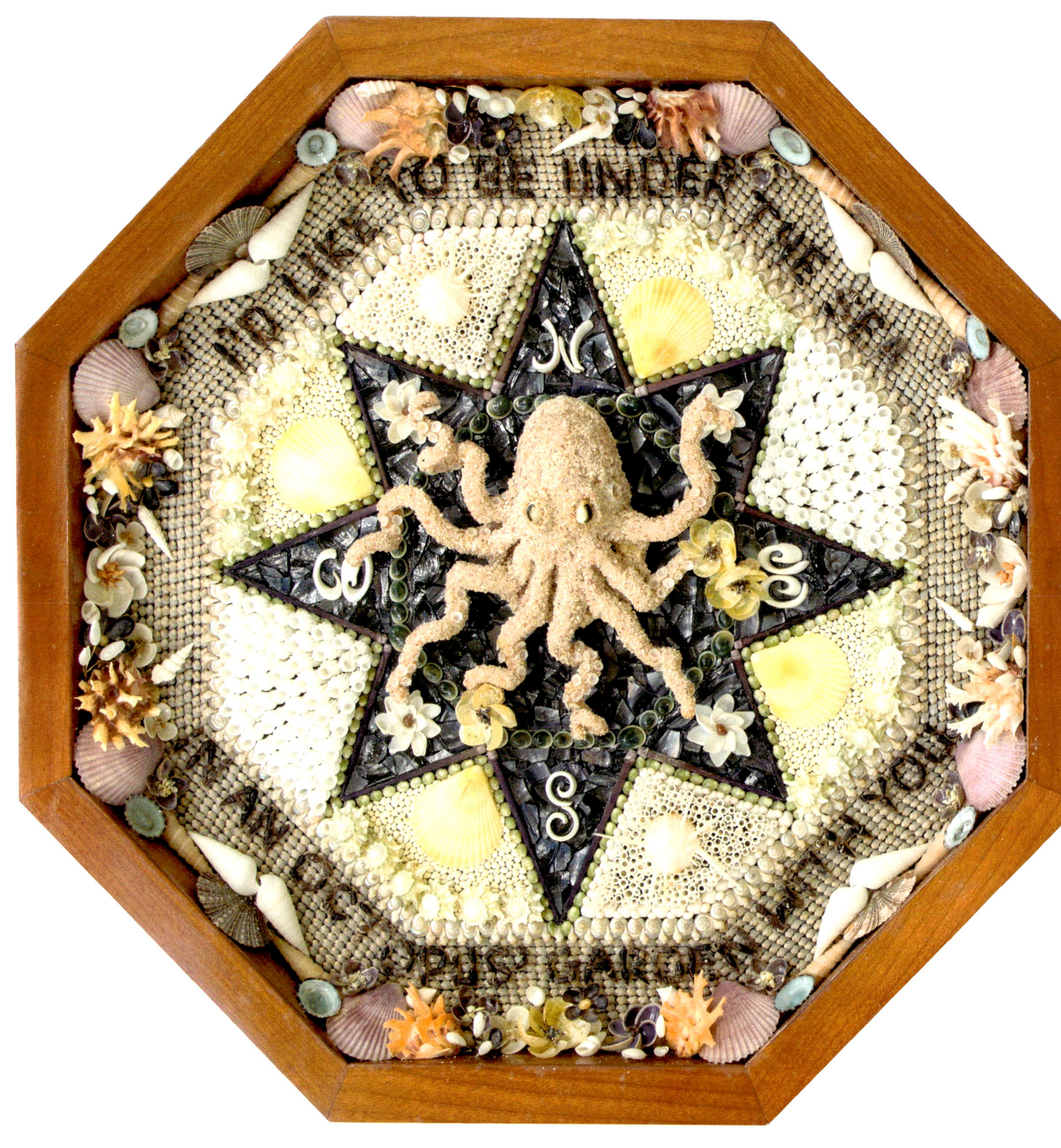

Inspired by the song "Octopus's Garden" by the Beatles.

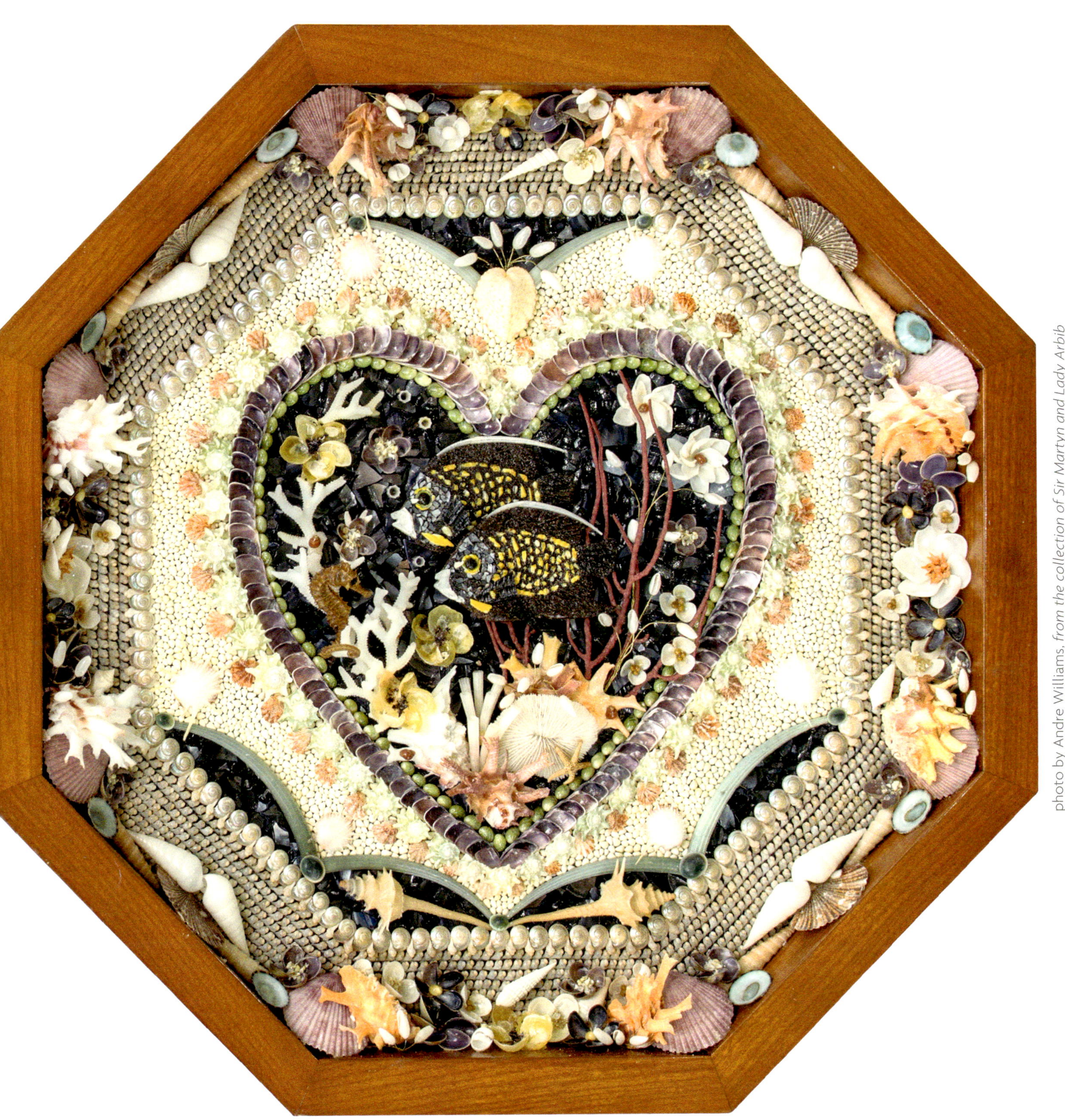

photo by Andre Williams, *from the collection of Sir Martyn and Lady Arbib*

Octopus's Garden

13-inch (each side) cherry case made by Bruce Chandler

The octopus was made from a cockle shell with worm shells attached to it. For the eyes, two limpet shells were filed down to put holes in the tops, where marginellas were inserted. The black accent is painted on. The octopus is covered with pink sand from Bermuda, and small white bivalves were glued on for the suction cups. He holds flowers made from yellow jingle shells.

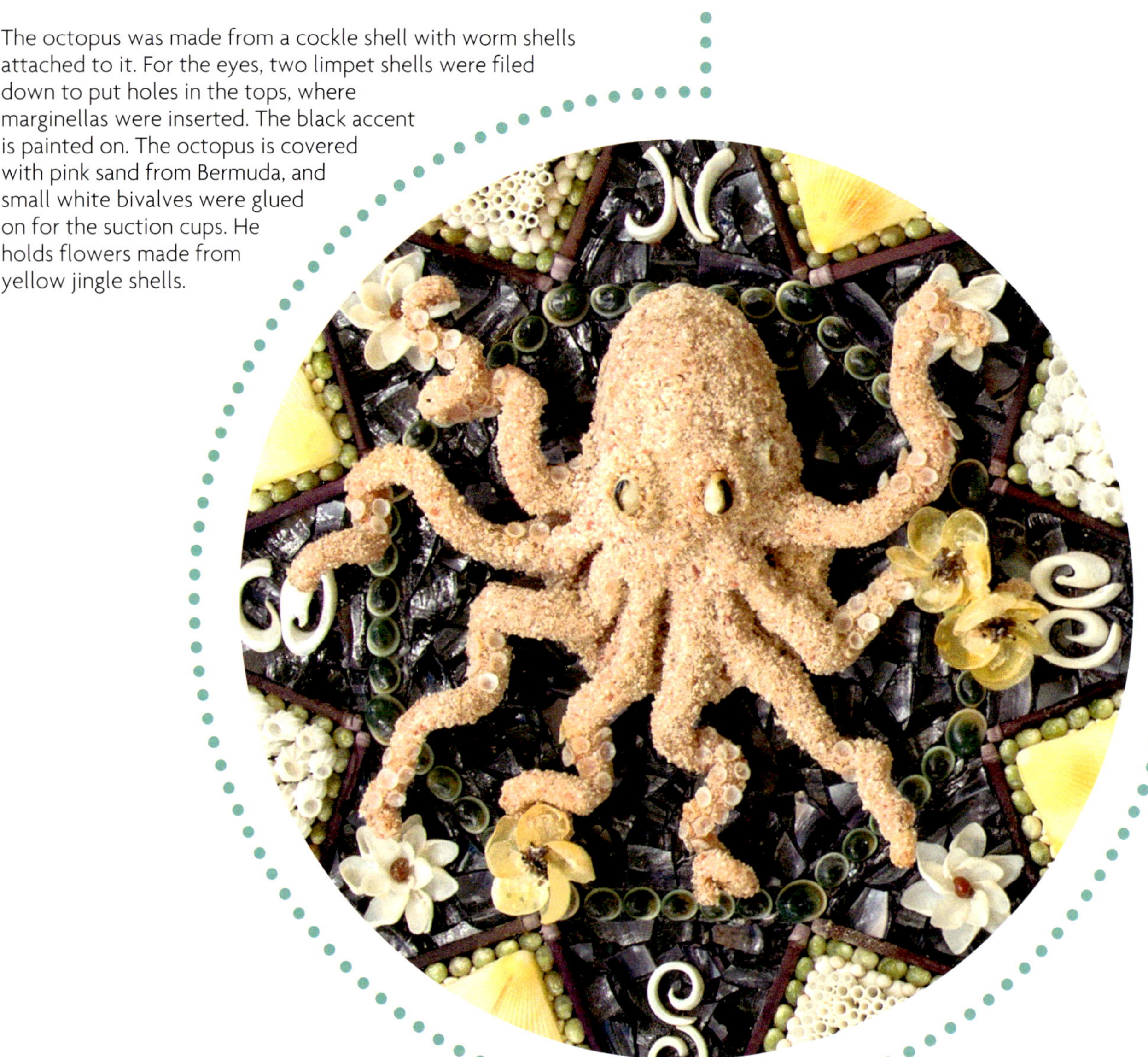

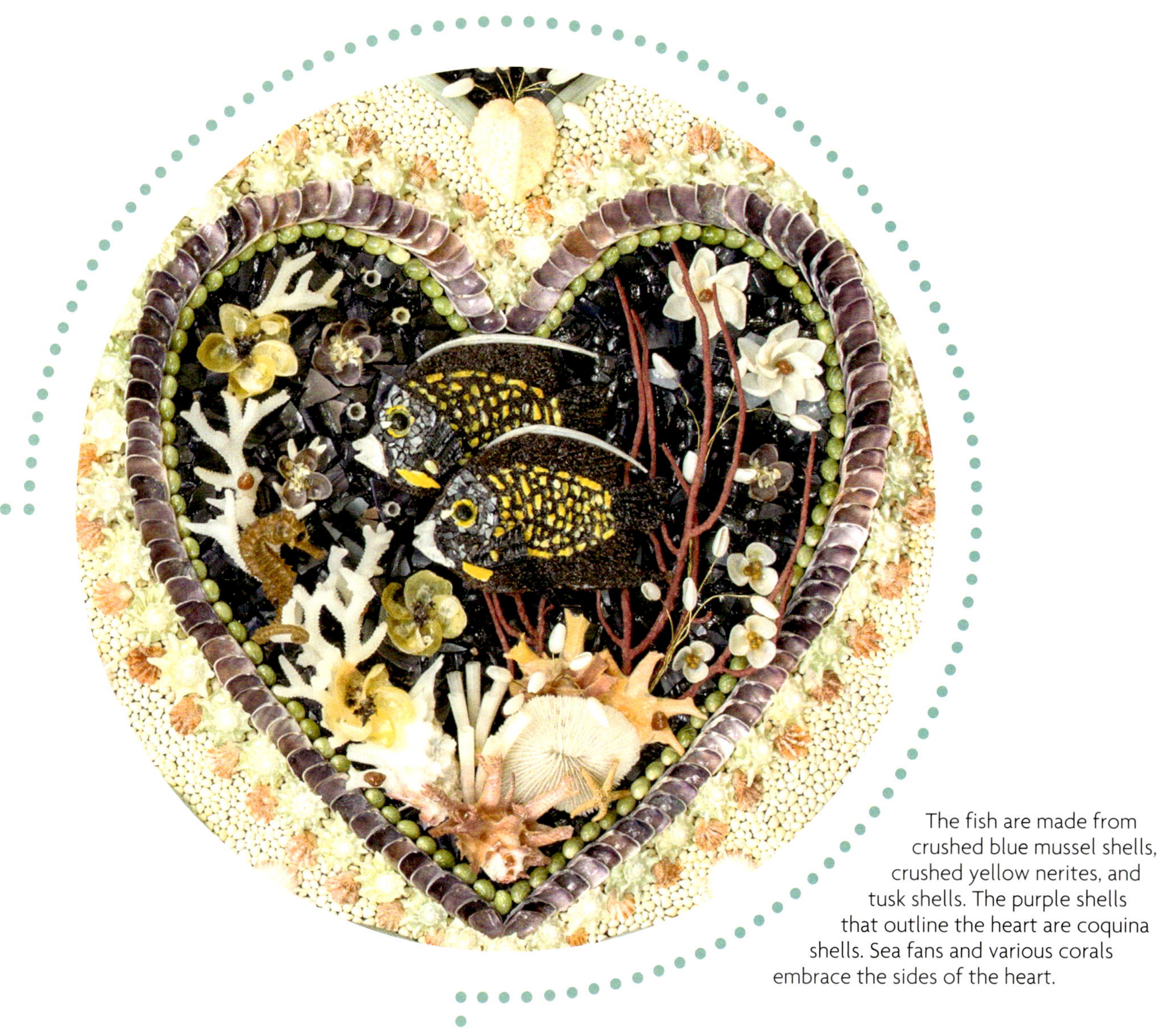

The fish are made from crushed blue mussel shells, crushed yellow nerites, and tusk shells. The purple shells that outline the heart are coquina shells. Sea fans and various corals embrace the sides of the heart.

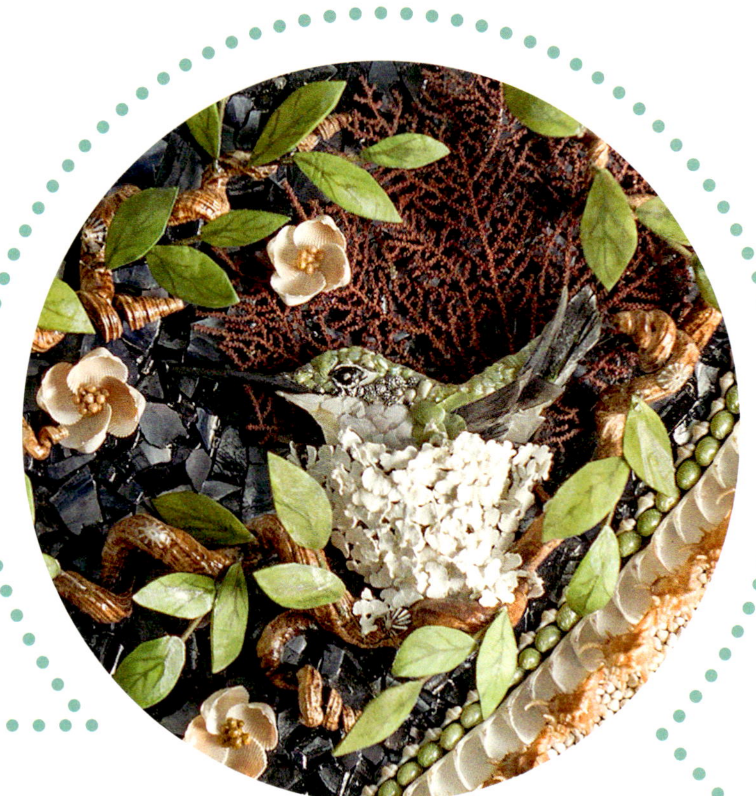

The female hummingbird sits in a nest made of large limpet shells found by the artist in Panama, which have been covered with white beach lichen. There are two eggs in the nest done with Caribbean milk moon snails. The leaves are cut and painted fish scales.

The large white flower is made of tellin shells, with small cockle shells and yellow mustard seeds in the center. The pink flower is done from rose petal tellins. A pale blue limpet, pink stylaster coral, and leaves made from painted fish scales complete the corner design.

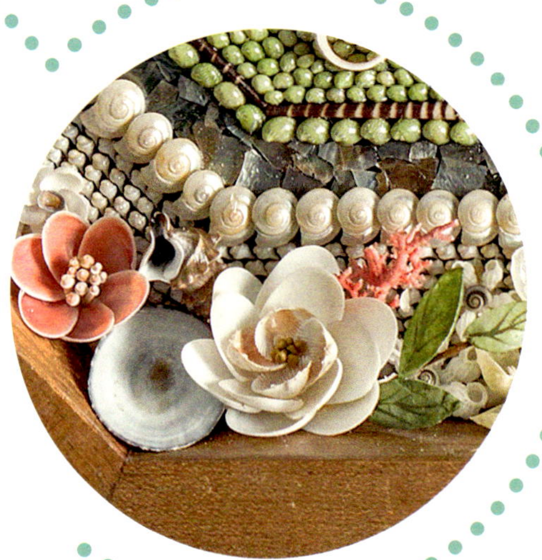

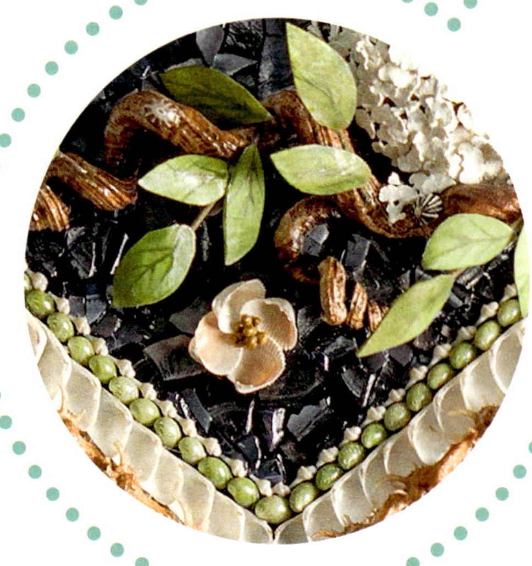

The baby lightning whelks that sit along the inside of the heart next to the emerald nerites are all freak right-handed ones that the artist found in an egg case in 2004. Lightning whelks are normally left-handed.

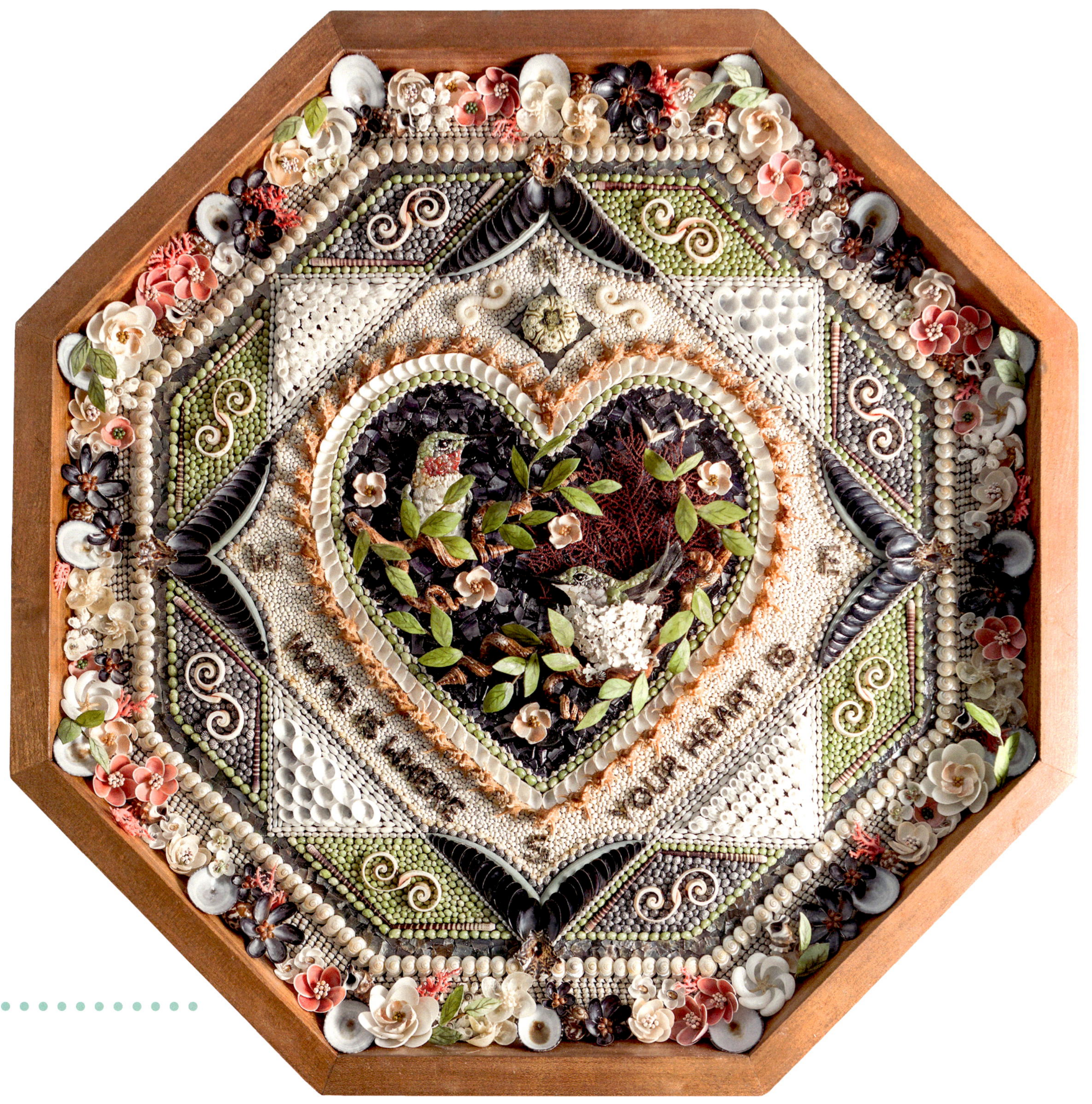

photo by Justin Nixon

Home Is Where Your Heart Is

Inspired by two hummingbirds that nested in a tree
at the Lewes Yacht Club in the summer of 2011.

22-inch cherry case made by Bruce Chandler

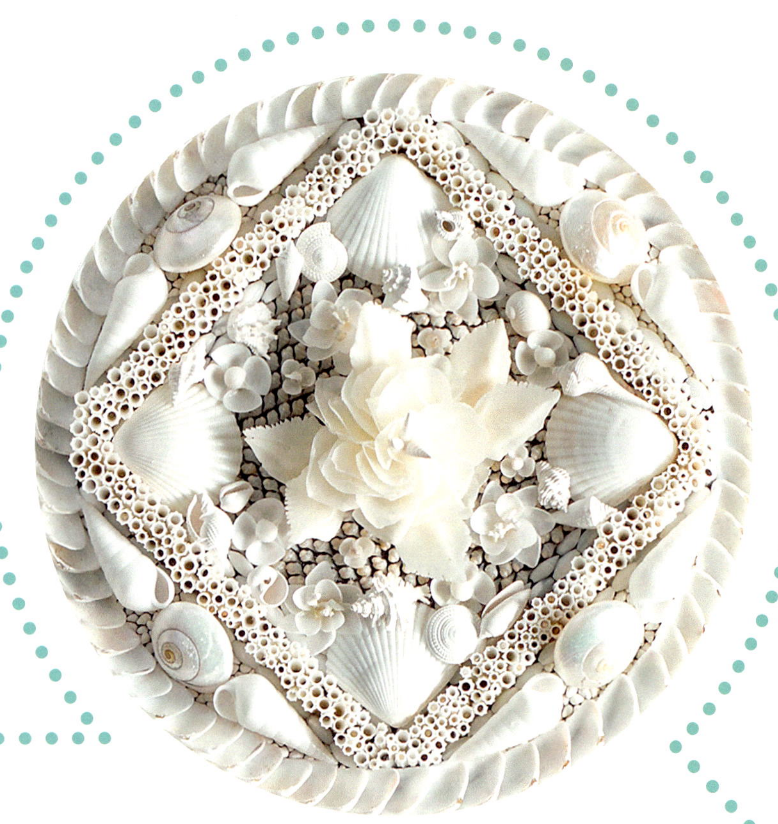

The use of white fossil shells adds a creamier shade of white. Cut tusk shells glued on their ends create a unique texture in the square.

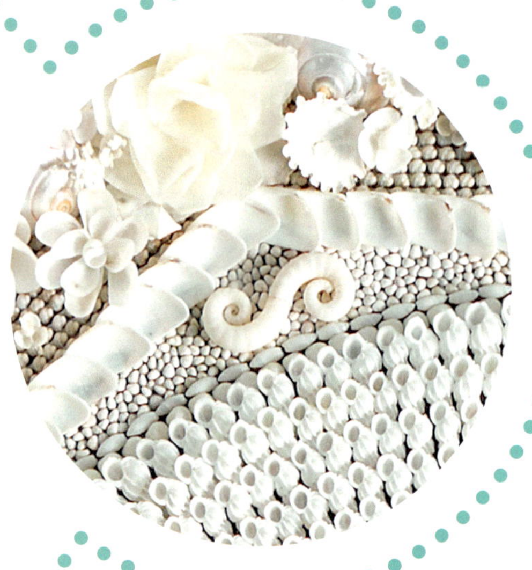

Baby lightning whelks, collected by the artist on Sanibel Island, are frequently used to create backgrounds in her pieces. Here, she also uses self-collected white coquina shells for the octagonal border.

Glistening tumbled bubble shells set upright create this marvelous triangle.

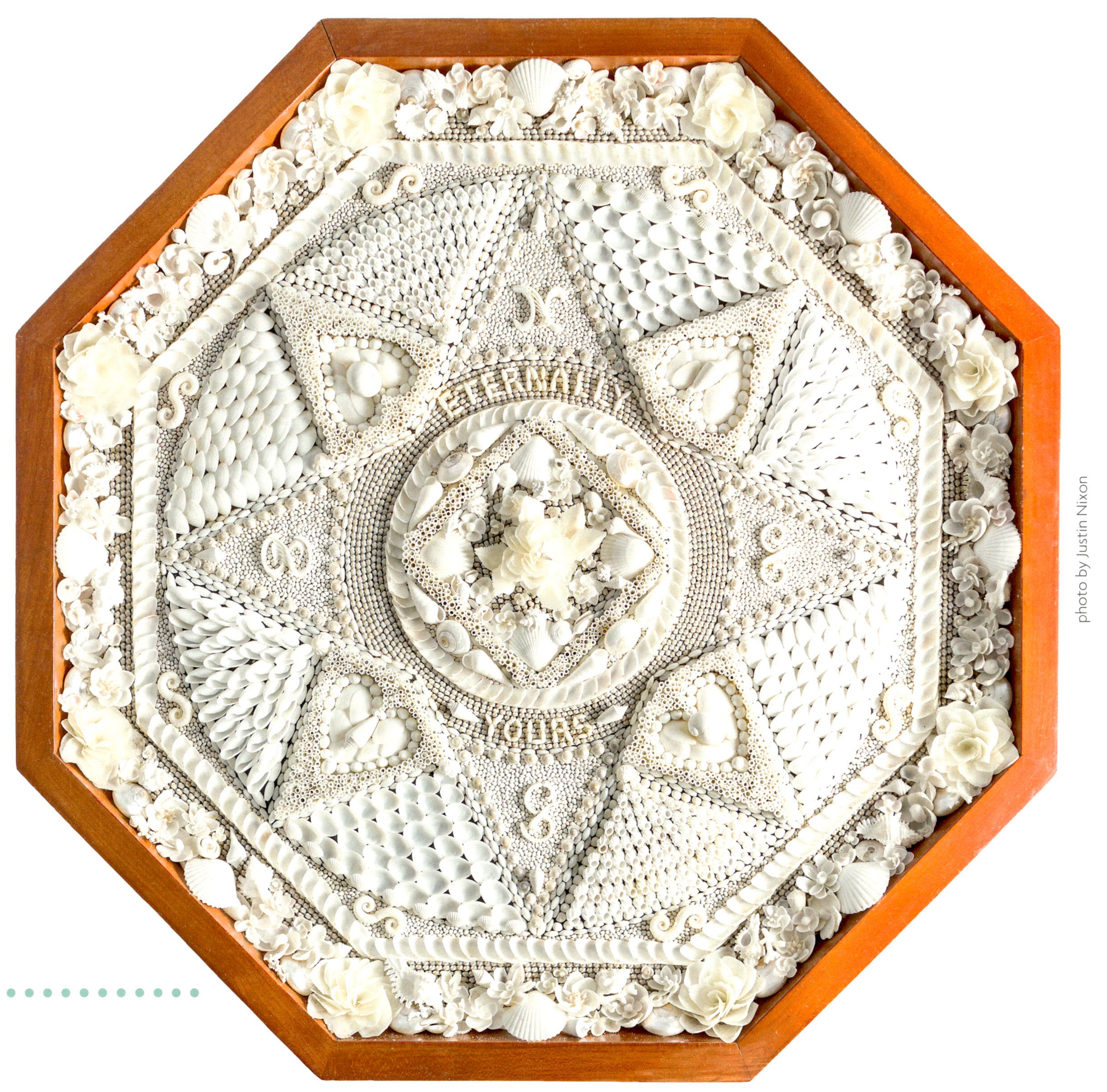

photo by Justin Nixon

Eternally Yours

Inspired by the striking effect that can be obtained with various shades of white shells and sealife.

22-inch cherry case made by Bruce Chandler

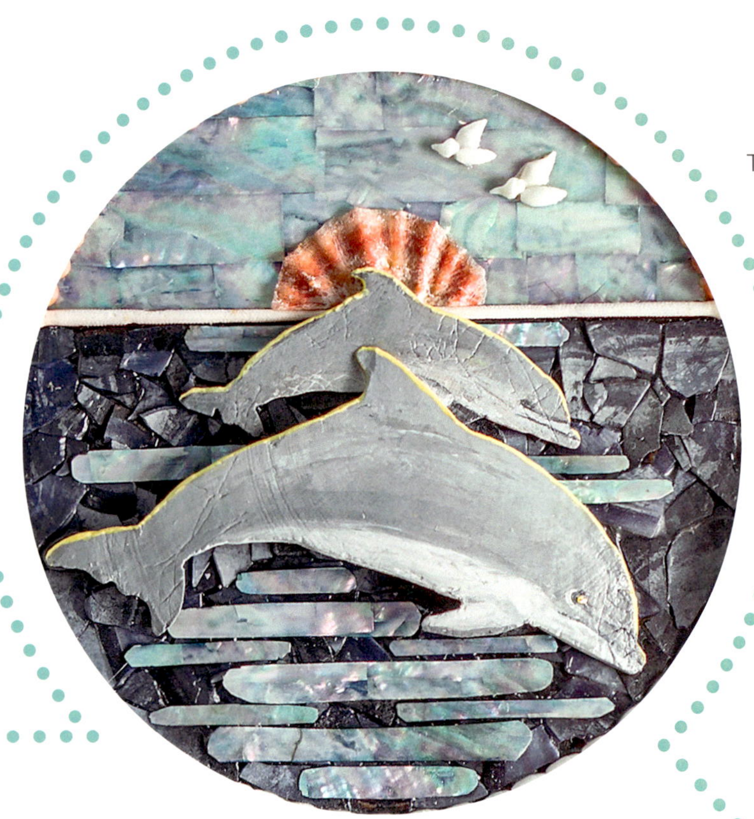

The sky and reflections on the water (made from crushed blue mussel shells) are cut from shell veneer. The dolphins were cut from a Japanese sun and moon shell. The pelicans in the sky are each made from a baby lightning whelk, a rice shell, and a Job's tear shell. The lush orange setting sun is a noble scallop.

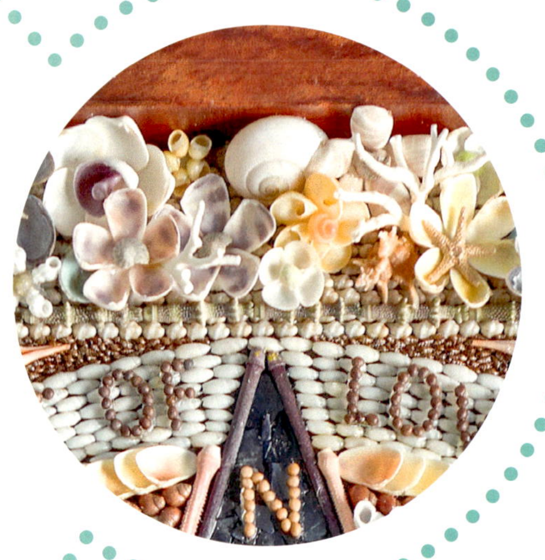

Coquina shells in various shades and different arrangements are used to create a variety of flowers.

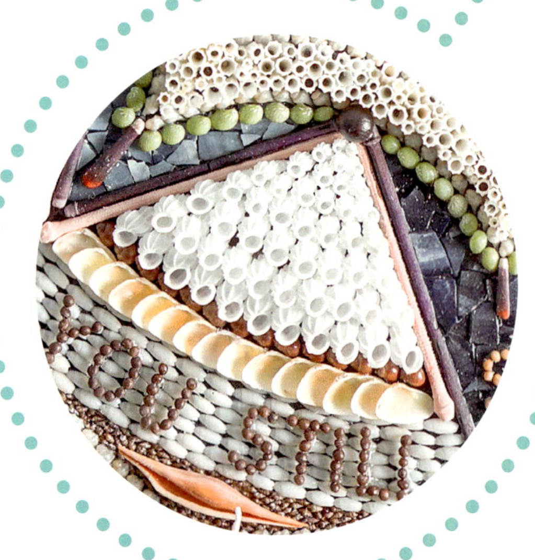

The artist uses wentletraps (seen in triangle here) in most of her Valentines, all collected on Sanibel Island by herself and her family.

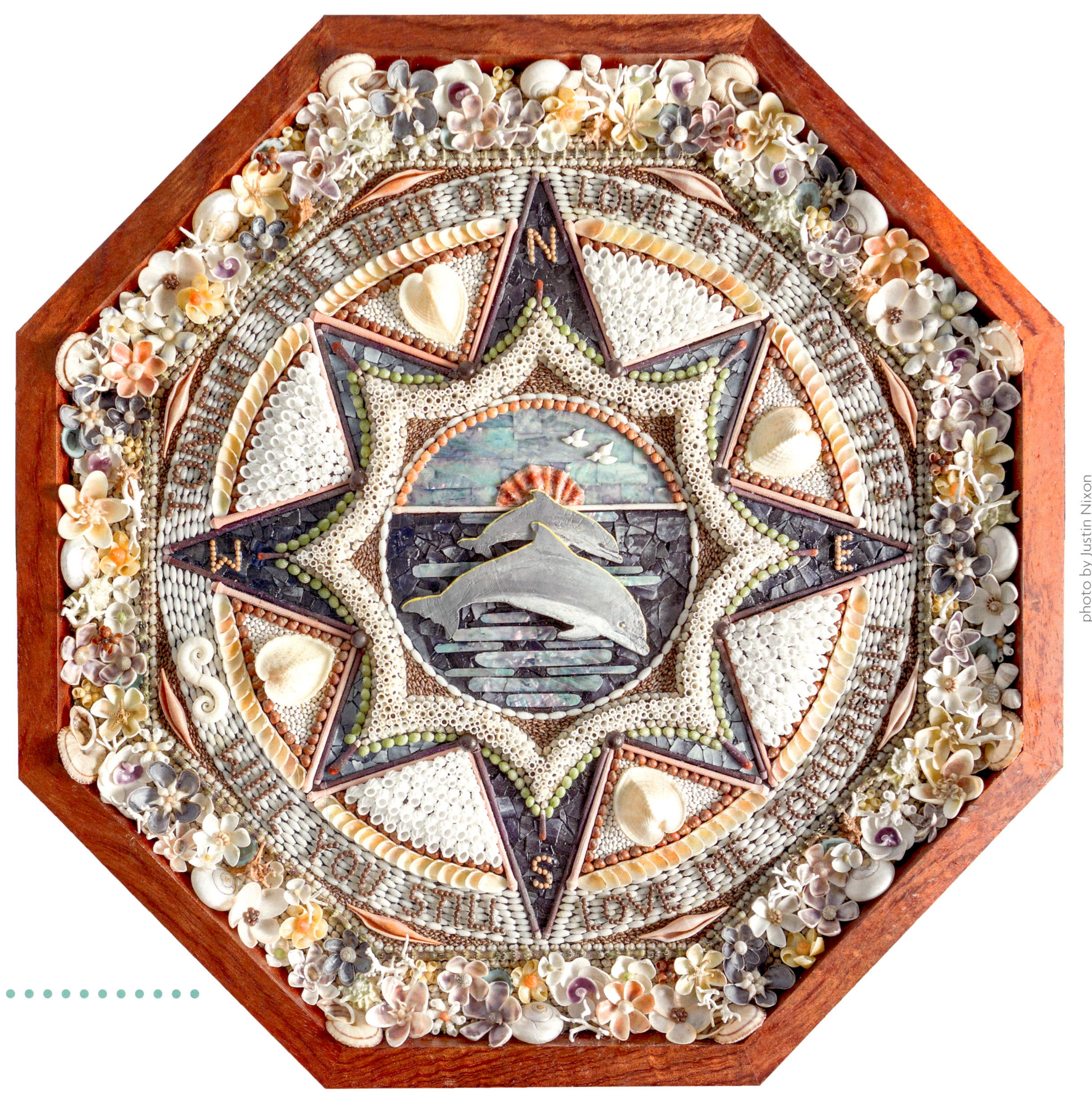

photo by Justin Nixon

The Light of Love

Inspired by the Shirelles hit "Will You Still Love Me Tomorrow."

15-inch walnut case with marquetry on the back, from the collection of Ann Schutt

photo by Dan Cutrona

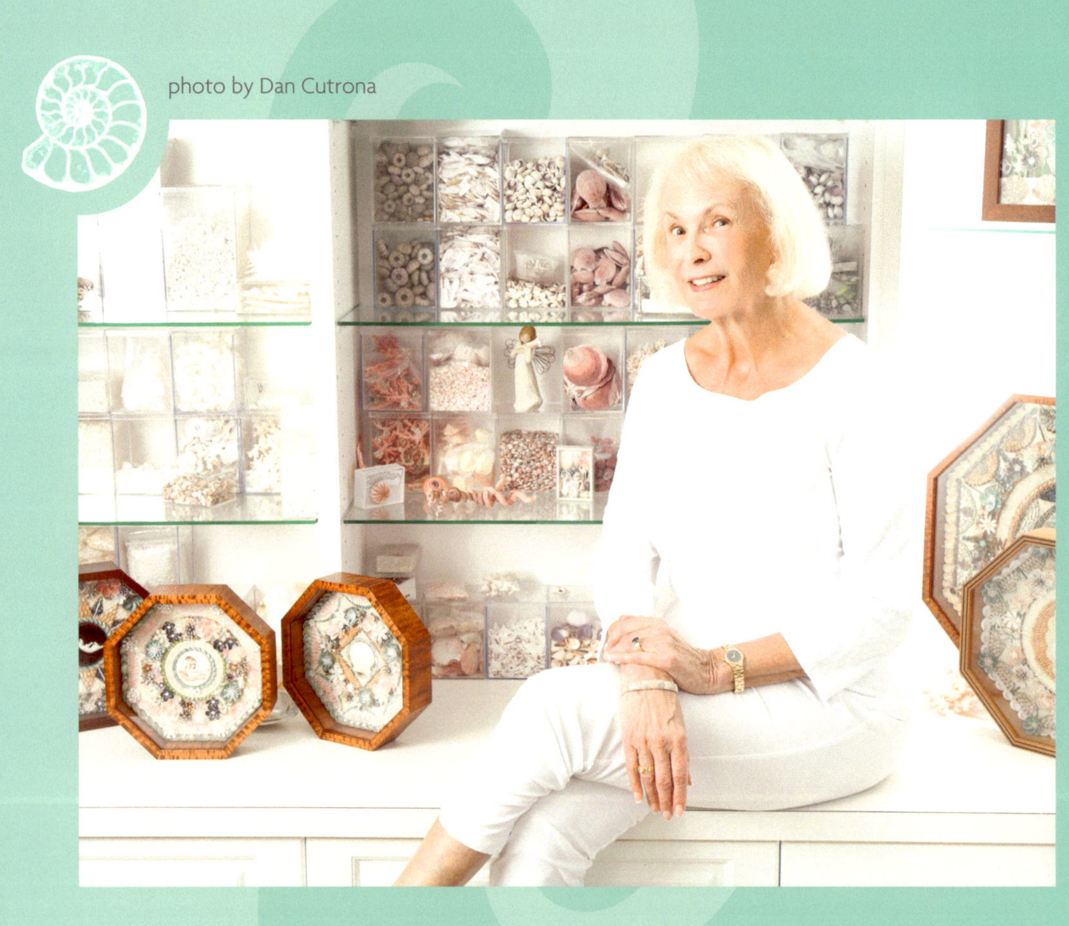

Sandy Moran

Sanibel Island, Florida

Having visited Sanibel Island for many years, I was continually called by the island's array of seashells, so in 1990 I moved there full-time and began a new chapter in my life with the creation of my business, Sailors' Valentine Studio. I have been creating Sailors' Valentines for 26 years now, and continue to have a steady stream of commissions and restoration work.

I was first inspired by these 19th-century works of shell art when I saw one at an antique show in Boston. I wanted to find out everything I could about Sailors' Valentines, shell art, and seashells. The stories behind the Valentines seemed so romantic. So I set out to see what colors and types of shells I could find to create my first piece.

After spending five years on Sanibel, I purchased a home on Cape Cod where I still spend the summer months. I have restored two antique homes on Cape Cod, but currently live and have my studio in a townhome in Yarmouth Port, Massachusetts. My northern and southern studios are both designed in the same manner, with white counters and cabinets, glass shelving, and clear acrylic containers displaying the hundreds of choices of shells available for my work.

My work is displayed in fine art galleries in Florida and on Cape Cod and Nantucket. I have been featured in national design and art publications such as the *Wall Street Journal* and *Martha Stewart Living*, as well as on the *Martha Stewart Show*. For many years I served as artistic chair of the Sanibel Shell Show, where I met many others who share a passion for this art. I recently started a new business, Seaside Productions, that will present shell shows throughout New England.

One of my favorite aspects of my business is offering workshops on Sailors' Valentines throughout the year on Sanibel and Cape Cod. It gives me pleasure to be able to share my years of experience with those just beginning or looking to improve upon their skills.

www.sailorsvalentinestudio.com

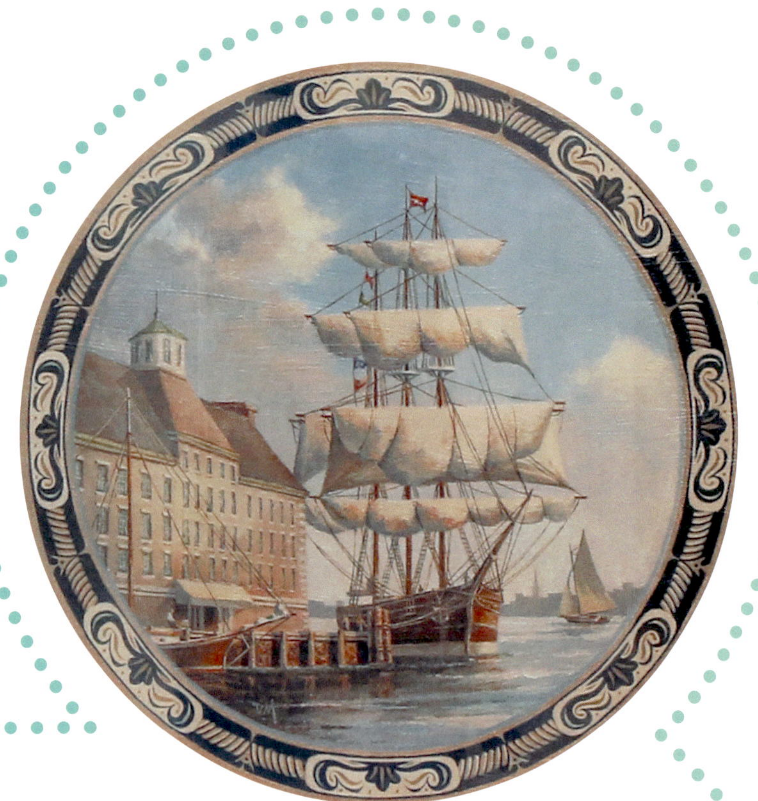

The painting of the Customs House in 1840 is oil on board done by David Monterio.

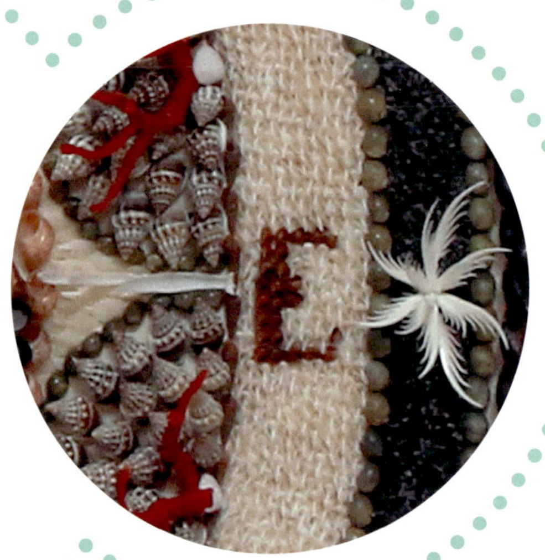

The directional letters are done with brown mustard seeds placed on baby whelk shells. To the right, a squilla claw flower adds movement; and to the left, pieces of red coral sit atop dove shells.

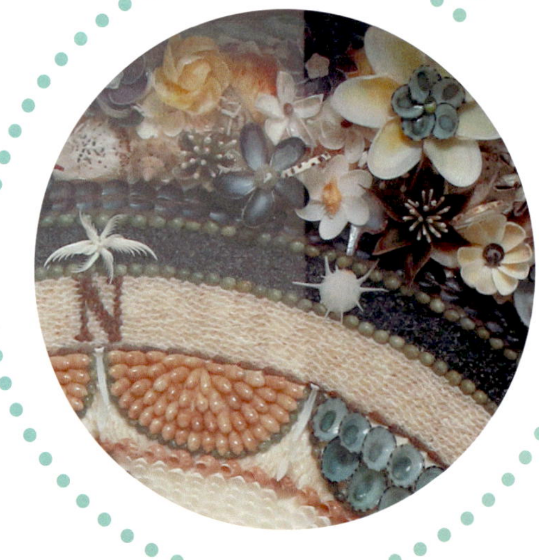

Around the outer edges, a peaceful feeling is imparted to this work through the blending of numerous colors of shell flowers (made from blue mussel shells, baby purple clams, yellow jingle shells, and coquina shells with blue-green operculums at the center).

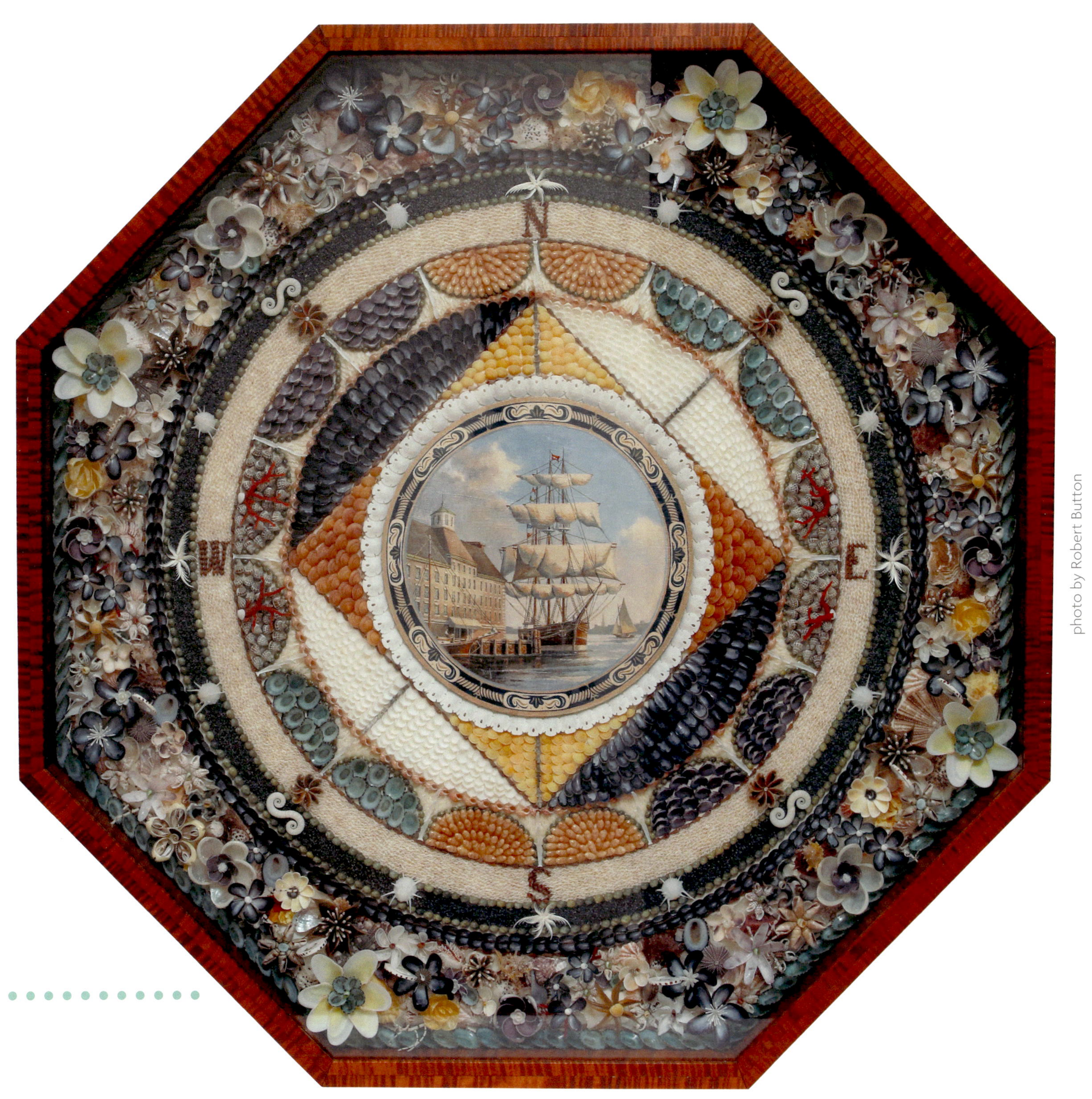

photo by Robert Button

Boston

Inspired by a photograph in the Nantucket Historical Association's archives of the Customs House on Long Wharf in Boston.

32-inch tiger maple case made by Jim Smith

A variety of different sizes and shapes of shells, dyed varying shades of blue, adds texture to the water behind the mermaid. She is carved from mammoth ivory. Green sea urchin spines stand upright at the top right, and blue mussel shells sit at the lower left. Small rocks collected by the artist on Cape Cod beaches are outlined with yellow land snails below.

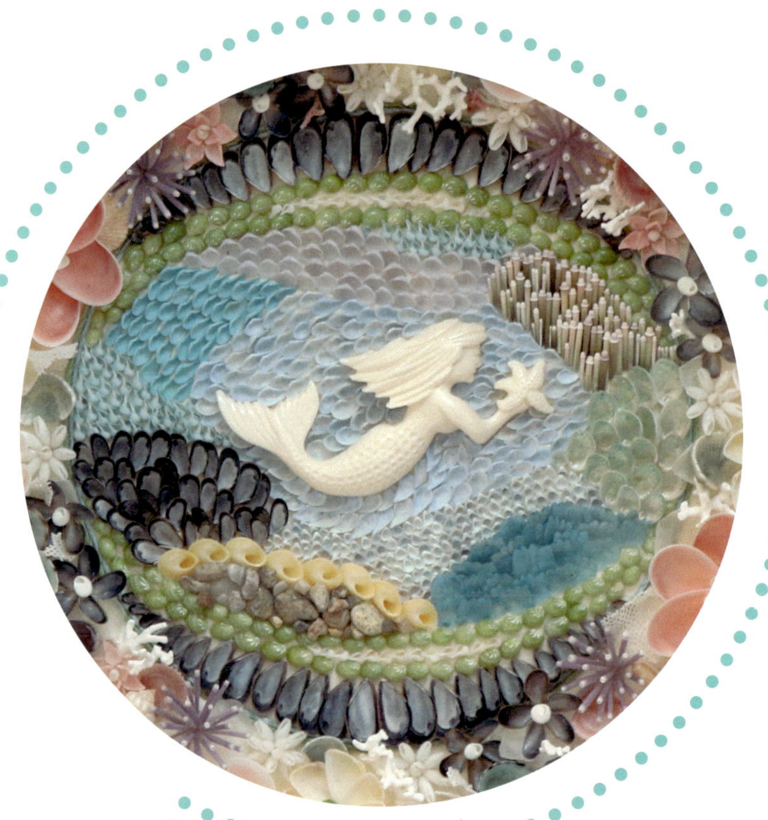

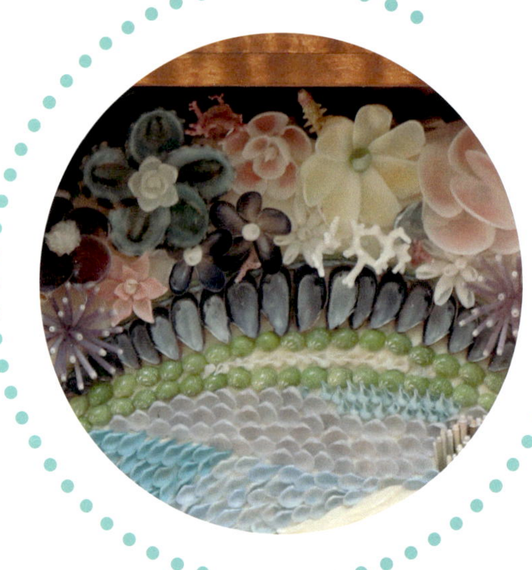

Striking blue-green limpets form a flower with a cup shell center. Beautiful pink rosecup and apple blossom shell flowers are scattered along the outer edges.

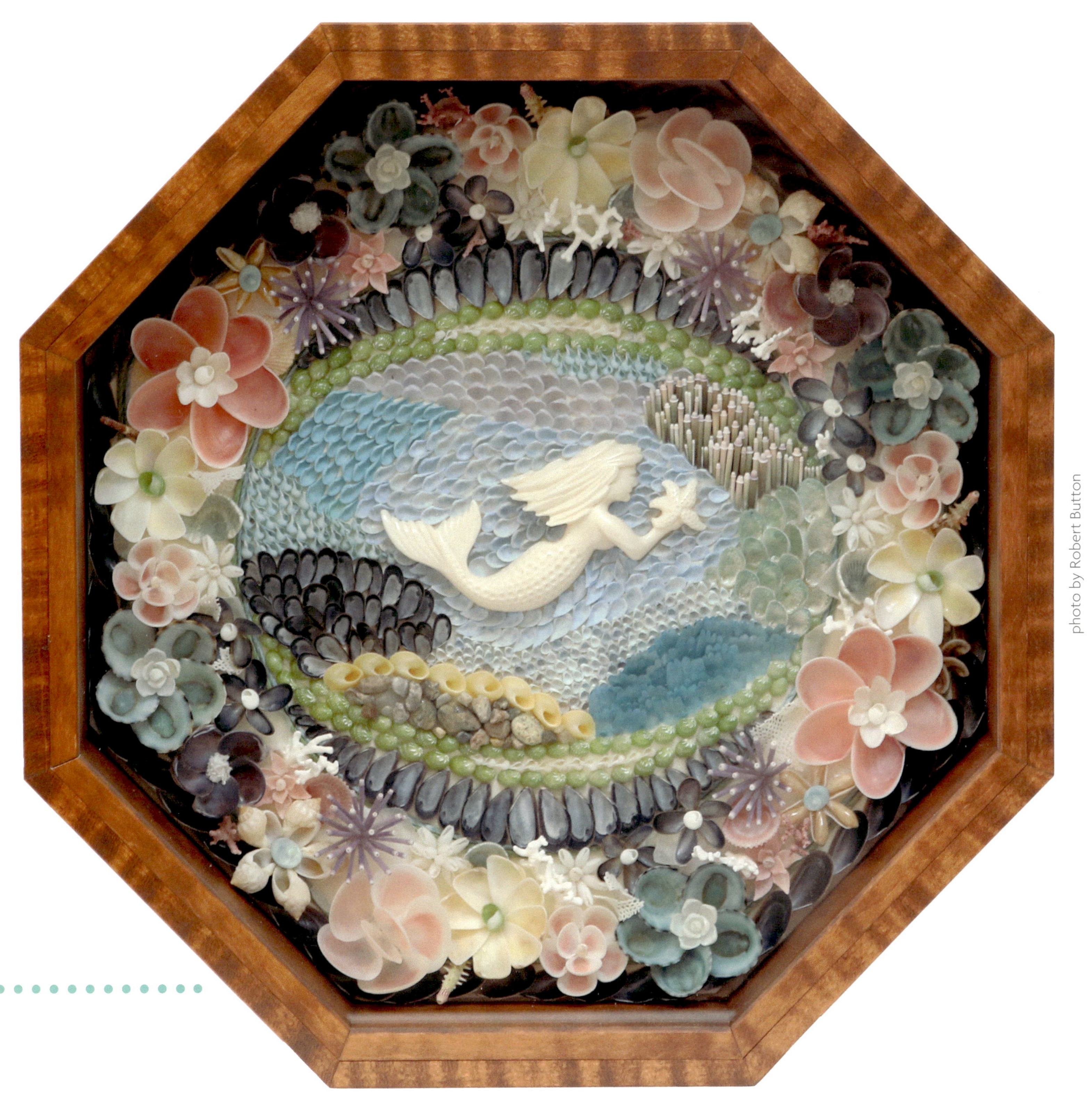

photo by Robert Button

Swimming Mermaid

Inspired by the gulf waters of Sanibel Island.

10-inch tiger maple case made by Jim Smith

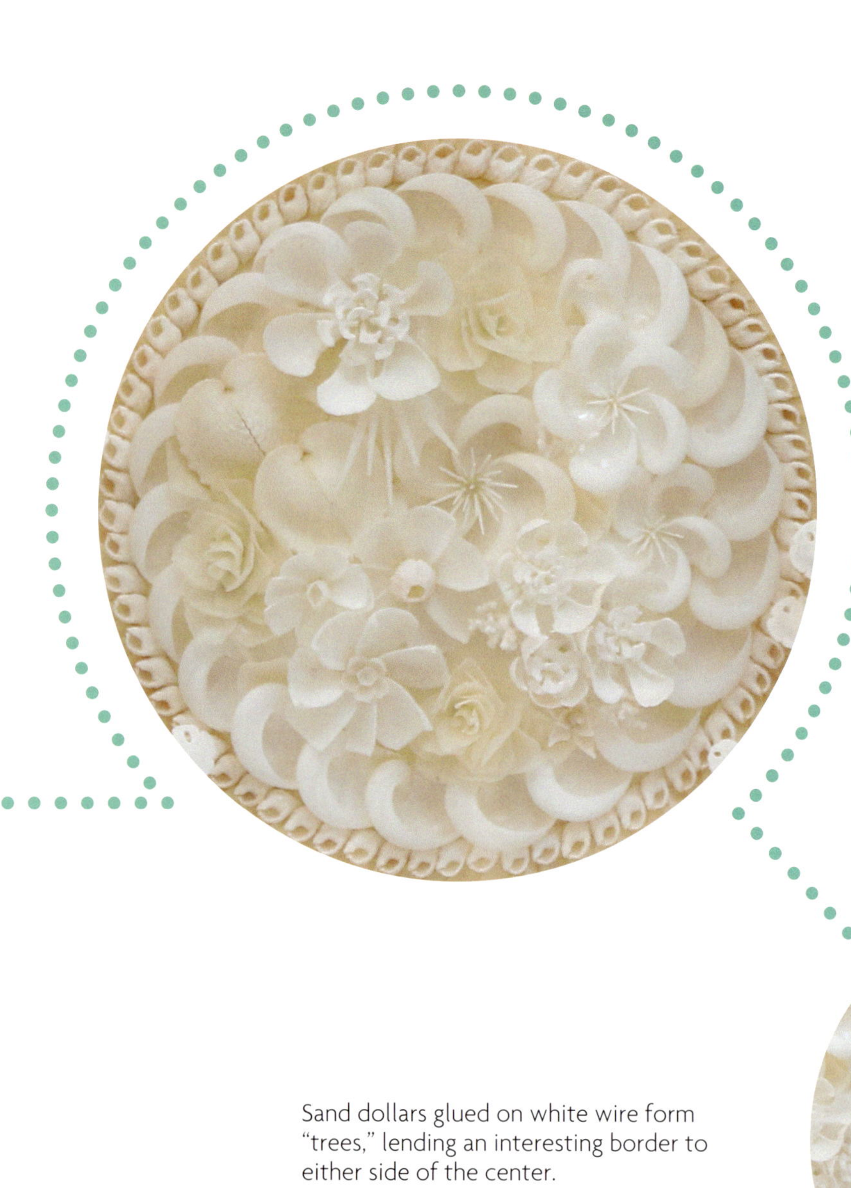

Upside-down baby's ear shells are laid in a circle around the center. Varying shades of white shell flowers, with heart cockles amid them, create a warmly colored centerpiece.

Sand dollars glued on white wire form "trees," lending an interesting border to either side of the center.

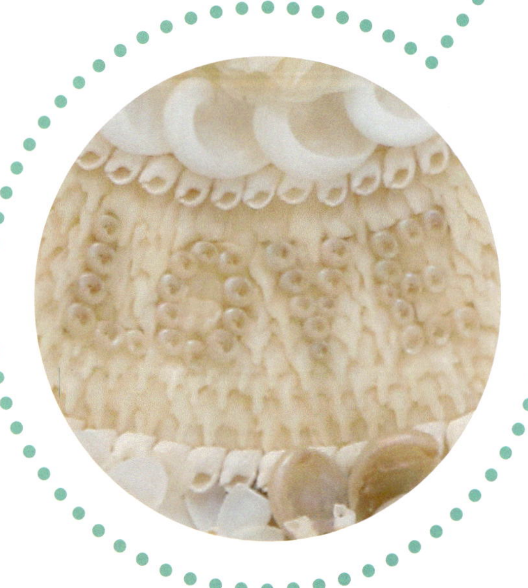

"Love" is spelled with upside-down Venetian pearl shells on top of hundreds of tiny ivory garfish scales that make up the circle surrounding the centerpiece.

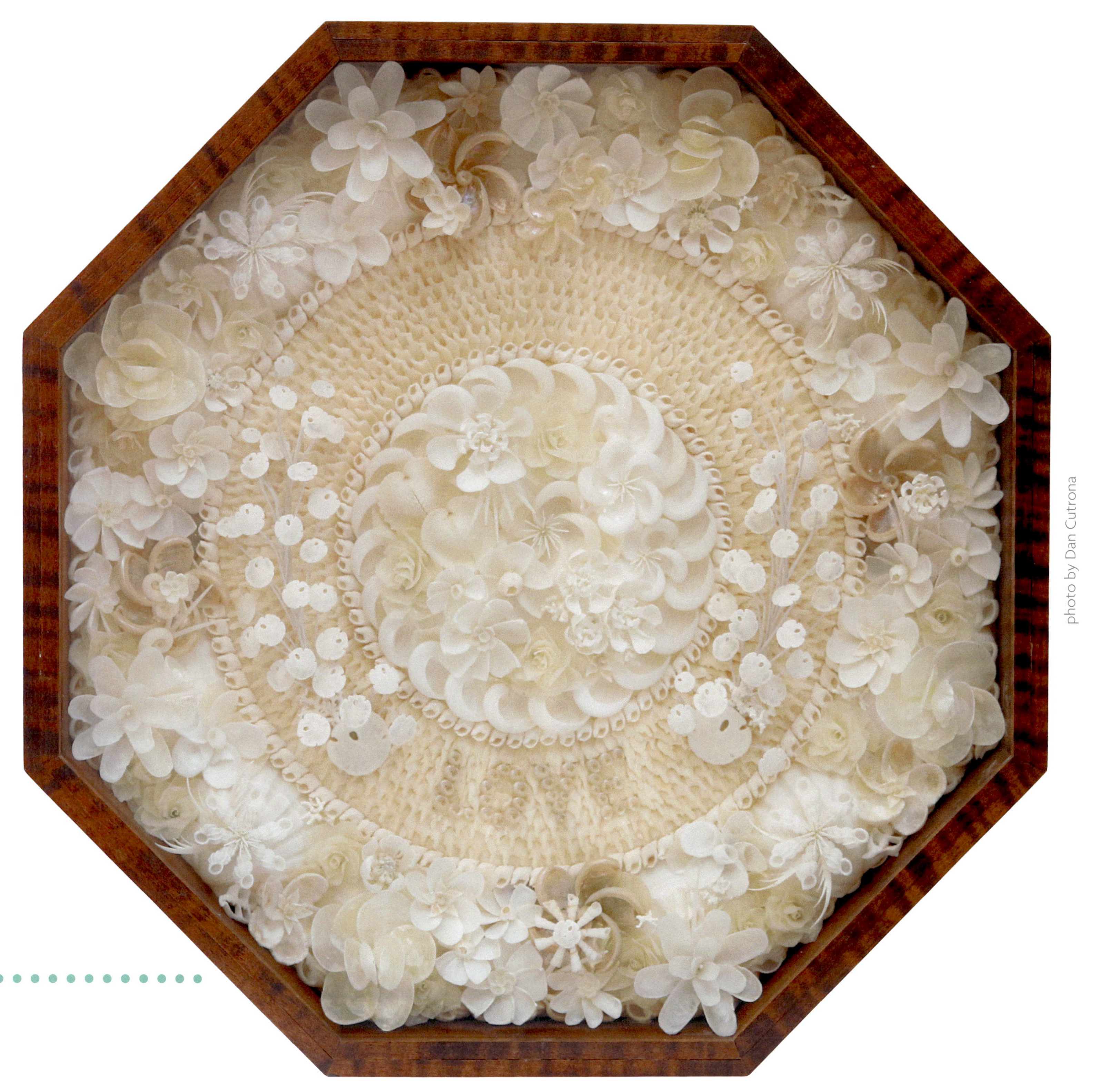

photo by Dan Cutrona

Love

Inspired by the wonders of weddings.

16-inch tiger maple case made by Jim Smith

The Nantucket basket was woven as a whole by Hank Haug, then cut in half to be filled with shell flowers. The basket sits on top of a layer of creamy white garfish scales. The circle outside the centerpiece was created with baby sand dollars.

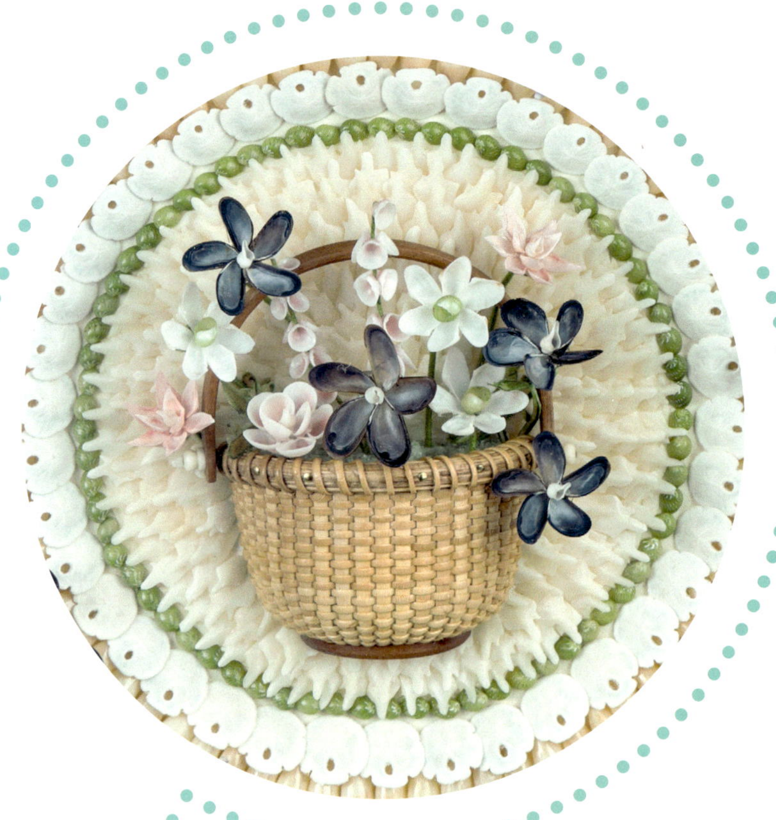

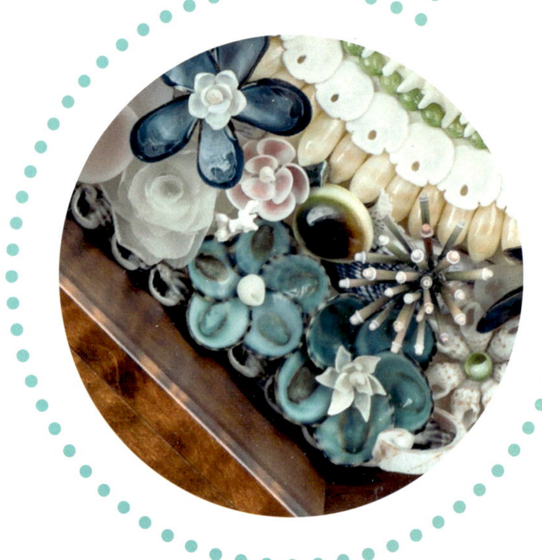

Blue-green limpet flowers add great depth of color to the outer edges.

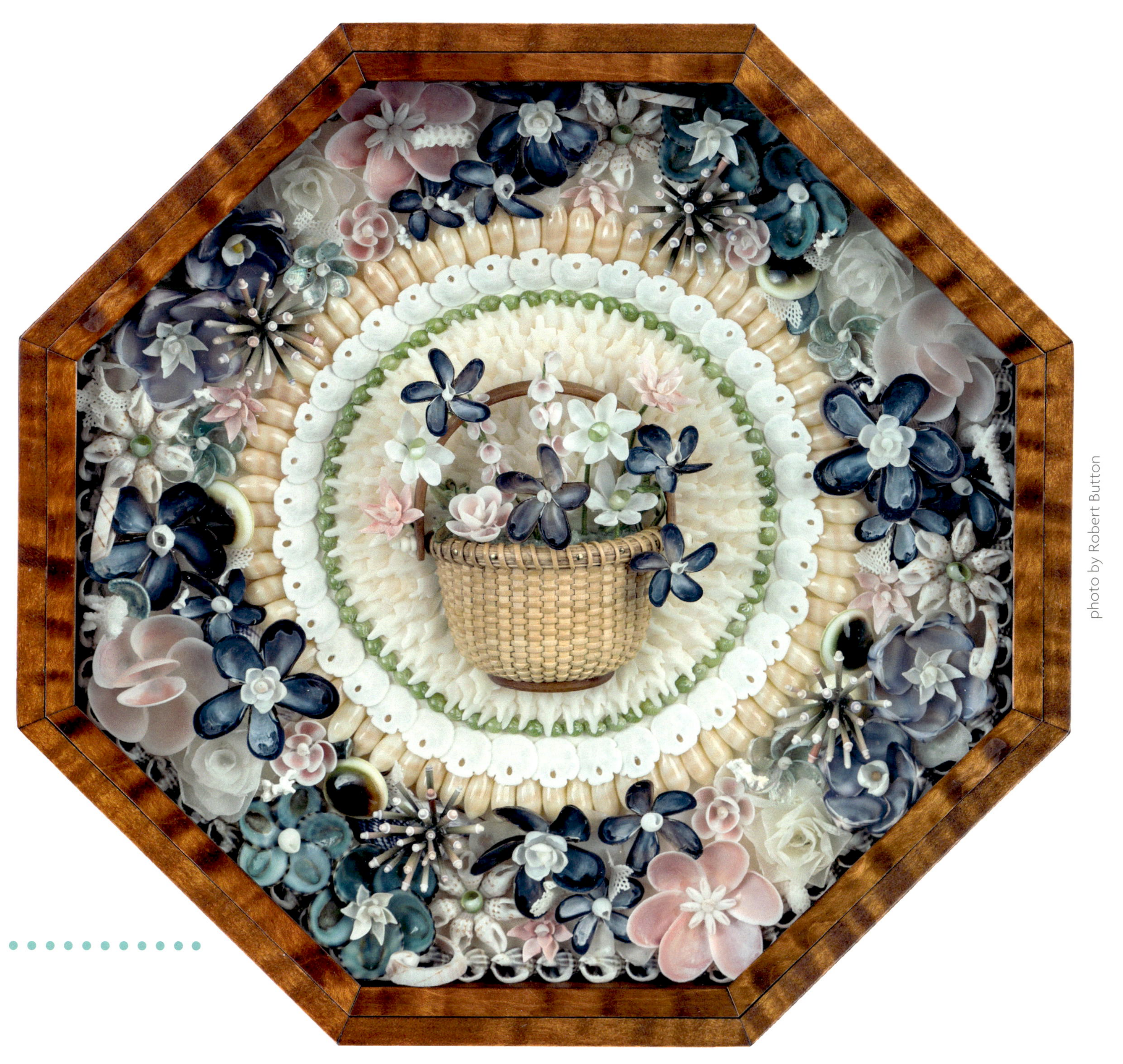

photo by Robert Button

Tiskit a Tasket

Inspired by a classic Nantucket basket handbag.

13-inch tiger maple case made by Jim Smith

photo by Lasting Impressions, Ft. Myers

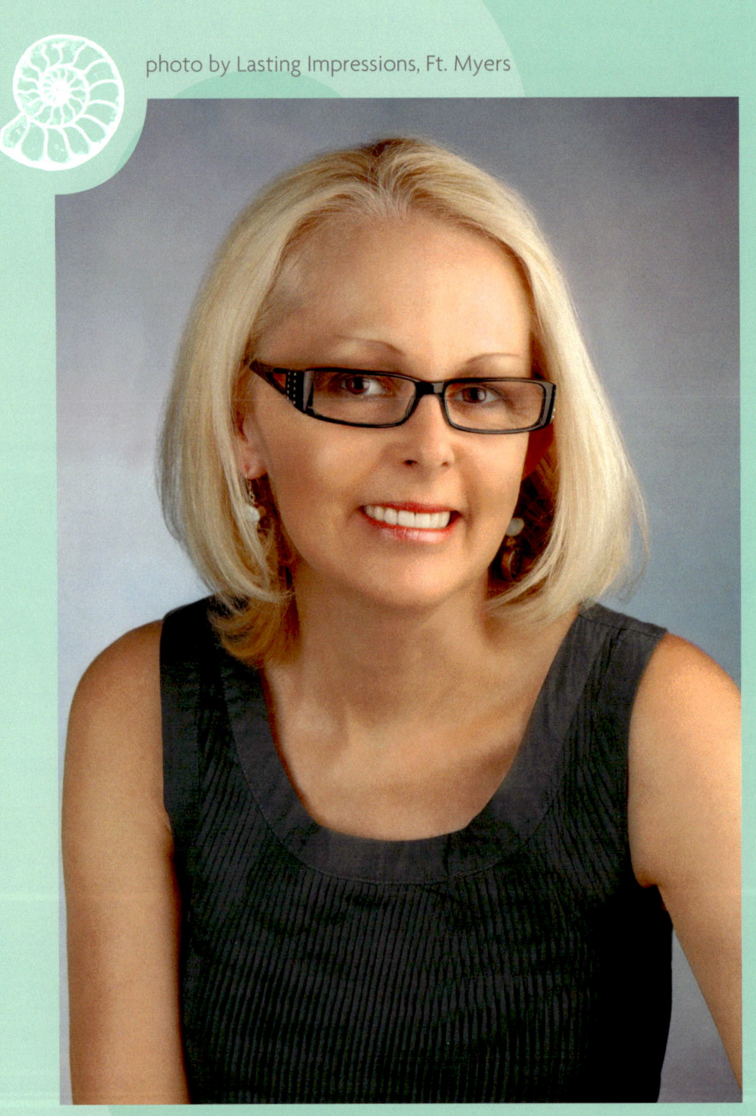

Audrey J. O'Donnell

Cape Coral, Florida

In 2003 I was visiting a friend in Barnstable, Cape Cod, and on the mantel was a Sailors' Valentine. My friend's mother was from Cotuit, Cape Cod, and was good friends with Bernie Woodman, the creator of this Valentine and one of the early contemporary Sailors' Valentine makers. Her family had a long history in Cotuit and also knew Ralph Cahoon, another of the early contemporary Sailors' Valentines artists who lived there.

I fell in love with the piece the moment I laid eyes on it and knew I had to make one. The owners were kind enough to allow me to borrow the piece so that I could study it, and this led me to doing research on Sailors' Valentines. I found information at the Falmouth Historical Society and the New Bedford Whaling Museum, as well as other maritime museums.

In 2004 I took a class on making Sailors' Valentines that was sponsored by the Cahoon Museum. I was hooked. I showed my piece from the class to a professional Valentine artist, who said, "It looks like a big mass of shells." I laugh now, but the comment inspired me to improve. My second attempt was a 20-inch case with a mermaid wedding party in the center. The mermaids' tails were all done with jingle shells self-collected on Cape Cod beaches. The piece was quite elaborate and a big undertaking for my second piece, but I learned a lot from the process and will never part with it.

My favorite piece is *Elegance*, a 14-inch Victorian-style Valentine that took more than 1,700 hours to make (see pages 158–159). It is my version of an 1850s Valentine that was in the collection of Queen Mary and was gifted to the Victoria and Albert Museum in London in 1923. This piece required thousands of white rice shells, which are my favorite shell to work with, as I love the wire-wrapping process.

My studio is like an art gallery. I have a collection of antique rice shell baskets as well as several I have made myself, along with other shell art and an endless collection of shell books. I never tire of spending time in this space.

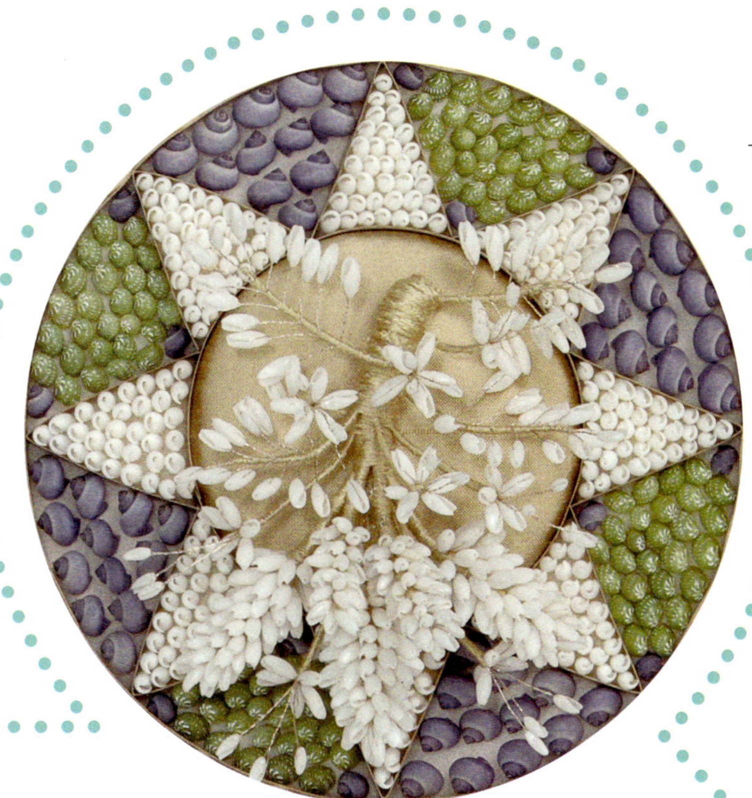

The center circle depicts flowers, leaves, and grapevines typical of Victorian-era Valentines. More than 1,000 rice shells are wired for the center and the outer circle, and they are surrounded by emerald nerites and purple janthinas. This Valentine is done on cotton batting, as was typical of the early 1800s pieces.

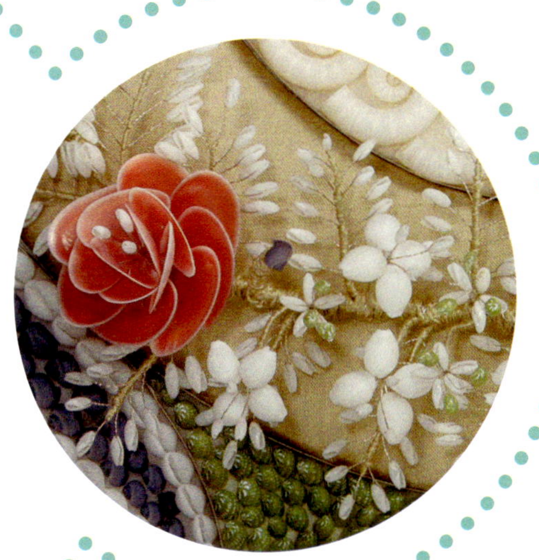

A flower made from rose petal tellins adds rich color, and white rice shells form the leaves. White trivia shell flowers are to the right. No glue was used in the center or outer gold silk circles; the work is all done with silk thread. This valentine took over 1,700 hours to create.

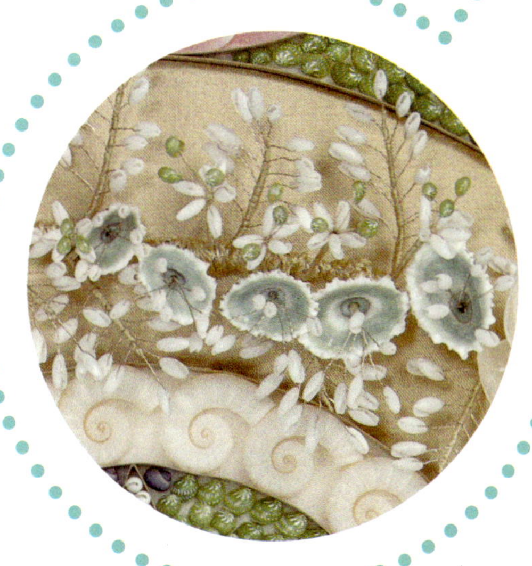

Keyhole limpets from Barbados form subtle greenish-gray flowers.

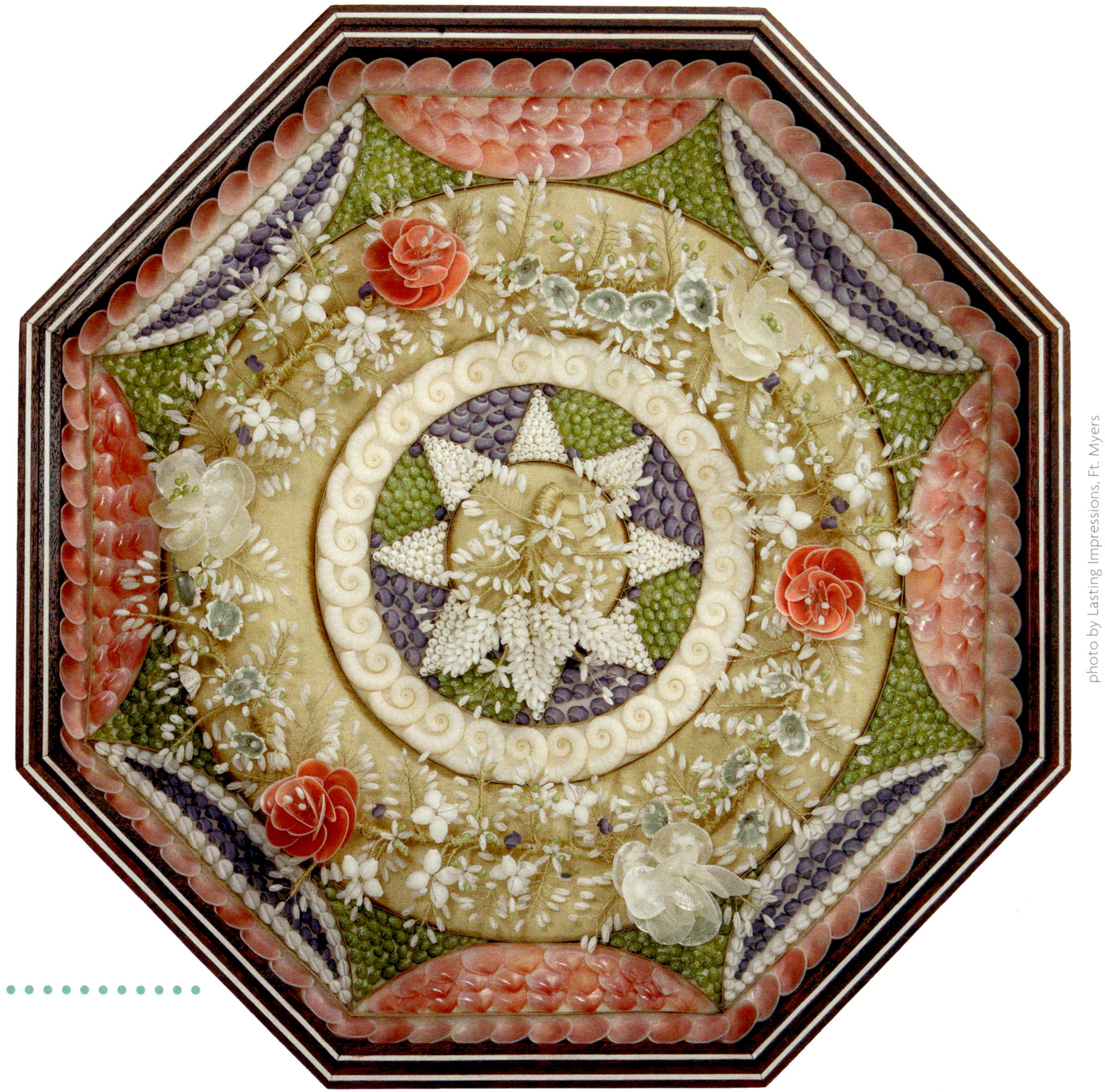

photo by Lasting Impressions, Ft. Myers

Elegance

Inspired by a Sailors' Valentine that was in the collection of Queen Mary and gifted by her to the Victoria and Albert Museum in London in 1923.

14-inch walnut case with white inlay made by Bill Jordan

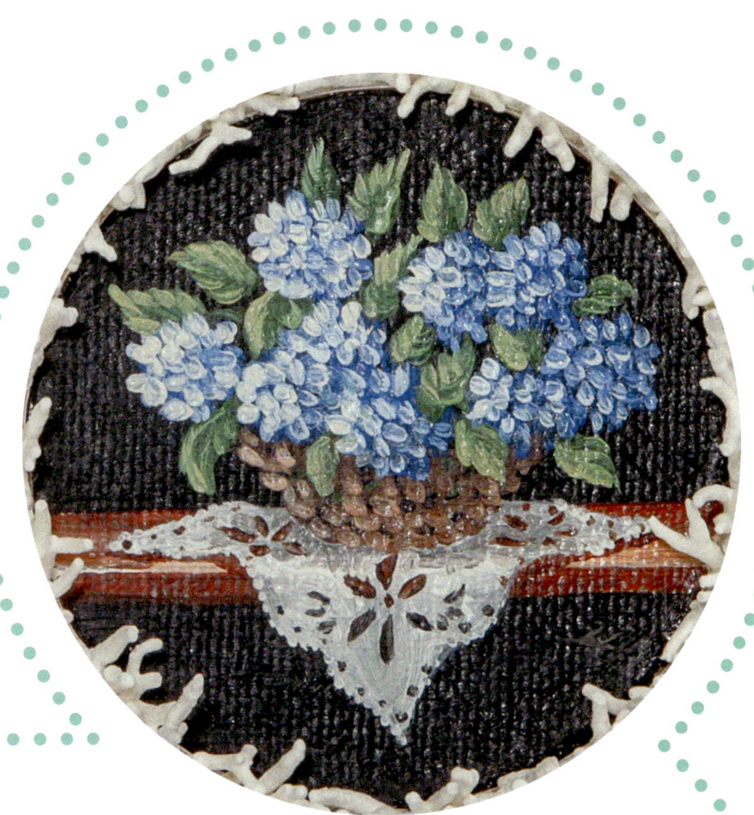

An oil painting by Anna Lowther features a Nantucket basket filled with deep blue hydrangeas on a table with a lace tablecloth. Coralized algae surrounds the painting.

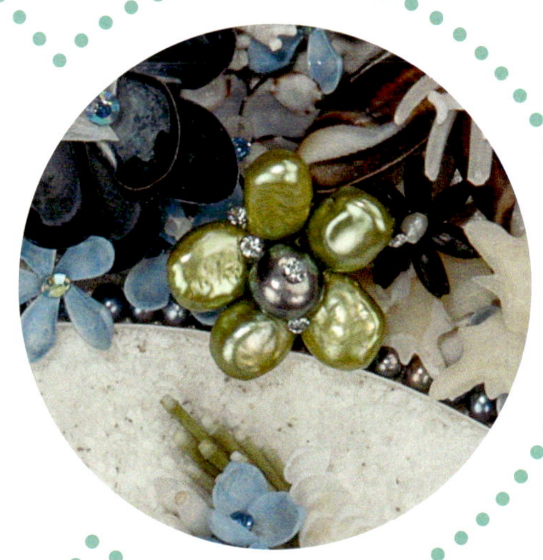

A keshi pearl flower with a black pearl center and faceted Swarovski crystals.

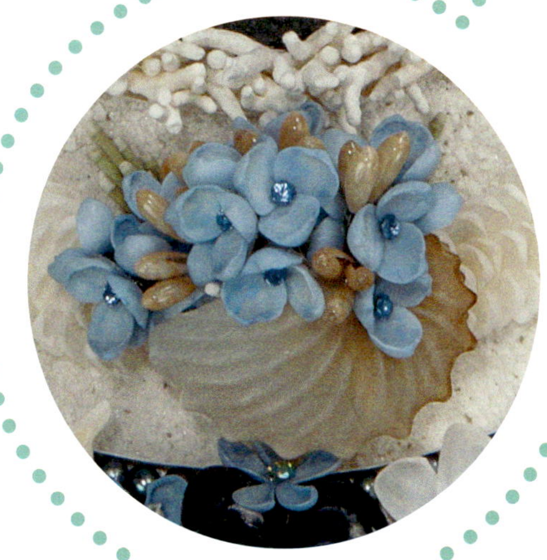

A paper nautilus shell holds a tiny bouquet of dyed blue cup shell flowers with vintage Swarovski crystals in the centers.

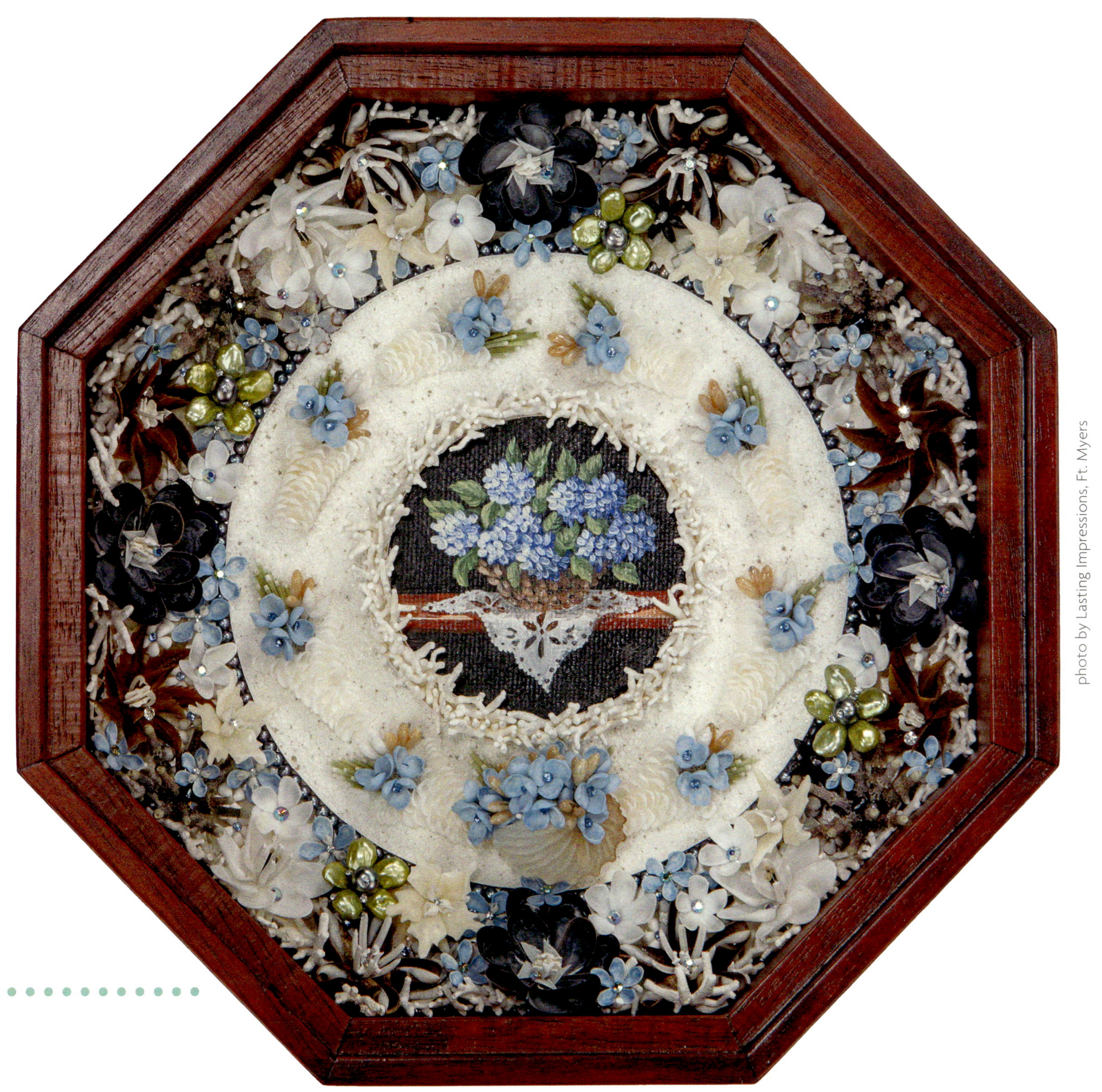

photo by Lasting Impressions, Ft. Myers

Endless Summer

Inspired by the endless blue hydrangeas on Cape Cod that bloom all summer long and on into October.

9-inch mahogany case made by Hans Sagemuehl

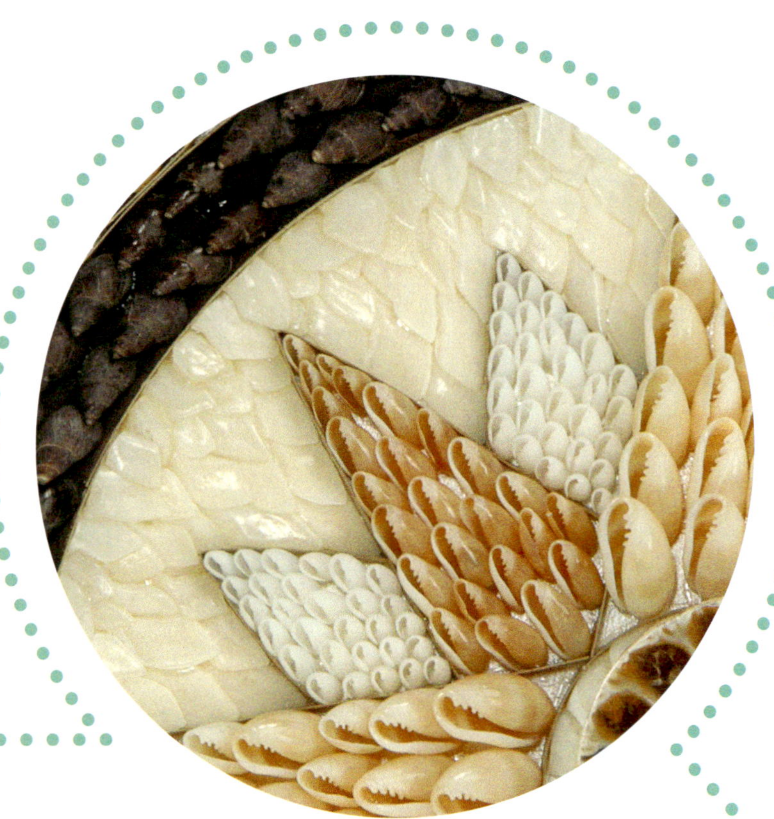

Texture is created by angled white rice shells beside tan Philippine rice shells.

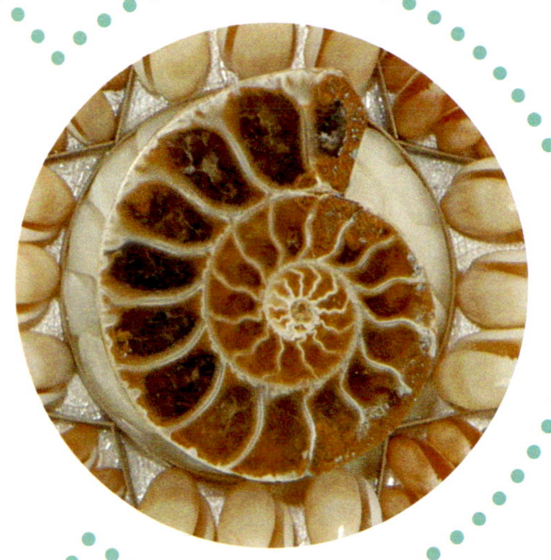

An ammonite in the center reveals the spiral shape of the internal chamber of this fossil shell.

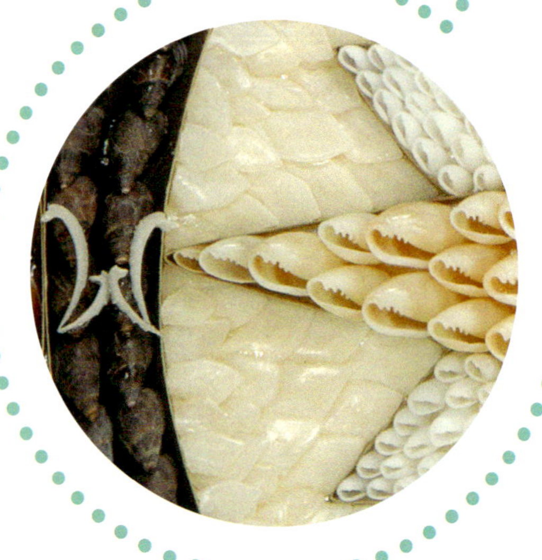

Garfish scales are filed to fit in the circular center, and gooseneck barnacle pieces form the "W" for west.

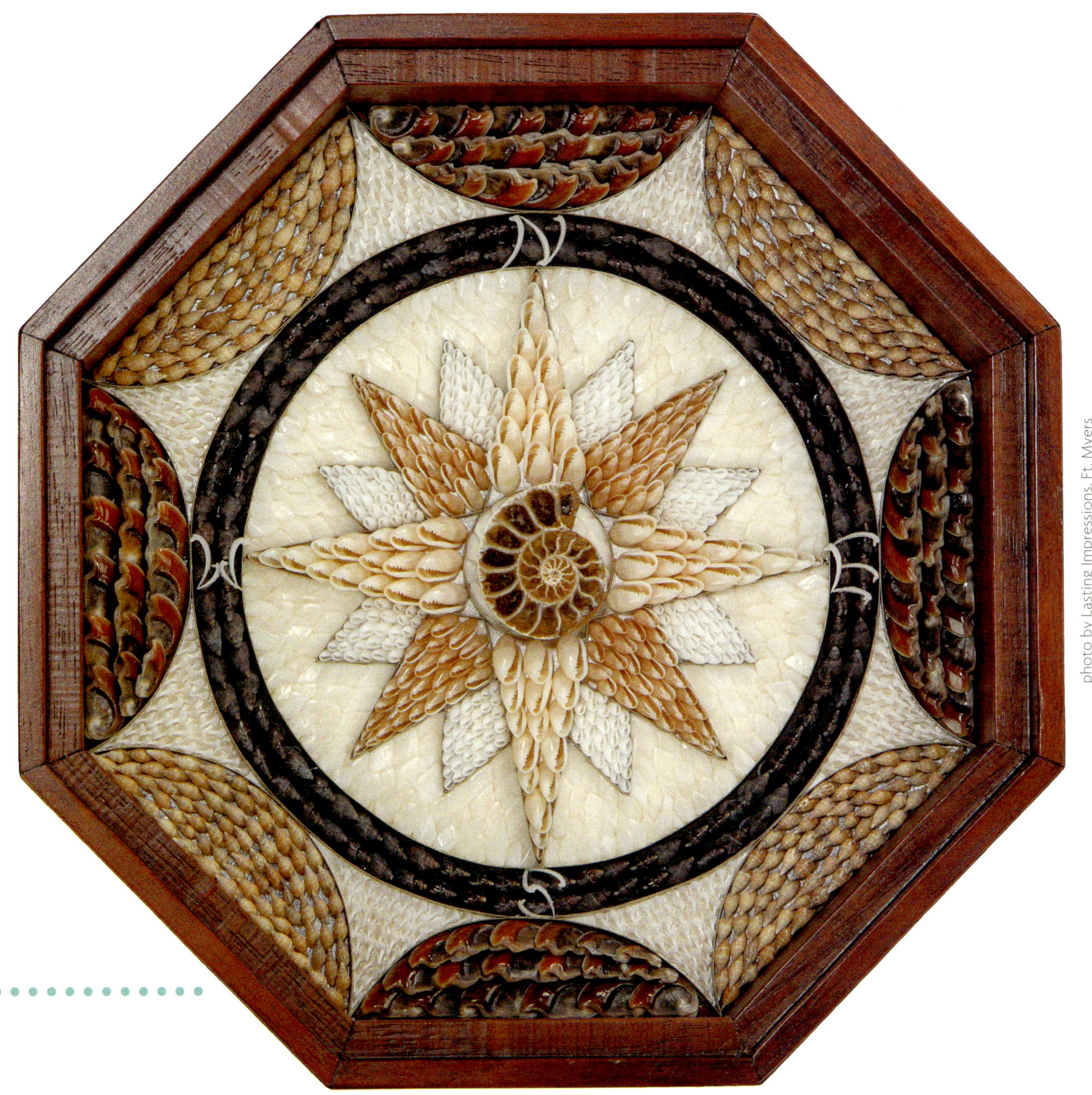

photo by Lasting Impressions, Ft. Myers

Latitudes

This piece was commissioned by the builder of the artist's home, called Latitude 26, in Cape Coral, Florida. He wanted the piece to include a compass rose with no flowers and asked that it be done in the colors of his travertine and onyx floors.

9-inch mahogany case made by Hans Sagemuehl

Fish scales with pieces of gooseneck barnacles in the center create delicate roses. They sit on top of a circle of sand dollars surrounded by a ring of freshwater pearls.

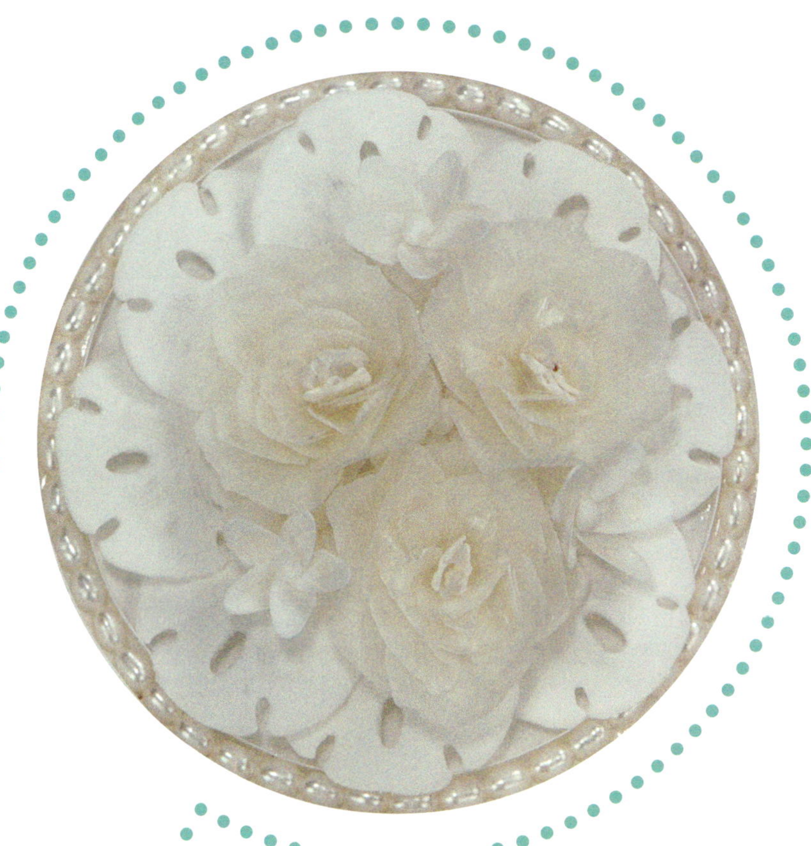

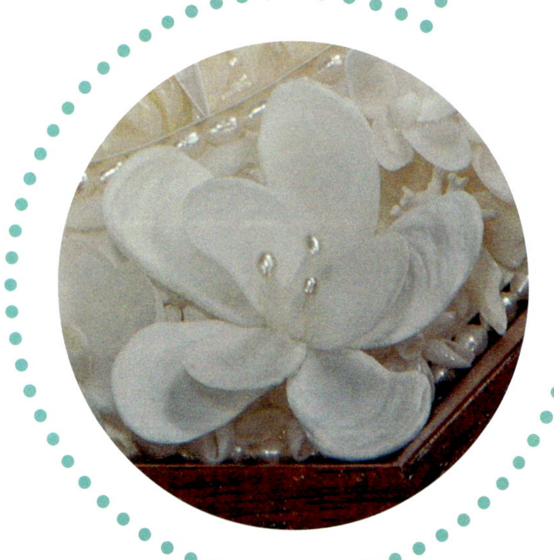

White slipper shells form this flower with a center of tusk shells that have pearls suspended on top.

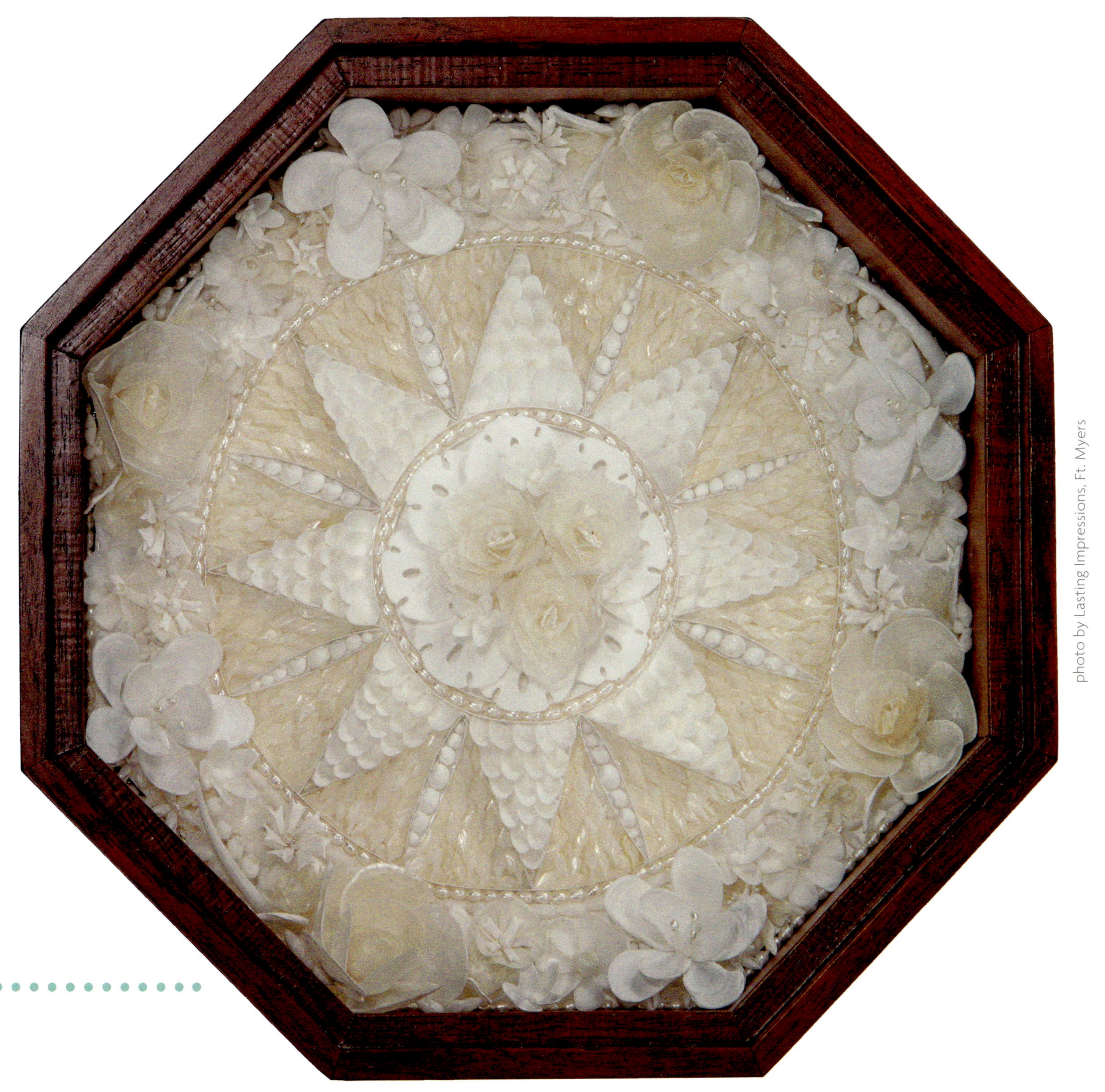

photo by Lasting Impressions, Ft. Myers

Everlasting Love

Inspired by romantic summer weddings on Cape Cod.

9-inch mahogany case made by Hans Sagemuehl

A small larimar heart sits on top of blue abalone inlay from New Zealand. Surrounding it are pieces of coralized algae and a row of blue pearls.

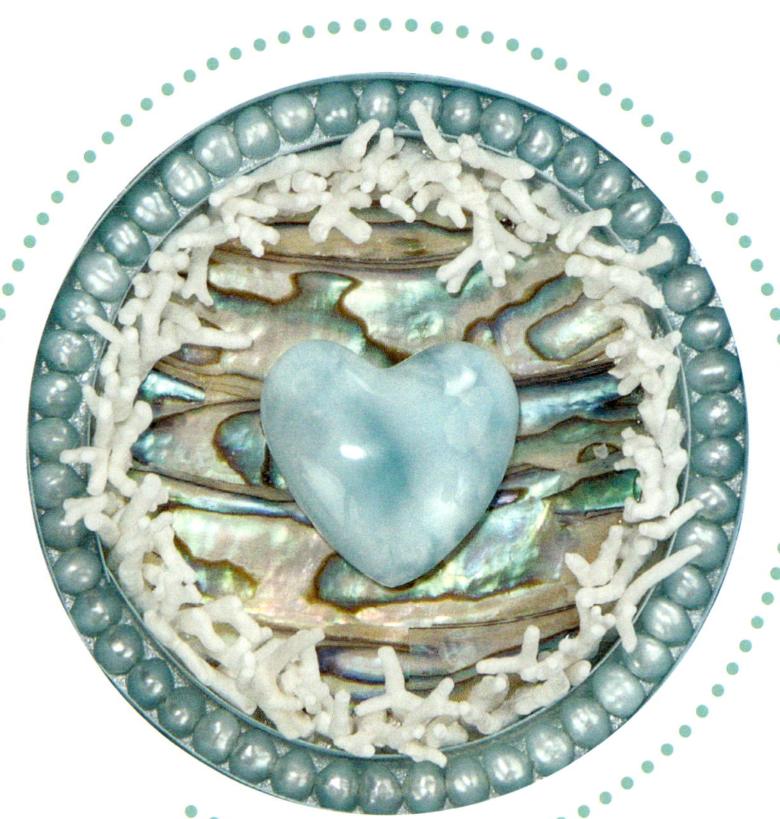

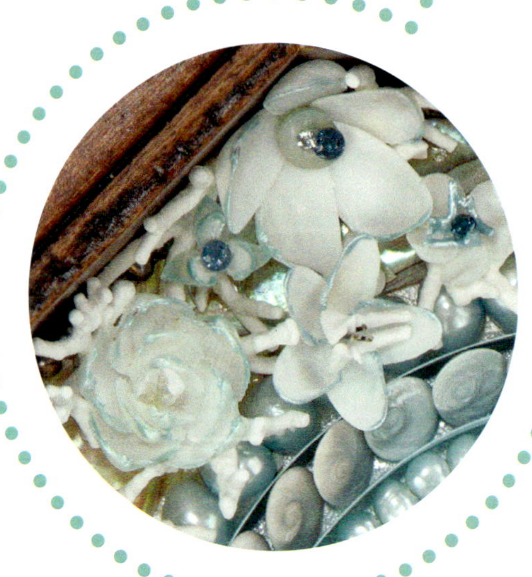

The artist has lightly painted the edges of various white shell flowers with metallic paint that matches the color of the larimar and inlay. Blue sapphires adorn the coquina shell and white operculum flowers. Layers of coralized algae collected from Key West beaches are placed throughout.

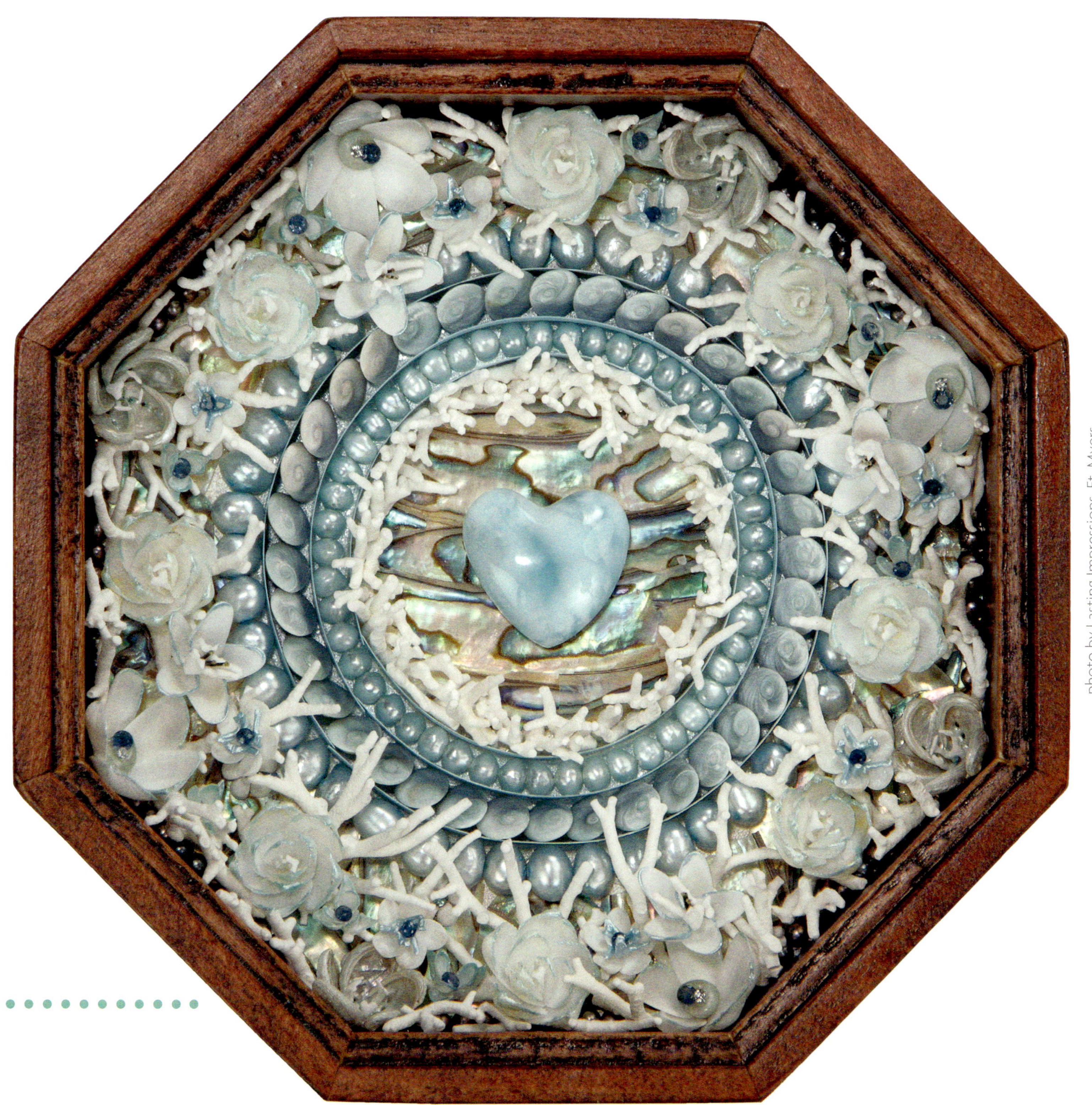

photo by Lasting Impressions, Ft. Myers

Heartbeat

Inspired by the colors of the sea and sky.

5-inch mahogany case made by Hans Sagemuehl

photo by Bruce Reid

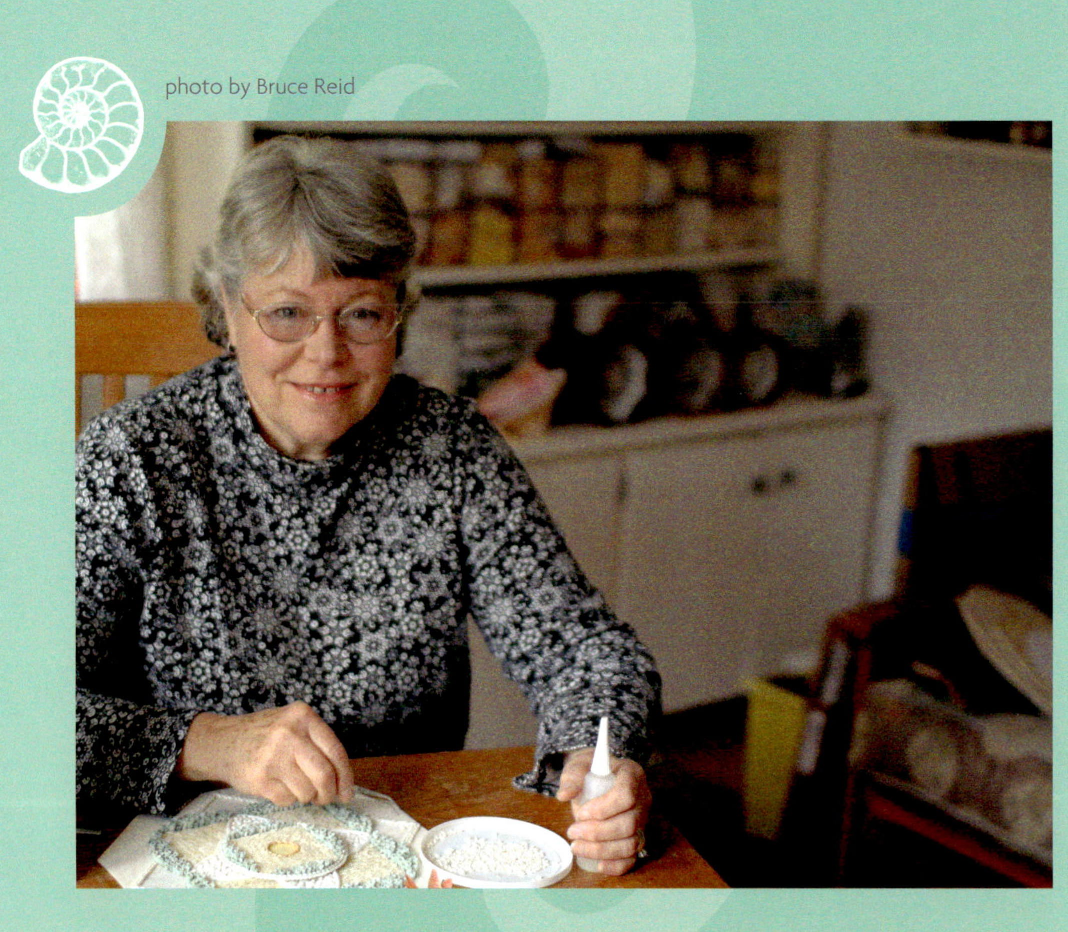

Gerda Reid

Marstons Mills, Massachusetts

I was fascinated when I first saw a Sailors' Valentine in 1999. A friend of mine had taken some lessons and proudly showed me her finished piece. I was taken with the depth, color, and variation of the shells, and I began to study Valentines at galleries and museums, taking note of techniques and design.

I am self-taught and my work is entirely my own creation, including shell work (mosaics), inlays, scrimshaw, and artwork. I also design and construct my own Valentine boxes from mahogany, cherry, maple, ebony, and other select hardwoods.

Much of my work contains shells I have collected on the beaches of Cape Cod, Florida, and Barbados. I only use shells that are natural in color; nothing is ever dyed. My designs are intricate and precise, bright and cheery, and very colorful, with attention to shading.

I was born in Germany and immigrated to the United States when I was six years old. My father, an artist and designer, passed on to me his love for the fine arts. I graduated from Kean University with a dual major in fine arts and biology. For years I worked as a biological illustrator for Kean, creating images from microscopic slides and live specimens. I have engaged in a variety of mediums in my life: ceramics, painting, pen and ink, marquetry, Ukrainian Easter eggs, quilting and other needlework, and silk screening. My hands are always busy.

I value my many friendships in the community of Sailors' Valentine artists and enjoy trading ideas, supplies, and techniques with them. With each new Valentine my methods and techniques improve, and participating in competitive shows constantly challenges my skills.

Following my husband's retirement we moved to Cape Cod, where we enjoy our many hobbies and sports. If I am not working on a Valentine at my dining room table, you'll find me in the garden, sailing, windsurfing, shelling, or repairing sails. But one of the things I enjoy most is sharing my interest in this art form with others by offering lessons, lectures, and demonstrations.

www.sylviaantiques.com

The catboat sail is made from baby whelk shells, as are the spars and hull. The sky is done with crushed bearded and green mussel shells, and the water with crushed blue mussel shells. The lettering is done from white rice shells and brown mustard seeds. Blue operculums and green urchin spines are used for the flowers on the sides.

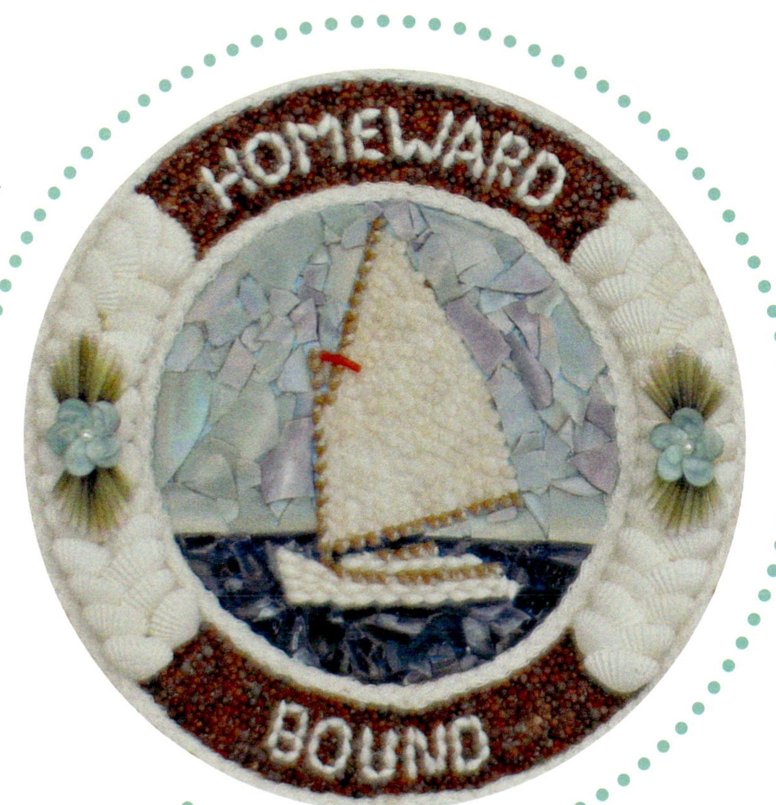

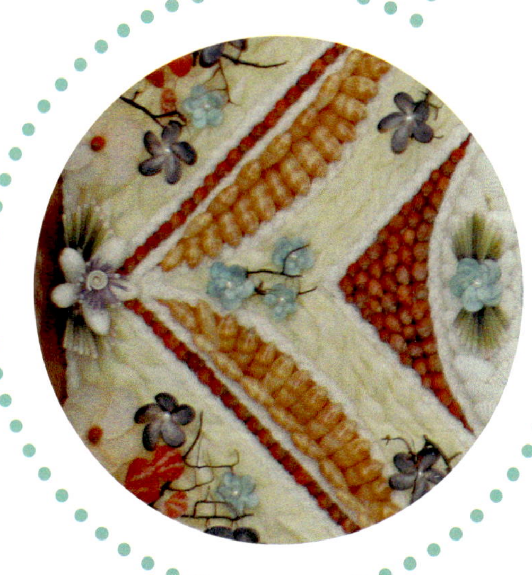

The outer flower is embellished with purple and green urchin spines. The tan shells are Philippine rice shells, and the triangle to the right is made with red snail shells. The background is done with garfish scales.

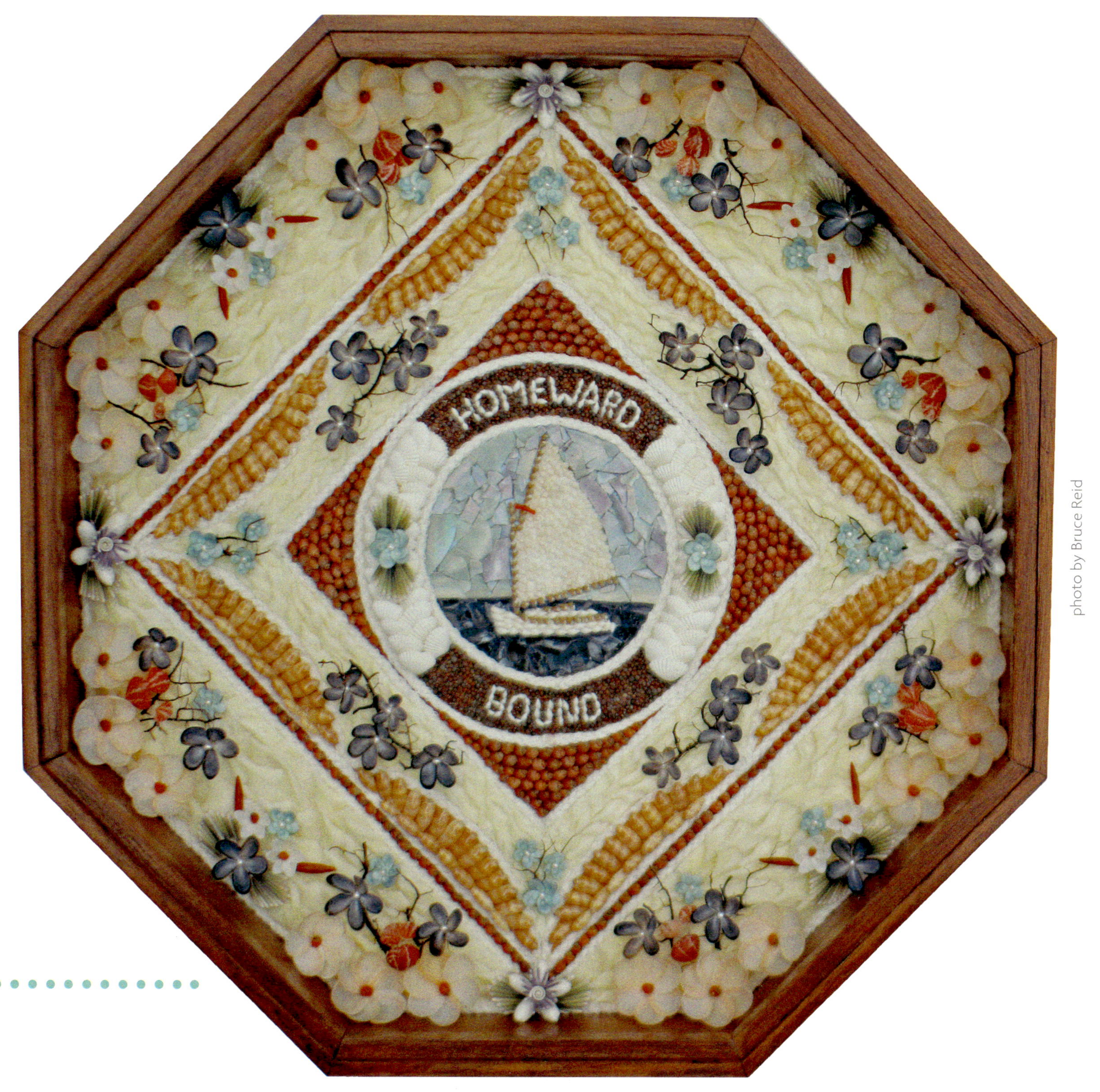

photo by Bruce Reid

Homeward Bound

The artist lives on Cape Cod very near the home of the Cape Cod Crosby catboat, and she is a lover of sailing. Thus, it is fitting that she used a catboat as a centerpiece.

14-inch mahogany case made by the artist

The large flower is done with yellow tellins with peach coquina petals in the center. Sprays of flowers including blue-green limpet shells, white cup shells, rose petal tellins, and tiny blue mussel shells surround it. These are accented by purple sea urchin spines and reddish simnia.

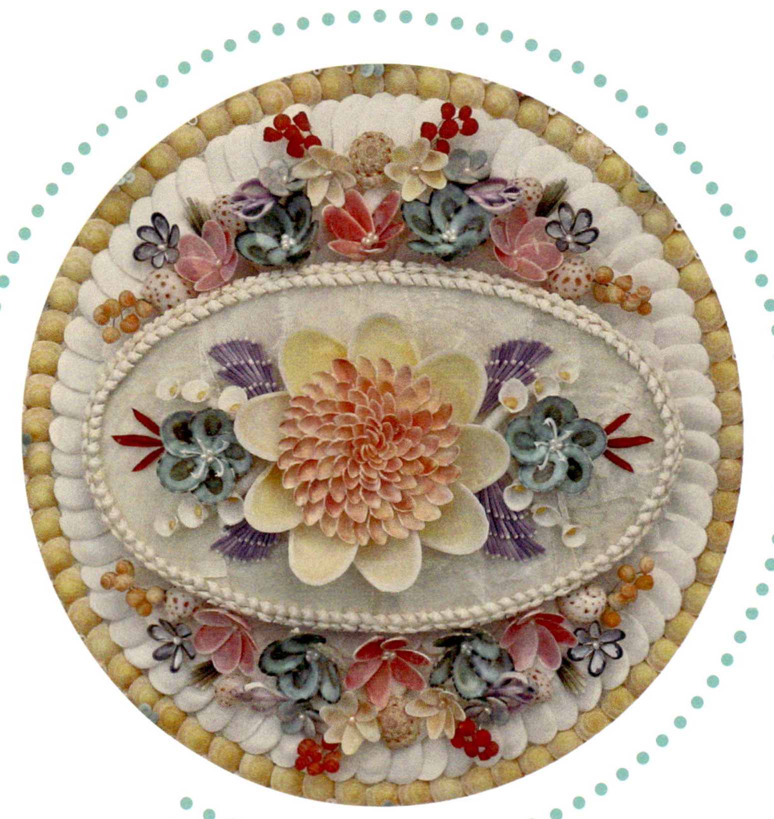

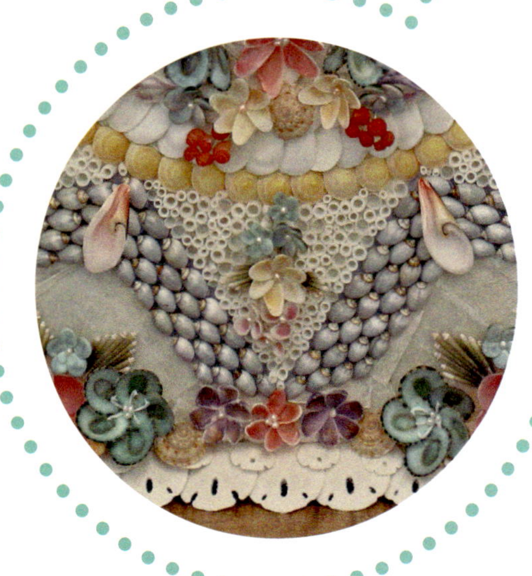

Each point is created from purple olive shells, inside of which sit cut white tusk shells that add interest with their varying heights and circles. At the base of the V are cut strawberry strombus shells showing off their beautiful pink coloring.

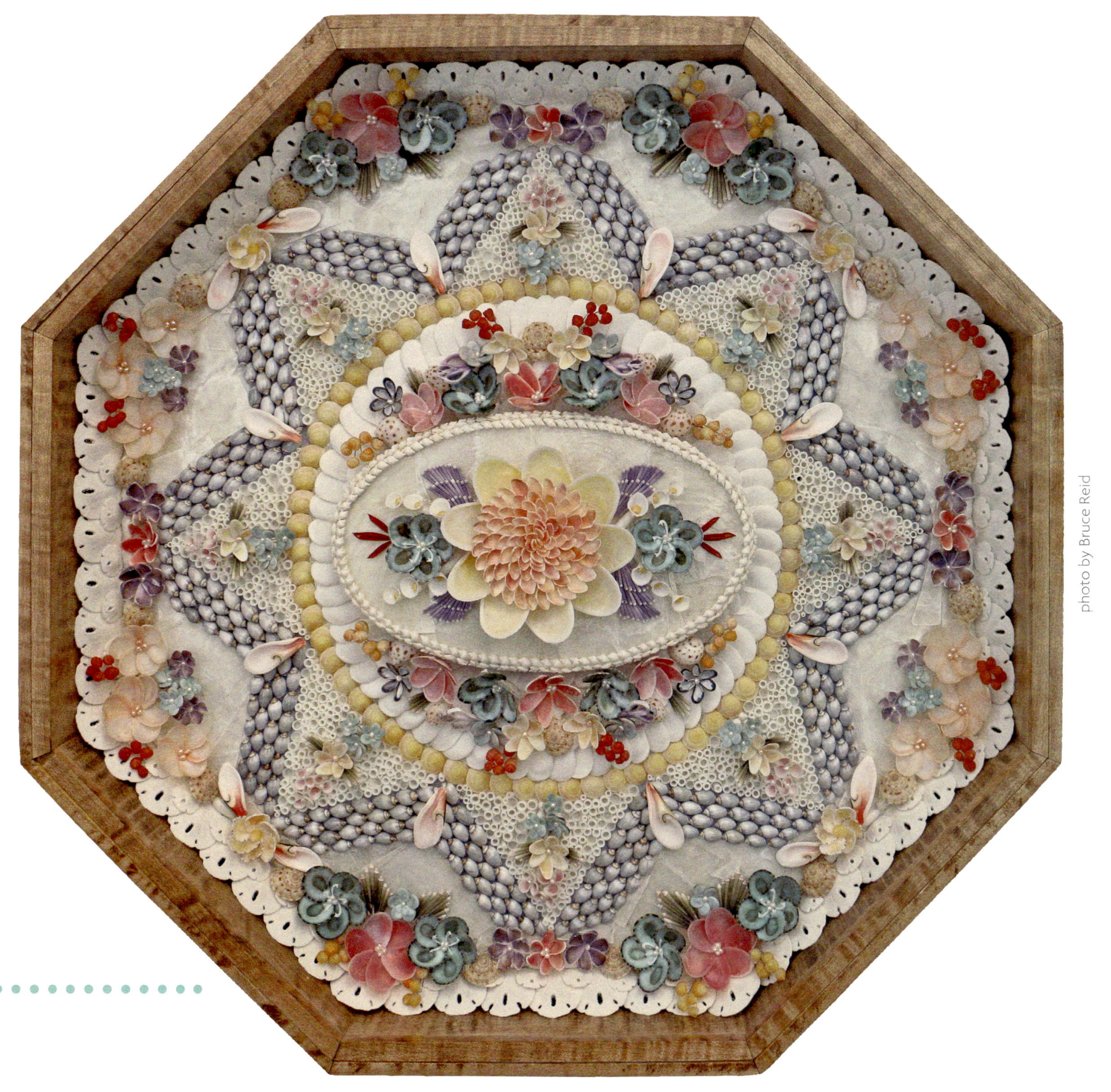

photo by Bruce Reid

Sometime

After constructing this case from curly maple, the artist was inspired to create a piece with bright, bold, and colorful shells to complement the beautiful grain.

17-inch curly maple case made by the artist

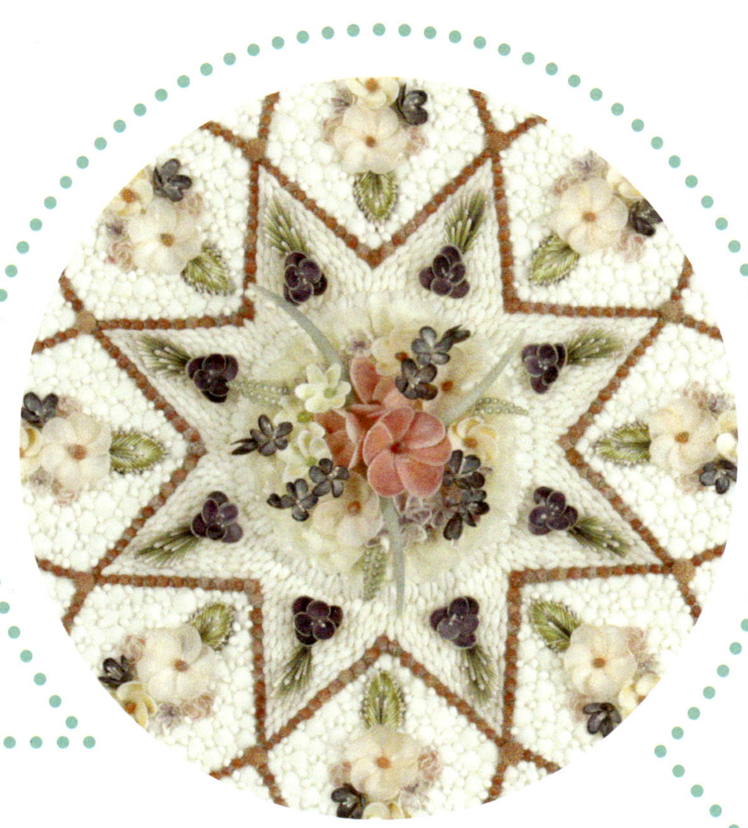

The center bouquet is created with rose petal tellins, yellow cay cay shells, and Tampa tellins. Little blue mussel shell flowers and long green tusk shells surround these. The foliage is created with green sea urchin spines.

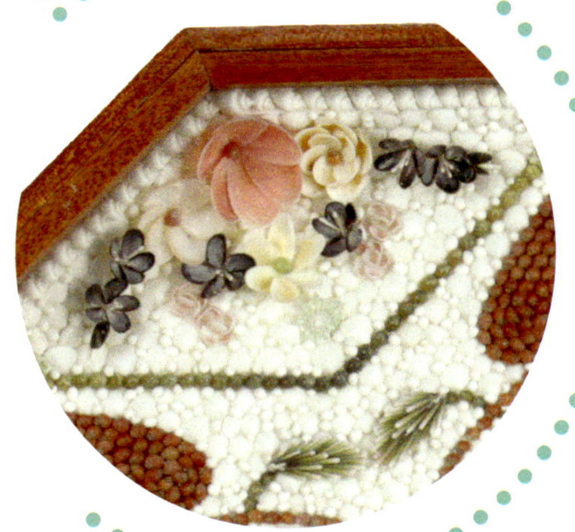

Each point of the Valentine has bouquets that mimic the shells in the centerpiece. The outer edge is done with white dove shells, and the background is comprised of thousands of tiny white littorinas and cup shells.

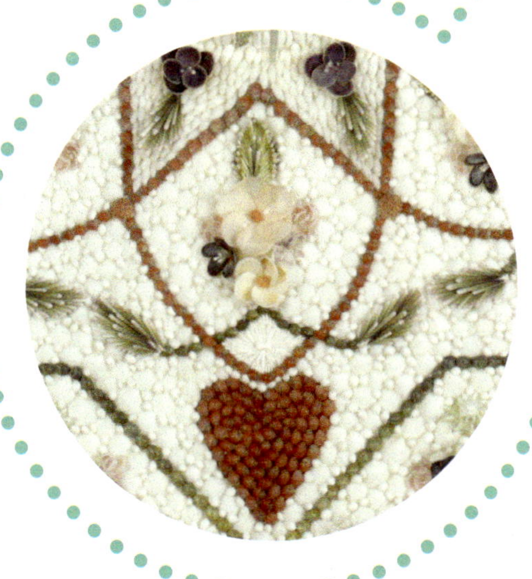

The hearts in each corner and the bands throughout are created with red moon snails. Tassels of green sea urchin spines sit above each heart.

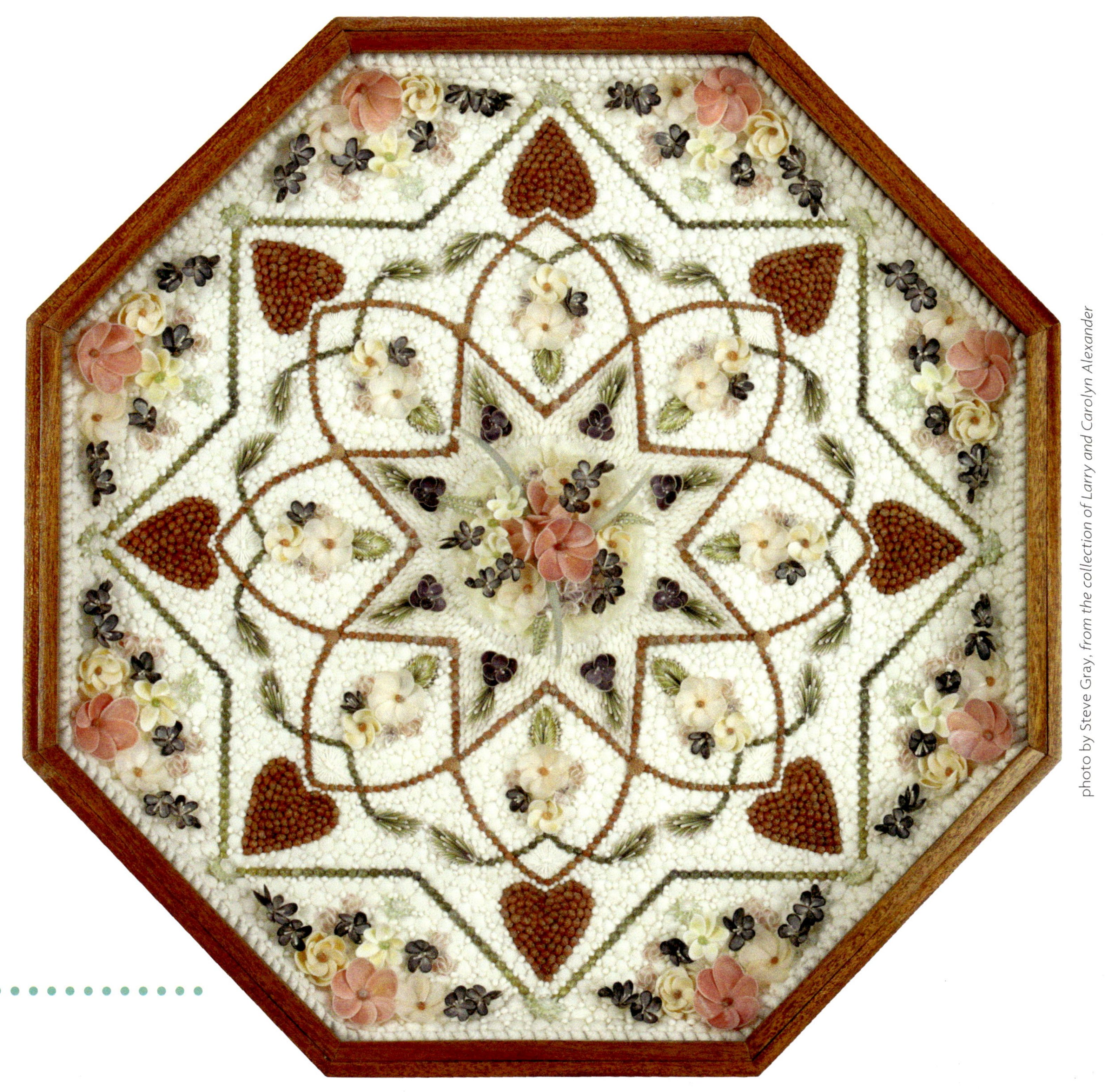

photo by Steve Gray, from the collection of Larry and Carolyn Alexander

Kaleidoscope

Inspired by a piece in a book of mandalas that the artist simplified and adapted using shell hearts and flowers.

19-inch mahogany case made by the artist

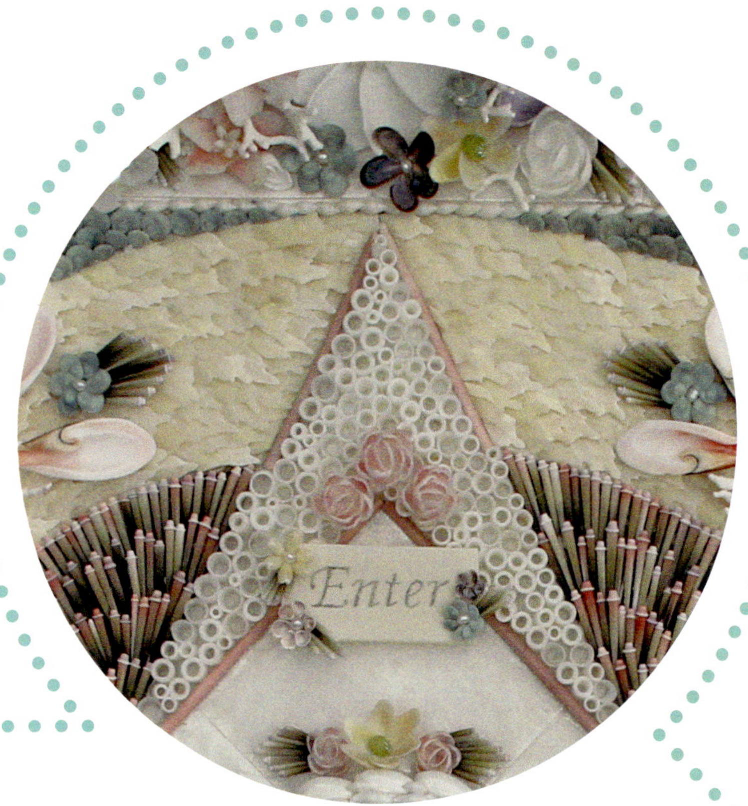

Points of cut tusk shells are outlined by pink sea urchin spines. "Enter" is written in scrimshaw on an antique ivory piano key. On either side of the point are flowers made of blue operculums atop a field of garfish scales accented with cut strawberry strombus shells.

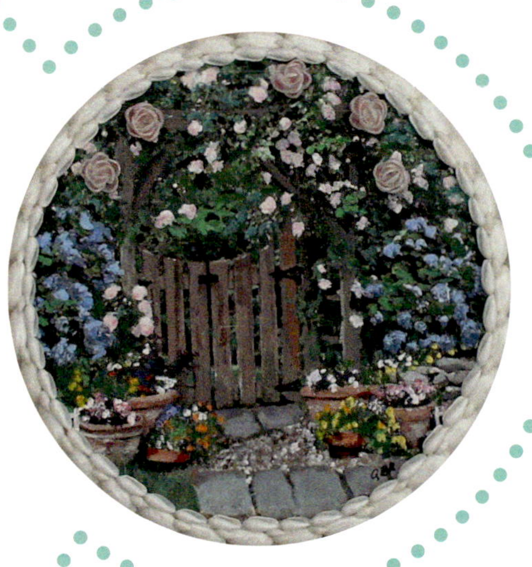

The artist did the acrylic painting of the rose arbor, which is surrounded by blue hydrangeas, pink roses, and pots of flowering annuals, inviting you to enter her world and discover the beauty that lies inside. The tranquil center of the Valentine balances the riot of color in the surrounding floral wreath.

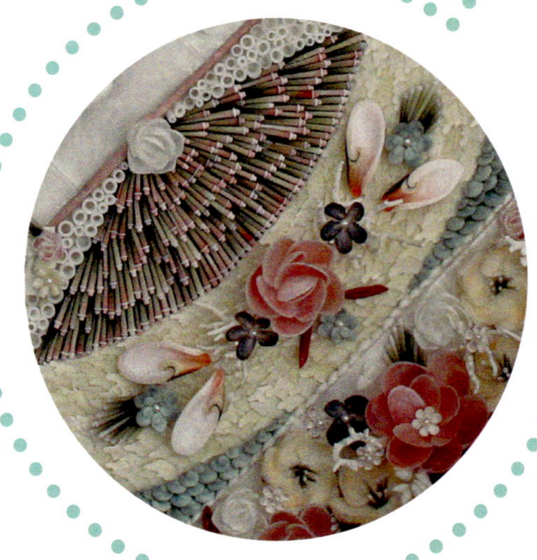

A wedge of pink-tipped sea urchin spines placed at random heights draws the eye to a flower arrangement of pink rosecup shells, strawberry strombus, blue operculums, and blue mussel shells.

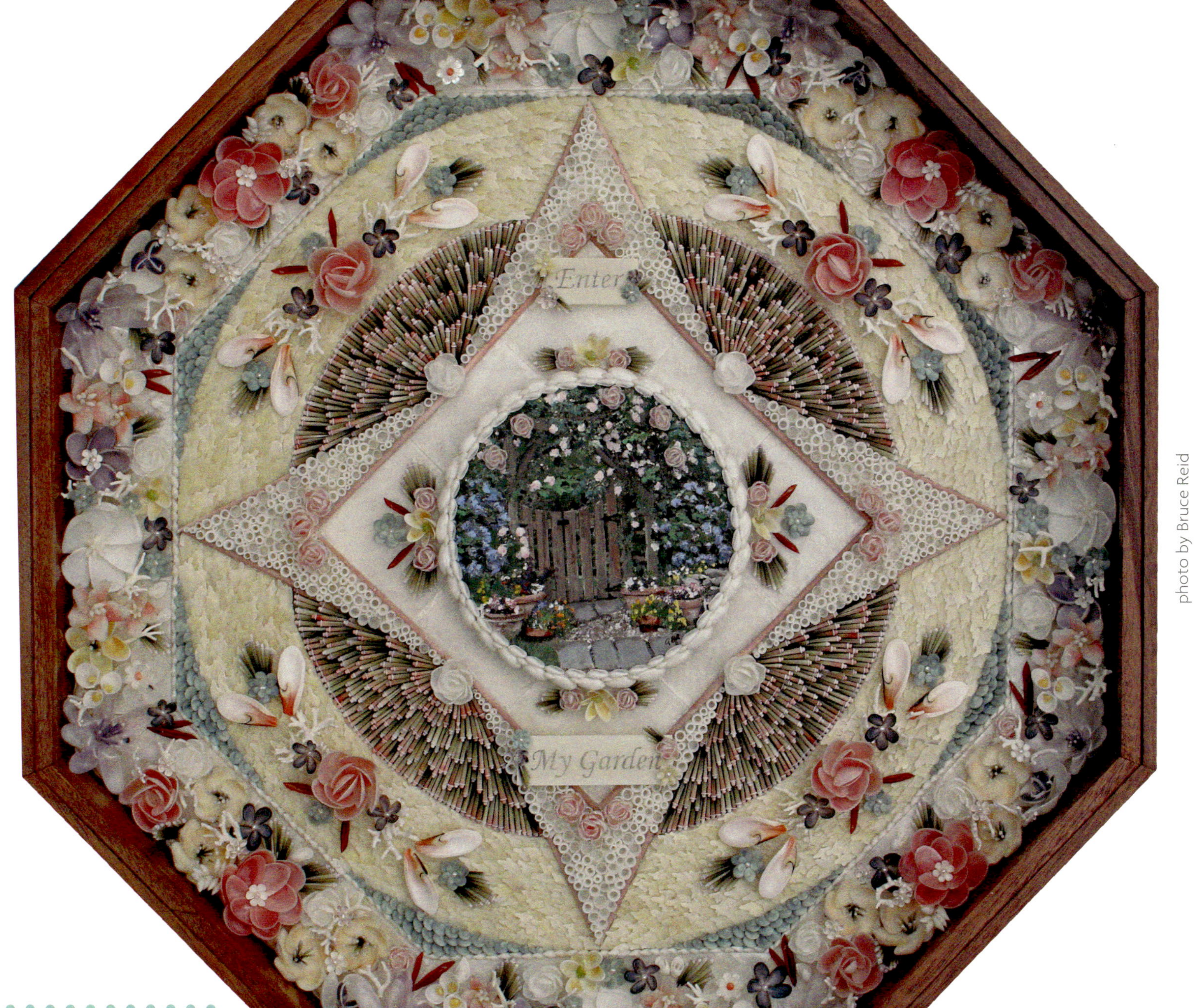

photo by Bruce Reid

Enter My Garden

Inspired by the artist's love of flowers and gardening, this Valentine uses a multitude of colorful seashells to create a permanent reminder of the beauty of her garden gate and the adjoining arbor.

17-inch mahogany case made by the artist

Central flowers of rosecup shells and white rice shell sprays lie on a pillow of silk fabric. The flowers are surrounded by a ring of yellow limpet shells from Barbados. Each point is filled with deep purple janthinas. The shell work is done on a bed of cotton, as in the antique Valentines.

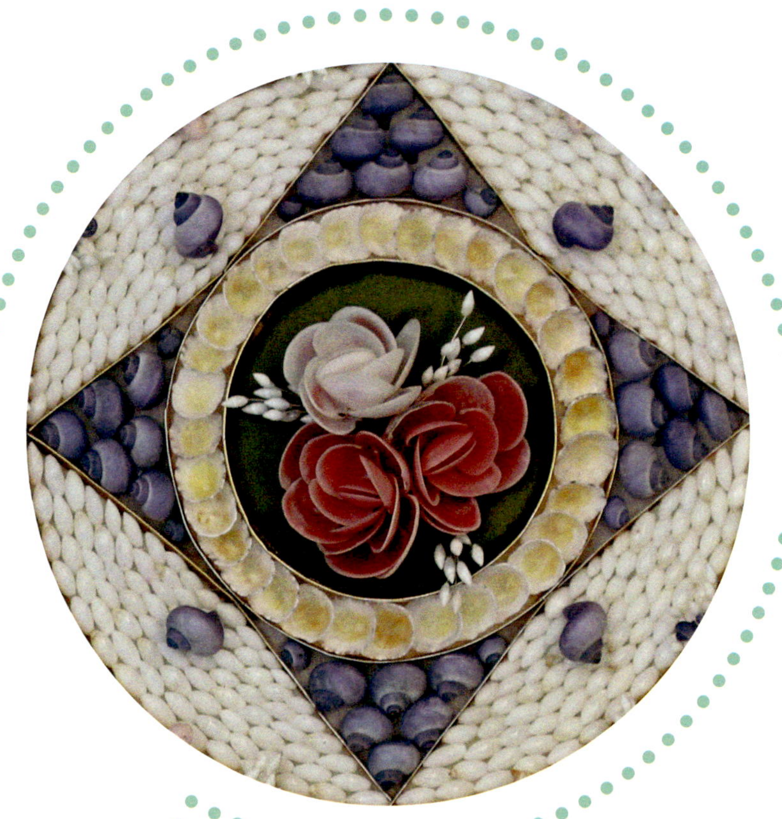

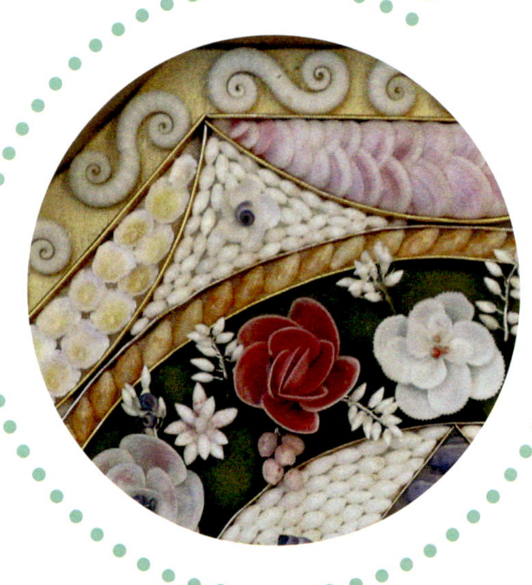

Pairs of spirula shells make up the border, and below that are yellow limpets and woven rosecup shells, with a triangle of white rice shells between them. A ring of orange miter shells encircles the wreath.

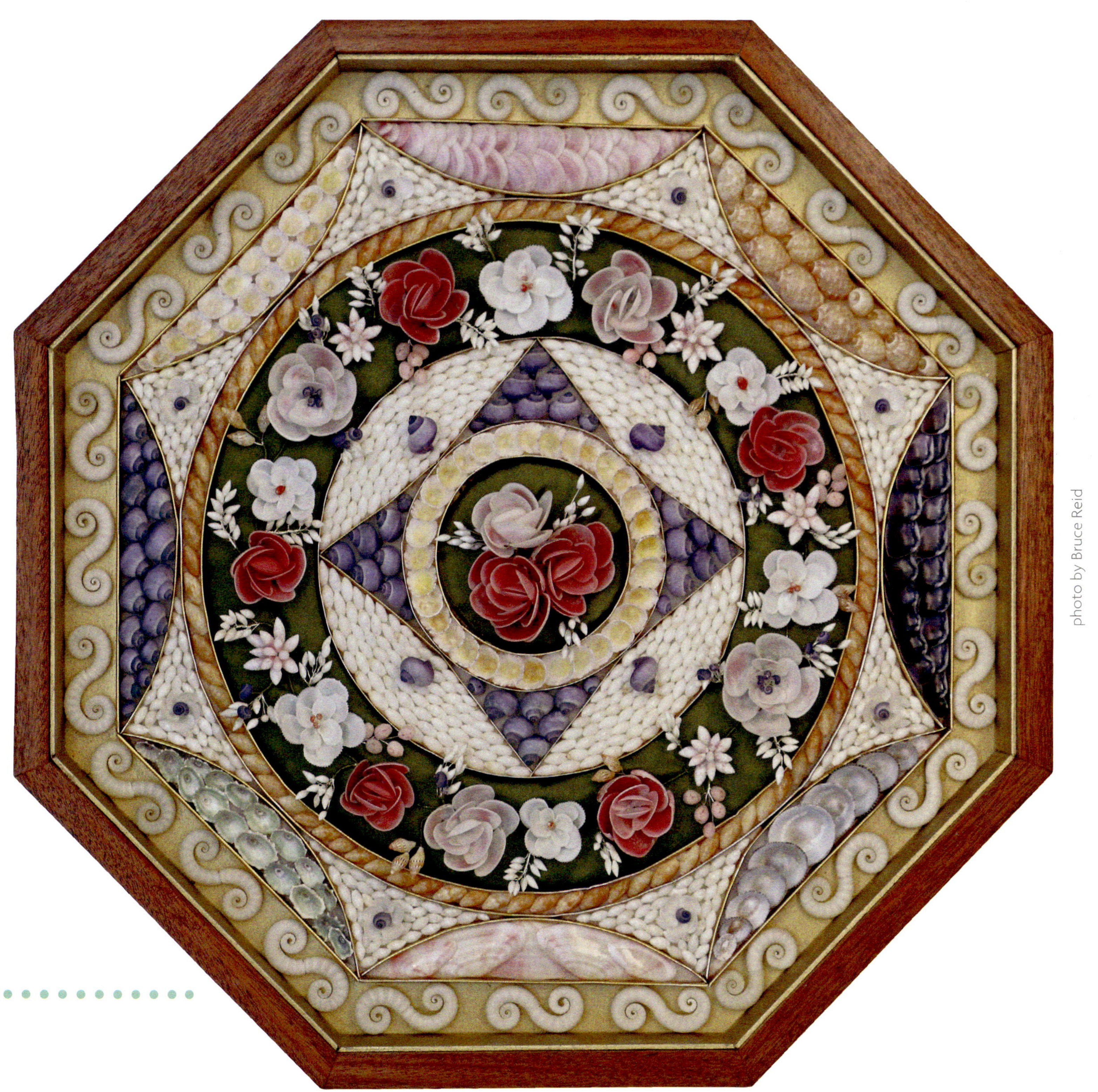

photo by Bruce Reid

Victorian Splendor

Created in the Victorian style using silk fabric, cotton batting, and gold foil. The artist hoped to capture the flavor of silk wreaths in Victorian Valentines with this modern piece.

14-inch mahogany hinged case with maple splines made by the artist

photo by Michael Gruttadauria

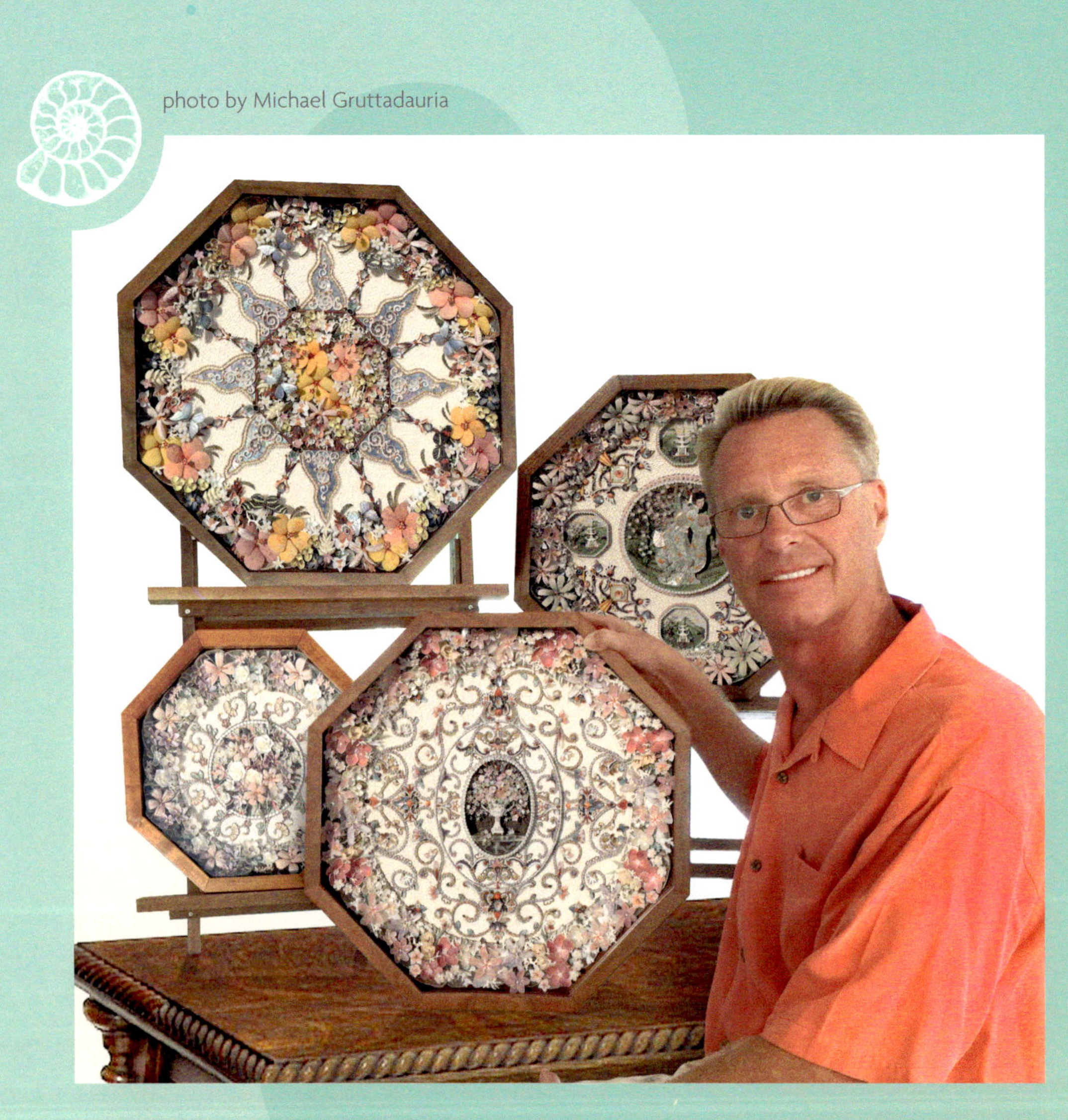

David Rhyne

Sarasota, Florida

I saw my first Sailors' Valentine at the New York City Winter Antiques Show in 1981. It was one of the original pieces from Barbados, and I loved it. I have always had a fascination with vintage shell work, and this was unlike anything I had seen before. At the time, my wife, Victoria, and I lived in the city, where we were designing bridal and evening shoes for Dyeables Shoe, Inc.

Shortly after I saw the Valentine at the antique show, we traveled to London, primarily to see the Victorian Valentines at the Victoria and Albert Museum, many of which were donated to the museum by Queen Mary from her personal collection.

I have a BFA degree from the Ringling College of Arts and Design in Sarasota, Florida, and throughout my life I have enjoyed painting and drawing. I saw Sailors' Valentines as a way in which I could combine these artistic talents with the detailed and intricate work that could be done with shells and sealife.

So in 2001, after moving from New York City to Sarasota, I made my first Valentine to enter into the Sanibel Shell Show. After attending the show I realized what path I needed to take to improve my work. I am totally self-taught.

Each of my Valentines takes between 100 and 450 hours to complete. My studio is located in my home and I take my work seriously, committing myself to hours in the studio almost every day. Many of the shells I use Victoria and I have collected, others are imported, and some are purchased. My preference is for very small and colorful shells, and capiz shells are the medium I use for my carvings.

One of my favorite pieces is *Victorian Vase*, filled with miniature shell flowers (see pages 182–183). It incorporates so many things that I love about the art of that era in history and that I also love about this art form.

www.davidrhyne.com

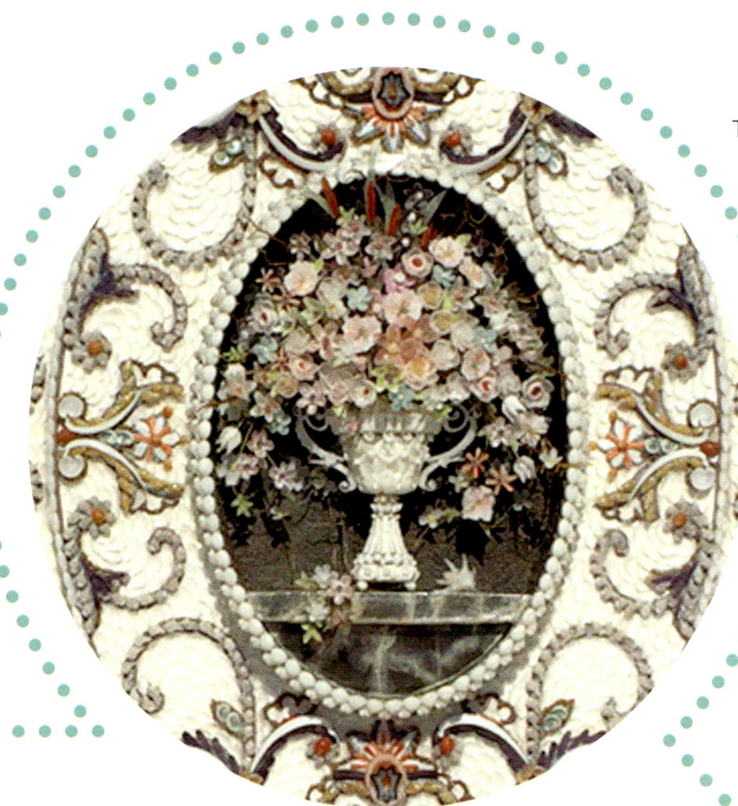

The center depicts a Victorian vase filled with miniature flowers. The vase is covered in sea urchin pieces and white littorinas. The handles are made from pieces of gooseneck barnacles and cut shells. The marble table is cut from capiz shell. Flowers of apple blossom shells, aqua and pink operculums, and pink chitons are included among the glorious bouquet.

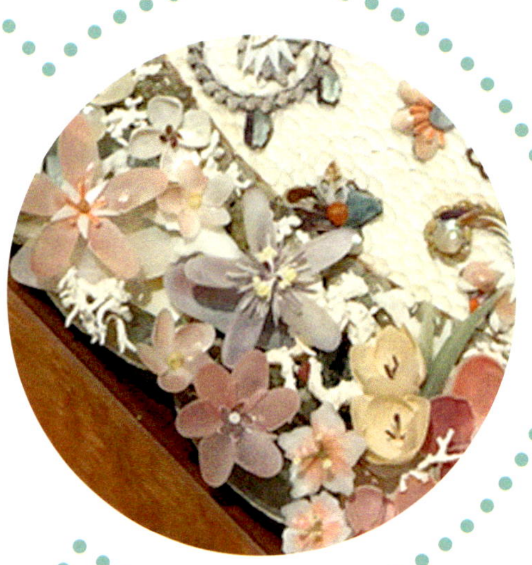

The lavender flower is made from tagelus shells with purple urchin spines, white tusk shells, and crushed yellow shell at the center.

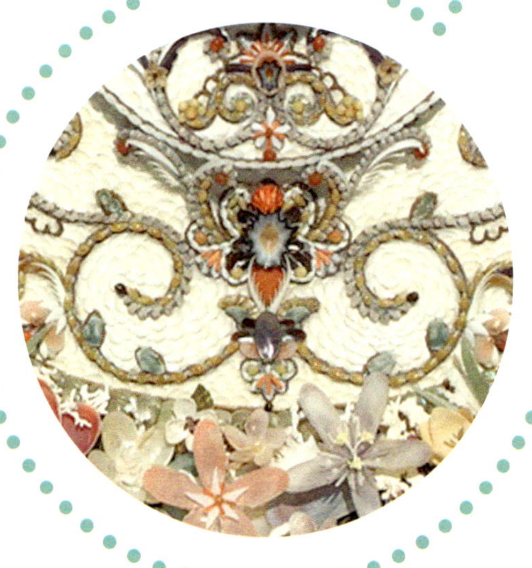

The scrolls and ornamentation include Philippine brown rice shells, baby whelks, limpets, squilla claws, and various abalone.

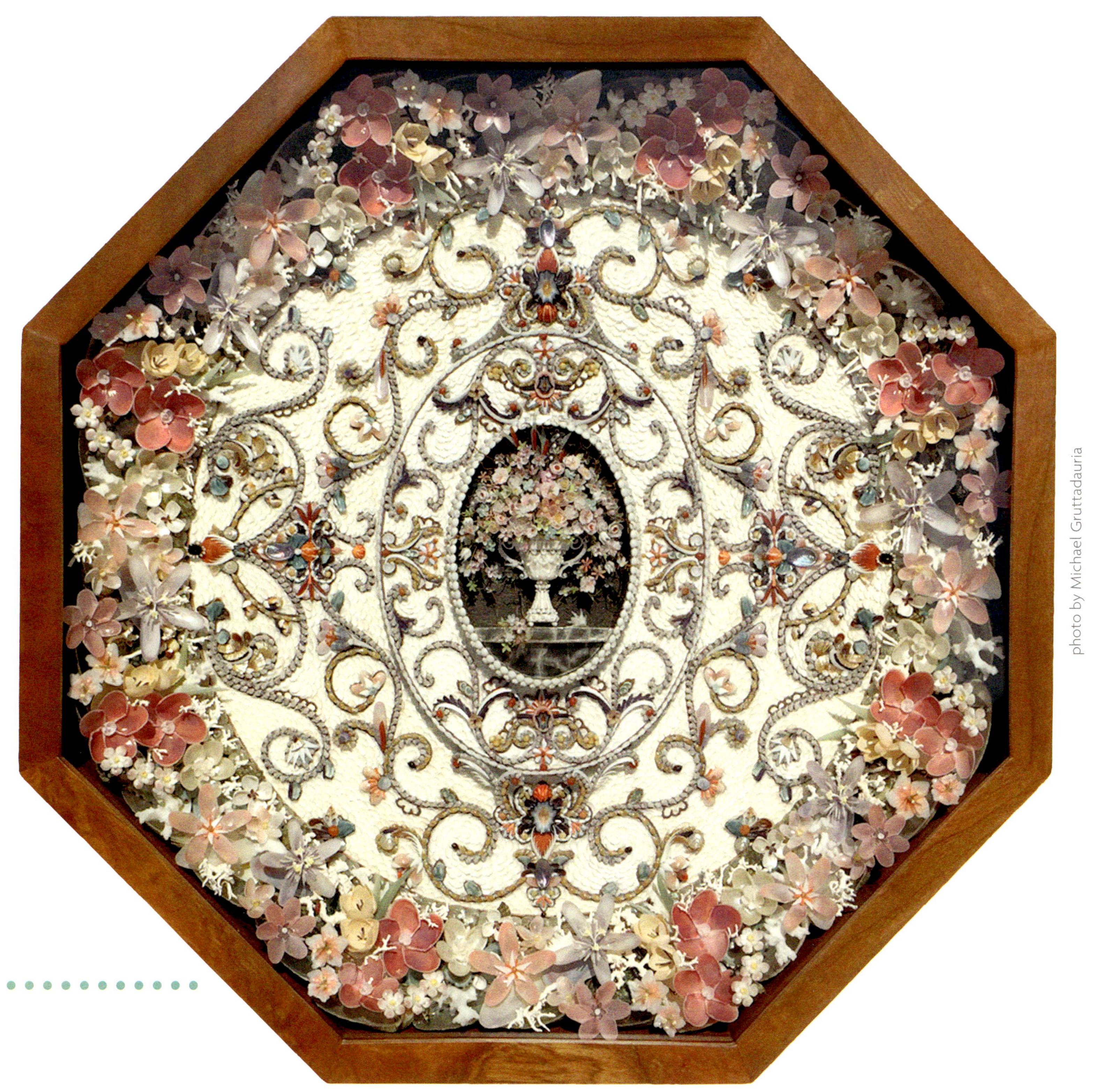

photo by Michael Gruttadauria

Victorian Vase

Inspired by a classic Victorian vase on a marble table.

19-inch cherry case made by David Rhyne Sr.

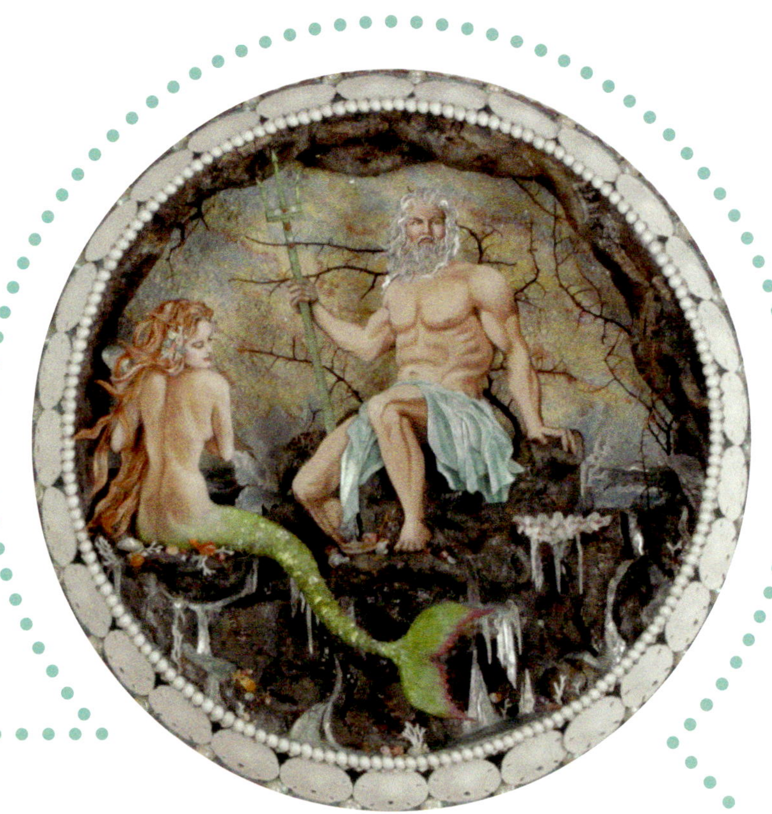

The artist carved Neptune and the mermaid from capiz shell, then painted them. The rock and cave setting are made from winged oyster shell.

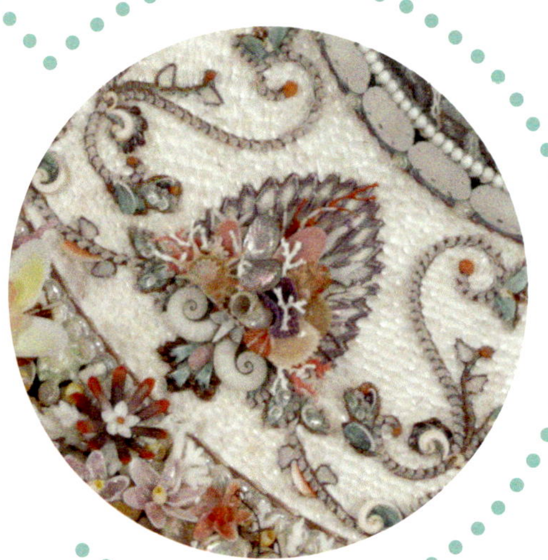

Neptune's bounty is an assortment of beautiful specimen shells: purple bryozoa, green abalone, coralized algae, pink stylaster coral, and red brachiopod shells, with curly spirula below.

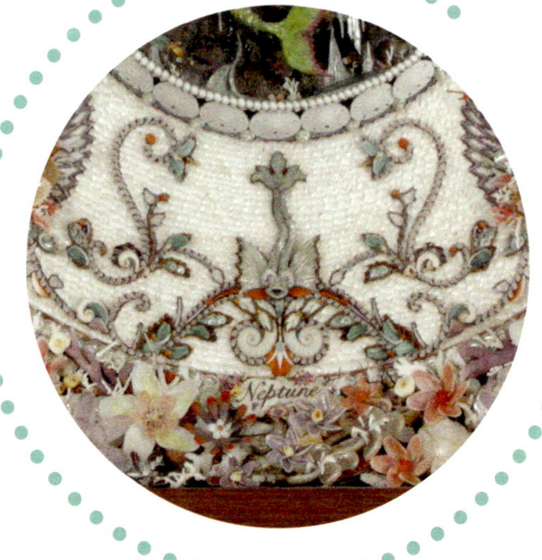

The stylized dolphin is taken from an 18th-century Italian fountain and is made from capiz shell. Flowers are created from yellow tellins, tiny green abalone, sea urchin spines, and pink coquina shells. "Neptune" is written in sea urchin spines.

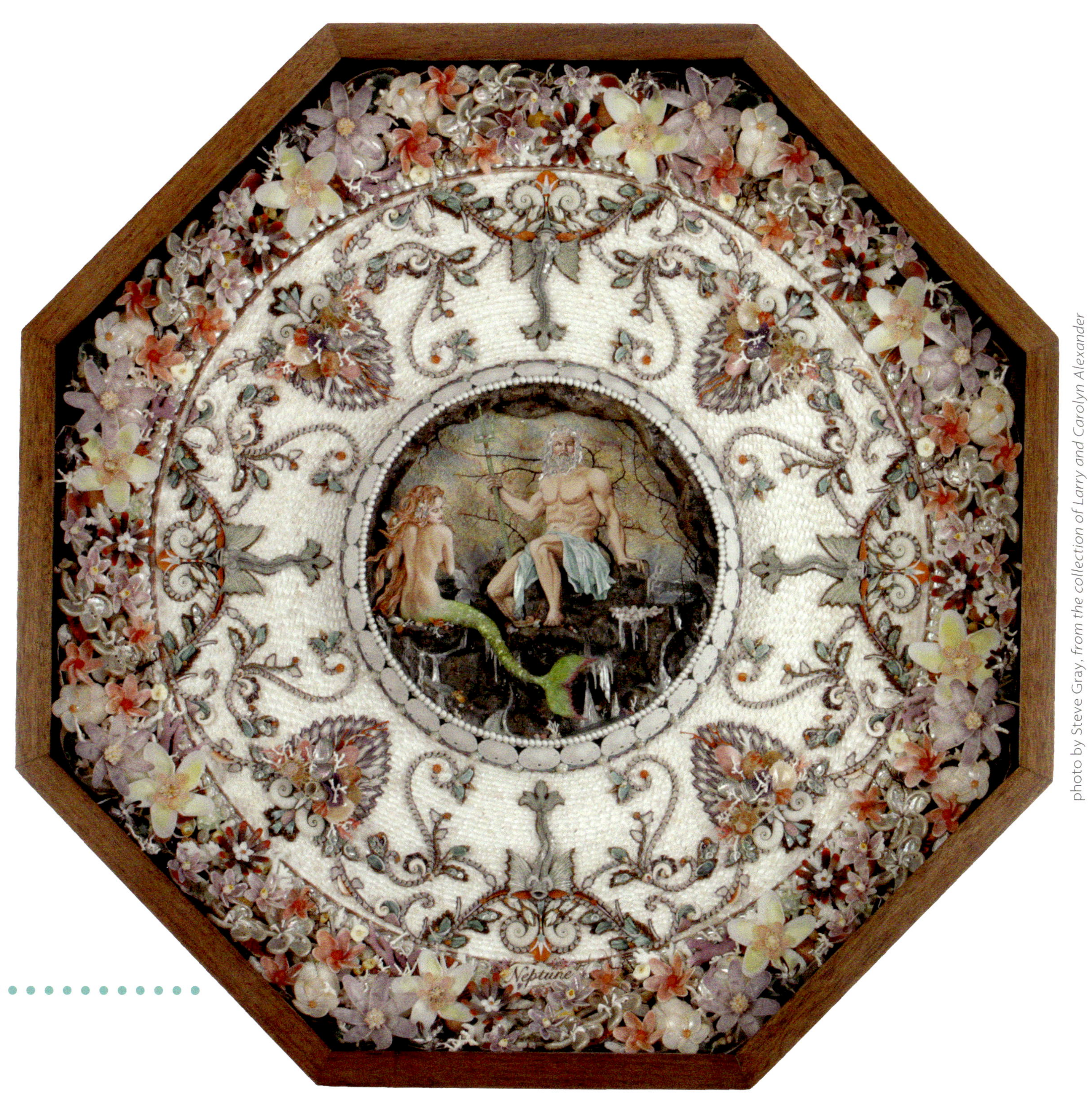

photo by Steve Gray, from the collection of Larry and Carolyn Alexander

Neptune

Inspired by the Roman god of the sea.

22-inch walnut case made by David Rhyne Sr.

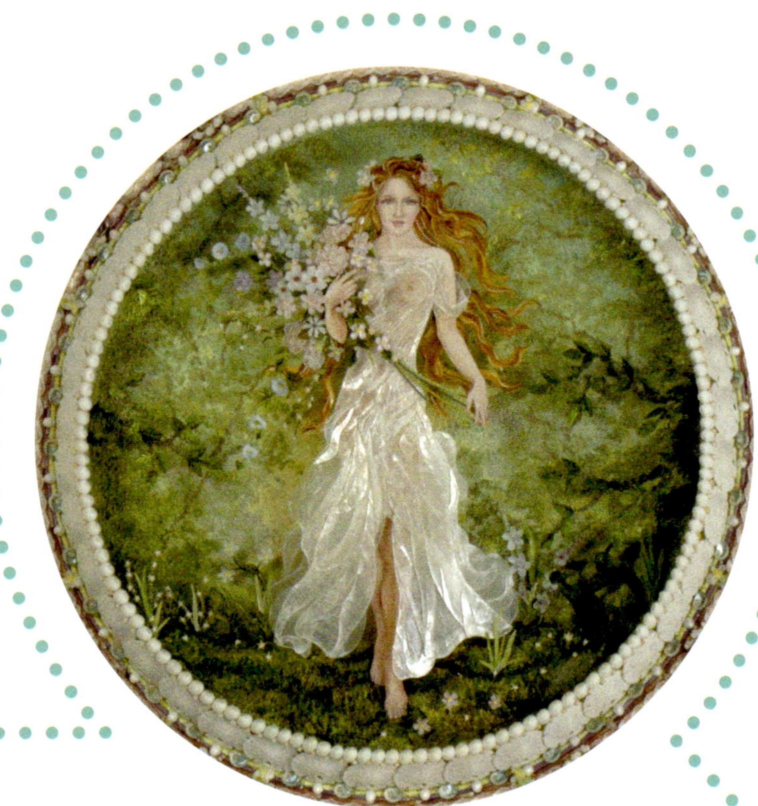

Flora has been carved by hand from capiz shell and painted by the artist, who also dressed Flora in hand-carved, hand-painted capiz shell. Her bouquet is done from both natural and dyed miniature shells.

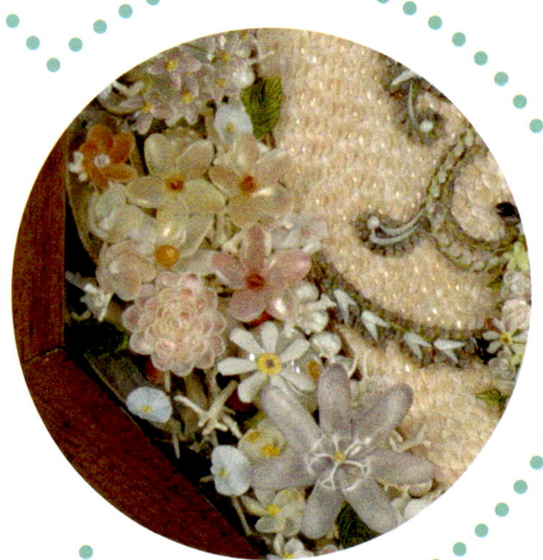

Baby pink coquina shells are used for the background. Pieces of a gooseneck barnacle form the curved floral image to the right. The delicate purple flower at the bottom is made from pale purple tagelus shells.

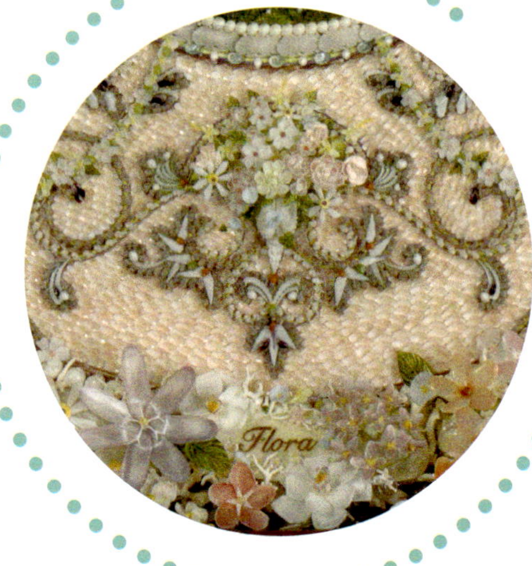

Baby whelk shells form the flowers and patterns, along with parts of a gooseneck barnacle and pink coquina shells. "Flora" is written in sea urchin spines.

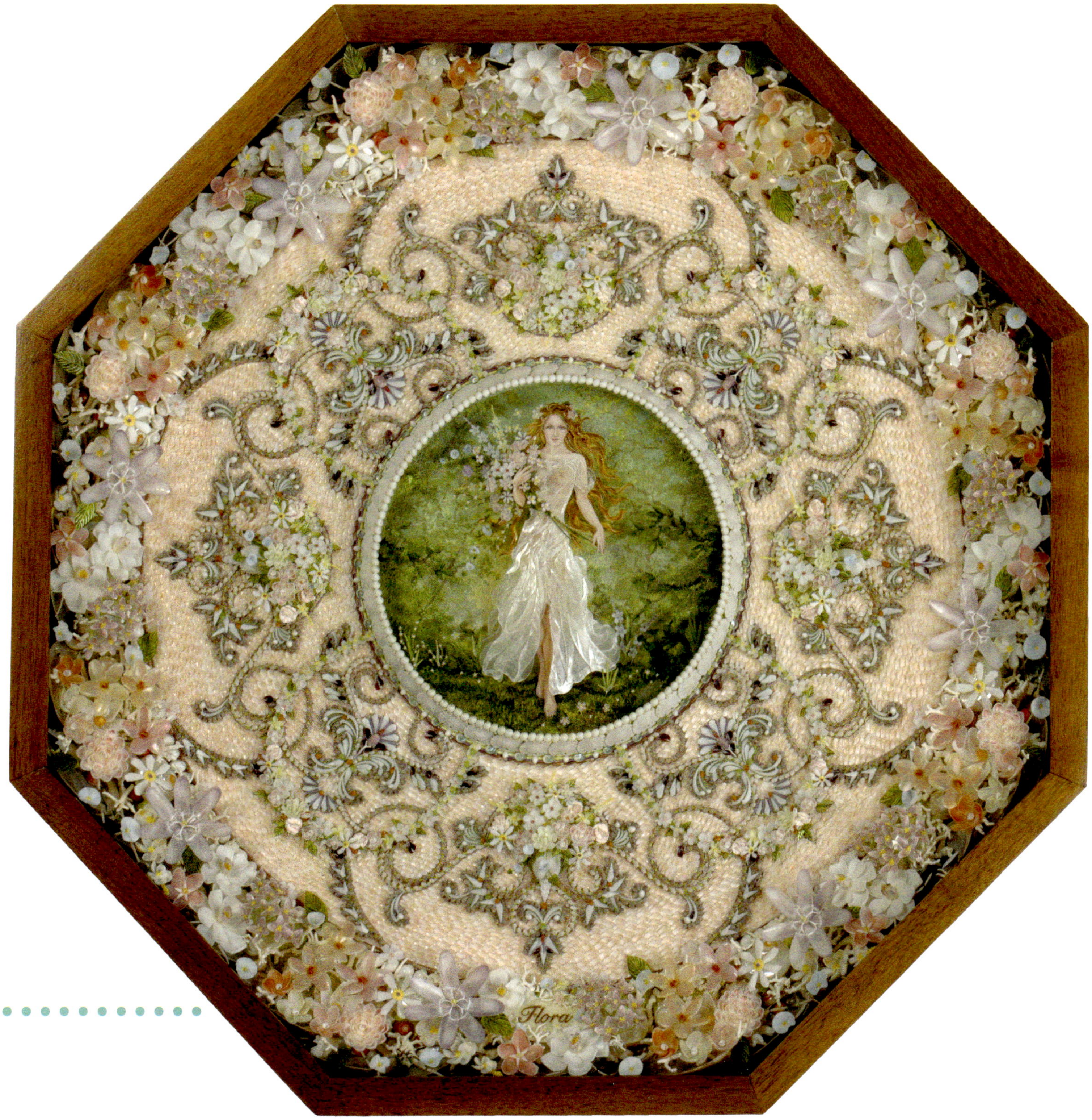

photo by Steve Gray, *from the collection of Larry and Carolyn Alexander*

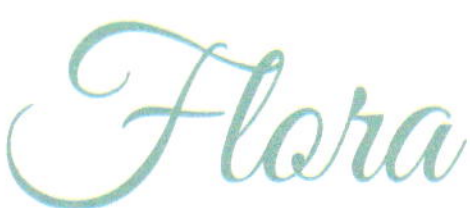

Inspired by the Roman goddess of spring.

22-inch walnut case made by David Rhyne Sr.

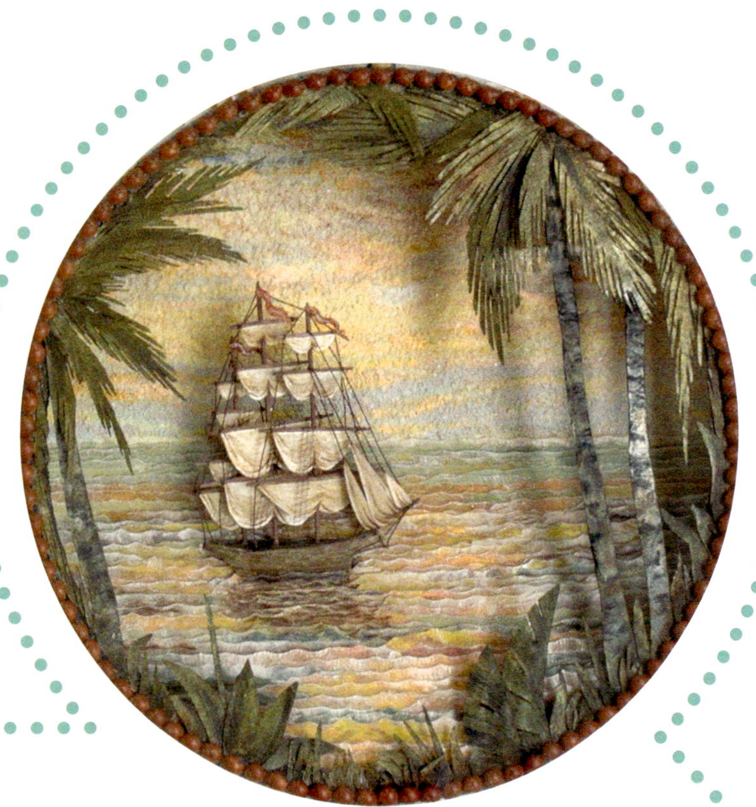

The ship is created from sea urchin spines, and the sails and water are carved by the artist from capiz shell. The colors of the sunset are done with various colors of crushed shell.

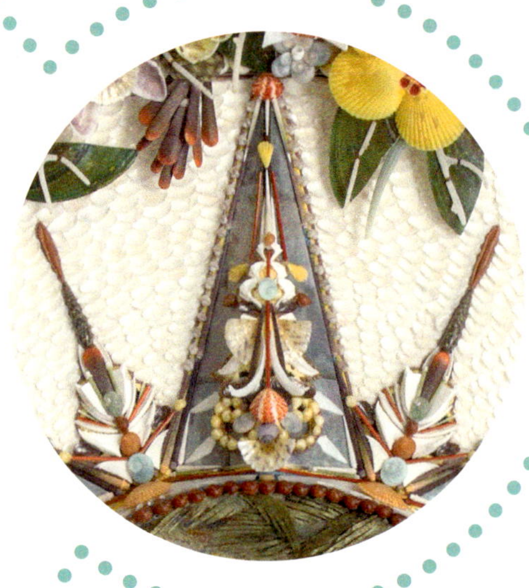

Thin sheets of mother-of-pearl have been carved by the artist to create the compass rose. It has then been decorated with yellow nerites, sea urchin parts, gooseneck barnacle pieces, blue operculums, and carved pecten shells.

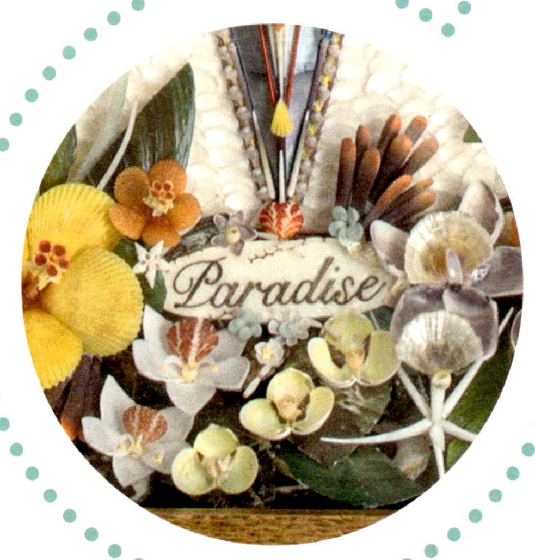

Striking yellow and orange pecten shells form the hibiscus flowers. "Paradise" is written with sea urchin spines.

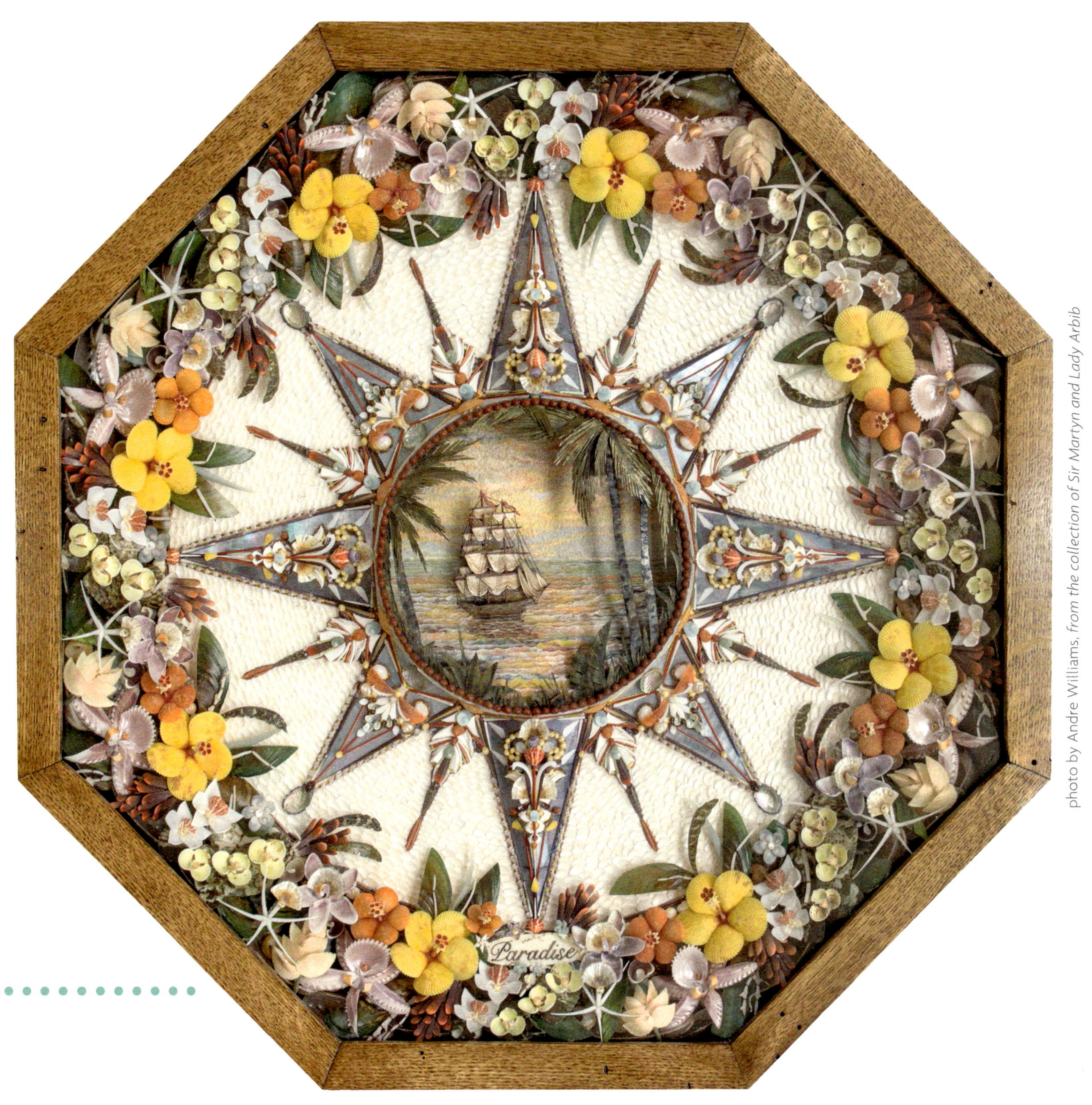

photo by Andre Williams, *from the collection of Sir Martyn and Lady Arbib*

Paradise

Inspired by a schooner anchored off the shore of a beautiful tropical island.

19-inch wormy chestnut case made by David Rhyne Sr.

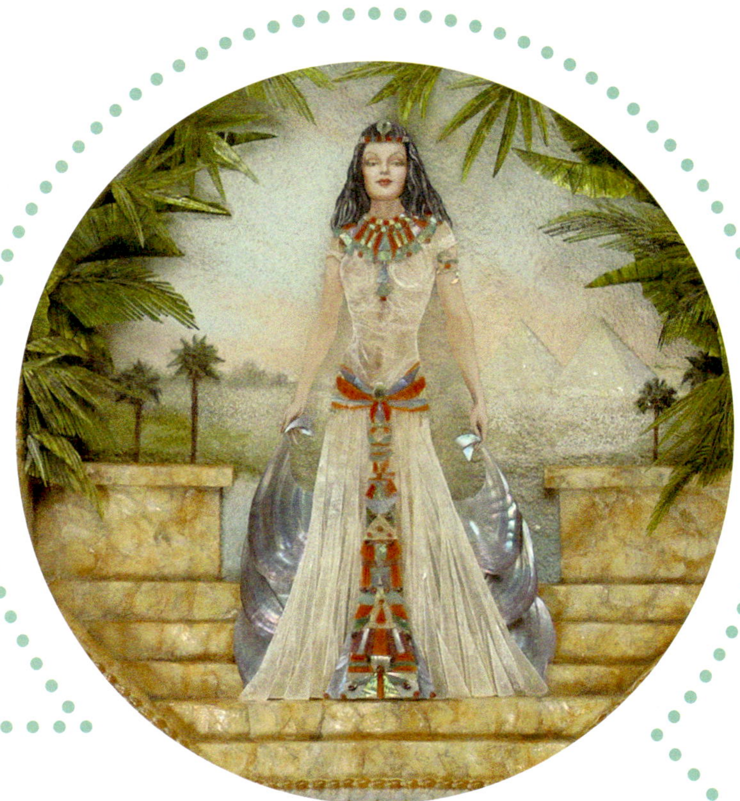

Cleopatra is carved from capiz shell. Her collar and the decorative part of her gown are done with carved shells to create a mosaic effect. The marble staircase is created from cut capiz shell.

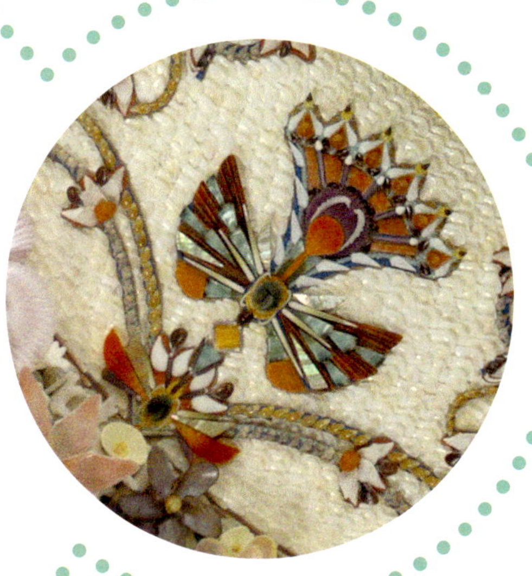

The winged scarab is created from pieces of cut pectens and other shells, then detailed with sea urchin spines. A carved blue operculum has been used to create the scarab in the center.

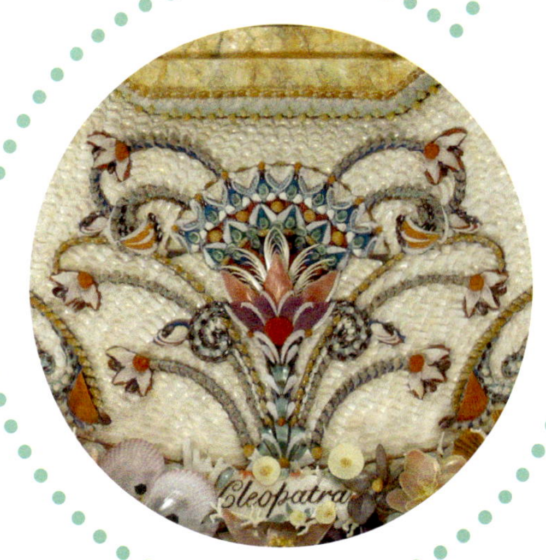

Purple pecten pieces are used to create the intricate lotus blossom, with squilla claws and pieces of the gooseneck barnacle adding texture. Cleopatra is written with sea urchin spines.

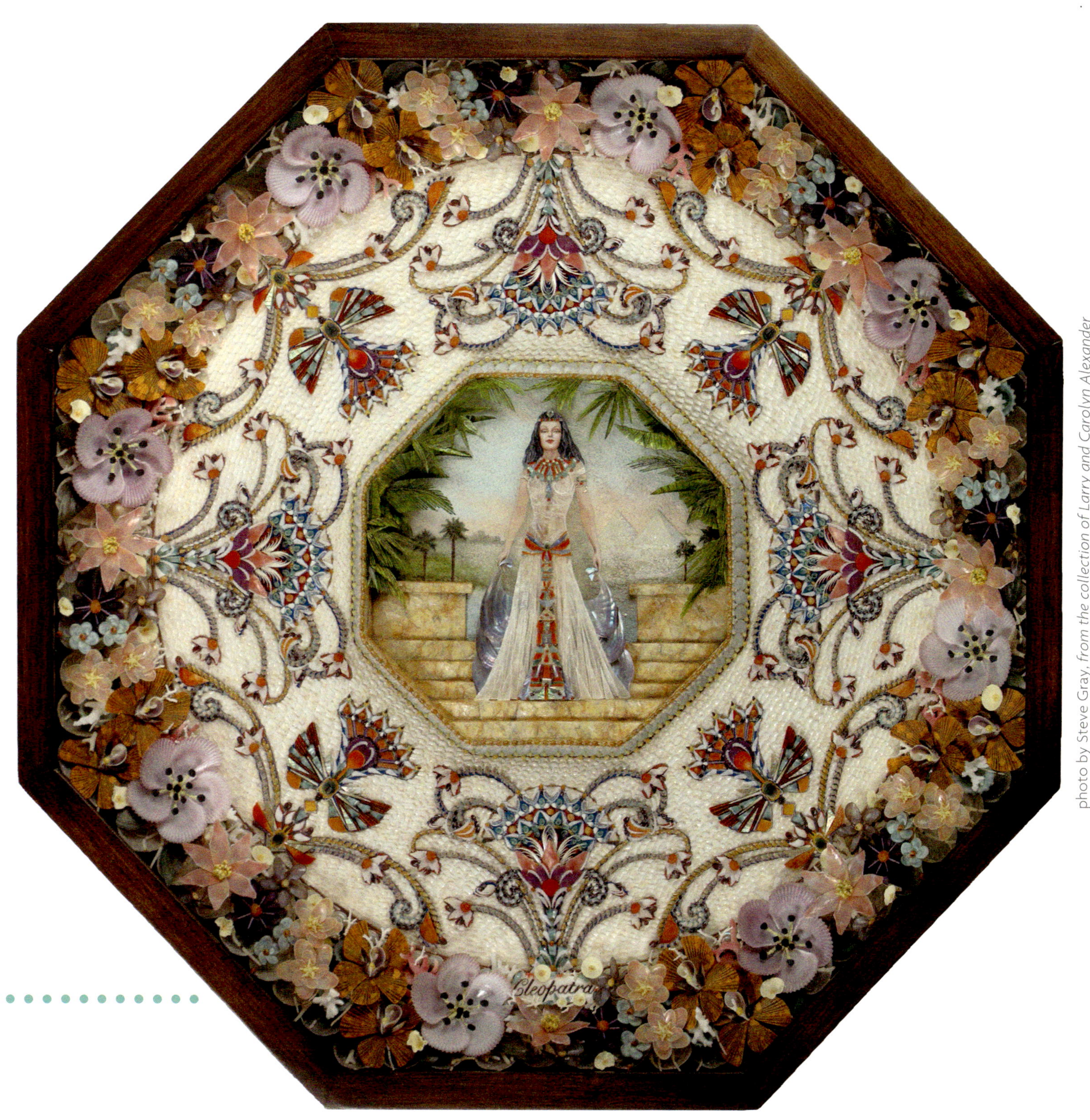

photo by Steve Gray, *from the collection of Larry and Carolyn Alexander*

Cleopatra

Inspired by the Queen of the Nile.

22-inch walnut case made by David Rhyne Sr.

photo by Melanie Moraga

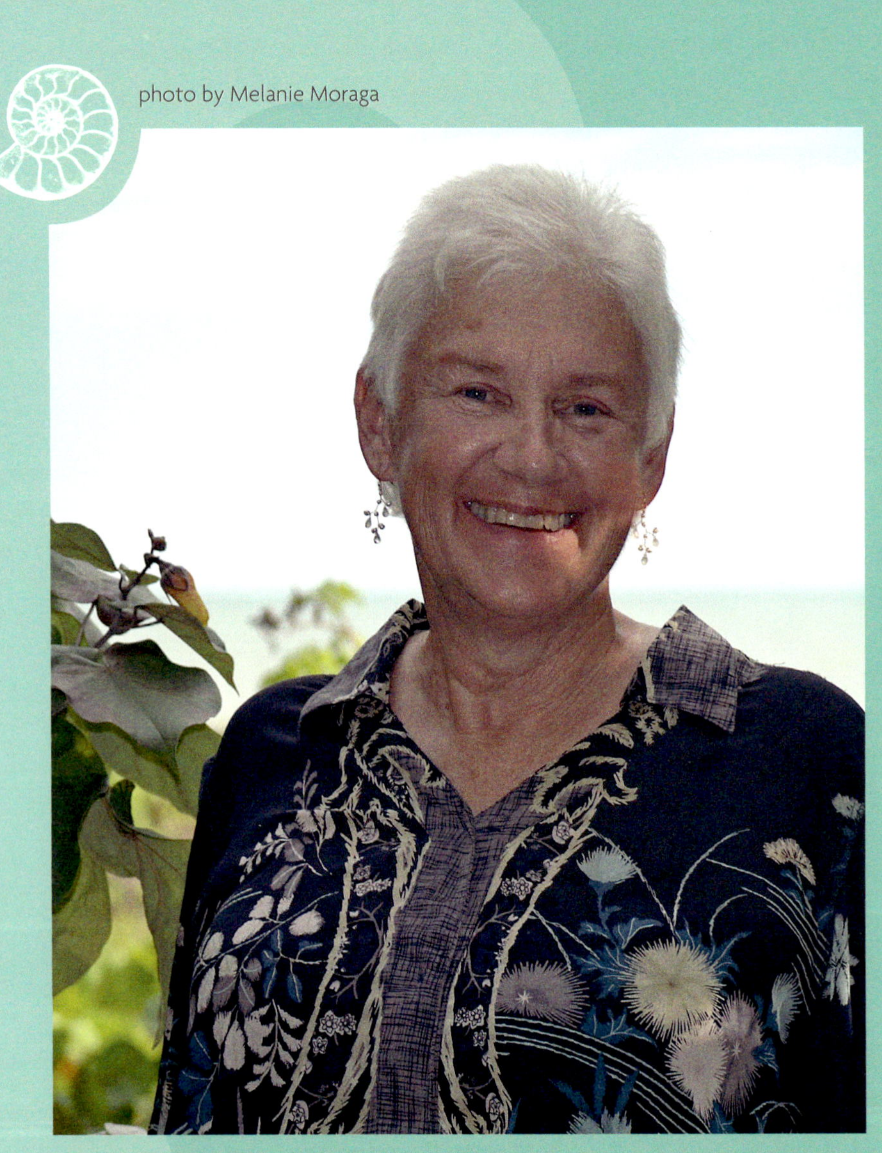

Jane Santini

Kingston, New York

In 1986, while vacationing with my children on Sanibel Island, I saw a Sailors' Valentine for the first time. I was struck by the incredible beauty of it and couldn't stop thinking about it. So I went on a quest for some books with information and found a few details about and photographs of the original Sailors' Valentines. I was so intrigued by the romantic stories of these intricate works.

My father's work kept him at sea for much of his life, and he would often bring me back shells from some faraway shore, which started me fantasizing about these places. (I was a solitary child, escaping into fantasy land frequently.) Because the sea and things associated with it were so much a part of my childhood, the appeal of Sailors' Valentines seemed a natural extension of this.

Shortly after discovering Sailors' Valentines, I was diagnosed with Lyme disease. There would be many years of recovery ahead, and I decided this would be a good time to make an attempt at one. Once I began, I loved the process and knew there would be many more Valentines to come. Over the next few years, my adeptness at handling these very small shells and the tools required to maneuver them improved significantly.

During these years I had a business in Rhinebeck, New York, cultivating plants in greenhouses. Some of the flowers we grew there inspired the flowers I made out of shells for my Valentines. Though I continue to love gardening, I no longer garden professionally. And due to some major changes in my life over the past three years, I have not had the chance to create a Sailors' Valentine. But recently, I have started to think about and make sketches for my next piece. Since my work almost always includes words or quotes, that is generally where I begin.

Of all the pieces I have done, my favorite is *Invictus* (see pages 200–201), inspired by the poem of the same name by William Ernest Henley. It was this poem that helped keep Nelson Mandela alive while he was imprisoned for 27 years, and it is this poem that has helped me through the darkest moments of my life: I am the Master of my fate; I am the Captain of my soul.

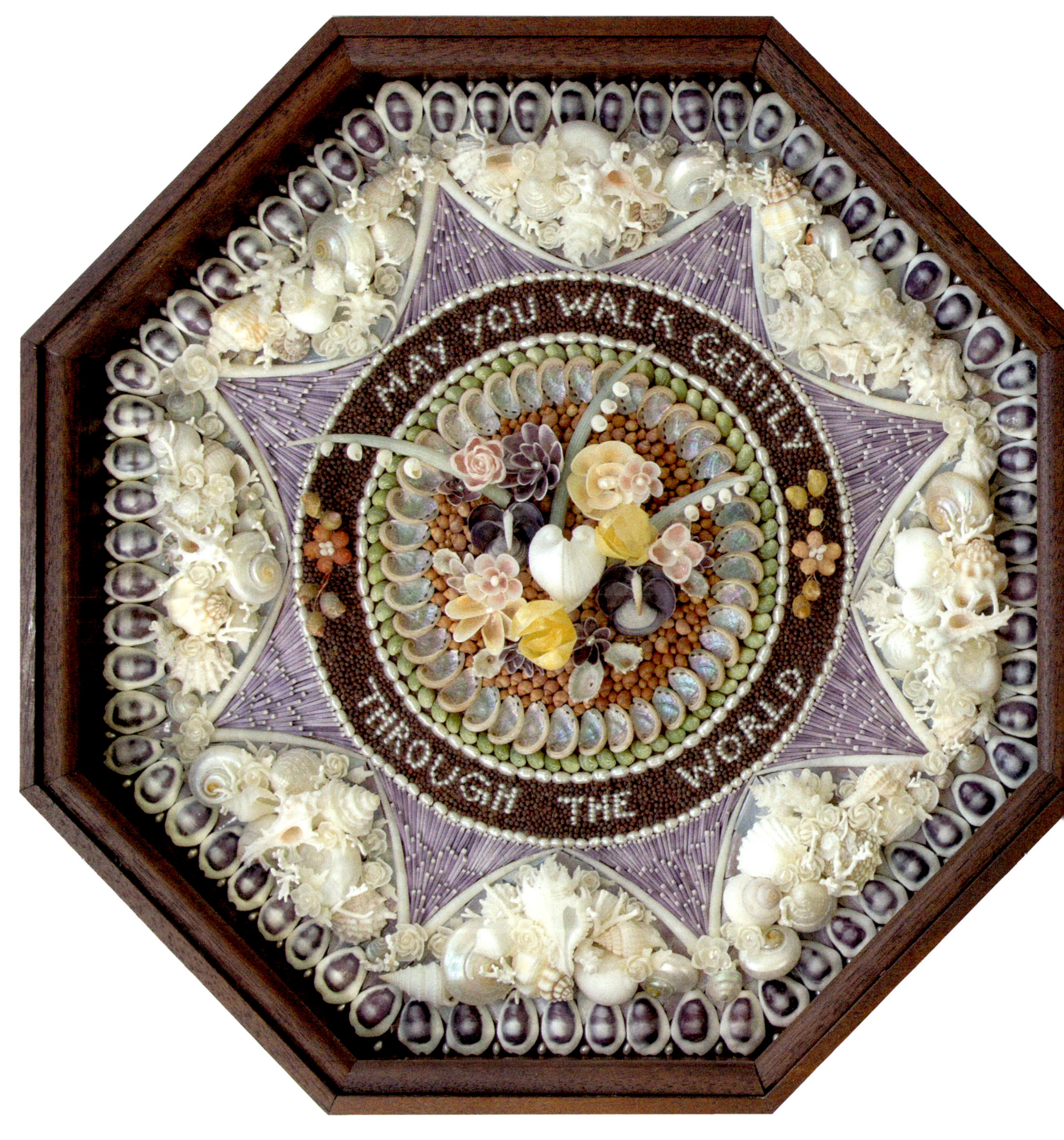

Inspired by words from an Apache blessing
in the 1950s movie *Broken Arrow*.

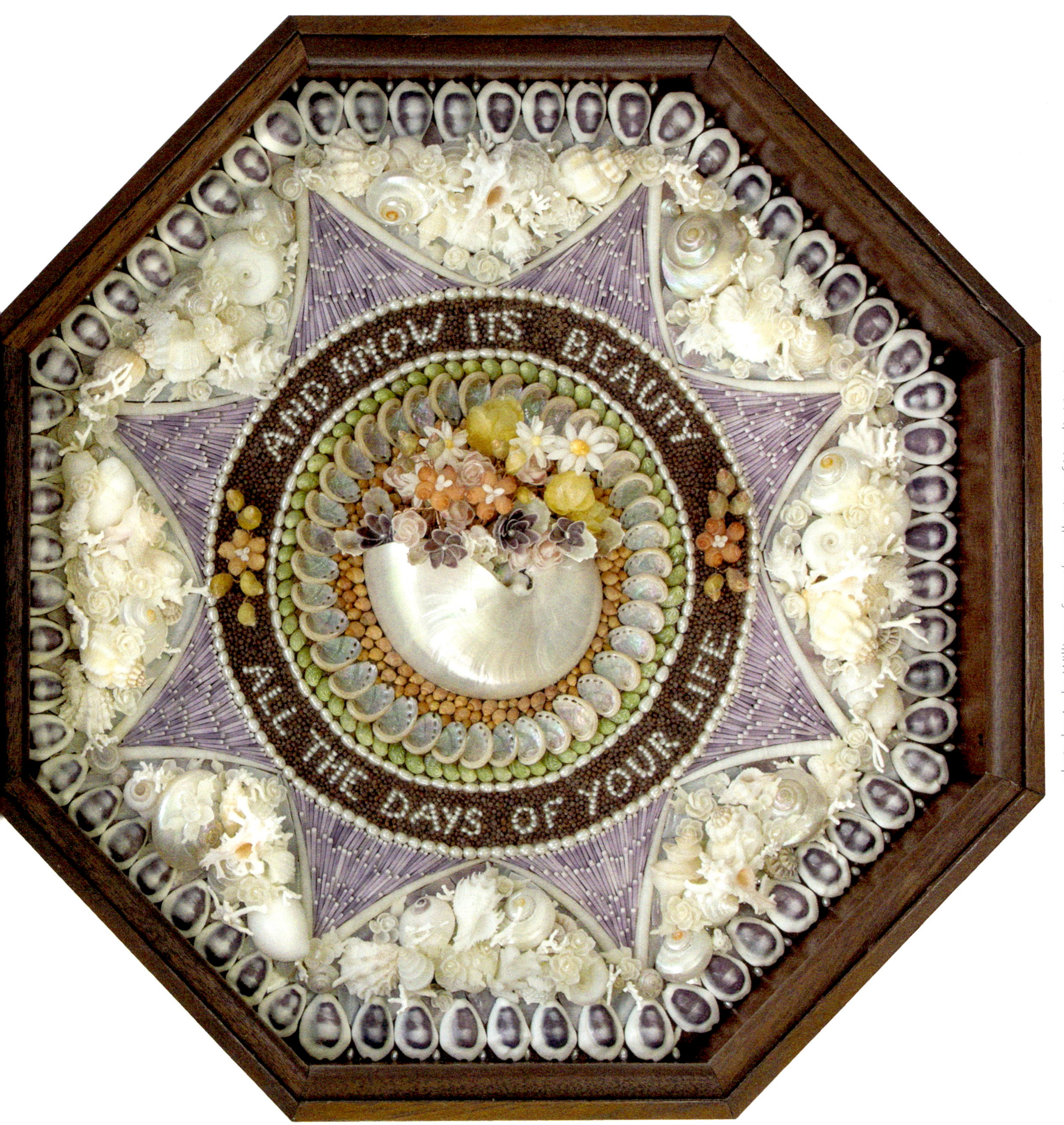

photo by Andre Williams, *from the collection of Natalie Manning*

May You Walk Gently

13-inch (each side) mahogany case made by Richard Gasper

The spray of flowers on the left side complements the bouquet on the right side. In the center is an ox heart cockle shell. Green tusk shells spring outward with tiny pikaki shells attached, as if to be lilies of the valley.

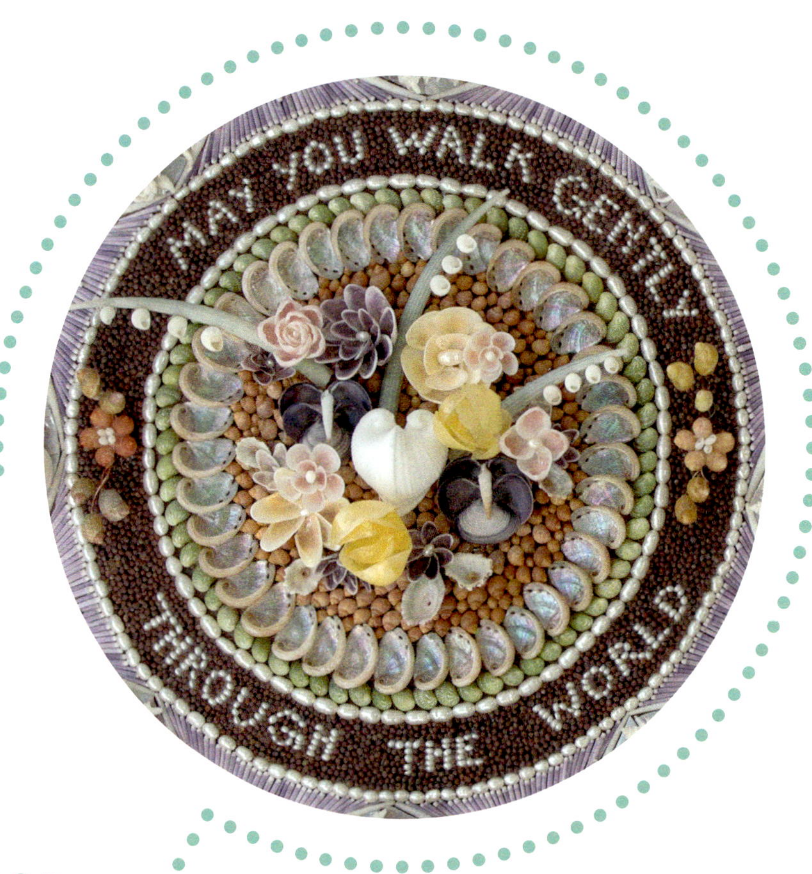

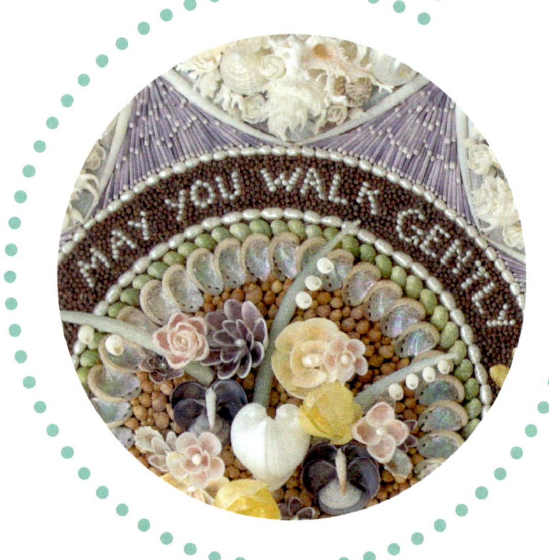

The lettering is done with white seed pearls placed amid brown mustard seeds.

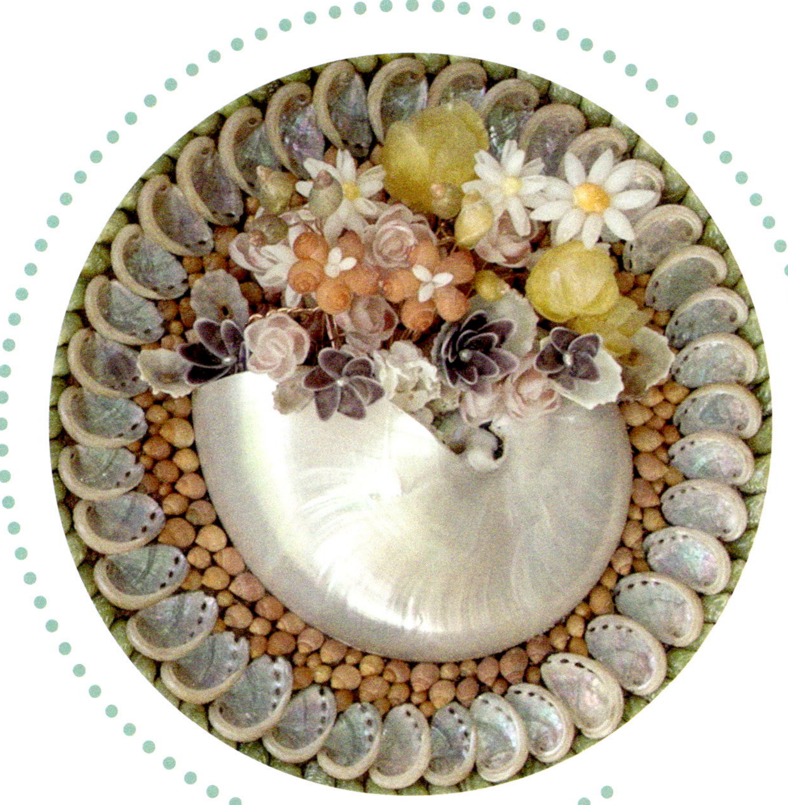

A polished nautilus shell serves as a vase for a bouquet of shell flowers made from yellow jingle shells, orange land snails, purple coquina shells, and white rice shells. Encircling the center is a row of upside-down abalone shells.

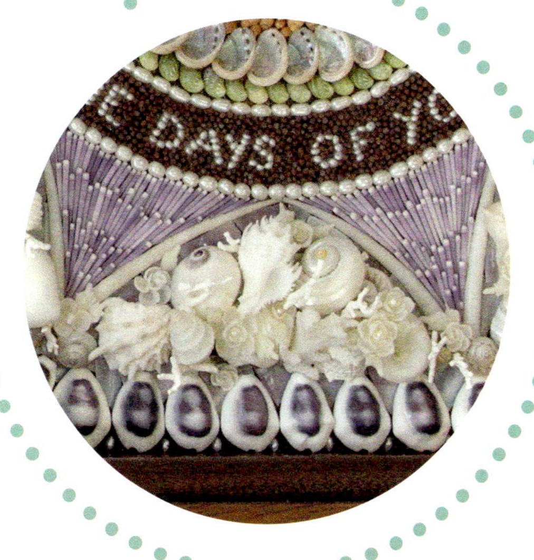

Pale green tusk shells form an arch within which sit shells and shell flowers in various shades of white. Beside the tusk shells, spaces are filled with layered purple sea urchin spines. Along the outer edge of the Valentine are purple top cowries.

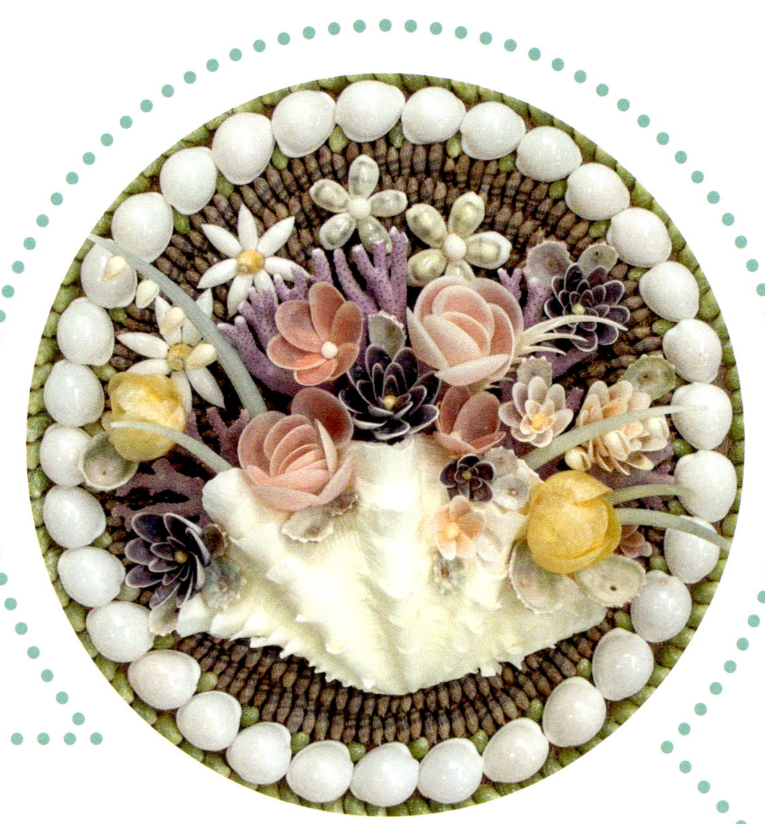

A magnificent fluted clam shell holds a bouquet of colorful flowers enhanced by the beautiful purples of corals and coquinas.

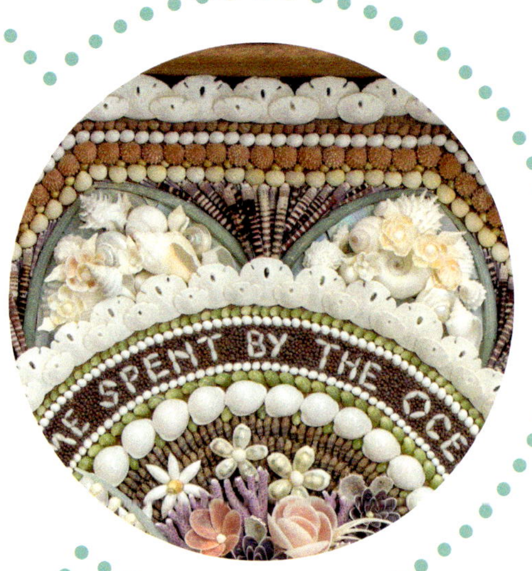

Green tusk shells form archways to showcase an assortment of white and cream-colored shells.

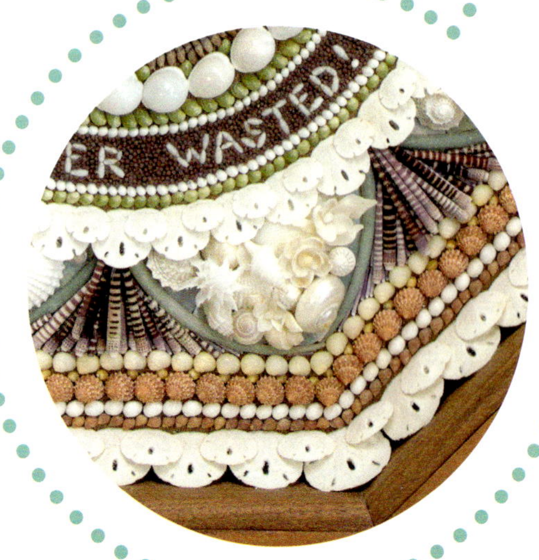

Layered sand dollars create a unique texture along the outside of the Valentine, as well as in the circle around the centerpiece.

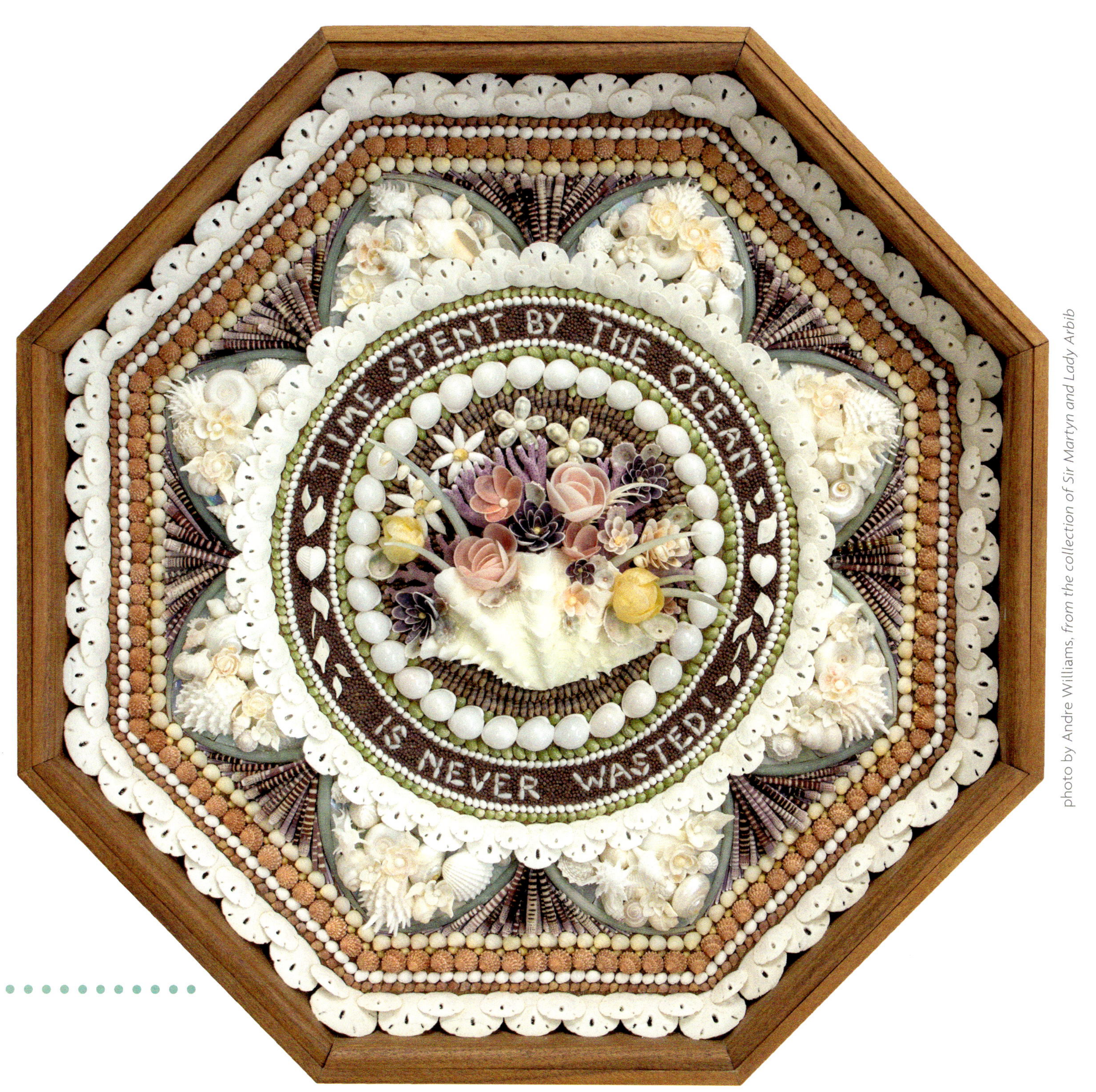

photo by Andre Williams, *from the collection of Sir Martyn and Lady Arbib*

Time Spent by the Ocean

Inspired by the lure of the ocean.

16-inch mahogany case made by Bill Jordan

A center star of varying sizes of auger shells is suggestive of a compass rose. It rests on little red snail shells defined by a circle of translucent white Pacific atys shells. At the center is the operculum of a shiva shell.

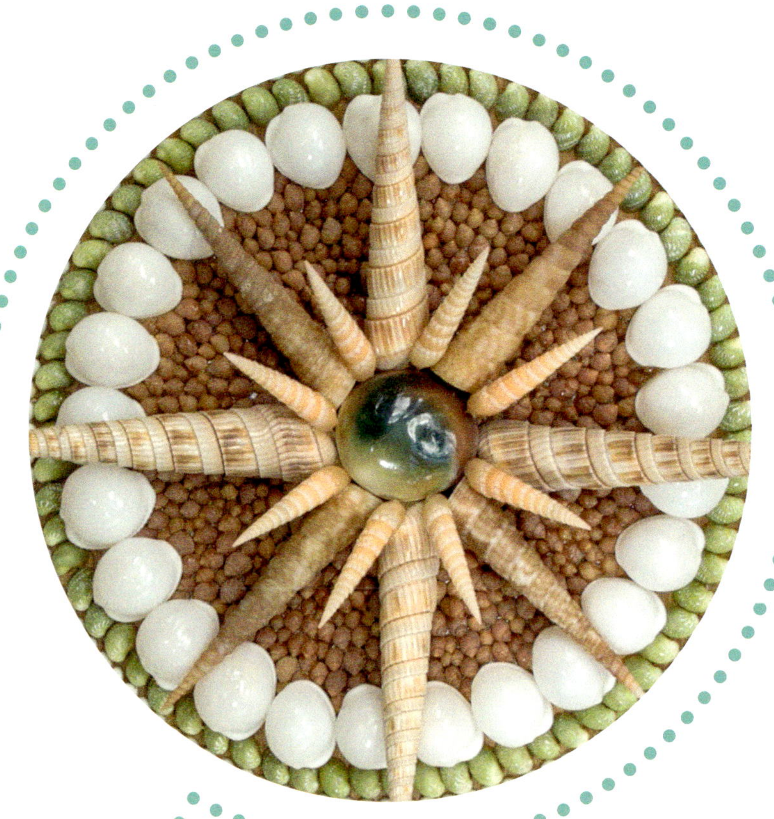

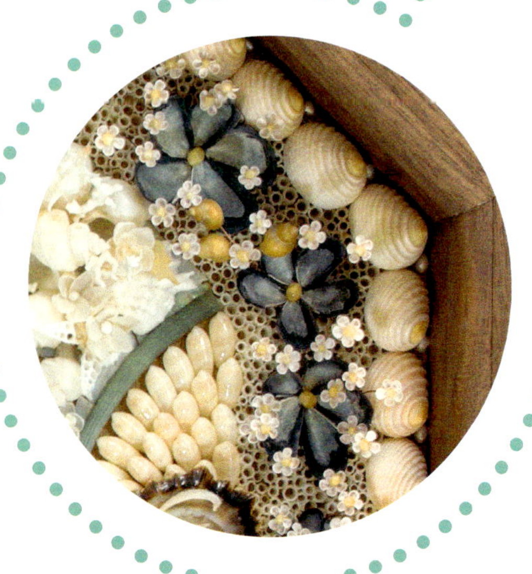

At the outer edge of the Valentine is a row of nerita plicata, and beside them lie blue mussel shell flowers with tiny white lilac shell flowers strewn among them. They sit atop cut white tusk shells standing upright.

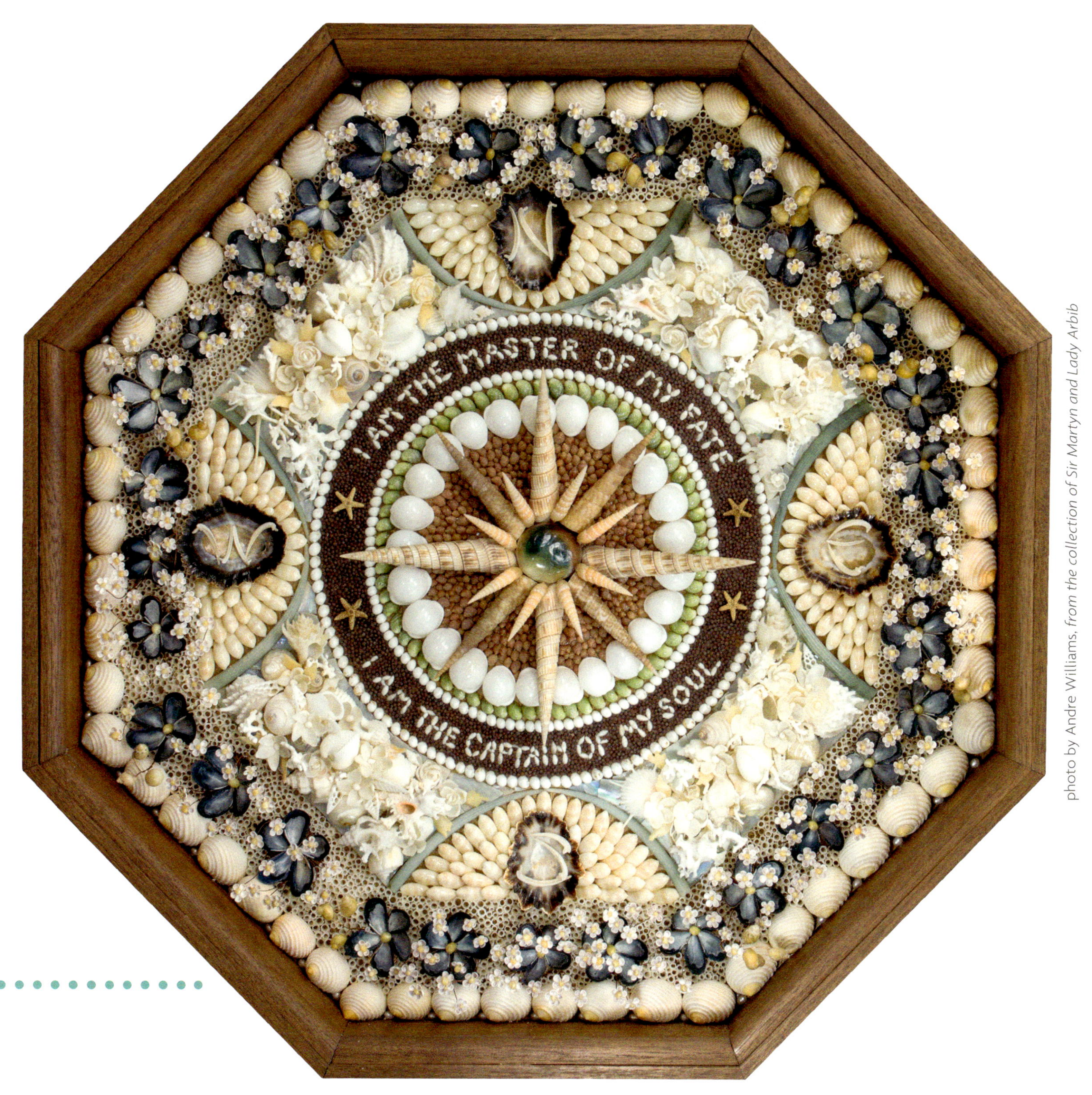

photo by Andre Williams, *from the collection of Sir Martyn and Lady Arbib*

Invictus

Inspired by the poem "Invictus," by William Ernest Henley.

18-inch mahogany case made by Bill Jordan

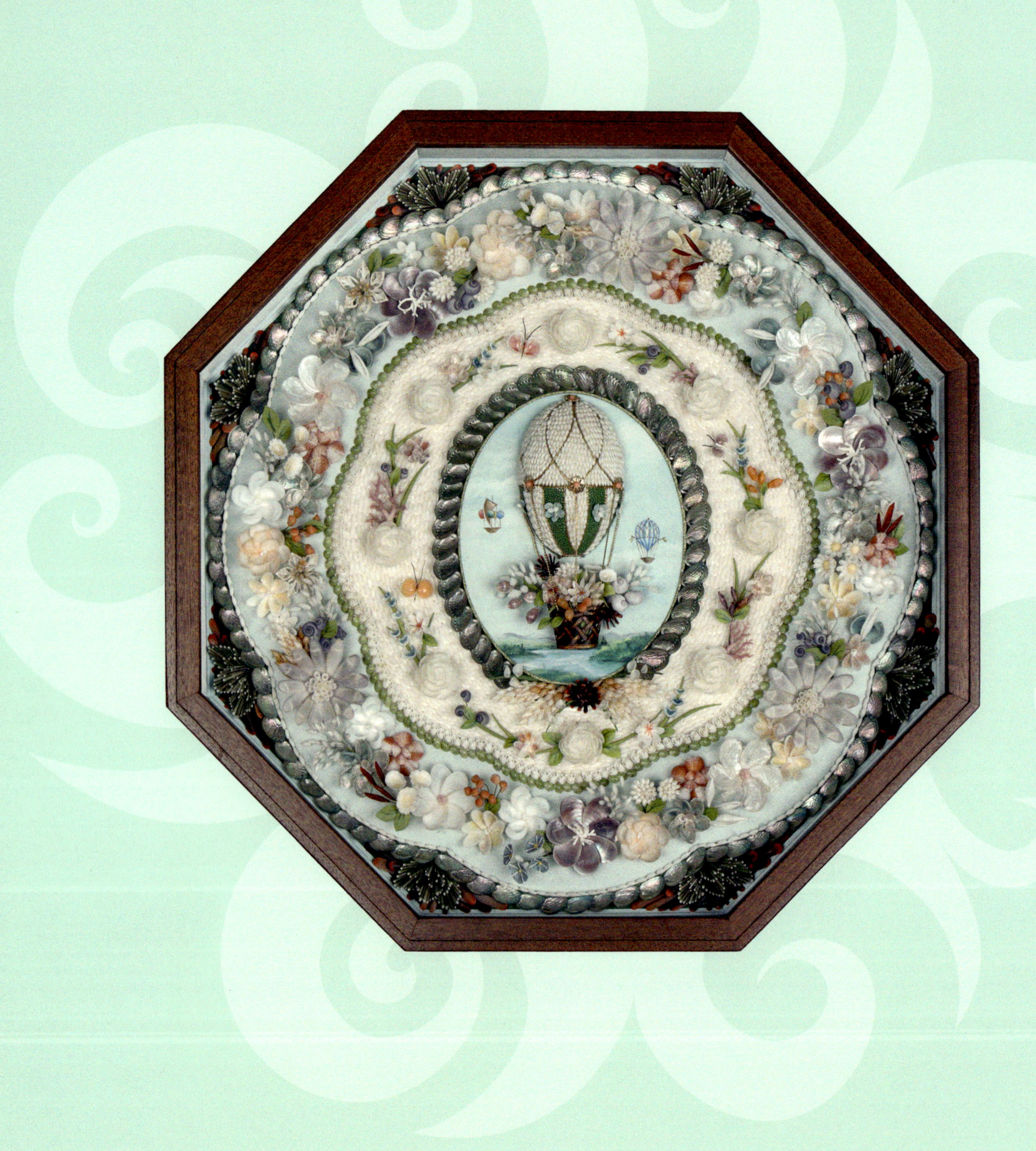

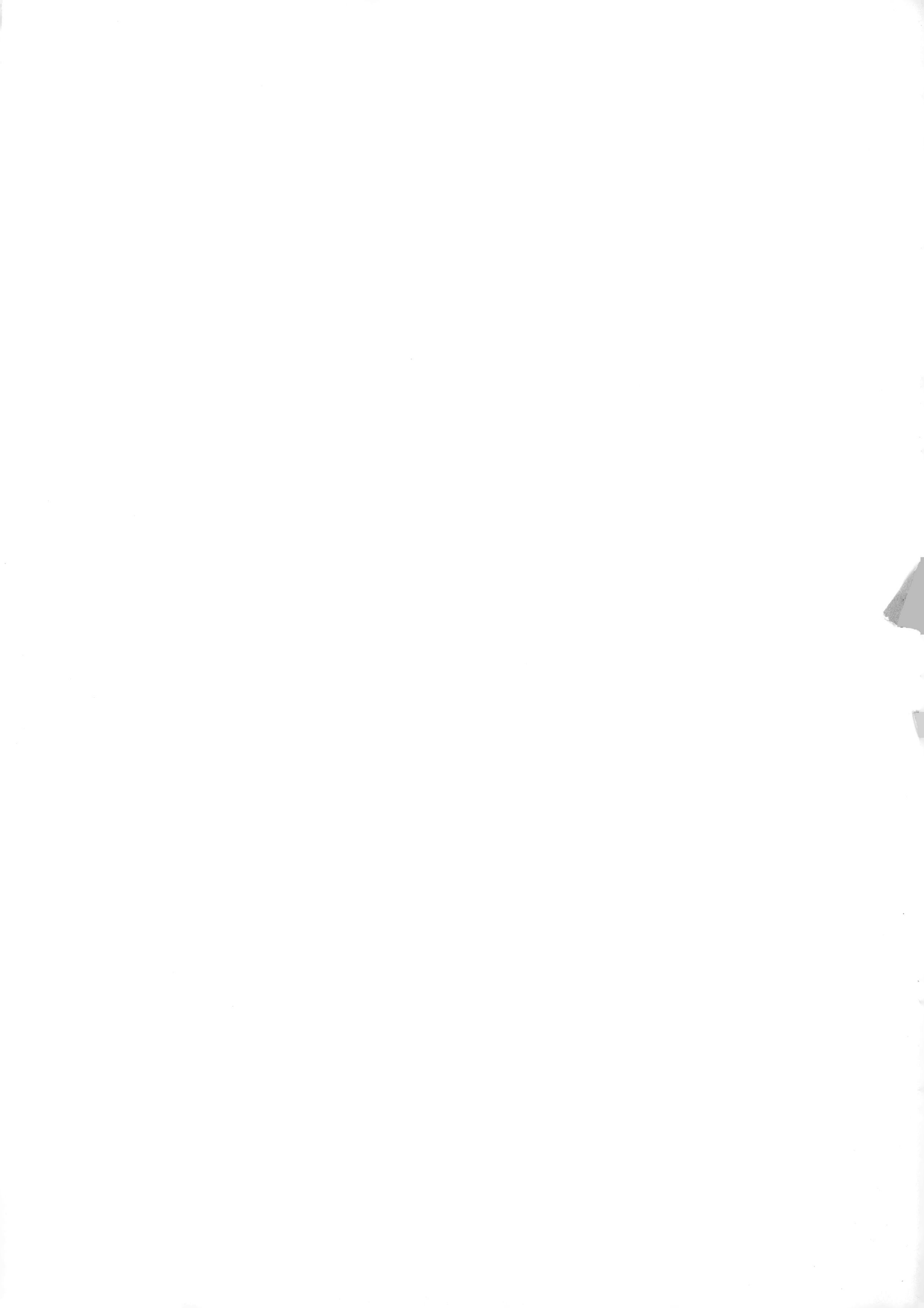